Y0-CBW-681

SNAPSHOTS

an introduction to tourism   fifth canadian edition

norma polovitz nickerson, University of Montana

paula kerr, Algonquin College

Pearson Canada
Toronto

Library and Archives Canada Cataloguing in Publication

Nickerson, Norma Polovitz
    Snapshots : an introduction to tourism / Norma Polovitz Nickerson, Paula Kerr.—5th Canadian ed.

Includes bibliographical references and index.
ISBN 978-0-13-502509-3

    1. Tourism—Textbooks.   2. Tourism—Canada—Textbooks.
I. Kerr, Paula, 1944–   II. Title.

G155.C2N56 2010   338.4'791   C2008-905390-7

Copyright © 2010, 2007, 2004, 2001 Pearson Education Canada, a division of Pearson Canada Inc., Toronto, Ontario.

Pearson Prentice Hall. All rights reserved. This publication is protected by copyright and permission should be obtained from the publisher prior to any prohibited reproduction, storage in a retrieval system, or transmission in any form or by any means, electronic, mechanical, photocopying, recording, or likewise. For information regarding permission, write to the Permissions Department.

Original edition published by Pearson Education, Inc., Upper Saddle River, New Jersey, USA. Copyright © 1996 Pearson Education, Inc. This edition is authorized for sale only in Canada.

ISBN-13: 978-0-13-502509-3
ISBN-10: 0-13-502509-5

Vice President, Editorial Director: Gary Bennett
Editor-in-Chief: Ky Pruesse
Acquisitions Editor: David S. LeGallais
Sponsoring Editor: Alexandra Dyer
Marketing Manager: Loula March
Associate Editor: Brian Simons
Production Editor: Patricia Jones

Copy Editor: Erica Fyvie
Proofreader: Lenore Latta
Production Manager: Peggy Brown
Composition: Integra
Art Director: Julia Hall
Cover/Interior Designer: Jennifer Stimson
Cover Image: Getty Images/Shannon Fagan

For permission to reproduce copyrighted material, the publisher gratefully acknowledges the copyright holders listed on page xiii, which is considered an extension of this copyright page.

Statistics Canada information is used with the permission of Statistics Canada. Users are forbidden to copy the data and redisseminate them, in an original or modified form, for commercial purposes, without permission from Statistics Canada. Information on the availability of the wide range of data from Statistics Canada can be obtained from Statistics Canada's Regional Offices, its World Wide Web site at http://www.statcan.ca, and its toll-free access number 1-800-263-1136.

1 2 3 4 5   13 12 11 10 09

Printed and bound in the United States of America.

CONTENTS

Travelling for business, to visit family and friends, or simply to relax is an important part of any industrial nation's lifestyle. While the last five years have taken their toll tourism continues to thrive as the number one global sector. Our job as tourism sector workers is to make business travel easier and vacations more fun!

The world has seen many disasters over the past decade, from terrorist attacks to devastating weather patterns. The events of September 11, 2001, clearly demonstrated how one component of tourism depends to a large degree on the others for economic growth. The tsunami that hit southeast Asia was devastating and deadly, but the tourism industry bounced back with amazing fortitude. It has taken longer for the areas hard hit by Hurricane Katrina to rebound, but that area is almost back to full tourism strength.

Other problems continue to trouble tourism. Airlines are still struggling fiercely to survive in the wake of costs. Crossing what was once the longest "unguarded border" in the world now requires full documentation, and that means long border delays during the hot summer months, which has caused a serious erosion in our major foreign market, the United States. Still Canada is fortunate. It is looking forward to the 2010 Olympic and Paralympic Games. VANOC (the Vancouver Organizing Committee) is working hard to create the first truly sustainable Olympic Games, and the excitement they have been creating with pre-publicity brings global recognition so badly needed at this point in time.

Most tourism textbooks tend to focus on one or two areas of the tourism sector, such as hospitality, travel, events planning, or marketing. This book views the industry as a whole based on the original eight components developed by the CTHRC (the Canadian Tourism Human Resource Council) in the mid 1990s. At the turn of the millennium, North American countries reviewed all of their business dealings and NAICS (North American Industry Classification System) adjusted the industry to create a simpler five components. By using the eight-component system, however, it is easier to delve more deeply into each component.

The text is divided into three parts. Part 1 includes topics such as reasons for the growth of tourism, theories of travel, the impact of tourism guests on a culture, planning and development, and marketing concepts. It is important that students first understand the basic concepts of travel before exploring the eight components of tourism, which are fully discussed in Part 2. Part 3 looks at the issues, challenges, and future of tourism in Canada.

New to This Edition

Key revisions in this edition include the following:

- Expanded coverage of recent occurrences affecting tourism, including terrorist attacks and weather events
- Information from research papers discussing cultural impacts of tourism, tourism's effect on the ecosystem (its carbon footprint), and new green programs being used by the sector
- Footprints, a discussion of specific programs undertaken by the industry to reduce our carbon footprint
- Additional discussion of travel patterns, including a closer look at ethics and serving travellers who have disabilities
- Travel statistics updates
- More comprehensive coverage of ecommerce and technology

Text Contents

Part 1 comprises three chapters. Chapter 1 introduces the Canadian tourism sector and provides general knowledge of tourism as a whole including NAICS and the impact of the WHTI. Chapter 2 looks at dealing with the "people factor" of tourism—guests and hosts. Included in this section are theories of motivation that affect travel and a summary of the positive and negative effects of tourism on a city, region, province, or country. Chapter 3 looks at planning for, developing, and marketing tourism including VANOC's planning and development strategies, with a look at the progress British Columbia is making toward successful, sustainable 2010 Winter Olympic and Paralympic Games.

Part 2 looks more closely at each of the eight components of the Canadian tourism sector. Chapter 4 discusses travel by land, sea, and air. It reviews the organizations, legislation, and trends that influence the transportation industry, as well as the theory of travel choice. Chapter 5 explores the lodging industry, including its variety, its organization, and its marketing techniques. Chapter 6 reviews the food and beverage industry, examining full-service restaurants, fast foods, and the contract food service business. The next three chapters look at recreation and entertainment—specifically attractions (Chapter 7), events (Chapter 8), and adventure tourism and outdoor recreation (Chapter 9). Chapter 9 also looks more closely at building sustainable tourism products. Chapter 10 discusses the important role of travel services—tourism's channel of distribution—and Chapter 11 looks at how tourism is supported by indirect industries such as the media, the government, and organizations and associations.

Finally in Part 3, Chapter 12 examines the current challenges and issues facing the industry. What is the projected future of tourism in Canada and what role will it play in Canada's prosperity?

I hope that the variety of teaching opportunities provided with each chapter will make this introductory course an exciting one for both instructors and students. Tourism can only be fully accessed when the big picture is understood.

How to Use This Text

A historical timeline, located on the inside front cover of the book, depicts the milestones of the ever-developing tourism industry. Not all important dates are covered, so students should feel free to add dates identified by their instructors as significant. Short biographies, called "Snapshots," are interspersed throughout the book and introduce students to the movers and shakers in the industry. These Snapshots focus both on early pioneers of the tourism sector and on Canadians making a difference in tourism today.

Some of the in-class discussion opportunities are the "In Practice" segments, the short case studies, and the new "Footprint" discussions. Chapters contain an array of features that provide extra resources to both the instructor and the student. Learning objectives and key terms are set out at the beginning of the chapters, while case studies and a summary end each chapter. There are also questions at the end of each chapter that are based on chapter material and may be used as out-of-class assignments, quiz questions, or small-group discussion questions. Web links can now be found in the margins for additional information on important topics.

Supplemental Materials

The **Companion Website** for *Snapshots* will benefit students and instructors alike. For students, this website provides timely updates, self-assessment quizzes for each chapter, and links to other internet resources.

The **Instructor's Manual**, provided free to adopters, includes lecture outlines, topics for discussion, and suggested projects and research assignments. In this new edition, suggested online research activities have been added. This supplement is available online and can be accessed through the instructor link on the Text Enrichment Site or through Pearson's Instructor Central site at www.pearsoned.ca/highered/instructor.

MyTest includes multiple-choice, true/false, and essay questions for each chapter and is available in both print and computerized formats.

New to this edition are electronic transparencies. Each chapter of the text is outlined in a series of **PowerPoint Slides**, which include key points, figures, and tables.

Pearson's **Technology Specialists** work with faculty and campus course designers to ensure that Pearson technology products, assessment tools, and online course materials are tailored to meet your specific needs. This highly qualified team is dedicated to helping schools take full advantage of a wide range of educational resources, by assisting in the integration of a variety of instructional materials and media formats. Your local Pearson Education sales representative can provide you with more details on this service program.

CourseSmart is a new way for instructors and students to access textbooks online anytime from anywhere. With thousands of titles across hundreds of courses, CourseSmart helps instructors choose the best textbook for their class and give their students a new option for buying the assigned textbook as a lower cost eTextbook. For more information, visit www.coursesmart.com.

Acknowledgments

No author can work in a void; writing this text has been made possible with the help and support of friends and colleagues. Many thanks to the Canadian Tourism Human Resource Council, and to the Canadian Tourism Commission, whose help and cooperation have been consistent and valued throughout the years. Over the years, my family has been my greatest support and a continued source of information: John, Nancy, Wendy, and my nephew Tom Hadley. Thanks to my friend Glenor Bogard, who started me on my journey into the world of tourism, to Erica Fyvie who makes my writing look professional, and to Alexandra Dyer whose faith in me may have wavered, but never disappeared. Working with Brian Simons, Patricia Jones, and Peggy Brown at Pearson Education Canada makes me aware of the care and concern they take with each and every textbook they publish. It provides me with confidence when I stand alone, in front of a class. A final thanks to our reviewers, who included the following:

- Christopher Lewis,
  Nova Scotia Community College

- Alita Brown,
  Southern Alberta Institute of Technology

- Janet Baker,
  Humber College

- Maureen James,
  Camosun College

Paula Kerr
Algonquin College

CREDITS

Chapter 1: p. 5, Canadian Tourism Commission; p. 7, Canadian Tourism Commission; p. 12, Paula Kerr; p. 18, Paula Kerr; **Chapter 2:** p. 29, John Wiley & Sons, Inc.; p. 34, Paula Kerr; p. 35, Canadian Tourism Commission; p. 35, Tom Hadley; p. 38, Canadian Tourism Commission; p. 39, Canadian Tourism Commission; p. 43, Canadian Tourism Commission; p. 44, Canadian Tourism Commission; p. 50, Canadian Tourism Commission; p. 55, Canadian Tourism Commission; **Chapter 3:** p. 64, John B. Kerr; p. 66, USTTA; p. 70, Canadian Tourism Commission; p. 73, Canadian Tourism Commission; p. 74, Paula Kerr; p. 83, Paula Kerr; **Chapter 4:** p. 96, Canadian Tourism Commission; p. 104, Canadian Tourism Commission; p. 105, Canadian Tourism Commission; p. 108, Canadian Tourism Commission; p. 113, Canadian Tourism Commission; p. 116, John Kerr; p. 118, John Kerr; p. 121, John Kerr; **Chapter 5:** 129, Canadian Tourism Commission; p. 129, Canadian Tourism Commission; p. 138, Canadian Tourism Commission; p. 141, Marriott Corporation; p. 142, Canadian Tourism Commission; p. 143, Paula Kerr; p. 146, Canada Select Accommodations Program; p. 149, Paula Kerr; **Chapter 6:** p. 164, Canadian Tourism Commission; p. 168, Canadian Tourism Commission; p. 170, Canadian Tourism Commission; p. 172, Paula Kerr; p. 173, Canadian Tourism Commission; **Chapter 7:** p. 178, Tom Hadley; p. 183, Canadian Tourism Commission; p. 185, Parks Canada; p. 186, Canadian Tourism Commission; p. 189, Canadian Tourism Commission; p. 196 (top and bottom), Canadian Tourism Commission; **Chapter 8:** p. 201, Canadian Tourism Commission; p. 203, Canadian Tourism Commission; p. 206, Ottawa Senators Hockey Club; p. 210, The Banff Centre; p. 211, Canadian Tourism Commission; p. 212, Canadian Tourism Commission; **Chapter 9:** p. 225, Canadian Tourism Commission; p. 227, Canadian Tourism Commission; p. 227, Wendy Booth: p. 230, Canadian Tourism Commission; p. 232, Canadian Tourism Commission; p. 233, Canadian Tourism Commission; p. 235, Canadian Tourism Commission; **Chapter 10:** p. 245, Canadian Tourism Commission; p. 250, Canadian Tourism Commission; p. 253, Canadian Tourism Commission; p. 258, Canadian Tourism Commission; p. 262, Paula Kerr; **Chapter 11:** p. 269, Canadian Tourism Commission; p. 272, Canadian Tourism Commission; p. 276, Paula Kerr; **Chapter 12:** p. 288, Canadian Tourism Commission; p. 291, Canadian Tourism Commission; p. 293, Canadian Tourism Commission.

Understanding Tourism

Key terms

agricultural tourism
common currency
culinary tourism
domestic tourist
ecotourism
excursionist
extreme tourism
foreign tourist

inbound tourist
leakage
le grand tour
medical tourism
multiplier effect
outbound tourist
same-day visitors
sector

spa tourism
tourism
tourist dollars
travel deficit
trip
volunteer tourism

Learning objectives

Having read this chapter you will be able to

1. Discuss the importance of tourism to the overall economic well-being of Canada.

2. Identify and explain the importance of the interaction between tourism industries.

3. Discuss the reasons for the growth of tourism over the past 100 years.

4. Discuss the impact of terrorist attacks on the sector.

5. Define the terms *tourism, trip, domestic* and *foreign tourist, inbound tourist, excursionist, sector, travel deficit, leakage,* and *multiplier effect*.

6. Identify prominent tourism organizations and their roles in the tourism sector.

No matter where you live in the world today, **tourism** plays an important role in the life of your community. Much of the world's population has had experience with tourism, and many nations depend on tourism to be one of their biggest revenue generators. In this text, we will look at how quickly the world is changing and how those changes have directly affected our lives and the way we use tourism and its products.

At the turn of the 20th century (1900), your life would have been very different from the one you are living now in the 21st century. Your great-grandparents likely heard about the Wright brothers' marvelous accomplishment—the first flight of an aircraft in 1903—but it would have taken weeks to see a picture of the event. Television for the masses was still 50 years away. Yet, in a brief 66 years, we not only built aircraft that could fly faster than the speed of sound (i.e., break the sound barrier), but we also placed men on the moon, a feat of which fairy tales were made. That event was watched live by millions around the world because television sets had become a standard home item. Today we have travelled even further—and are making "space tourism" a reality! Communication? Methods are changing so fast that "breakthrough" technology is often old news in six months.

The first half of the 20th century was filled with discord—two world wars fought with millions of young men and women killed. After World War II, nations demanded that lasting world peace be a united goal. To this end, the United Nations was formed. At the heart of the United Nations charter is the belief that understanding another culture's identity and beliefs leads to greater understanding of each other and hopefully a peaceful existence. Peace and an absence of conflict are the cornerstones of tourism, and peace has allowed tourism to reach the global heights it has, providing jobs and revenue to nations of all sizes.

What has been the impact of global tourism on today's world? Tourism represents approximately 33% of the world's exports (revenue generation) and for smaller nations, it can represent almost 3/4 of their yearly national income.[1] According to the World Tourism Organization (UNWTO), tourism reached an all-time high in 2007, with 898 million international travellers.[2] Even in these difficult times, tourism has had a sustained growth of 4-6% over the past three years. In 2006, tourists funnelled $733 billion into the finances of the countries they visited, and this revenue helped sustain and improve individual lives in the global community.[3]

All regions of the world increased their tourism numbers in 2007 and despite the concerns regarding uncertainty in some markets (e.g., the rising price of oil, the U.S. subprime mortgage crisis, and regional conflicts), the prospects for 2008 remain good. Based on recent experience, the World Tourism Organization believes tourism will remain resilient and projects a continued growth rate of 6%.[4]

How has Canadian tourism faired over the past two years? Concern over the passing of the Western Hemisphere Travel Initiative (WHTI), legislation requiring both Americans and Canadians to carry valid passports when crossing the border, appears to be waning. This legislation was aimed at stopping terrorists from gaining access to U.S. soil by crossing the Canadian border, and while it has created longer border waits it has apparently had little impact on our overall revenues. Revenues from long haul travel were up from $6.9 billion in 2006 to $7.1 billion in 2007, and our world ranking rose from 12th to 11th in overall tourism revenue generation.[5] In addition, there has been a 2% rise in the number of available jobs, with current employment in the industry equalling 633 600 jobs.[6]

THE CANADIAN TOURISM PRODUCT: AN OVERVIEW

Why are these figures important to Canadians? They are important because tourism is a "product" we sell, and the revenues from this product are used to help balance the budget and reduce the deficit.

Tourism can be referred to as an industry or a **sector**, which is a part or division of a national economy. For example, you have probably heard the terms "manufacturing sector" or "private sector." Tourism as a sector is very fractured. The products it produces can vary from an attraction like Disney World to a historical site outside of Red River, Manitoba; from a simple bedroom in a bed and breakfast to a luxurious five-room suite in the Fairmount Vancouver; from a gourmet meal to a hot dog bought at a local hockey game. The comparisons continue, but one point can be made—tourism products are *integrally connected*, meaning one product does not flourish by itself but needs other, different components to help sell it.

In 1993, the Canadian government took a big step toward better understanding the industry by appointing a committee to review the scope of the industry and its impact on Canadian society. The Buchanan Report, a white paper requested by the Chrétien government to review the tourism industry, was issued in 1994; although the numbers have changed, many of the points it made are valid today. The Buchanan Report[7] stated that:

i. As an industry, tourism had the ability to create more jobs at a faster pace than any other industry in Canada.

ii. The dollars created by the industry benefited all levels of government with nearly 40% of revenues split between federal, provincial, and municipal organizations.

iii. Tourism employed more females, more young adults, more visible minorities, more people re-entering the workforce, and more new immigrants than any other industry in Canada.

iv. The quality of jobs created by the industry ranged from entry level to highly paid executive positions, many of them requiring a strong set of personal skills and a higher set of work skills than generally understood by the public.

v. The value of tourism was vastly underrated and misunderstood by all levels of the government as well as the Canadian public.

Over the next several years, two steps were taken to ensure the continued growth of this industry: the establishment of the Canadian Tourism Commission (CTC) and the establishment of the Canadian Tourism Human Resource Council (CTHRC). The CTC became responsible for promoting all areas of the industry both at home and on a global basis. The CTHRC was charged with identifying and developing training standards and programs for all areas and levels of the industry. At that time, the tourism sector was identified as being made up of eight interlocking sub-sectors or components: *transportation, accommodations, food and beverage, attractions, events, adventure tourism and outdoor recreation, travel services,* and *tourism services* (Figure 1.1).

FIGURE 1.1
The eight
components of the
tourism sector

Transportation

The transportation industry provides the visitor with a way to get to a destination and to get around once the destination is reached. Businesses within this industry include airlines, railroads, cruise lines, tour bus companies, and car rental companies. More so than in any other industry, skills developed in one area of transportation are easily transferred to another. A reservation agent for an airline, for example, could work for a cruise ship or a railroad with little additional training. Jobs in this industry include pilot; reservation agent; cruise director; car rental agent; customer service agent; purser on a train, ship, or plane; and captain of a charter boat.

Accommodations

This component provides travellers with a place to sleep and includes any type of lodging available to the travelling public. Its products range from deluxe hotels in major cities to fishing camps in the Yukon, igloos in Greenland, or a treehouse in Costa Rica. Services required also differ. The business traveller in Vancouver requires a comfortable room with full service, a family on vacation may require a room that sleeps four, and the fisher wants a rustic cabin near a lake that promises good fishing. Some of the jobs you will find in this industry are front-desk clerk, hostel manager, health-club manager, valet, camp counsellor, night auditor, groundskeeper, concierge, and housekeeper.

One of the North's most interesting historical sites—the inuksuk. This is being used as a "brand" for the 2010 Olympics in B.C.
(Photo courtesy Canadian Tourism Commission.)

Food and Beverage

The food and beverage component is the largest in the tourism sector and provides perhaps the greatest opportunity for the entrepreneur. This industry includes all full-service restaurants (fine dining, family style, specialty, and theme); all limited-service eating places (fast food); all drinking establishments (bars, pubs, and taverns); food service that is contracted out in lodging facilities; contract food service in airports and arenas; catering firms; and deli and gourmet shops.

Some of the jobs in the food and beverage industry are wine steward, banquet chef, baker, bartender, nightclub manager, food service director, catering manager, and food and beverage server.

Attractions

The attractions component entertains and educates the visitor. Attractions are permanent, which means they can be visited at any time of year, and they may be natural or manufactured. Canada's geography provides many world-class natural attractions, such as Peggy's Cove in Nova Scotia, Magnetic Hill in New Brunswick, Niagara Falls in Ontario, and the West Coast Trail in British Columbia. Manufactured attractions provide an even broader choice for the tourist. They include historical sites, museums, theatres, casinos, water parks, gardens, and zoos. Some of the jobs in the attractions component are travel guide, casino dealer, heritage interpreter, attraction facility guide, amusement park supervisor, sales manager, and public relations manager.

Events

Events also educate and entertain the traveller, but events are available for only a short period of time. If you want to visit the Calgary Stampede, you must plan your visit for July because the Stampede is not available in mid-October. Festivals, conferences, sporting events, conventions, and meetings provide a growing number of Canadians with employment. Professionals in this industry need good organizational skills, strong people skills, and the ability to focus on details. Some of the jobs found in the events component are destination services representative, program specialist, registration supervisor, catering coordinator, special events manager, trade show operator, meeting planner, exhibit designer, and convention centre manager.

Adventure Tourism and Outdoor Recreation (ATOR)

ATOR is the component of recreation and entertainment that provides hands-on, physical activities for visitors. Much of the growth in this component is based on the desire to stay fit and healthy through exercise. The ski industry alone generates more than $5 billion in revenue yearly, and tennis, golf, hiking, and fishing are all popular with tourists. Hunting, while slipping in its importance as a driver for international tourists, still attracts the very high-end tourist, willing to pay dearly for the experience. Choices for a Canadian trip packed with adventure are as diverse as the country's landscape: whitewater rafting on the Fraser River, heli-skiing or hiking in the Rockies, and whale watching off the coast of New Brunswick are all part of adventure tourism.

Ecotourism also falls into the recreation and entertainment industry. **Ecotourism**—travel that is intended to support the study of earth's biodiversity—is of great interest to many visitors, and Canada's geography makes this country a fascinating destination. Polar bears, tide pools, archaeological sites, and vast wilderness put Canada high on the list of places to visit for many. Some of the jobs in this industry are local tour guide, ski lift operator, park warden, avalanche control trainee, lifeguard, tennis pro, recreation director, and marina manager/owner.

Travel Services

Who sells tourism? Who creates that neat package of flights, hotel reservations, and attractions? Travel services! There are more than 4500 travel agencies in Canada and hundreds of tour operators. A love of travel, an interest in geography and other cultures, and a love of people all combine to create the perfect job for someone who wants the best of both worlds—a chance to travel and still work near home. Some of the jobs available in the travel services industry are reservations agent, tour guide, sales representative, incentive travel specialist, tour planner, package tour coordinator, destination development specialist, tour operator, and travel agency owner/operator.

Tourism Services

This industry provides support services for the tourism sector. Some of its major components are federal, provincial, and municipal governments; associations and organizations; research, marketing, consulting, and education professionals; the media; and manufacturers. Other businesses, such as information centres, gift shops, travel insurance agencies, and duty-free shops, may provide services directly to the tourist. Some of the jobs found in this industry are teachers, accountants, researchers, reporters and writers, photographers and cinematographers who specialize in tourism, customs officials, designers and developers of tourism products, and souvenir and duty-free shop-owners.

Many tourists come to Canada to enjoy our climate and recreational activities.
(Photo courtesy Canadian Tourism Commission.)

These eight components, while still valid, have since been adjusted by Statistics Canada.

The North American Standard Industrial Classification (NAICS)

Several years ago, Canada and Mexico engaged in discussions with the U.S. Department of Labor to update and refine its Standard Industrial Classification System. This allows all three countries to produce statistics using the same terminology and sector information, giving them the ability to determine the health of their own economy and its projected growth rate, based on the two other economies.

This review also provided the United States with a chance to update its classification system to reflect the rapid changes that have occurred in the last 40 years. The North American Industry Classification System (NAICS, pronounced "nakes") has classified all economic activity as either goods-producing sectors or service-producing sectors. It recognizes tourism as one of the service-producing sectors. The system subdivides tourism into five sub-sectors: accommodations, food and beverage, recreation and entertainment, transportation, and travel services.[8] In doing so, NAICS has redistributed tourism industries from the eight components, used by Canada in the past, to five by combining attractions, events, and ATOR as "entertainment." The text, while mentioning NAICS, continues to use the more explicit eight-component model.

Canadians are often unaware of the magnitude of the tourism sector, and do not fully understand how important tourism is to their community, region, province, or country. In fact, people actively working in the tourism sector are often unaware they are part of tourism. For example, if you ask your local bartenders if they work in tourism, many will say no. Yet they will all agree that they work in food and beverage, which is the largest single industry in the tourism sector.

Although bartenders may serve mostly local customers and very few tourists, because they belong to the food and beverage industry, they are considered to be an integral part of tourism in Canada.

Understanding Tourism Terminology

The World Tourism Organization (UNWTO)—a specialized agency of the United Nations—defines **tourism** as "the activities of persons travelling to and staying in places outside their environment for not more than one consecutive year for leisure, business, and other purposes."[9] Put simply, the tourism sector transports people, provides them with accommodations, food and beverages, and then entertains or educates them. Tourism continues to expand, and as visitors generate new interests, new tourism product groupings appear. Here are a few of the better known and newer tourism groupings.

www.gocanada.com

Agricultural Tourism Agricultural tourism gives the visitor the chance to enjoy the chance to work on a family farm, learning more about the production of a specific product.

Examples of **agricultural tourism** might include a visit to an organic farm in Ontario's Holland Marsh, the granaries of Saskatchewan, or a vacation on a working ranch in Alberta.

www.exodus.co.uk

Ecotourism One of the oldest and largest types of focused travel is called **ecotourism**. With the real concern of climate warming, people are beginning to want a better understanding of our biosphere—how the varying "pieces" that create the world we live in today work together to produce either positive or damaging results. People more and more are wanting a vacation that helps them to understand this relationship, to become involved in nature-related experiences, and/or to see a sight that scientists have identified as fragile before it disappears. These vacations are often expensive as well as informative, so you can see why some entrepreneurs have focused on ecotourism.

FOOTPRINT

The David Suzuki Foundation has been a leader in creating and promoting environmental awareness since 1990. The foundation's main goals are solving global warming, protecting human health, and conserving the oceans. One of the main concerns that the foundation is currently working on is the salmon industry in B.C. The sea lice proliferating in salmon farms are causing the wild salmon to become extinct. What does this have to do with tourism? Tourists visit B.C. primarily to take part in wilderness and wildlife activities. These activities are challenged by the reduction in salmon because "healthy wild salmon feed the bears, eagles, orcas, and even the old-growth riparian forests which derive the majority of the nitrogen fertilizing their growth from the carcasses of wild salmon." Without salmon, the traditional reasons for visiting B.C. will themselves become extinct. (Source: www.davidsuzuki.org/files/CAAR_Economics_Factsheet.pdf)

Culinary Tourism **Culinary tourism** is a broad topic and might include enjoying the cultural cuisine of Quebec, attending a seminar on growing and using herbs, taking a short course in Chinese cooking techniques at one of Canada's culinary schools, visiting a sugar bush, or touring the vineyards in B.C.'s Okanagan Valley.

Volunteer Tourism **Volunteer tourism** is one of the newer products in the tourism sector. With a desire to give back to the world community, to learn more about a culture, or just to change their daily life patterns for a short period of time, some tourists are paying for the opportunity to volunteer. Organizations like Globe Aware match the interests of volunteers with special needs around the world. Tourists might visit a remote area of Nunavut to help build a new school, join a research group that is studying dolphins in the Caribbean, or travel to Kenya to build a water system that provides a town with clean, fresh water.

Spa Tourism **Spa tourism** focuses on the overall health and well-being of the traveller. Many of the world's resorts have now adopted spa programs for their clients. Guests enjoy spa services like nutrition programs, massages, and facials, while still having access to the resort's other activities like golf or tennis. Dining rooms can cater to appetites for organic, health-oriented dishes as well as to those for a more rounded menu.

Medical Tourism A branch off spa tourism, **medical tourism** involves travellers choosing a destination to gain access to a specific medical practice unavailable at home.

Extreme Tourism One of the newer, more exotic tourism products has people paying to put their lives at risk. **Extreme tourism** appeals to those who enjoy the adrenalin rush of danger and includes activities such as storm chasing, swimming with sharks, or ice diving.

REASONS FOR THE GROWTH OF TOURISM

Tourism has experienced phenomenal growth over the past century. Much of this growth has taken place during the past 50 years for the following reasons.

1. **The advancements made in our transportation systems.** Clearly, the way in which we travel today is very different from that at the beginning of the 20th century. Humans had not taken their first flight in 1900, but by 1971, the Concorde (the first British/French supersonic passenger jet) travelled from London, England, to New York City in just under 2.5 hours! (Due to the overall cost of operation, Concorde service was discontinued in 2003.) Planes are bigger, faster, safer, and more comfortable than ever before. Cruise ships are larger, with new designs and technologies that provide more entertainment and amenities for customers, helping to make

rough seas smoother and the trip more enjoyable. Cars, which most North American families now own, are also faster, safer, and more spacious. European and Japanese trains can travel at speeds of more than 350 km an hour. Modern tour buses boast large viewing windows, snack bars, and television sets, allowing passengers to watch their favourite TV shows, movies, or educational videos during their trip. Continued improvements to modes of transportation will make travel less expensive and more accessible to tourists, adding to the growth of tourism around the world.

2. **The advancements made in media coverage.** Our media systems have become global and instant through the use of satellite technology. Now as events happen around the world, we watch them unfold live on networks like CNN. Televised sporting events such as the Olympics, the Super Bowl, and the Kentucky Derby allow those of us who cannot be there to experience the thrill of the event. The excitement generated on the screen helps create a desire to experience the event in person.

3. **The introduction of computer systems.** The introduction of the computer in the 1960s heralded a whole new way of doing business throughout the world. Tourism has benefited enormously from this technology. From how guests are checked in and out of a hotel to how meals are prepared, from how airline tickets are purchased to how air traffic controllers track the flights landing at their airport, computers have aided the traveller. It would take an entire textbook to describe the ways in which computers have changed world business practices. In today's world, lifelong learning is essential, and computer literacy is imperative for all businesses to remain competitive.

4. **The internet and ecommerce.** The most significant advancements in computer technology have to be the internet and the World Wide Web, which together are the major tools we use to exchange information. Today, a business that does not have a website or is not otherwise accessible to its marketplace via the internet is likely losing customers. In June 2005, the Tourism Industry Association of Canada (TIAC) announced the finalization of plans for a "sponsored top-level domain exclusive to the tourism and travel industry."[10] Its purpose is to assist consumers who are looking for travel-related internet services, but it will also allow buyers and sellers of tourism products to connect more easily through the travel directory. Using the web, tourists can not only "visit" a destination in advance to look at the variety of available entertainment and recreation facilities, they can also check out their hotel options, look at the variety of restaurants in the area, and make bookings! Airlines and tour operators can make available last-minute sales on flights or tours that are scheduled to leave within a day or two, which in turn allows them to sell space that would otherwise have been empty, recouping at least a portion of their costs. Websites have been developed for many museums, attractions, and other tourist facilities in Canada and around the world, making the dispersal of information fast, efficient, and inexpensive. The uses of and possibilities for the internet are so vast that it is impossible to list all the benefits it brings to the tourism sector, but knowledge of the internet is essential for any student entering the sector. Throughout each chapter you will find several websites that you might wish to explore.

Will this technology replace existing means of information distribution? Experts believe that, in the foreseeable future, new technologies will be used to enhance, not replace, the way information is distributed. Although the younger generation is comfortable using these new technologies, tourism's swelling baby boomer market still enjoys looking through glossy travel brochures and magazines, with the personal attention of a travel counsellor. It is clear, however, that tourism companies not using the internet and the other latest technologies will be left behind.

5. **Better educational systems.** Higher education has become the norm for many young adults. The value of continuing lifelong learning in today's technologically oriented workplace cannot be ignored. Research shows that the more education people have, the more willing they are to travel. Learning broadens a person's perspective and often creates the curiosity that will motivate that person to travel in search of new personal experiences.

6. **More disposable income.** The amount of disposable income (money left over after bills are paid) available for travel has increased because of the rising numbers of two-income families. With two adults working in one household, even in recessionary times, vacation means travel.

The emerging market of retirees is important in any discussion about disposable income. The baby boom generation (many of whom have chosen early retirement), as well as the generation that precedes the boomers, have a dramatic effect on tourism sales. These two generations are in good health, have money to spend, and have already travelled more extensively than any other seniors group in history. With their mortgages paid off and their children educated, they are ready to continue their travel adventures. These two generations will have plenty of time and disposable income to spend on tourism.

What will they be looking for? David Foot, a professor at the University of Toronto and author of the book *Boom, Bust and Echo*, has this to say about the "other" generation:

> These young seniors, born in the 1930s, they really had a rough beginning. They were pre-teens in the Second World War . . . [they] really did pay their dues up front but they didn't have to serve. Then they entered the job market in the post-war reconstruction of the 1950s. Did they ever have to worry about getting a job? No. They had their choice of jobs . . . [and] did better than they ever expected to do. . . . The richest people in Canada today are in their late 50s and 60s, and these are people who are now retiring."[11]

7. **A more stressful lifestyle.** Stress, a by-product of the pace of modern life, creates the physical and emotional need to get away. At the same time, as companies attempt to keep costs down, benefit packages often include longer vacation periods, and overtime work may be repaid not with dollars but with additional time off. So, although the extended vacation seems to be disappearing, the long weekend and the 10-day holiday provide vacationers with the opportunity to travel more often.

8. **Declining cost of travel.** The cost of travel has declined, making it more accessible to everyone. Modes of transportation vary from the least expensive

(private vehicle or bus) to the most expensive (air). Deregulation has allowed new transportation companies to compete for business, and, as a result, low-cost carriers have given the consumer an alternative to the major airlines. This, in combination with the Open Skies Agreement, has provided North Americans with a wider choice of flights and destinations as well as lower-cost tickets. Frequent-traveller plans and the partnerships that have developed between destinations and the airlines have resulted in better packaging, which reduces the overall cost of the vacation.

9. **Better marketing and promotion.** Products sell better when they have strong marketing programs, and the tourism sector, with its many industries, has become more active and creative in this area. New tourism advertising campaigns focus on fun, education, activity, and information. Electronic marketplaces bring up-to-date information not only to agents and operators but also to clients. From the federal government's perspective, lack of promotion has hurt tourism in the past, giving the Canadian Tourism Commission its primary mandate of promoting the Canadian experience. Across Canada, all levels of government are forming partnerships with local tourism operators to produce proactive marketing plans that feature state-of-the-art promotional materials.

10. **Common worldwide currency.** Travel also flourishes when a **common currency** exists. Since World War II, the introduction of credit cards, travellers' cheques, automated banking, and currency exchange machines has created easy access to money and credit while on vacation. Nowadays, currency can be easily obtained using the INTERAC® banking machines located in just about every major destination around the world. American Express, Visa, and MasterCard all focus on the pleasures of tourism as they promote the use of their cards.

Shopping is usually a part of every tourist's vacation and is made even easier by the fact that credit cards serve as a common currency. Here tourists enjoy the shopping arcade at Jasper Park Lodge, Alberta.
(Photo: Paula Kerr.)

11. **Easing of government travel restrictions.** The fewer regulations a country places on international travellers, the stronger the prospect for a sound international tourism market. In Europe, where unification, started in the late 1980s with the destruction of the Berlin Wall, has eased tough border requirements for documentation, tourism has flourished. With the implementation of the Bush government's Western Hemisphere Travel Initiative (WHTI) legislation, forcing valid Canadian passport requirements for the first time ever, Canada has seen a loss of 4.2% of its largest international market—the United States. In dollar terms, that translates into $5.7 billion for the year 2006.[12] Few Americans have valid passports and the long waits at border crossings are discouraging our U.S. tourists. With harsh weather a constant factor in Canadian winters and many residents seeking the pleasures of Florida, the United States has not seen as dramatic a decline, but U.S. border towns are feeling the pinch of fewer Canadian spenders despite the rising value of our loonie.

12. **Political stability.** Peace and tourism go hand in hand. The world has been, for the most part, peaceful over the past 50 years, but in countries where terrorism, civil unrest, or war is a daily threat, tourism seldom plays an important economic role. Countries such as Israel, for which tourism is a significant revenue generator, have seen tourism revenues drop significantly. Terrorist attacks in the past five years have had a negative impact on tourism, with events on September 11, 2001, being the most harmful. Analysts predicted and tourism statistics showed that the fear of terrorism, coupled with SARS and a weakened world economy, had driven international tourism spending down, with significant increases only in the past few years. On the bright side, economists now believe that tourism is much more resilient than expected.

We are fortunate that Canada has earned a reputation as being a safe and peaceful country. Although we felt the backlash of the terrorist attack on the World Trade Center with falling tourism revenues, Canada remains a country that inspires traveller confidence.

The tourism sector itself has become user friendly, providing travellers with access to many components with a single email or phone call. Transportation systems are linked with accommodations, accommodations are linked with the food and beverage industry, and the food and beverage industry is linked to all aspects of tourism. The sector is beginning to see the benefits of working together as a single tourism unit.

SPEAKING THE SAME LANGUAGE

To begin our discussion on tourism, we need some common basic terminology. We have already looked at the new NAICS and seen some of the numbers it has produced. To make these figures understandable to any person reading and using them, parameters have been set. Here are some of the key terms used in Canada and other countries around the world when discussing tourism: *trip*, *foreign tourist*, *domestic tourist*, *excursionist*, *travel deficit*, *multiplier effect*, and *leakage*.

In Canada, a **trip** is defined as any travel that takes a person 80 km from their place of residence for any reason other than a commute to work or school, travel in an ambulance or to a hospital or clinic, or a trip that is longer than one year.[13] This definition excludes the trip within your own country that is shorter than 80 km.

www.hospitalitynet.org

In 1937, the Committee of Statistics Experts of the League of Nations defined **foreign tourists** as persons visiting a country, other than that in which they usually reside, for a period of at least 24 hours. Foreign tourists may also be called **inbound tourists** (likewise, Canadians who visit other countries may be described as **outbound tourists**).

Domestic tourists are people travelling in the country in which they reside, staying for at least 24 hours, and travelling at least 80 km from their home.[14]

Here are some guidelines the United Nations uses to clarify the term "tourist."[15]

You *are* a tourist if

- you are travelling for pleasure, for family reasons, to learn more about the world in general, or for health or religious purposes
- you are travelling for business reasons other than direct remuneration by the country you are visiting
- you are visiting the country as part of a sea cruise or travel package

You *are not* considered a tourist if

- you are actively going to take up an occupation at your destination
- you are establishing residency in the country
- you are attending an educational institution and establishing a residence
- you are staying less than 24 hours

As travel has become faster and easier, people will often travel 80 km from their homes for recreation or entertainment without staying overnight. By definition, they cannot be called tourists because they are not away from home for a long enough period. The tourism sector calls these travellers **excursionists**, or **same-day visitors**. In Canada, an excursionist is any person who travels at least 80 km from the place of residence, stays less than 24 hours, and is not commuting to work or school, or operating as part of a crew on a train, airplane, truck, bus, or ship.[16]

Canadians love to travel, and they like to travel outside Canada. Here are some of the reasons: (a) our cold winter weather makes sunny, warm climates popular; in winter, (b) many Canadians have relatives who live outside the country, whom they must travel to visit; (c) foreign countries promote their attractions more effectively than Canada does; and (d) Canadians are not aware of the tourism treasures within their borders. However, every time Canadians leave the country, their tourism dollars are lost to Canada. This loss in tourism revenues is called a **travel deficit**. More simply put, a travel deficit is the difference between the amount of money spent by visitors travelling to Canada and the money spent by Canadian residents travelling abroad, and is referred to as our International Travel Account.[17]

Tourism is a revenue producer, and much of this revenue goes back into the local economy. The **multiplier effect** of tourism dollars shows the beneficial effect this revenue has on nearly everyone in the community. For example, when tourists stay in a Ramada Hotel, they pay the hotel for their room. The Ramada takes these "**tourist dollars**" and uses them to pay for salaries, supplies, mortgage payments, and electricity, etc.

Sally Hyung is a front-desk agent at the Ramada. She uses her salary to pay for rent, food, entertainment, transportation, dry cleaning, and so on. The grocer takes the money he receives from Sally and uses it to help pay for his rent, to buy supplies (such as eggs from local farmers), and to pay his employees' salaries. You can see that the ripple effect of tourist dollars in a community benefits just about everyone.

Leakage occurs when the community cannot support the influx of tourists and must import workers and goods in order to sustain the industry. For example, the town of Banff does not have enough residents to support the throngs of tourists who arrive each summer. Every year, Banff's hotels, restaurants, and shops must hire workers from outside the community. Banff also needs to purchase supplies from larger centres like Calgary.

Bill James, a college student from Vancouver, B.C., is working in a Banff hotel for the summer. The tourist dollars spent in his hotel are used to pay for salaries, supplies, and the mortgage. Bill uses some of his salary to pay for his living expenses in Banff, but he is also saving some of his pay to use for his last year at college. Part of what he makes is being spent in Vancouver, not Banff. This is an example of leakage. When leakage occurs, the community that hosts the tourist does not get the full benefit of the revenue generated. Leakage is particularly harmful in countries such as the Bahamas, an island group with few resources to support its large tourism sector. Most of the products needed to build and sustain its tourism industry must be purchased from other countries. This reduces the amount of tourism revenue the country is able to retain and, therefore, reduces the amount that is to be shared amongst its communities.

HISTORICAL AVENUES

The history of travel is as old as the human race itself. In the early days of civilization, people travelled by foot and were exposed to many dangers. They seldom travelled for pleasure but rather to find new food sources, to adjust to climatic changes, or to escape other stronger, threatening tribes. Yet historical research suggests that people in early civilizations, often linked by marriage and common ideals, did travel occasionally for the purpose of business and pleasure. Archaeologists have unearthed artifacts from digs in North and South America, Europe, and Asia that indicate that tribes would meet at certain times of the year to perform religious celebrations, to conduct tribal business, to trade, and to dance and socialize.

As civilizations developed, the strongest tribes would seek to control the resources of an area. Armies conquered entire regions, enslaving the inhabitants and taking their possessions, which increased not only the conquering tribe's influence, but their wealth as well. Traders travelled to different lands to find goods to bring to their homes.

Two peoples of ancient times who became noted as traders, not warriors, were the Sumerians and the Phoenicians. They focused on industry to increase their wealth, and they established early trade routes in the African/southern European corridors. The Sumerians were the first nation to develop coinage, used as payment for goods. The Phoenicians, noted sailors, were responsible for creating some of the first maps, showing their system of water routes, to help guide others.

Three major civilizations dominated the world (as they knew it) between 4800 BCE and 300 CE: the Egyptians, the Greeks, and the Romans. Each civilization in its own way provided for the advancement of travel activities. Ancient people travelled frequently to conduct trade, to complete government business, and for educational, religious, and social reasons. The Egyptians developed strong central governments and large flourishing cities, which attracted travellers. Many of their cities were built along the Nile River, with its northward currents and southward breezes. Travel by boat was easy and safe, making these urban centres accessible.

By 900 BCE, groups of Greek-speaking peoples had formed city-states that exchanged goods and maintained open ports and roads. A network of city-states emerged. As researchers, explorers, traders, and philosophers, the Greeks made travel part of their education and way of life. City-states and shrines flourished, becoming destinations in themselves. As tourists do today, the Greeks loved to shop, eat, and drink. They loved the theatre and spectator sports, and they travelled great distances to partake of these forms of entertainment.

By 400 BCE, a new culture was on the rise and was to grow into one of the most successful empires in the history of the Western world. Great conquerors, administrators, and engineers, the Romans established colonies across Europe ranging from North Africa and Asia Minor to France, Germany, and Great Britain. Wherever they moved, they built roads—more than 80 000 km of them! The Romans also brought with them their culture, their language, and their way of life. A strong, central government and well-established Roman laws and local magistrates provided peace and security for the empire for many years. Roman coinage became the universally accepted currency. During this period of peace and prosperity, travel became both easy and safe. Inns and taverns sprang up to care for travellers in towns and along the roads. Restaurants, bars, and a wide variety of entertainment flourished in the cities. Roman shrines and baths became destinations for recreational travellers, and Roman business people established fast-food style restaurants to accommodate them.

More than any other ancient civilization, the Roman Empire clearly illustrates the conditions under which tourism may flourish—peace and prosperity. Travel modes must be easily accessible and safe. Common currency, a common language, and a well-established legal system are essential. As long as these conditions exist, people will be encouraged to travel. If any of these conditions are missing, travel will be diminished. As Roman society began to break down and the central government became unable to keep up with the demands of its extensive empire, the peace and prosperity that made travel easy crumbled. By 400 CE, the Roman Empire had fragmented, and the officials and soldiers who maintained the Roman peace had been recalled to Rome. Few people risked travel.

By the turn of the millennium, the Roman Catholic Church had gained political and social control in many areas of Europe. The growth of towns and a class of people with disposable income combined with the influence of the church to create an interest in pilgrimages to religious sites. Inns and hostels grew up along pilgrimage routes to support these medieval tourists. However, feudal society had created a class of wealthy warriors without any lands to govern. When the Byzantine Emperor asked for help, the church organized these warriors and sent them on crusades—a sort of large-scale military pilgrimage.

The crusades had a profound influence on medieval culture. One effect was the return of knights and their retinues with stories of and souvenirs from faraway lands and cultures. Another was the growth of industries to serve travellers—inns, blacksmiths, traders, and others—along the routes that the travellers followed.

Over the course of the Middle Ages, much of the known world was being carved up into kingdoms, with strong families uniting their lands under one rule of law. Towns and cities became larger and stronger. Merchants, less fearful for their safety than most, began to venture farther into the countryside in search of luxury goods for the wealthy classes. One of the best known of the early travelling merchants was Marco Polo, who travelled from Europe to the Far East. The spices, silks, and merchandise with which he returned created great interest in foreign lands and cultures.

As governments and towns became stronger, travel became easier, and more destinations for travel became popular.

In the 17th and 18th centuries, England's nobility, recognizing the lack of educational opportunities at home, and valuing the cultural opportunities available in France, Italy, and Greece, began to send their sons to the European continent to be educated. This strategy, dubbed **le grand tour**, prepared heirs for the future by teaching them languages and financial skills, and ensuring a knowledge of religious and legal institutions. The trips lasted several years and included stays in Paris, Florence, Rome, Zurich, and Vienna. *Le grand tour* still plays a part in modern tourism, but modern tourists complete it in days, not years.

Between 1800 and 1939, there were many changes in modes of travel. Steamships and steam trains made crossing the oceans and continents easy. The invention of the automobile provided a means for people to travel independently, choosing their own time and destinations. And, in 1903, the era of air travel was born. By the late 1920s and early 1930s, air routes had been established and travel across the oceans had been reduced to days instead of months. With fast and accessible modes of travel available, tourism grew.

In 1939, with the outbreak of World War II, safe travel once again became difficult. Those who travelled for pleasure were few. Canadian men and women, pulled from their Prairie homes or from the fishing fleets of British Columbia and the Maritimes—people from across the country, representing all ages and occupations—were shipped overseas to fight. Many did not return. Those who did brought back experiences of other cultures and lands to share with the folks at home. In the shadow of war, the age of modern tourism had begun and great advances were made in modes of transportation. Bigger and faster planes and automobiles, and faster and more comfortable ships and trains were necessary to the Allied victory. After the war, these modern machines fuelled a new growth in tourism. Industrialized nations became prosperous, and with that prosperity came more discretionary income and time. Time, money, peace, safe and accessible transportation systems, and common currency—all of these things have helped build today's tourism sector.

No history of tourism will ever be complete without mentioning the modern risks posed by terrorist attacks. In the attacks on the World Trade Center (WTC) and the Pentagon on September 11, 2001, more than 2800 people from 86 countries, including 24 Canadians, were killed. The visual impact of watching two jumbo jets hit the twin towers and explode, followed by the collapse of the World Trade Center, stunned the world. Commercial airlines have been hijacked in the past. Bombs have been placed on commercial airliners causing midair explosions, as with Pan Am's Flight 101 over Lockerbie, Scotland, in 1992. However, the use of fully fuelled jumbo jets as guided bombs to attack a specific target shocked the world and brought home to many how insecure travel can be.

As tourists we may also be caught in the violent struggles of warring factions in a foreign destination. Two Canadian travellers enjoying a night out in Indonesia were killed in October 2002, when terrorists bombed the nightclub they were in. London, England, has experienced a series of bombings, and in July 2005, terrorists bombed the Egyptian luxury resort Sharm El-Shaikh, killing 83 and wounding 200.

Tourism has become a target for terrorists, and in the future, tourists will choose destinations with greater concern for their personal safety.

Despite these events, the United Nations and the World Tourism Organization still hold to the belief that one of the ways to build a peaceful world is for people from different nations to meet and learn more about each other. Tourism can provide a formula for friendship that no amount of government legislation can match. There is no better umbrella under which to foster such friendships.

TOURISM SECTOR ASSOCIATIONS AND ORGANIZATIONS

Good food and drink and a place to sleep are essential parts of a trip. Tourists have a wide variety of accommodation choices, from elegant hotels through country inns to local campgrounds.

(Photo: Paula Kerr.)

There are many tourism associations and organizations responsible for (a) legislation and control of the industry; (b) research, development, and marketing; and (c) professional development of workers. Some of these groups will be highlighted in Chapter 11. Described below are five international organizations and five Canadian organizations that will be referred to throughout the book. You should be able to recognize their names and acronyms. Some will represent one or more industries, and many have more than one role to play. Some are strongly supported by government funding, while others support their activities using funds received from their membership base.

International Organizations

World Tourism Organization (UNWTO)
The UNWTO is the official consultative organization to the United Nations on tourism. Its fundamental aim is the promotion and development of tourism, with a view to contributing to economic development, international understanding, world peace, prosperity, and universal respect for and observance of human rights and fundamental freedoms for all, without distinction as to race, sex, language,

SNAPSHOT

Conrad Hilton

First truly international hotelier, first to "gold dig" in his own hotel lobbies, first to set job and safety standards, first to set pricing programs for his properties: Conrad Hilton, hotelier extraordinaire!

Conrad Hilton began his career in 1907 when he started work as a hotel operator to help his family face some very hard times in his hometown of San Antonio, New Mexico. But, it was not until after World War I that Hilton bought his first hotel. He had been a soldier, a politician, and a banker, and in 1919, Hilton went to Cisco, Texas, intending to buy a bank. Instead, he purchased the Mobley Hotel. The oil boom had just begun and the hotel's owner had caught oil fever. He sold his property to Hilton, and left to strike it rich. Had he realized the Mobley Hotel would be the stepping stone to wealth and fortune for one of the richest hotel tycoons in America, he might have charged more!

By 1929, Hilton had seven properties, but instant riches were not his destiny. The Depression found him penniless and in debt. At one point, his bellhop loaned him $300 for "eatin' money." It was during this phase of his career that Hilton learned to operate economically, and this lesson served him well. In 1946, Hilton Hotels Corporation was formed, and in 1949, Hilton International was established with its first operating contract at the Caribe Hilton in Puerto Rico. In 1954, he acquired the Statler Hotel chain. It was not until the 1960s that Hilton saw the advantage of franchising, and, in 1967, he sold Hilton International to Trans World Airlines. In 1969, Hilton began a partnership with the University of Houston. To honour his support, the Houston school changed its name to the Conrad N. Hilton School of Hotel Management.

What did Hilton give to the hotel industry?

- He was the first hotelier to insist that each hotel prepare daily year-to-date reports summarizing all the financial actions of the day, such as revenues, expenses, and profit and loss.

- He set up one of the first computerized hotel reservation systems.

- He was a master at identifying lobby space that could be revenue-producing; he would rent it to shop owners or develop a new bar or restaurant.

- He had an instinct for finding "white elephants"—hotels that had not been financially productive—buying them at bargain prices, and creating profitable properties just by implementing simple cost controls.

What kind of a man was he really? He was energetic, he loved beautiful women, he learned quickly, he was an incurable optimist, and he believed strongly in equality. He also believed in working hard and playing hard. At age 90, he still held the position of chair of the board of Hilton Hotels Corporation. He passed away at the age of 91. A giant in his time, Hilton is still recognized as one of the world's leading hoteliers.

www.world-tourism.org

or religion. Activities of the UNWTO include providing international technical support, education, and training to member states; facilitating tourism by removing obstacles to tourists; providing security and protection to tourists; encouraging environmentally sound planning; and marketing and promoting global tourism.

International Civil Aviation Organization (ICAO) ICAO is another consultative organization to the United Nations. Its members are governments that have a vested interest in the safe, orderly growth of the world's airline industry. Its mandates include encouraging development of safe airways and airports, discouraging unreasonable competition among the airlines, and meeting the needs of the global community by providing safe, regular, efficient, and economical air transport.

International Air Transport Association (IATA) Established in 1919 and completely reorganized in 1945, this organization has been responsible for much of the ease of air travel in the last 50 years. The airlines themselves created and run IATA. IATA is responsible for the one-ticket/one-trip concept and takes an active role in the safety and security of global air travel. Additional information on IATA is also found in Chapter 4.

World Travel and Tourism Council (WTTC) Established in 1990 and headquartered in London, England, this private organization works with governments around the world, helping them to realize the full economic impact of tourism. Its members are executives from all branches of the tourism sector. The department that focuses on tourism's human resources is located in Vancouver, B.C.

www.wttc.org

Pacific Asia Travel Association (PATA) Founded in 1951, PATA is a good example of countries uniting for the benefit of the tourism sector. Its members come from all components of the tourism sector, and its mandate is excellence in travel and tourism through promotion, research, education, development, and marketing. PATA represents 34 countries in the Pacific Asia area, and it meets annually to present research papers, discuss common problems, and examine and adjust its long-range activities to meet changing needs.

www.pata.org

Canadian Organizations and Associations

The following organizations are just a few of the many that contribute to the smooth operation and the future development of Canada's tourism sector.

Canadian Tourism Commission (CTC) The CTC is a working partnership of tourism businesses and associations, provincial and territorial governments, and the government of Canada. It plans, directs, manages, and implements programs to generate and promote tourism in Canada. The CTC was established in 1994 and is discussed in Chapter 2.

Canadian Tourism Human Resource Council (CTHRC) The CTHRC provides a national forum to facilitate human resource development activities that will support a globally competitive and sustainable Canadian tourism sector. This organization brings together the work of the provincial tourism education councils (TECs) under a national framework. You will learn more about these organizations in Chapter 2.

Tourism Industry Association of Canada (TIAC) TIAC was founded in 1931 to encourage tourism in Canada. It is a not-for-profit industry association representing tourism-related businesses, associations, institutions, and individuals. TIAC provides representation at the national level and up-to-date information on tourism-related issues. TIAC works closely with the CTC and in 1996 was given the responsibility of running Canada's largest tourism trade show, Rendez-Vous Canada. It also works with customs to improve reception of all travellers, is a member of the CTHRC board of directors, lobbies the federal government on tourism issues, and supports research in co-operation with the Canada Tourism Research Institute (CTRI). TIAC will be discussed again in Chapter 11.

Association of Canadian Travel Agents (ACTA) ACTA is the not-for-profit trade association for much of the travel sector in Canada. ACTA's name was changed from the Alliance of Canadian Travel Associations in June 1997. Retail travel agencies, tour operators, as well as any travel or tourism-related companies provide a broad cross-section of tourism-related member groups.

Canadian Tourism Research Institute (CTRI) The CTRI is an integral part of Canada's foremost research institute, the Conference Board of Canada. CTRI is

CASE STUDY

The Lap of Luxury

It was their honeymoon. The wedding had gone without a hitch, and all their guests said it was one of the most beautiful weddings they had ever attended. Tanasha and Josh Proulx had saved for their honeymoon and they were going first class! They had booked into one of the world's most luxurious hotels in Tahiti for a week-long stay. They were greeted with wild orchid leis, chilled champagne in their room, a box of Godiva chocolates, and two soft,

burgundy bathrobes. It was a week full of pleasures, from the fabulous meals to the activities supplied by the resort. They sailed the blue sea, walked along silvery sands, and danced into the early dawn. Now it was time to go home. But, while Tanasha and Josh were checking out, the front-desk attendant received a call from a member of the cleaning staff, who reported that the two terrycloth bathrobes were missing.

1. As front-desk attendant, how do you suppose this company trained you to respond to situations like this?
2. What response do you think you would get from the honeymooners if you searched their luggage? How would the other people in the lobby react?
3. The resort's guest bathrobes are truly luxurious and could be a fond reminder of a pleasant stay, but each robe costs $125. What could the company do to stop guests from taking the robes? How well do you think it would work?
4. Are Tanasha and Josh guilty of stealing? Why or why not?
5. If they are guilty of stealing, would you, as a company, prosecute? Why or why not?

privately funded and engages in extensive research on the tourism sector, followed by reports written to inform other tourism organizations, the industry, and the public on tourism's past performance and its anticipated future.

In addition, each province and territory of Canada has an organization comprising government workers and sometimes private industry members. The focus of their work is the development, growth, and promotion of tourism at the provincial level with one main goal: to make that province the number one destination in Canada. For example, Tourism Saskatchewan is a partnership that is industry-led, market-driven, and dedicated to all aspects of tourism in the province.

Municipal Organizations

The smallest but perhaps the most active tourism organization in your own community will be your local convention and visitors bureau (CVB). Much of the support the local tourist industry receives is from the city's chamber of commerce or its CVB. These groups are responsible for developing and promoting local events, bringing large tours or conferences to the city, and marketing a community's tourism products to a broader regional audience. Municipal organizations are part of tourism services (see Chapter 11).

Summary

Tourism has seen many changes over the past 100 years, from the methods and speed with which we travel, to the wide variety of new destinations and activities available to the average citizen. Although travel is still an important part of our lives, the threat of terrorism will change some of our travel patterns.

There are many terms in the industry that should be understood before beginning to study the subject, including *tourist (domestic* and *foreign)*, *excursionist*, *visitor, trip, leakage, multiplier effect,* and *travel deficit*.

In 1994, Canada created a new agency, the Canadian Tourism Commission, to market and promote tourism industries to Canada's many tourist markets. Many other diverse organizations help tourism grow, including the UNWTO, IATA, ICAO, PATA, WTTC, CTHRC, TIAC, ACTA, and the CTRI.

Questions

1. a) Define the term *sector*.
    b) Why is tourism considered to be an important sector to Canada?
    c) List the eight components of the tourism sector identified in Figure 1.1 and the role each one plays in tourism.

2. Explain how the eight components of tourism satisfy all of a tourist's needs while on vacation.

3. a) List 10 reasons for the growth of tourism.
    b) Explain how, in your opinion, any five of the growth factors you listed above will affect tourism over the next 20 years. Defend your answer, using examples.

4. Have recent terrorist activities or weather disasters changed your desire to travel or your destination? Why or why not?

5. Define, in your own words, the following tourism terms: *tourism, trip, domestic tourist, foreign tourist, excursionist, leakage, multiplier effect, cuisine tourism, agriculture tourism, volunteer tourism.*

6. Canada's travel deficit has fluctuated over the past five years.
   a) Define the term *travel deficit.*
   b) Identify the reasons for this fluctuation.
   c) Suggest one measure that you think should be taken by the CTC in order to help reduce the travel deficit.

7. a) Discuss four global tourism organizations and four Canadian tourism organizations that you feel have the greatest impact on Canadian tourism products, explaining why you have chosen them.
   b) Looking at the eight components of tourism (Figure 1.1), with which component is each of these organizations associated?

Notes

1. UNWTO World Tourism Barometer, Volume 6, No.1 January 2008 p. 1.

2. World tourism exceeds expectations in 2007, www.traveldailynews.com/show_page/24316, printed Wednesday January 30, 2008.

3. UNWTO World Tourism Barometer, Volume 6, No.1 January 2008 p. 1.

4. World Tourism Exceeds expectations in 2007, www.traveldailynews.com/show_page/24316, printed Wednesday January 30, 2008.

5. Tourism, 2007 Annual Report p. 7, www.canada.travel/research

6. Ibid.

7. The Buchanan report of 1994, Snapshots, 2nd edition.

8. US Department of Labor/Bureau of Labor Statistics, North American Industry Classification System (NAICS), www.bls.gov, modified December 7, 2007.

9. www.unwto.org

10. Deadline looming for travel, www.tiac-aitc.ca, August 31, 2005.

11. Tourism Industry Association of Canada conference proceedings, 1996 National Conference on Tourism, Jasper, Alberta.

12. www.canada.travel/research Year-in-review 2006 facts & figures.

13. Statistics Canada, Cat. no. 87-4023, p. 140.

14. Ibid, p. 141.

15. Robert W. McIntosh, Charles R. Goeldner, and J.R. Brent Ritchie, *Tourism Principles, Practices, Philosophies,* 7th ed. (New York, NY: John Wiley & Sons, 1995), p. 9.

16. Statistics Canada. Cat. no. 87-4023, p. 141.

17. www.corporate.canada.travel/en/ca/glossary

Tourism Guests and Hosts

Key terms

allocentric
business guest
certification
code of ethics
cultural motivators
demographics
discretionary income
discretionary time
emerit
empty nest
ethics

external locus of control
extrovert
family life stage
guests
hosts
internal locus of control
interpersonal motivators
introvert
midcentric
motivator
occupational standards

physical motivators
psychocentric
psychographics
pull factors
push factors
status and prestige
  motivators
tourism education
  councils (TECs)
tourism illiteracy

Learning objectives

Having read this chapter you will be able to

1. Explain the differences between business and leisure tourists.

2. a) Define the terms *motivators*, *demographics*, and *psychographics*.
   b) Explain how motivators, demographics and psychographics help determine travel choices, giving one example for each.

3. Identify four business market segments and four life stages (see Figure 2.1) explaining how the demographics of each market segment impact travel decisions.

4. Define the term *tourism illiteracy* and discuss its effect on a community.

5. a) List seven of the reasons people choose not to travel.
   b) Identify which of these reasons would be most difficult to override.

6. Identify and evaluate the 10 benefits of tourism to a community.

7. Give a brief analysis of the nine negative impacts of tourism on a community.

8. Identify the roles of the six federal government departments that interact with the tourism sector.

9. Discuss the roles in tourism played by the Canadian Tourism Commission (CTC), National Capital Commission (NCC), and the Canadian Tourism Human Resource Council (CTHRC).

10. Identify 10 human resource issues currently faced by the tourism sector.

11. Explain the terms *certification* and *emerit* and briefly discuss their value to business owners and to individual staff.

12. Explain the term *ethics* and why it is so important to the tourism sector.

In the study of tourism, it is important to understand the psychological and sociological composition of guests and hosts. **Guests** are the outside visitors who have come to be entertained by the people of a community or region. **Hosts** are individuals, communities, or regions who entertain the visiting guests. The correlation between host and guest is an interesting one. When we are guests, we expect to be treated with dignity, respect, fairness, and honesty. We generally will not accept anything but considerate treatment. However, when we are hosts, we sometimes forget how a guest should be treated, especially if our role as members of a host community or region is passive.

THE TOURISM GUEST

The first half of this chapter will focus on the guest. Guests are as diverse as humankind. Trying to define and understand the characteristics of guests is like trying to put together a giant jigsaw puzzle with pieces missing.

We all enjoy being guests, and part of that enjoyment comes from the care and service that we are given during our stay. Canadians as hosts have developed a great reputation for friendliness and hospitality, and how we approach each guest is determined by many factors.

Guests are most commonly grouped in three ways, depending on the purpose and the study source:

- by their **motivators** (business or pleasure)
- by their **demographics** (age, occupation, education, income level, and marital status)
- by their **psychographics** (personality, behaviours, likes, and dislikes)

Motivation: The Business Guest

Business travel is generally non-discretionary travel, in that the guest has few choices of where, when, how, and how long to travel. **Business guests** fill nearly 35 percent of all airline seats and are usually members of one or more frequent customer programs. Meetings and conventions continue to be the two main reasons for business travel, as they have been for many years. Other reasons for business travel include consulting, sales, operations, physical functions (maintenance), and management.

Four major types of traveller make up the business market:

1. **Frequent business traveller.** These guests may often stay repeatedly in the same hotel, which offers them specialized services such as instant check-in, and whose staff members are encouraged to remember the guests, their likes and dislikes, and to address them by name whenever possible.

2. **Luxury business traveller.** Desiring the best of travel experiences, these guests are not concerned with cost but consider service attitude extremely important.

3. **Female business traveller.** In 1970, only 1% of business guests were female. In 2000, women made up 50% of the business tourism market. The female guest, travelling alone, has somewhat different needs. She is more concerned with safety issues and is more likely to order room service than to venture outside for meals.

4. **International business traveller.** Travel in this segment is down due to higher costs, a weakening global economy, and the threat of terrorism. Many international companies are using internet conferencing as a viable alternative to travel. Having services available in the language of the guest is an important feature.

An interesting trend that appears to reflect the state of the economy is that business travel is being consolidated—that is, travellers tend to stay on the road a little longer to maximize accomplishments while minimizing cost. Many hotels go to great lengths to ensure the needs and expectations of business guests are met. Some will provide services like a full on-site business office to take care of incidental needs, or give the eco-conscious client the opportunity to purchase carbon credits, helping offset some of the damage to the global environment any trip incurs.

Motivation: The Pleasure Guest

Pleasure travel is very different from business travel and is affected by discretionary time and income, as well as family life stage.

Discretionary time is time away from work and other obligations. Vacations obviously involve discretionary time. **Discretionary income** is the money people may spend as they please. The relative value of personal income has grown sluggishly in the last decade, and we have seen a drop of approximately 13% of our U.S. tourism revenues, likely due to American concerns about a recession, their mortgage crisis, and the rising price of gas. On the positive side, these factors have encouraged more Canadians to vacation at home, in Canada. One trend seen by the industry is the rise of the "mini-vacation." Experts believe our more hectic lifestyles have left us with less discretionary time, and guests must be satisfied with 3–5-day vacations taken several times a year rather than the extended 14-day trip.

Family life stage is a second variant that helps determine when, where, and how a person takes a vacation. One important aspect to note is that the amount of

FIGURE 2.1

Life stages

www.checkin.com

discretionary income and time ties directly to each life stage. Generally speaking, people in the young-single and the **empty-nest** stages have more discretionary income (with neither mortgage to pay nor children to support) and time (with fewer family obligations) than do those in the other stages. In addition, empty nesters who are still working have more vacation days than do younger workers. Families spend their time and money differently than single pleasure guests do. Children have different needs, and if the children are happy, so are their parents. Therefore, family vacations are normally child-oriented. Figure 2.1 illustrates the different stages in life.

The amount of discretionary income and time available will dictate how much of each a guest can spend. Family life stage, however, is the best predictor of what guests will do on particular pleasure trips.

How do you think Jon's vacation choices will differ as he ages and moves up the lifestyle ladder? (See In Practice box, page 28.)

Demographics

Another method of classifying clients, loosely based on life stage, is by demographics. Tourism businesses should be aware of a guest's domicile, age, occupation, income, marital status, education, and gender, as this demographic information can then be used to further categorize the guest. This in turn helps the business determine the type of facilities and services that best suit a guest's needs.

In Practice

Example 1: Jon is in his early 20s and has just graduated with his diploma/degree. He and three friends are planning on taking a trip to Nova Scotia to see the sites and visit family. What type of activities and choice of food service options, accommodations, and activities/sites do you think they will choose? Explain your choice.

Example 2: Jon is in his early 30s and is married with two children, ages 2 and 4. He and his family are going to Nova Scotia to visit relatives and take a short vacation. How does this life stage affect his choices for accommodations, food service options, and activities and sites? Explain your answer.

Example 3: Jon and his wife have just retired. They have paid off their mortgage and own two cars. With the money they have saved for this trip, they will return to Nova Scotia to visit family and do some sightseeing. What type of accommodations, food service options, and sites/activities do you think will meet the needs of Jon and his wife now?

Do your choices for activities and sites change if you know both Jon and his wife are allocentrics? Explain how this personality will change their choices. Which life stage do you think will be interested in the most risky activity and the safest activity?

Knowledge of where guests come from may suggest where advertising might be most effective. Depending on the choice of strategy, advertising can be placed in the home cities and regions of current guests to continue to attract these visitors, or in other cities and regions in an attempt to expand market areas.

Psychographics

Using motives or behaviour to categorize travellers is also useful. Psychographic information helps hosts to understand the activities, interests, opinions, personalities, and likes and dislikes of guests. It is clear that guests at golf and tennis resorts come because of the activity provided. What is not as clear are the reasons guests come to a particular city with many different activities available to them. Psychographic data help cities or regions determine in what categories their guests may be grouped.

The use of personality as psychographic data was first introduced by Stanley Plog.[1] Plog designed a sliding scale with allocentrics at one end, psychocentrics at the other; most travellers are midcentric and fall somewhere in the centre of this scale. (see Figure 2.2). The **allocentric** is a risk-taker. This traveller prefers to go where no foot has trod before and is willing to go without the normal conveniences of life in order to gain a fuller travel experience. Allocentrics, often referred to by marketers as *innovators*, are the first to try a new travel destination. Once a destination has been established with a broad market base, they move on to a site yet to be "discovered" by the average tourist. Of course, some sites, such as Mt. Everest, will likely always remain on the "allocentric list of challenges." At the other end of Plog's spectrum is the **psychocentric** traveller. **Psychocentrics** are "armchair travellers," some of whom prefer to get their travel experience watching television and specialty travel networks. In fact, they are often reluctant to travel at all. When they do travel,

FIGURE 2.2
Psychocentric–
allocentric
continuum

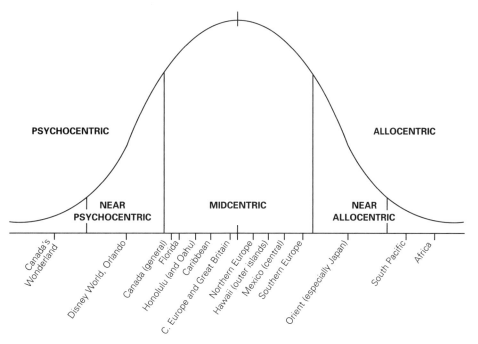

Source: Stanley C. Plog, *Leisure Travel* (New York: John Wiley & Sons, 1991), p. 83. Reprinted by permission of John Wiley and Sons Inc.

they prefer places that feel like home. The host community will speak the same language, food will be familiar, and the mode of travel they choose will be one with which they are comfortable (i.e., their car, a bus, or perhaps a train). For a Canadian psychocentric, learning about the "French culture" means a trip to Montreal or Quebec City. If they are finally convinced to travel to a foreign country like Germany, they will often choose to eat at a McDonald's and sleep in a U.S. brand-name hotel like Marriott. Visiting friends and relatives (VFR) is a common motivation for them. Travelling psychocentrics make great repeat customers because once they have visited an area and enjoyed themselves, they are comfortable returning. **Midcentrics** travel to obtain a break in their routine. Although they enjoy the change of pace, they are not likely to choose a vacation that deprives them of the basic comforts of life. One final note on Plog's theory: as we age, we are more likely to fall nearer the centre of his continuum.

Fiske and Maddi[2] have extended the personality theory by adding the two personality dimensions extroversion or introversion, as well as external or internal locus of control.

Travellers may also be categorized by their extroversion or introversion. An **extrovert** is an individual who is outgoing and uninhibited in interpersonal situations. They look to interact with the locals and go to their bars and restaurants to intermingle and make new friends. An **introvert** is more concerned with personal thoughts and feelings and is most likely to eat in a quiet, comfortable restaurant. Introverts get to know the culture of the destination by observing people on the streets, or visiting their national museums. While this factor may not actually determine the chosen destination, it will determine how they react once there. An internal or external locus of control describes a certain belief in life. People with an

FIGURE 2.3 The new consumers

1. They are more experienced travellers, more discerning purchasers, and willing to seek novel, adventurous, and niche-related activities.
2. They have changed values reflected in a desire for authenticity, a concern for environmental quality, and a search for personal fulfillment.
3. They have changed lifestyles manifested in healthy living, flexible work hours, higher household incomes, and travel as a way of life.
4. They are products of changing population demographics with an aging population, smaller households, couples without children, and those whose children have left home.
5. They are more flexible and are characterized by spontaneous and more frequent travel purchases, less planning, less rigidity, and markedly changed booking behaviours and specialized or niche product purchases.
6. They are more independent and need to be in control of their travel decisions and want to embrace their own identity."[3]

internal locus of control believe that they are in charge of what happens in their lives and that they control their own destiny. With an **external locus of control**, people believe that events are predetermined by other powerful individuals, fate, or chance and accept that what will be, will be. This personality trait helps determine travel choices like destinations and activities.

The Emerging Modern Traveller So much in life has changed over the past 50 years: how we communicate with each other, how we source information, and how we buy things, so it stands to reason that attitudes are changing, too. Figure 2.3 highlights some of the ways in which new consumers have changed according to Poon.

Finally, Epperson[4] has identified two factors that are also important in helping travellers choose a destination—push and pull factors.

The **pull factors**—external things such as scenic beauty—draw guests to a destination and continue to be an important reason for travel. Pull factors include people, places, and activities such as those listed on the following page.

In Practice

Identify yourself in the following terms:
- psychocentric, midcentric, or allocentric
- high or low activation or energy
- seeker or avoider of change
- introvert or extrovert
- internal or external locus of control

Based on how you identify yourself on each of these personality dimensions, choose your dream vacation and justify your choice.

friends	scenic areas	cultural events
relatives	historic areas	sports events
celebrities	educational events	
public figures	recreational events	

Push factors are those forces, needs, motivations, and ways of thinking that come from within us. Push factors are generated from our inner selves and include such factors as the following:

adventure	kinship	rest and relaxation
challenge	novelty	self-discovery
escape	prestige	

IMPACT OF TERRORISM ON THE GUEST

Tourists travel only when they feel secure in taking the trip, as the events of September 11, 2001, clearly illustrated. On September 1, occupancy rates in the Rockies were at their normal 95%, but by September 15, they had fallen 30%. Cross-border travel also fell dramatically, forcing border towns like Windsor to lay off staff in hotels, in the food service industry, and even in the casino. Business travel around the world dropped by 63% in the weeks that followed the attack, and vacation travel patterns changed. Tourists chose to travel by car, motor coach, or train and stayed closer to home.

The world's global tourism organizations quickly formed a coalition to deal with the problems of falling revenues, prompting Jean-Claude Baumgarten of the WTTC to appeal to governments "to work together in partnership to ensure that measures to strengthen security are effective, harmonized internationally, and applied globally. This will help restore consumer confidence in travel and tourism, the economic health of our industry, and the livelihood of all those who work in it."[5]

However, September 11 was only the beginning of Canada's tourism troubles. The country regained some of its lost market in 2002, but then a series of events put tourism into a negative spin again.

The first event was the Iraq war. Not only did people stop travelling in this period of unrest, but some American proponents of the war felt that patriotic Americans should put off visiting Canada. The second event that had an impact on tourism to Canada was the SARS epidemic in Toronto. While the disease was kept tightly controlled, the World Health Organization issued a six-month travel advisory for Canada. Canadian officials put forth a strenuous argument against the action—to no avail. Tourists responded by cancelling business trips, conferences and conventions, and of course vacations. In the middle of high season, Toronto hotels were running at 25% capacity. Then in June of that year, BSE (mad cow disease) was discovered in Alberta. While no people contracted the disease, the negative publicity did not help convince foreigners that we were a safe country to travel in. By 2004, most of the negative publicity had disappeared and it looked as though it was going to be a normal year. But new concerns arose.

The September 11 attack created great concerns in the United States about their borders. The Mexican border has historically been seen as an entry point for illegal aliens and drug smugglers. However, the U.S.–Canada border was proudly, for over 200 years, the longest "unguarded" border in the world, and proof of citizenship was simply a birth certificate. Passports were used for foreign travel, and travelling to the United States was definitely not considered foreign. Cross-border shopping was done with ease, and unless you chose a busy time period to cross, the border was a simple, friendly welcome. Since September 11, 2001, passport requirements have been in effect for those entering the United States by aircraft. Now, with the passing of the WHTI, anyone coming from Canada to the United States must have a valid passport. A vast majority of Americans (83% according to CNN) and Canadians do not have passports, and as our southern neighbour is our largest and friendliest foreign market, the loss of revenue has already been high. Fortunately, loss of revenue from the U.S. market has been compensated for the last year with an increase in both Asian and Australian visitors.

How have the events orchestrated by the United States changed their tourism industry? In March 2008, CNN aired the first of a series of discussions on the future of their tourism foreign market should the hard line border/visa stance remain in place. The high state of alert of the U.S. borders, the increasing difficulty in getting visitor visas, and the demand for passports and more thorough border checks have cost the U.S. tourism industry $130 billion. Tourists from China wait a minimum of 35 days and tourists from Brazil wait 85 days for the initial tourist visa interview to enter the United States. The visa itself may take as long as two years to get. Long lines at the border have taken their toll on Canadians visitors as well as other foreign visitors. These higher end tourists from Europe and Asia spend approximately $4000 per visit, and the losses continue to add up for America. The image of the United States as a "great place to visit" is gone, with 74% of Europeans stating it is no longer on their list of places to visit.[6] Canada has always been seen as a comfortable destination to visit, and with the loss of our U.S. markets and with our tourism revenues down, this could well be the perfect time for Canada to be gearing up to host other foreign markets to the 2010 Olympic Games.

WHY TRAVEL?

Demographics and personality have a great influence on where people travel to and what activities they do when they get there. But what actually gets a person travelling? A **motivator** is a *promoter of action*; it is what helps people decide what they want to do and when. A need or a want creates the motivation in a person to satisfy that need or want. If the need is for food, the motivator is to find something to eat. The need to conduct business is the motivator for business travel, but what motivates pleasure travel?

Physical motivators to travel, such as the need to escape a particularly cold winter, are easier to identify than psychological needs. Psychological needs are often theoretical and may be difficult to pinpoint in an individual. Understanding psychological needs, however, leads to a better understanding of the superficial reasons for travelling.

www.seetorontonow.com

Maslow's Hierarchy of Needs

Abraham Maslow first developed the theory of motivation based on a hierarchy of needs. Five levels of need are specified, from lowest to highest order (see Figure 2.4). According to Maslow, an individual will satisfy the lowest motivational level (that is, physiological needs) first. Once those have been satisfied, a higher-order need

FIGURE 2.4 Maslow's hierarchy of needs

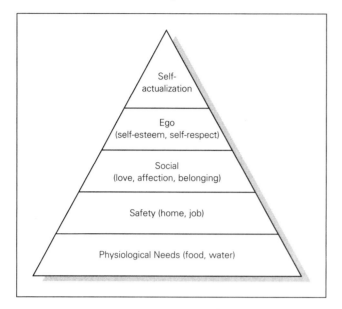

will emerge to direct behaviour. Thus, it is the unsatisfied need that leads to action. In advanced economies such as those in Canada and the United States, most tourists' physiological and safety needs have been met. According to Maslow, however, few people satisfy their social and ego needs sufficiently to move to the fifth-level need, self-actualization. Therefore, the most important motivating forces in travel are social and ego needs.

To apply these principles to tourism, let's look at each step and how it might affect the traveller. *Physiological needs* are simple and generate motivations such as escape from a cold climate, a break from the stress of work, and physical relaxation. These are the first needs the industry tends to—transportation, accommodations, and food. *Safety needs* must be met in order for travel to take place. Few tourists would knowingly make a travel choice that would endanger their lives. Safety for the traveller rests with governments, with those who provide police, medical, and similar services, and with individual tourism businesses. Nothing brings tourism to a halt faster than war or the threat of terrorism. News—of a plane crash, fatal food poisoning in a restaurant, a fire in a hotel, or a theme park ride that has malfunctioned and injured passengers—has an immediate negative impact on that business. *Social needs* are by far the most common motivators, and VFR (visiting friends and relatives) is the most common pleasure motivator. The need for companionship and belonging may be identified by the choice of a trip. For example, a tour package offers group activities with other people who share similar interests, and a sense of belonging may be fulfilled by a trip to trace a person's ancestral roots. *Ego/self-esteem* deals with a person's need to feel important and special. Included in these motivators might be a trip to see special events such as the Olympics or a concert, incentive travel vacations (awards for high performance), and the need for special services such as gold memberships or first-class service. The ego/self-esteem category also includes the "keeping up with the Joneses" or the "all my friends have been there" motivator. Finally, *self-actualization needs* focus on achieving one's full potential as a human being. These motivators might see a tourist choosing a self-guided walking tour through the vineyards of Bordeaux to learn the language and discover more about French wine, travelling to Toronto to help build homes for Habitat for Humanity, or climbing Mount Everest.

McIntosh and Goeldner have looked at motivators from a different perspective.[7] They have divided motivation into four basic categories: physical motivators, cultural motivators, interpersonal motivators, and status and prestige motivators.

1. **Physical motivators** are directly related to health. Sports participation, relaxation, and recreation are preventive health maintenance motivators, whereas medical exams, health treatments, or "fat farm" attendance are curative health motivators. Both types are seen as tension releasers through physical activity or attention to a health problem.

www.statcan.gc.ca

The Citadel, one of Nova Scotia's National Historic Sites, sits near the centre of the city making it easily accessible for tourists.
(Photo courtesy Canadian Tourism Commission.)

2. **Cultural motivators** are a desire to learn more about the music, architecture, food, art, folklore, or religion of other people. These motivators stem from a curiosity to experience another way of life through travel rather than just through books or television.

3. **Interpersonal motivators** are the strongest motivators of all and include two extremes: visiting friends and relatives (VFR) or escaping from family and friends. People who live close to family sometimes feel a need to get away from the family influence, even if only for a short time. Those who live far from family sometimes feel a need to get back in touch through vacation time.

4. **Status and prestige motivators**, which were discussed earlier in this chapter as ego and self-esteem factors, concern the need for recognition, attention, appreciation, and good reputation.

Travelling with a Disability

While motivations and needs may differ from one guest to another, all travellers expect one thing: that their expectations be met regarding the quality of their trip. Fifty years ago, working with disabled guests was not of great concern for the tourism sector. Few people with major disabilities travelled; modes of transportation were not easily accessed, and hotels and restaurants did not have the facilities to provide quality service. Today, disabled travellers form the single largest minority group in North America. Guests with disabilities come from all walks of life and all life stages, and as travellers, have a keen sense of adventure and a desire to participate fully in life. A Harris poll done for the Society for Accessible Travel and Hospitality (SATH) estimated that this market spends over $81.7 billion on travel products. In a 2004 news release, Harris reported

TABLE 2.1   *Top Activities Participated in* by International Tourists to Canada in 2003*

Activity	U.S. Residents %	Overseas Residents %
Shopping	62	87
Sightseeing	51	75
Participating in an outdoor sport or adventure tourism	32	32
Visiting friends and relatives	31	59
Visiting a historical site	28	39
Visiting a national or provincial nature park	23	47
Going to a party or nightclub	23	33
Visiting a museum	23	37
Attending cultural events	11	14
Visiting a zoo, aquarium, or botanical garden	11	27

* more than one activity may be participated in while on a trip

Courtesy Canadian Tourism Commission

www.pc.gc.ca/Banff

that 75% of people with disabilities eat out at least once a week, adding nearly $35 billion to the revenues of the food and beverage industry. With financial figures like this available, why is the tourism industry still neglecting the needs of this group?[8]

Table 2.1 shows what tourists actually do in Canada. For a variety of reasons, people do want to travel. They look forward to their next trip and talk about previous trips. Reasons for travelling always exist and often lead to actual experience.

Tourists travel to Canada from around the globe to experience the awesome natural beauty of such destinations as Athabasca Glacier, Banff National Park.
(Photo: Tom Hadley.)

THE BARRIERS TO TRAVEL

We've just talked about the reasons people choose to travel, but what stops them from travelling? Seven common barriers to travel are very difficult to overcome. You will note that often one factor influences another. For example, time, cost, and distance are often interrelated. If you live in Halifax, a trip to Agra, India, to see the Taj Mahal not only will be costly, but also will include a long airline journey. In a typical two-week vacation, you would likely spend at least 20% of your vacation on a plane.

Cost At no point can the average traveller avoid considering the cost of a trip. In times of economic difficulty, destination, length of stay, and travel method will all be modified by the amount of discretionary income people have to spend on their vacations. Occupation and education may determine whether someone can afford the trip because these factors are often related to wage scale and time off the job. Two other factors that affect cost are the number of people travelling and the price structure at the destination. A family of four interested in learning more about French culture may find a trip to Paris too expensive, while a trip to Quebec City provides them with a similar cultural experience at a fraction of the cost.

Lack of Time No matter where you decide to go for vacation, travelling takes time. If you have a three-day weekend and live in Halifax, you may go to Sydney, Nova Scotia, to see family, but you will not be visiting family in Sydney, Australia. Time limits the choice of destination and, often, the mode of travel. The farther the destination is from home, the more likely you are to travel plane rather than by car. This allows you maximum time to spend *at* the destination rather than travelling *to* it.

Accessibility, Distance, or Ease of Travel Can you reach your destination easily? Do you have to fly or can you drive? Many tourists who come to Canada to fish are looking for pristine lakes, like those in our north. These lakes are exactly what the fisher wants, but they are inaccessible by car and must be reached by float plane. Distance and time are so closely related that they can stop travellers from picking their first-choice destinations.

Health and Disabilities Of course, if you have the flu, you should not be travelling. Travelling is one of the ways that disease is spread and epidemics occur. Disabilities, on the other hand, are not communicable diseases but may be caused by an injury, a non-communicable disease, or simple aging. Obesity can also be disabling for travellers. In 2007, the Supreme Court of Canada ruled that an airline could not charge for a second seat if needed by a particularly large person, but that the body mass must be considered as one entity when selling space on an airline. Large people may now travel using two seats for the price of a single fare.

Travel Tastes and Experience Personality and age affect this barrier to travel. For instance, psychocentrics are not fond of travel at all. In fact, if they take a trip, it will likely be within their own province. Border crossings, a foreign language, and strange food are not on their agenda.

Education Education also influences the decision to travel. Generally speaking, the more education you have, the greater your knowledge of the world and the more likely you are to seek out new experiences.

Age When we are young, travel is an exciting adventure. As we age, it becomes more difficult to handle change; eventually, travel stops altogether. A 96-year-old woman in a wheelchair is not likely to travel at all. If she does, it is with great preparation and usually with a younger travelling companion.

Fear The most difficult barrier to overcome is fear—fear of new places, fear of water, fear of flying, fear of terrorism. Fears can paralyze activity, are seldom based on concrete experience, and may be real or imagined. For example, the beautiful beaches in Israel have fewer vacationers because of continued terrorist activities in that region. As for flying, the vast majority of flights safely carry passengers to their destinations; in fact, flying is still considered to be the safest mode of transportation. Unfortunately, knowledge does not always overcome fear. In 2008, the Canadian government issued a warning to tourists travelling to Mexico due to an increase in crime against Canadian tourists. When travelling to a foreign country, you should be aware that the country's rule of law governs not only the citizens, but tourists as well. There is little the Canadian government can do to release from a foreign jail a Canadian charged with a criminal offence in a foreign country.

THE TOURISM HOST

What is the role of a host? Think of inviting guests for an overnight stay. You want to be sure they are warmly greeted and made to feel comfortable and at home. You want your dwelling to be clean and tidy, and you may add fresh flowers to enhance its beauty. The food will be prepared specially, the beds will be made with clean sheets and pillows, and the towels will be freshly washed. Your conversation will be friendly and polite and you will likely not try to engage in an argument that leaves bad feelings between you and your guests. In other words, you treat your guests as you would like to be treated.

Destination communities use a similar strategy for greeting tourists. Streets are kept clean, and flower boxes, gardens, and parks make the destination pretty. Hotels endeavour to provide first-class service and restaurants to provide safe, wholesome food. Travellers also hope to receive a warm welcome from the people in a community. But do they? Have you ever driven behind a car that is obviously searching for a street name or the proper turn, and grumbled, "Learn how to drive"? Have you overheard foreign tourists trying to explain what they need when they do not speak French or English? How helpful has the listener been?

A positive attitude toward guests is crucial if guests are to enjoy their stay. Negative attitudes are often caused by **tourism illiteracy**. The major cause of tourism illiteracy is a lack of understanding of the benefits tourism brings to a community. For example, people are often unhappy when tax dollars are used to fund new tourist attractions or events instead of health, educational, or social programs. People and communities can also be illiterate in the sense that they don't see tourism as an economic benefit—they don't see the large number of full-time and part-time jobs tourism creates, and they don't realize how the economic multiplier spreads tourist dollars to nearly every member of the community. The public is unaware that tourism brings in more than $50 billion in revenue yearly, and they don't see the amount of additional tax dollars that tourists generate (Table 2.2). What they do see is that tourists intrude on their way of life. Sadly, even governments can show signs of tourism illiteracy. When was the last time a politician spoke up for the needs

TABLE 2.2 *Canada-U.S.A. International Travel Competitive Review 2007*

Trips from	Canada number (#)	Canada 07/06 % change	U.S.A. number (#)	U.S.A. 07/06 % change
Total international	17 768	-2	48 359	11
Americas				
United States	13 371	-3		
Mexico			6 732	15
Overseas Key Markets				
France	358	-1	998	26
Germany	298	0	1 524	10
United Kingdom	892	6	4 498	8
China	151	9	540	18
Japan	310	-15	3 531	-4
South Korea	188	-1	806	6
Australia	208	17	670	11
Canada			17 735	11
Total Key Markets	**16 006**	**-3**	**37 034**	**10**

Tourism Snapshot Year-in-Review 2007

Courtesy Canadian Tourism Commission

of the tourism sector? Did the Bush administration even consider its tourism industry when it put the strict border and visa requirements in place? Northern states that depend on Canadian tourism spoke out against the proposed legislation, but their words were unheeded. Today, the United States is just beginning to feel the impact of these changes.

Tourism illiteracy is hard to overcome. People who are illiterate about tourism may have developed this attitude because of a bad experience with tourists and may, therefore, label all tourism as bad. These people seem to enjoy expressing their negative feelings to others in the community or directly to tourists, which encourages more anti-tourist sentiment. How can we deal with this negativity? The best way to overcome tourism illiteracy is for tourism professionals to educate their community about the great value and benefits of this sector. Table 2.2 illustrates the positive gains made by the United States vs. Canada in regard to the number of visits, not the dollar revenue.

www.go2hr.ca

Benefits of Tourism

Here is a short list of some of the more important benefits tourism brings to a country and a community:

1. **Economic diversification.** The tourism sector provides a community with a wider variety of both full-time and part-time jobs than any other sector, including the hiring and promotion of minorities as well as people with different levels of education. Tourism also provides part-time work for those who cannot accept a full-time job.

Throughout the summer, tourists flock to Parliament Hill to see the Changing of the Guards, a ceremony similar to the one held daily at Buckingham Palace in London, England.
(Photo courtesy Canadian Tourism Commission.)

2. **Cultural preservation.** One motivation to travel is the chance to learn about other countries and ways of life. Canadian culture has been influenced by many different cultures, and this diversity gives tourists a mosaic of cultural experiences to enjoy while on vacation here. Canadian Heritage oversees the protection and development of many of Canada's cultural and historic sites.

3. **Better choices in entertainment, shopping, and food service.**

4. **Enhanced travel.** Roads, airports, ports, and public transportation are built or improved.

5. **Area beautification.** Tourists choose Canada as a destination because of its image as a clean, natural, and healthy environment. Destination communities take care to ensure that their region is planted with trees, flowers, and lawns; that towns and roadways are cleared of waste; and that, through unicipal legislation, the area maintains its beauty and uniqueness.

6. **Tax revenues.** For every billion dollars of tourism income earned in Canada, $230 million goes to the federal government, $160 million to provincial governments, and $60 million to municipal governments. This money helps reduce our taxes.[9]

   In the last five years, some municipalities have introduced a lodging/room tax. The revenues that are generated pay for additional advertising for the area, bringing in more tourists without using local tax dollars.

7. **Foreign capital.** When an international company invests in Canada, its foreign dollars help to build the Canadian product. Jobs are created and revenue is produced for Canadian tourism workers, with less investment needed from the region or municipalities.

8. **Recreational and educational facilities.** Many public universities and colleges would have financial difficulty were it not for government

support, and most hospitality schools have had some form of government financing. National and provincial parks, historic sites, and attractions are also funded in part by tourism dollars.

9. **Modernization.** A strong tourism market means roadways must be maintained, new airports built, and other infrastructure regularly upgraded. Local residents as well as tourists enjoy the benefits of these upgrades. Better infrastructure also helps public services such as the police and sanitation crews do their jobs.

www.otec.org

10. **A favourable world image.** The value of hosting a large international event such as the Olympics cannot be underestimated. British Columbia is already enjoying promotions focusing on their hosting of the 2010 Winter Olympics, and as we become more aware of how to host a profitable event, large losses such as those from the Olympics in Montreal in 1966 are rare. Events such as these strongly support a positive global vision of the hosting nation—who had heard of Lillehammer, Norway, prior to the Olympics in 1994? The Summer Olympics in Beijing in 2008 brought forth negative attitudes in certain international circles, with demands that the event be boycotted due to the Chinese attitude regarding human rights. The Olympics were awarded to China with the hopes that the world would gain a glimpse of the people of China and not just the government policies. The influx of foreign tourists and media may have helped other nations see the positive side of Chinese culture and helped the people of China by bringing revenue to individuals and not just the Chinese government.

FOOTPRINT

Both the First Nations communities and the environment were front and centre for Vancouver's Olympic Committee when they were designing the Olympic mascots for 2010. There are three mascots: (1) Miga, who is part Kermode spirit bear and part killer whale; (2) Quatchi is a hockey-loving sasquatch; and (3) Sumi is a fusion of animals—orca head, thunderbird wings, and black bear legs. Protection and preservation of the environment have been cornerstones of First Nations cultures since their beginning. Animals and the Earth are honoured for their beauty, sustainability, and giving of life. Historically, when an animal was hunted, its entire being had a purpose: meat for eating, skins for dwellings, and fur for clothing. Some Canadians think the mascots are good representatives of the diversity that thrives in this country, while also honouring our ecology and Aboriginal culture. Others think they are too cartoon-like and will appeal only to children.

Do an Internet search for Miga, Quatchi, and Sumi—what do you think of the official Olympic mascots?

Barriers to Tourism Acceptance

The fact is that tourists do have a negative impact on a community. Some barriers to the acceptance of tourism discussed here are based on fact; others are based on suspicion. All of them are concerns that a community, region, or country might voice against becoming more actively involved in the tourism sector:

1. **Crime and unwanted behaviour.** Tourists come to a destination with money, credit cards, and other valuable belongings. In any host society, there are those who wish to take advantage of people who are unfamiliar with the customs, the area, or potential dangers. *Crime against tourists has no national boundaries.* Protection of the tourist is an important part of maintaining a safe image to show to the rest of the world. Also disturbing to the host community are unwanted behaviours such as prostitution and drunkenness, which often become more prevalent in a town that focuses on tourism as its main source of revenue.

2. **Air, water, land, and noise pollution.** Adding a million additional people to a region during a short tourism season puts a strain on the ecosystem. Banff is one of the best examples of the problem. To minimize this damage, tighter controls have been established that limit new development and the number of visitors, and reinforce regulations to ensure that the ecosystem is safe.

3. **Congestion of roadways, parks, shopping areas, recreational centres, attractions, and restaurants.** Although a region may benefit greatly from tourism revenues, a feeling of ill will can be created when locals are forced to compete for a seat in their favourite restaurant or deal with the crowds and disruption of daily life brought about by a large event.

4. **Local resentment.** Tension may develop when cultural or economic differences exist between guests and their hosts. For instance, resentment may occur if tourists do not follow the social or cultural norms of the host country, or if young residents begin to question the values of their own cultural traditions. Some members of the community may also resent guests' extravagant lifestyles.

5. **Inflation.** Inflation increases when tourists come to town. During high season, hotels charge full rates, shops are less inclined to offer bargains, and the general cost of living tends to rise.

6. **Seasonality.** Regions that experience a seasonal tourist influx, such as Cape Breton and Prince Edward Island, will also experience high unemployment once the season is over.

7. **Leakage.** When demand for the tourism product is greater than the destination's local resources, leakage occurs (Chapter 1), and the community does not get the full benefit of tourism dollars.

8. **Increases in the cost of services.** Most tourism events require additional police service and may require on-site paramedics. During World Youth Day in July of 2002, the hot weather meant that additional staff were needed to hand out bottles of water, more paramedics were required to deal with sunstroke victims, and more police were needed to ensure the event happened in an orderly fashion.

9. **Diversion of government funds.** Tourism may divert government money and attention from needed projects in order to build and renew a country's tourism products. In 2003, forest fires destroyed some of the historic train trestles that attracted hikers to the Kelowna area. Much to the dismay of many living in that area, Canadian Heritage provided a one-time grant of $50 million to repair them. The tsunami that struck Southeast Asia in 2004 resulted in the rapid rebuilding of resorts, compared with a slower move to rebuild homes and local lifestyles.

TOURISM'S IMPACT ON CULTURES AND SOCIETIES

Many studies have been done on the impact of tourism on the host nation and its people. The impact tourism has on a community is largely based on the community's ability to absorb tourists. Larger, modern communities found in countries with looser cultural regulations adjust better to a sudden influx of foreigners. For this reason, while tourists do impact the society of New York or Paris, the population handles the inconvenience more easily. Smaller towns such as Banff or Niagara-on-the-Lake—or where the living environment of the destination is very different from Canada's such as Nairobi, Kenya, or Kingston, Jamaica—have a great deal more difficulty. Edward Inskeep suggests that the following differences determine the depth of the difficulties:[10]

- basic values and logic system—how is life viewed, what facets of life are deemed important? Education? Finances? Family lifestyle?
- religious beliefs—does religion play an active or a passive role in the society?
- traditions—traditions are often an important part of the lure for tourists, but are they compatible with foreign ideas and traditions? e.g., if alcohol consumption is frowned upon or completely illegal
- customs—do customs meet the norms of the visiting population or are they so different they cause conflict? e.g., bargaining at the local market or shops
- lifestyles—can tourists adjust easily to the local lifestyle and vice versa? e.g., siesta time interferes with the tourists' need for activity
- behavioural patterns—e.g., women are not allowed the same freedoms as men
- dress codes—can women show their bodies without being considered immoral?
- sense of time budget—"don't worry, be happy," tomorrow is soon enough
- attitudes toward strangers—can visitors move freely, comfortably among the local population?

Colouring these differences is the simple fact that when people travel, their own customs change, including spending and dining habits. Researchers have also concluded that the faster a tourism industry develops, the more difficulty local residents have in adjusting to the changes.

A second approach to looking at cultural impacts of tourism has been developed by G.V. Doxey. His "Index of Tourist Irritation" identifies five stages that smaller destinations are likely to experience even if cultural norms are similar.[11]

Stage 1: *Level of euphoria* Positive vibrations occur as tourist dollars begin to flow, the additional jobs and financial resources have a positive impact on the community, and there is an enthusiasm for the development of the tourism industry. Visitors are greeted happily and both tourist and resident enjoy mutual satisfaction.

Stage 2: ***Level of apathy*** As the industry grows, residents begin to take advantage of the tourist, inflation may have a negative impact on locals, or a two-tier system of pricing develops. Tourists and their financial resources are taken for granted. The warmth first experienced between tourist and local becomes more formal.

Stage 3: ***Level of irritation*** This stage is reached when the industry is nearing the saturation point and local residents begin to be annoyed by the number of tourists taking advantage of their town and its facilities. As long as the number of tourists is kept at a tolerable level, dealing with the irritation factor is simpler.

Stage 4: ***Level of antagonism*** Irritation becomes more vocal and tourists are blamed for all of the negative occurrences such as increase in crime and bad behaviours, disrespect of property, and a feeling that the townsfolk are being taken advantage of. At this stage, there may be irreversible changes in local culture and moral attitudes.

Stage 5: ***The final level*** The local residents forget that the way they lived was what first attracted the tourist, they are unable to deal with the changes brought about by the increase in tourism and its trappings, and they must live with the fact that their life has changed, never to be the same again. If the destination is able to make the adjustments and can cope with mass tourism, it will continue to thrive.

If tourism experiences a high and low season, locals can often tolerate the change, knowing it comes to an end with the season. However, if seasonality has little impact on tourist flows, this is not a benefit locals can count on. Once tourism has a foothold on a town or a country, its progress is difficult to stop without some sort of government interference, however, if the tourist is made to feel uncomfortable or threatened, the industry flounders. It is in the hands of the government to control the direction tourism takes, and its decisions determine the positive and negative impacts dealt with by the local residents and their environment.

Tourists prefer their souvenirs to be authentic, and this often provides income for local artists.
(Photo: Canadian Tourism Commision.)

In Practice

If you were placed in a leadership role in your hometown and were trying to persuade residents of the benefits of tourism, who would be your strongest allies and who would be your toughest opponents? How would you try to sway the opinion of those opposed to tourism?

CANADA'S ROLE IN THE DAYS AFTER SEPTEMBER 11

Canadians have gained a reputation for being ready to take an active role in global events when needed. In the first 12 hours after the September 11 attacks, Canadians welcomed more than 35 000 unexpected visitors to their cities. With airports and airspace across the United States closed, inbound airliners had little option but to land at Canadian airports. The small town of Gander, Newfoundland (population 10 500), was a good example of how communities put on their "host hats" for these stranded travellers. In less than 10 hours, the region around Gander received 6600 tourists needing lodging, food, and comfort. With far too few hotel rooms available, private homes and community centres were opened. U.S. fears of more attacks forced passengers to stay on their aircraft for as long as 24 hours before getting off. Newfoundlanders made sure that when passengers were allowed to disembark, they had clean blankets, fresh food, and beds. The warm hospitality of Newfoundlanders helped passengers cope with the horrors of September 11, and in 2006, five years after the attack, many of the U.S. passengers returned to Newfoundland to express their gratitude once again. Included in their thanks was a significant donation to an educational trust, set up by the passengers in the year following the attack, that provides bursaries and scholarships for the children of their hosts.

www.tourismhrc.com

Friendly, helpful staff provide a positive experience for tourists.
(Photo courtesy Canadian Tourism Commission.)

As noted earlier, September 11, 2001, was only the beginning of Canada's tourism troubles. Fortunately, shortly afterwards, the Canadian government and the CTC announced a one-time $20 million cash infusion for the promotion of tourism. This allowed the CTC to quickly put together a new marketing plan addressing recent events and reassuring travellers that Canada was still a safe destination. These efforts paid off. In the first quarter of 2002, there was a surprising resurgence of tourism. In Canada, 7 of our top 12 foreign markets (not including the United States) rebounded, with the number of visitors up 11.3 percent. However, because our largest market, the United States, stayed home, final 2002 tourism numbers were up only marginally by the end of the year.

National and global events continued to put Canadian tourism into another negative spin. Canada's annual travel deficit for 2003 was $3.9 billion, but by 2004, it had risen by 7.7% to $4.1 billion.[12] Since the poor showing of 2003, tourism prospects have improved. Between 2005 and 2006, overall tourism revenues increased by 6.5% to an all-time high of $66.8 billion. While there was a decrease in visits from the United States, overall foreign travel was up by 2.4% and this helped offset the U.S. decline. Visitors from Mexico and China registered the highest increase in the number of travellers, but showed the lowest average spending per night (Mexico $68/night).

In 2008, we celebrated the 400th anniversary of the founding of Quebec, and a higher number of French tourists were expected to visit the province. Many of France's deluxe tour operators focused their products on this anniversary year, developing high-end (and profitable) tours. While it was unlikely this group of visitors would be visiting the western regions of Canada, the Maritime provinces, and Ontario enjoyed some of the revenue. Acadian history is one of the colourful eras of our past that intrigues the French. For our Western provinces, the booming Australian economy and the continued strength of the Australian dollar against the U.S. dollar has brought with it an increase in Australian visitors. The Australians tend to be older, spend more money per night, and stay longer than most other visitors. The CTC projects a continued decline in U.S. visitors as their economy weakens, and new legislation slows cross-border traffic. The Summer Olympics in Beijing also siphoned some visitors off, but the next four years, with the increasing chatter of the 2010 Olympics, are shaping up to be financially rewarding for the tourism sector and Canadians.[13]

THE FEDERAL GOVERNMENT AND TOURISM

The major host in any country is its national government, which plays an extremely important role in tourism. If the tourism sector does not have the support of the government, it cannot flourish. For instance, when the Shah of Iran was overthrown in 1979, the new government closed the borders of Iran to foreigners. The streets of Tehran, once bustling with tourists eager to spend their money in the city known as the "Paris of the East," suddenly had no visitors. Many of its beautiful shops, hotels, and restaurants went bankrupt, and those that survived had great difficulty and were forced to make major changes in how they did business. Tourism, once a very profitable industry in Iran, became virtually nonexistent. Japan provides another example of the impact of government regulations. Until the 1960s, travel to and from Japan was tightly controlled. The Japanese were seldom allowed to vacation outside the country, and foreigners were not encouraged to visit Japan. When the ban on travel was lifted, tourism began to flourish, opening Japan to the world and providing new revenues for the Japanese government and its people.

Governments not only hold power over their own tourism industry, but also can have a major impact on other nations' tourism. The new Western Hemisphere Travel Initiative (WHTI) security measures passed by the U.S. government have had a devastating effect not only on their own tourism industry but on tourism in foreign countries, especially Canada. How much does the average member of Parliament know about the tourism industry? Past history indicates not much. For this reason, organizations like the Tourism Industry Association of Canada (TIAC) and the Hotel Association of Canada (HAC) constantly examine pieces of legislation that could have a negative impact on the industry. They are ready to lobby "on the hill" to ensure that changes are made or that the legislation dies on the floor, and, fortunately, they often have some success.

Here are the federal government departments that have the most impact on the Canadian tourism sector:

- **Industry Canada** is responsible for the overall well-being of the tourism sector. The Canadian Tourism Commission operates as a Crown corporation under the auspices of this department.

- **Foreign Affairs Canada (FAC)** is responsible for issuing Canadian passports and Canadian entrance visas. Passports are official documents that allow holders to travel from and return to their own countries. The federal government has redesigned Canadian passports to make forgery more difficult by digitally printing the bearer's picture on a secure page and adding a hologram. Children used to travel on their parents' passports, but must now carry their own. Background checks on new applicants are more vigorous, and tighter security measures at all border crossings are now in place. Of course, with these changes came an increase in the cost and turnaround time of processing a passport. For business travellers who frequently cross the border, Canada and the United States are considering a special identification card that will allow expedited access to both countries. To qualify for these cards, the business person must first submit to a rigorous background investigation. Iris identification scanners and visual scanners that can quickly identify travellers as "safe" or "safety risks" are also being considered.

  Visas are official documents that give travellers permission to enter a country for a specified period of time. For example, a Hungarian who wishes to visit Canada must now go to the Canadian embassy in Budapest to obtain a visitor's visa. FAC has imposed new, tighter restrictions on all visas issued and has added eight countries to the "visa required" list. The easiest visas to get are those granted to students enrolling in a school or university—and most of the terrorists involved in the attacks on the World Trade Center and the Pentagon entered the United States on student visas. If you have any questions, your travel agent can provide you with correct visa or passport information.

  On October 4, 2005, new regulations were instituted at borders and airports. These new regulations require Canadian travellers heading to the United States to give additional specific information to U.S. Immigration prior to their departure. Now Canadians visiting the United States must also provide U.S. authorities with the full address of their destination, including telephone number and zip code. Simply providing the name of a hotel is no longer sufficient. Legislation expected to pass the U.S. Senate by 2009 will require that all Canadian citizens have valid passports. Currently, passports are not mandatory, but strongly recommended.

Because of growing tensions throughout much of the world, the government of Canada has created a website covering recent developments in 220 foreign countries (Voyage.gc.ca). The information provided on this website includes developments that might put the Canadian traveller in jeopardy—from current conflicts to weather problems or health concerns.

www.voyage.gc.ca

- **Canada Border Services Agency** The first Canadians that a foreign tourist meets are employees of the CBSA, who in turn report to Citizenship and Immigration Canada. These employees are responsible for checking the travel documents of every person arriving in Canada—including Canadians. Prior to September 11, 2001, this office's computer system was not linked to any other law enforcement agency. In recent years, several terrorists have entered Canada first, then crossed the border into the United States. To try to stop this human traffic, immigration officials will now be linked to the RCMP system, which will in turn link to U.S. law enforcement agencies.

  Every country requires arriving travellers to pass through customs control, where purchases being brought into the country must be declared. The CBSA is responsible for customs services. Airline passengers who reside in a foreign country must complete declaration forms and immigration forms upon entering Canada. For returning Canadians, proof of citizenship and the declaration form serve as both entry and customs declaration documents. At airports, Canadians must list on their declaration form all items purchased abroad. Canadians entering the country by private vehicle may be able to make a verbal declaration. However, drivers may be asked for proof of ownership or for the rental agreement for the vehicle. Customs inspectors, constantly on the lookout for missing children, often query children accompanying adults.

- **Parks Canada Agency** is now an independent agency reporting to Environment Canada. It is responsible for overseeing all of our national parks, 131 national historic sites, historic railway stations, and more than 650 historic sites; it oversees operation of our seven historic canal systems; it coordinates the federal–provincial co-operative program for the Canadian Heritage River Systems; it directs and implements heritage tourism opportunities and programs; and it provides services to the more than 20 million visitors who use the national parks system every year. More detail on its role is given in Chapter 9.

- **Transport Canada** oversees the regulation of our transportation systems and helps with the building and maintenance of the transportation infrastructure. It is responsible for overseeing all accidents involving death where any form of transportation has been used. In 2002, a tour bus from Ottawa called the Lady Duck sank just offshore from the city of Hull in the River Ottawa. With four people killed in this incident, the Transportation Safety Board investigated and determined that the vehicle was unsafe for water transportation and charged the tour company. For information on Transport Canada's role in air traffic, see Chapter 4.

A Crown Corporation: The Canadian Tourism Commission (CTC)

The most significant development for Canada's tourism sector has been the establishment of the Canadian Tourism Commission (CTC) in 1994. Now a Crown corporation, its headquarters are in Vancouver, B.C. The CTC provides a good example of how the federal and provincial governments can partner with an industry to ensure its growth and success. This partnership provides a unique opportunity to develop and coordinate programs that benefit the industry and the country as a whole. The tourism sector matches government promotional funding dollar for dollar. This 50/50 formula has allowed the advertising budget to increase to $100 million in 2003, from just under $20 million in 1993. Some of the activities that the CTC supports include gathering and maintaining data on potential markets, analyzing international and domestic marketplace opportunities and issues, market research and analysis, advertising, public relations, promotional projects, and travel trade activities.

There are several activities the CTC does not engage in. It does not lobby the government or provide direct subsidies or grants to the industry. Those activities are performed by tourism associations, organizations, and provincial and municipal governments. An interested Canadian may judge the performance of the CTC by looking at the yearly results in five areas: overall tourism revenue increases, growth in visitor volumes, reduction in the travel deficit, market share changes, and job creation. Certainly the five-year results shown on page 38 in Table 2.2 are encouraging.

www.canadatourism.ca

A Crown Corporation: The National Capital Commission (NCC)

The capital of a nation always holds a special position, for it is the heart of a country. As such, it hosts the central government and is the site of many historic events that helped to shape a country's culture and heritage. A capital city is the showcase

---

Mandate and Mission Statement for the Canadian Tourism Commission

Vision
Canada will be the premier four-season destination to connect with nature and to experience diverse cultures and communities.

Mission
Canada's tourism industry will deliver world-class cultural and leisure experiences year-round, while preserving and sharing Canada's clean, safe, and natural environments. The industry will be guided by the values of respect, integrity, and empathy.

Strategic Objectives
The main thrusts of the commission are to market Canada as a desirable travel destination and to provide timely and accurate information to the industry to assist in their decision making.

of a country's vitality, talent, creativity, and accomplishments. There were many reasons for Queen Victoria's choice of Ottawa as Canada's capital: the natural beauty of the region with its rolling hills and waterways; its inherently bilingual nature due to its closeness to Quebec; and its distance from the U.S. border, which provided the new capital with military security.

The NCC is an independent legal entity created by Parliament to ensure that public policies pursued on behalf of the National Capital Region benefit all Canadians. The NCC has the broad goal of maintaining the integrity and beauty of the capital region, which extends over a large area of western Quebec and the Ottawa area. It has the following mandates:

- to use the capital to communicate Canada to Canadians and to assist in developing and highlighting the Canadian national identity
- to safeguard and preserve the capital's physical assets and natural setting for future generations

To preserve the natural beauty of the area, an aggressive plan for parks and green space was developed. A wide band of undeveloped land circling the capital was designated to ensure that the city maintained its sense of beauty. Gatineau Park, located on the Quebec side of the Ottawa River, provides the area with the largest wilderness park in the capital region. It offers visitors paths and nature trails for biking and walking, downhill ski areas and cross-country ski trails, and beaches for swimming and picnics. One of the capital region's largest tourist attractions is the *Fall Rhapsody*, a celebration of autumn's colours in Gatineau Park. The NCC is also responsible for maintaining that portion of the Rideau Canal that lies within the city. This historic canal is one of the longest artificial waterways in the world. The NCC donates the land on which many new museums and cultural centres are located and acts as a guardian for heritage treasures such as the Aberdeen Pavilion at Lansdowne Park. It is impossible to walk through the older neighbourhoods of Ottawa without stumbling across unique buildings or sites designated by the NCC as part of Canada's history. The NCC also helps sponsor events in the region such as the Canadian Tulip Festival and Winterlude.

The board of directors for the NCC consists of 14 appointed members: seven represent the National Capital Region and seven represent the interests of all other Canadians. The board meets several times a year, but in the past has come under criticism for its lack of an open forum. NCC meetings are now open to the public.

www.capcan.ca

In Practice

Why should a country's capital city be a showpiece? List the capital cities of five foreign countries. What sites do they have that create a cultural/historical ambience or a positive world image? Are Ottawa's pull factors competitive with the foreign capitals you have chosen? Why or why not? Should the NCC continue to make decisions for the city of Ottawa, or should the citizens of Ottawa be given the sole power to shape Ottawa's future tourism development? Justify your decision.

Canada's National War Memorial is located in the heart of the city.
(Photo courtesy Canadian Tourism Commission.)

SNAPSHOT

Judith Cabrita

When Judith Cabrita walks into a room, her energy quickly spills over into conversations. Here is a woman whose love of tourism has guided her career and life over decades of endeavours. Judith epitomizes the new tourism professional, successfully manoeuvring her career through three tourism sectors: accommodations, food and beverage, and tourism services. No one knows better the flexibility and transferability of tourism skills. A native of Toronto, she is Nova Scotian at heart. Judith was educated at Ryerson University, where she became active in the student association, serving as its secretary and graduating as a silver medallist. Her career began in the accommodations industry. Working first in the hotel business and then the resort business, she gained skills in a variety of different positions. Looking for additional challenges, she then accepted the position of chef manager at the Voyageur Restaurant in

Halifax. Judith's next step was into the tourism services sector where she worked her way up to vice-president of a hospitality consulting group. Her continuing quest for challenge turned her career path toward education and innovation. Teaching a class for youth with special needs, she took over the management and training of these students and successfully turned their classroom into a small, profitable dining room, which provided them with valuable hands-on skills. Judith then worked as a consultant to the government of Nova Scotia, helping design and implement a hospitality curriculum. Her lastpositions in education were as industry coordinator and co-op coordinator at Mount St. Vincent University.

"Learning is a lifetime experience" has been Judith's personal mission statement. She not only believes in education and training, but she has also used her strong convictions to improve the tourism product of Nova Scotia through the development of skills upgrading and training for the province's tourism workers. Judith was one of the original members of the Tourism Industry Standards and Certification Committee (TISCC), and in 1989 she initiated development of the Education and Training Department branch of the Tourism Industry Association of Nova Scotia (TIANS), now its Human Resource Council. In 1995, Judith was appointed director of TIANS, Nova Scotia's tourism education council. Under Judith's leadership, it is one of the most active councils in Canada. Judith strongly believes in the power of people and in investing in tourism employees by providing them with continuous educational opportunities and training based on industry standards. TIANS has helped in the development and implementation of 14 occupational standards for the industry, including Responsible Beverage Service and Gambling.

Today, TIANS operates the largest tourism industry trade show in Canada and works with the industry to establish environmental guidelines to ensure that tourism remains a viable, sustainable product. Judith remains active in many different industry associations, such as the Canadian Food Service Executive Association and the Halifax and Nova Scotia chambers of commerce. She sits on the board of directors of both the Canadian Tourism Human Resource Council (CTHRC) and the Tourism Industry Association of Canada (TIAC).

Ask Judith Cabrita what she believes life's most important lesson is and her quick response will be "lifelong learning." Most of her working life has focused on education and training and she can give no higher compliment than that of a job well done. This focus on excellence has driven Judith all her life, and she has passed her energy on to those around her, helping develop Nova Scotia into one of Canada's most successful tourism destinations. In 1993, she was awarded the Canada 125 Medal, and there is a scholarship in her name—the Judith B. Cabrita Tourism Professional Scholarship. Judith's work with TIANS, the CTHRC, and occupational standards is helping the industry develop a more professional workforce—making an imprint that will last well into this century.

TRAINING THE TOURISM HOST

Over the past 20 years, the tourism industry has become a major revenue producer for Canada. The fact that there is such a variety of small, independently owned and operated businesses creates problems that are not faced when an industry produces just one product—such as the auto industry. This fragmentation hinders united efforts at improving the quality of the product; however, this same diversity allows the industry to offer a broad-based market appeal.

Measuring the dollar value of tourism is easy, but the real economic importance of tourism to Canada also includes the number of jobs it creates. Tourism is a very labour-intensive industry. Tourists do not drive home in the product; when they purchase a trip to Prince Edward Island, they are purchasing experiences and services. Returning home, they must leave behind the island's beautiful beaches, historic sites, and entertainment. So what *do* they get for their money? They get memories. These memories may be warm and friendly—or they may not.

No machine or technological advancement will ever replace the warm and caring interpersonal communication that takes place between a tourist and a professional tourism host. For this reason, when Canada began a review of its tourism industry product, its focus was on people resources. Listed below are 10 of the major problems this review identified.

Human Resource Challenges, Issues, and Concerns

1. **Industry image.** Most Canadians have never viewed tourism as a true profession, instead perceiving tourism workers as hamburger flippers or bed makers working long hours in a dead-end job with low wages and few benefits.

2. **Unskilled labour.** In some areas of Canada, the shortage of trained workers is so great that employers are forced to hire applicants who have little or no training.

3. **Poor training practices.** Since training is often regarded as an expense, employers often do not take the time to provide their new employees with the skills needed to accomplish the job. Although training does take time and money, professionals know that not only will trained staff be more productive, they will also provide customers with a positive experience which, in turn, increases revenues.

4. **Poor attitudes/self-image.** Workers who have not been trained not only lack the skills to perform their jobs well, but also are often unsure about what they are supposed to do. This leads to frustration and negative responses from both customers and management and can culminate in feelings of inadequacy or apathy on the part of the worker.

5. **High turnover.** The poor attitudes described above lead to discontent, causing workers to quit. Turnover rates are often 35 percent or higher, with some businesses experiencing more than a 100 percent change in staff on a yearly basis.

6. **Shrinking labour pool.** Tourism has always depended on the labour pool that is less than 35 years of age. Although the demand for labour is increasing, the number of younger workers and unskilled immigrants is declining.

7. **Demand for qualified workers.** As the industry grows, so does the demand for skilled workers. The CTHRC forecasts that between 2005 and 2015, over 280 000 new tourism jobs will be created.[14]

8. **Poorly trained managers.** Many managers have been placed into their positions without benefit of training themselves. They have not developed the skills to deal with personnel problems and do not understand the value of training.

9. **Language barriers.** Tourism is a business that deals with many cultures and languages, both in the marketplace and in the workforce. Language problems will always require additional attention from businesses wishing to maintain a competitive advantage in tourism.

10. **Lack of recognition for institutional training.** Business operators, who themselves may lack formal training, often do not recognize the importance of institutional training.

How will tourism continue to grow if it is unable to find qualified workers? How does an industry that undervalues training and education and yet requires long hours from a dedicated workforce stay in business? How does it attract and keep the best staff? The answer is, it doesn't. Many businesses within this sector, especially in the food and beverage industry, face bankruptcy within a few years.

For today's managers and for those training to be tomorrow's managers, understanding the problems just discussed is essential. The federal and provincial governments are doing their share to help solve these problems by developing industry-based training programs and national **certification** for employees who have demonstrated their competence in specific tourism occupations. Now owners and managers must take a proactive stance and put real solutions in place for tourism workers. It is up to the industry to make use of these inexpensive training programs, to develop and use reasonable work hours, appropriate pay scales, and advancement opportunities for their staff. Without these changes, growth in the tourism industry faces what may be an unbeatable challenge.

Tourism Education Councils (TECs)

Between 1983 and 1990, a series of studies were undertaken, focusing on human resource needs and challenges for the tourism sector. Many of these studies recommended that government, industry, and education co-operate to restructure the current education and training practices in the industry. In addition, several of the studies advocated identifying all the occupations found within the tourism sector, developing occupational standards for each one, training programs to ensure each standard was taught, and a system for certifying as qualified tourism professionals those people who successfully passed the training. The task was originally taken on by **tourism education councils (TECs)** established in each province and territory.

In 1993, the CTHRC was established to serve as a national forum bringing together all the TECs in order to facilitate the development of national occupational standards and training programs. The CTHRC is not responsible for development of these programs, but instead, with the help of Human Resources and Skills Development Canada (HRSDC, now Human Resources and Social Development Canada), provides leadership and support for the TECs. The federal and provincial governments, along with the tourism sector, believe that a trained workforce is the best way to ensure that the Canadian tourism product is both sustainable and globally competitive. (For more details about TECs, see the Appendix.)

Occupational Standards

Occupational standards are documents outlining the skills, knowledge, and attitudes (SKAs) that an individual must demonstrate and practise to be deemed competent in a given occupation. The process of developing occupational standards ensures that industry members from across the country identify and validate the SKA components they feel are most relevant to performance. TECs then ensure these SKAs form the critical mass of each occupational standard document. This satisfies employers who have had some disdain for the term "certificate-based training," which in the past has attached less importance to actual credentials. The current term, "competency-based training," focuses on experiential learning as well as knowledge.

The *Emerit* Program

In order to make certification accessible to every tourism worker, the CTHRC has developed online training courses that teach participants what they need to know for each occupation. This training is interactive and reasonably priced. But students must also have the skills that come from hands-on experience in the occupation of choice. Students who graduate from a tourism-based college or university program and wish to certify immediately will likely have the required knowledge base; however, unless they have worked in the industry over a period of time, they will not have the required hours, skill sets, or competencies needed. If they have practical lab experience, such as working in the school's kitchen or restaurant, these hours can be counted toward the total number of working hours needed to finish the certification process.

The value of certification is its portability and its national recognition. A certified food and beverage server from Winnipeg has met the criteria established by the industry and accepted in all other provinces and territories. As a manager, a certified applicant will have the skill sets needed to immediately provide quality service for customers, saving both time and money by reducing or eliminating training costs. Certified individuals gain an edge in an increasingly competitive job market. Having successfully completed the CTHRC program of choice, the student is then permitted to place a designation after his or her name that signifies the level achieved. For example, a student who completes the Tourism Certified Supervisor level may use the designation TCS. These new designations will soon be recognized by employers both across Canada and globally.[15]

Standards serve the industry in many ways: they help with the development of job descriptions; they streamline the recruitment and selection process; they result in a well-trained workforce that is committed to the industry; they provide recognition of the value of tourism occupations; they increase service levels, thereby meeting or exceeding client expectations; they serve as a basis for training programs; and they address some of the issues identified by HRSDC as challenges for the future.

The *emerit* program offered by the CTHRC makes training easily accessible from your home computer. As a registered member, you may log onto the website, which gives you access to the complete set of standards for over 60 different occupations. You can see what knowledge is required for certification and determine if that occupation is one you might enjoy. In addition, you have the opportunity to pull up and try one of the lessons. For example, do you know the correct procedure for opening a bottle of wine, for making a specific sauce, or for handling a reservation over the phone? Your lesson will identify the learning objectives, illustrate the standards, then let you self-test. Enrolment costs are clearly identified, should you decide to begin the certification process, and are handled by the TEC in your province or territory (see Appendix).

Ethics and the Host

Ethics are an important part of how we view the world and conduct our lives. As tourism professionals, we need to know what the term *ethics* means, why we should have a code of conduct, and how to put it into action. We sell a product that is purchased unseen and untried, our customers pay a great deal of money for the product, and they place their lives in our hands.

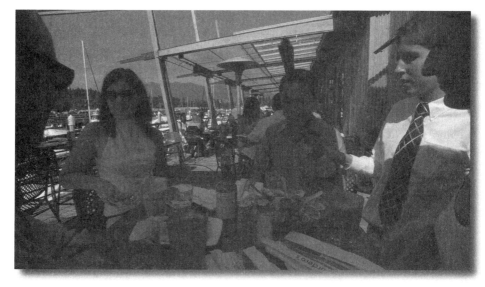

Training your staff is essential if you wish to develop a reputation for excellent service.
(Photo courtesy Canadian Tourism Commission.)

To begin a discussion on ethics, we must first understand two key words: *morals* and *ethics.* According to *Webster's New World Dictionary,* morals are "the ability to make a distinction between right and wrong conduct." **Ethics,** on the other hand, involves "a system or code of morals of a particular person, religion, culture, group, or profession." It sounds simple, but we all view the world from different standpoints. Your concept of right and wrong may differ dramatically from your parents' or friends' ideas of right and wrong. What one culture views as wrong, another may view as right.

Cultures today may be based on religion, race, or even business. Many corporations have a specific culture created by company founders and executives who set the ground rules or **code of ethics** by putting into words their beliefs on how the business should operate and on the proper treatment of guests and employees. A business code of ethics should be printed and prominently displayed, and everyone, including the president/CEO, must understand it and live by its tenets. Often this means a training session or two for employees, but the easiest way to teach ethics is to live by them. When you research the different companies you would like to work for after you graduate, find out if they have and live by a code of ethics. It is also important that employers have faith in their workers' abilities to put the corporation's code of conduct into action, even if some instances require an unexpected expense.

One of the positive impacts the UNWTO hopes will arise out of tourism is the development of a better understanding between cultural groups, a lofty dream at best. While on vacation, tourists hope to slip from the bonds of their life at home and live vicariously in a place where no one knows them. Big problems can arise when the difference between the cultural norms of the visitor and host is very different. This has already been pointed out when we looked at the negative impacts of tourism but, because of the rise in concerns and problems associated with differing codes of conduct, a closer look should be taken. The two areas of wide concern are sex tourism and crime rates. For a Third World country, with high poverty and poor job prospects for women in particular, prostitution is a simple, easy way to make money—money that provides for their families the necessities of life. Some destinations, like Thailand and the Philippines, have gained a reputation for their sex trade, which can mean interaction not only with consenting women, but with children. Where prostitution is illegal, some countries, such as Pakistan, have allowed "red light districts" to form. This type of destination may be chosen by participants for the very reason that what is unacceptable in their home community is more easily attained and less likely to bring about legal action at their vacation spot. In Thailand, half a million women work in this trade with most of them basing their operation in Bangkok. It has such a positive financial impact on the woman and her family that the risks are ignored. Rising rates of sexually transmitted diseases and HIV have been documented. What is not clear, however, is the role tourism plays as records of the activity are not kept. This also brings about a variety of sociological and religious issues. Forced prostitution is a human rights concern, and sex tourism is seen as one of the ways traditional family structures in these countries are breaking down. Enforcing legal issues or outright banning prostitution can cause tremendous hardship for families who depend on that form of income, and suggestions that legislation protect prostitutes could improve both the health and welfare of those earning money in this, one of the world's oldest jobs.

The other side of this negative coin is crime. Tourists are easy prey in a foreign land where customs are not understood and visitors on vacation often participate in such activities as excessive drinking, gambling, and using drugs or prostitutes, and this opens the door to crimes such as theft, credit card fraud, beatings, and death. There is no destination in the world that can guarantee that crime against tourists never occurs. Mexico has recently been in the Canadian spotlight as two sets of brutal murders have taken place and remain unsolved. In Aruba, a young girl enjoying spring break with classmates disappeared and is presumed dead, but the perpetrators remain free. Cruise ships are also targets for criminals. Most of the sailing a ship undertakes is in open water, under no specified legal authority, so rapes, robberies, and murders continue to go unsolved. In the past, cruise lines have merely fired the perpetrator or requested they disembark at the next stop, and while local police may be brought in, they have no jurisdiction over a crime that took place in international waters.

Tourists are also targeted by terrorists—they are considered easy targets for abduction or other harm and the event receives worldwide attention. All of these problems are costly for a destination and require that it increase its expenditures on law enforcement, security systems, and fire and emergency personnel.

CASE STUDY

Determining the Manager–Employee Relationship

The kitchen of this large food service contractor reflected the population of Canada, with 23 culinary staff representing 12 ethnic groups. Communication was often difficult, and dealing with the different cultural values of his staff was a challenge for Roberto, the unit manager. However, his staff knew he treated them fairly, and they seemed to work well together.

Roberto's company was part of a massive program started by the provincial government to provide challenged workers with paying jobs. One of his best workers was Carlos, his dishwasher, whose family had emigrated from Costa Rica 10 years earlier. Despite his learning disability, Carlos was hard-working, and once he learned a task, he performed it well and without shortcuts. Carlos kept the pots and pans area clean and orderly, and seldom allowed dirty dishes to stack up. His father had opened an account for him in the bank located nearby and had instructed Carlos to deposit his weekly wages before he came home on Fridays. One day, Roberto received a disturbing call from Carlos's father. Carlos was not depositing his cheques; his father wanted to be sure the company was still paying Carlos his wages.

Roberto found that all of Carlos's cheques had been cashed by the bank, and for the next three Fridays, Roberto watched Carlos take his cheque down to the bank.

On the third Friday, Roberto finished his paperwork early and headed to the kitchen for a cup of coffee. The steward had not replenished the paper coffee cup supply, so Roberto went to the storage room to get some. There he found the answer to the mystery: five of his kitchen staff were busy playing poker with Carlos, who was happy to be "one of the boys," despite the fact he was rapidly losing all his money.

Working with challenged adults can be very rewarding. These adults usually take great pride in what they do and are dependable, getting to work on time and seldom missing a day.

1. Is this problem an ethical dilemma for Roberto or a cultural one? What factors helped you make your decision? Is this type of employee interaction acceptable? Why or why not?
2. Should management become involved, or is this a family affair?
3. If Roberto decides to take action, what do you think he should do? What impact, if any, will his decision have on the work staff?
4. As a manager, how might you avoid facing a similar problem?

Summary

Guests and hosts comprise the people factor in the tourism sector. Guests are the entertained and hosts are the entertainers.

In a broad sense, there are two types of guests. Pleasure guests visit an area by choice. The business guest is on non-discretionary travel—visiting for meetings, sales, or conventions. Beyond the business and guest profile, however, the guest can be categorized by demographics and psychographics. Demographics provide basic information about where the guest is from, family income, age, occupation, and education level. A psychographic profile provides insight into the motives, behaviours, interests, and personality of the guest. An understanding of personality dimensions such as activation, variety seeking, and degree of introversion or extroversion allows a destination to provide the experiences the tourist seeks. Understanding why people travel and the barriers they face when they choose to travel can help the host provide a satisfactory travel experience.

The host is the second half of the "people factor" of tourism. Members of a community might not understand their role as hosts, nor the important role tourism plays in their community's welfare. These *tourism-illiterate* people, including many political leaders, usually do not support tourism initiatives, seeing only the negative impact of the tourism industry on their neighbourhoods. In fact, such people can make the tourists' visit rather unpleasant. It is important that the industry continue to educate residents about the benefits of tourism, including its role in bringing employment opportunities to the community, as well as revenue in the form of additional tax dollars and wage earnings. Many community concerns could be alleviated through this education process.

One of the hosts' responsibilities is to market their destination. In order to do this effectively, hosts must understand the unique characteristics of the tourism product. They must have a good knowledge of the marketing mix and how to use it effectively to attract an increasing number of tourists. Hosts must also be able to identify target markets and provide these groups with the products and services that best suit their needs.

Canada has strong new tourism initiatives in place, and both federal and provincial governments play an active part in creating a positive experience for the tourist. Industry and government have identified 10 problems in the human resource component of the industry. The industry acknowledges that it needs trained professionals delivering both products and services in order to overcome these problems. TECs and the CTHRC, working together with industry, have created certification programs and training products that are fast gaining international respect for their thoroughness and relevance. Convention and visitors bureaus (CVBs) and chambers of commerce have also become an integral, proactive part of the tourism product.

Questions

1. Plan a trip to your hometown for a business guest and a pleasure guest. Explain how their motivations, needs, and expectations (MNEs) differ.

2. Define the following terms in your own words: *demographics, psychographics, motivators, external locus of control, push and pull factors, discretionary income, discretionary time.*

3. Explain how your tourism region can best fulfill the needs of
   a) a psychocentric
   b) an allocentric
   c) Compare the needs and expectations of each. Justify your answer by defining the terms and choosing an activity that would match the individual personalities.

4. List five different disabilities you might encounter in customers in a restaurant. As a server, what might you do to help make their stay more comfortable?

5. Is your local government "tourism illiterate"? Define the term and justify your answer, using local examples.

6. Tourism has both negative and positive effects on a region/country.
   a) List nine negative effects of the tourism industry and ten positive effects.
   b) From each list choose the three effects (for a total of six) that you believe are most important in your region, and explain why you have chosen them.

7. a) What is the NCC and why was it established?

   b) Should Canadians from across the continent have input regarding the development of the city of Ottawa (National Capital Region)? Why or why not?

8. List, with a brief explanation of each, the 10 issues and concerns identified by the tourism sector regarding its human resources.

9. a) What are "occupational standards" and how were they developed?

   b) Log on to the *emerit* website: www.emerit.ca. From the left side of the home page, click on "Sample Training Tools." Run through the "Frontline Training Samples" lesson and then briefly list five aspects of making a bed that are critical to ensuring it meets customer expectations.

   c) Take the quiz and log your score here. _____

10. What is a code of ethics? List eight items you would include in your code of ethics (conduct) if you were opening a small hotel or restaurant.

11. As a tourist, you are a prime target for criminals at your destination.

    a) Why are tourists so vulnerable?

    b) Identify three types of crime you believe you might encounter on a trip to a foreign country. How best might you avoid getting into trouble with local criminals?

    c) Do the criminal activities discussed on page 56 occur in Canada? If so, where would these events likely take place?

Notes

1. Stanley C. Plog, "Why destination areas rise and fall in popularity." Paper presented to the Travel Research Association Southern California Chapter, Los Angeles, CA, October, 1972.

2. D. Fiske, and S. Maddi, *Functions of Varied Experience* (Homewood, IL: Dorsey, 1961).

3. Poon, cited in Geoffrey Wall and Alister Mathieson, *Tourism Changes, Impacts and Opportunities* (Essex, England: Pearson Education Limited), p. 32.

4. Arlin Epperson, "Why people travel," *Journal of Physical Education, Recreation and Dance*, 31 (April 1983), pp. 53–54.

5. *Canadian Travel Press*, October 11, 2001, CTX article 32609.

6. CNN, *The Situation Room*, October 25, 2005, 6:00 p.m.

7. Robert W. McIntosh, and Charles R. Goeldner, *Tourism Principles, Practices, Philosophies*, 6th ed. (New York: John Wiley & Sons, 1990), p. 131.

8. "Open doors communication—a new Harris Poll of US disability population," June 2002. Available by emailing info@opendoorsnfp.org.

9. J. Judd Buchanan, "Report on the tourism industry," in *Report from the Honourable J. Judd Buchanan*, October 1994.

10. Edward Inskeep, *Tourism Planning: An Integrated and Sustainable Approach* (New York: John Wiley & Sons, 1991).

11. G.V. Doxey, "When enough's enough: The natives are restless in Old Niagara," *Heritage Canada*, 2(2) (1976), pp. 26–27.

12. "Travel deficit reaches 11 year high," *Tourism Magazine*, www.canadatourism.com.

13. *Research/Canadian Tourism Facts and Figures 2003*, www.canadatourism.travel.

14. Canadian Tourism Human Resource Council, *Total Tourism Sector Employment in Canada: 2004 Update*, March 2005, p. 28.

15. www.emerit.ca.

Planning, Developing, and Marketing a Destination

Key terms

balanced development
catalytic development
channel of distribution
centralized development
city gateway
clustering
coattail development
elastic demand
environmental protection
destination life cycle
forecasting
functional form
hospitality of host
inelastic demand
infrastructure

intangible
integrated development
interdependency
isolation
market match
marketing plan
market segmentation
natural resources
niche marketing
partnerships
planning
product capacity
product, price, place,
  promotion
qualitative forecasting

quantitative forecasting
rapid development
secondary developers
sense of place
supply and demand
suprastructure
target marketing
TDA
transportation systems
trend
trend analysis
USP
perceived value

Learning objectives

Having read this chapter you will be able to

1. Describe the five essential components of a tourist destination.

2. Explain how the life cycle of a product affects tourism destinations.

3. Identify the five priorities the Canadian government uses to help plan future tourism growth.

4. Describe the role of communities and regions in tourism planning and development.

5. Identify the eight steps of the planning process.

6. Describe how British Columbia is using the eight steps to create successful 2010 Olympic and Paralympic Games.

7. Explain why communities differ based on type of development.

8. Explain the differences between the three types of development.

9. Identify seven constraints on the future growth of Canada's tourism industry.

Tourism facilities, sites, and events do not become tourist destination areas (**TDAs**) overnight. An abundance of formal and informal planning, developing, and marketing is required before an area is known well enough that the number of people choosing the TDA have made it profitable. A century ago, tourism simply "developed" with little or no knowledge of how it was happening. If the TDA already had a home base of residents, tourism was simply another way to make money. If, on the other hand, few people lived in the area but some natural (or ancient cultural) aspect intrigued visitors enough for them to want to visit, then development was a huge change in lifestyle for locals. Planning the tourism experience, ensuring that you provide your market base with the facilities and activities they want, and presenting an exciting marketing program that describes your TDA well will help ensure the desired marketplace segment(s) will hear about it and decide to visit.

This chapter looks first at what good planning is and why planning is essential; three basic methods of development are discussed, and curbs to the growth of your TDA are identified. Six factors that help create a tourist-friendly TDA are considered with the understanding that even in a fully developed city like Victoria, Edmonton, Winnipeg, or Halifax, positive changes can be made that will make your TDA more enjoyable. Finally, we look at the "odd" product we sell called tourism. It is like the goose and the golden eggs—maintain your product and it is always with you to sell again and again. Is there any other product that people are willing to buy without the pleasure of adding it to their collection of toys?

Planning is an essential component of profitable tourism. Where and how do you start adding to or developing a new TDA? Is the community ready to embark on a "tourism venture"? How do we determine what our customers want now and what they will be looking for in the future? These are some of the questions that must be answered, to the best of our ability, during the planning process. Ignoring one of them may doom the project to failure. However, the same concepts apply whether the group is looking to add a whole new level of industry in a TDA, to add a new activity or site, or to create a totally new product from the beginning. The concepts discussed may be used by any business or region—from a small entrepreneurial tourism business to an entire country. In this chapter, tourism destination area (TDA) may be that single unit or it may refer to a more diverse product for simplicity's sake.

THE FIVE COMPONENTS OF A TOURIST DESTINATION

There are five essential components or pieces that must be initially in place if the TDA is to host the traveller. A TDA that is already developed will have these components so the processes move forward at a faster pace. In the case of a TDA that has not been developed, these components must be in place if the TDA is to entice the midcentric and psychocentric traveller. The allocentric, however, ready to give up some of life's "comforts" just to be one of the first, may visit before the TDA is even being considered.

1. **Natural resources.** A destination needs to have the physical means of supporting the tourist. It need lands, a habitable climate, a water supply, and natural beauty to attract the tourist. Hawaii is an example of a destination that has many **natural resources** available—soft sands, beautiful waters, and flora and fauna that have intrigued people from early times. The Jasper and Banff valleys are good examples of spectacular Canadian scenery, and although they lack the warm temperatures of Hawaii, their majestic snow-capped mountains, unique wildlife, and changing seasons have helped create a huge tourist market. Not all destinations need such a dramatic backdrop to entice the tourist, but they must all have the natural resources available to support life and the tourist's needs.

2. **Infrastructure.** Often called the "guts of the city," **infrastructure** is the first component put in place in any area that is being developed for habitation. What makes up the infrastructure? Roads, telephone wires, electric wires, sewage and drainage pipes, docks, railroad tracks, runways—all those essential services that are seen or unseen.

3. **Suprastructure.** A community's **suprastructure** consists of all the buildings found at the destination. Lodging facilities, restaurants, terminals, sport complexes, stores—these are all examples of the suprastructure of a site.

4. **Transportation system.** A **transportation system** consists of the actual vehicles that use the infrastructure. What good are railroad tracks if there are no trains? Transportation systems are completely dependent on infrastructure; together, they provide the guest (and host) with access to and around the destination.

5. **Hospitality of the host.** The **hospitality of the host** destination includes the social and political climate, but involves much more than laws and culture; it is the genuine warmth shown by the local population—the smiles and greetings and the willingness to tolerate the changes that tourism brings. The host city may have the finest hotels, the best restaurants, and the most modern methods of transportation, and yet not attract the tourist market because of a less-than-welcoming attitude.

As an example of how these components fit into an area that has already seen some development, consider Newfoundland and Labrador, which is gearing up for new tourism growth. This province has an abundance of natural beauty to attract the tourist. Gros Morne National Park on the west coast is a UNESCO (United Nations Educational, Scientific, and Cultural Organization) World Heritage Site. Nicknamed "the Galapagos of the tectonic plate," the park has an abundance of wildlife, spectacular mountains, and fiords carved by glaciers from a distant time. Infrastructure and transportation systems are already in place—Newfoundland and Labrador have many beautiful scenic roads to travel, and airplanes and ferries connect cities on the island to one another and to the mainland. Gros Morne National Park also offers the tourist a unique infrastructure—more than 65 km of hiking trails! Newfoundland and

www.unesco.org

Labrador's suprastructure intermingles the modern hotel with bed and breakfast inns, historical forts with state of the art museums, craft stores with shopping centres, and ski lodges with golf courses. But, it is the outgoing, warm hospitality offered by Newfoundlanders that makes this province a great, exciting tourist destination.[1]

FOOTPRINT

The "Greening" of Fairmont Hotels

Canadians should have tremendous pride for one of its "own"—Fairmont Hotels. In the early 1990s, Fairmont began to establish a green program unlike any other in the world. With many of their hotels placed in ecosystems such as the Banff and Jasper Valleys, they decided to do something about the environment long before other hotels were even thinking about it and published a booklet called *The Green Partnership Guide*. In it they itemized publicized programs they were embarking on to reduce waste and to reuse and recycle products when possible. Here are some of the objectives they have met over the past decade:

Name of hotel	Overview	Example of one measure implemented	Total savings per year
Delta Toronto	296 rooms $700 000 in upgrades	Centralized energy management system	$80 000
Fairmont Château Laurier	429 rooms Over $3 mil in energy retrofits	Installation of high-efficiency incremental units in all guest rooms	$575 000
Fairmont Banff Springs	770 rooms $600 000 in retrofits	Retrofit of all guest room lighting and heating systems	$315 000
Fairmont The Queen Elizabeth	1000+ rooms $3 million in upgrades	Lighting retrofit of all guest areas and installation of ventilation waste-heat recovery system	$500 000

Fairmont hotels recycle just about everything possible from food service leftovers (sent to soup kitchens or to become fertilizer); unused guestroom soaps (melted down and reformed into bars that are donated to agencies working in developing countries); and pamphlets that encourage guests to think wisely about water conservation during their stay (fewer hot baths, reusing towels, and sleeping on sheets for more than one night). (Source: www.oee.nrcan. gc.ca/publications)

Planning for tourism means providing wide, clean walkways, and streets with accessible local transportation.
(Photo: John B. Kerr.)

THE LIFE CYCLE OF A DESTINATION

Every product, like every person, has a life span. In a **destination life cycle**, the first stage is called *conception*. This is when the creative entrepreneur comes up with a new concept that is different and exciting. Ideas flow, plans are made, and research is done to ensure that there is a demand for the product. The second stage of the life cycle is the actual *building* of the product. If the product is a new destination—the area is undiscovered and there will be few if any tourists visiting—this stage may interest the allocentric traveller. The further along development moves, the more tourists the product may attract. The third phase is *maturity*. During this phase, all components of the destination are fully developed, the product is being marketed successfully, and visitor use is high.

Once a site has enjoyed several years of high activity, it begins to lose visitors as they move on to newer destinations they have not yet experienced. This phase is called *decline*. The product itself may be well used and beginning to look a little rundown. At this point of its life cycle, the destination can choose to close, to become a second- or to third-rate activity, or to rethink the product—returning to the conception stage, and reinventing and renewing the destination to attract a new set of visitors and to bring past visitors back again.

The Disney theme parks provide good examples of how tourism products avoid the decline phase. Every few years, new attractions are added, such as their new Animal Kingdom in Florida, and older sites are upgraded. Marketing focuses on themes that send the message: "come back and see us through different eyes."

In Toronto, the CN Tower has added lights at night for visitors and a new glass elevator so they can enjoy the entire ascent/descent—from floor to ceiling.

No product is free from its life cycle. Tourism professionals must be constantly looking to improve and renew their product and excite their target markets if they wish to stay competitive in the global world of tourism.

PLANNING FOR TOURISM

Planning is an activity all businesses must do, whether it is on a daily basis, by the month or year, or 10 years into the future. Government plans usually focus on long-term activities five to ten years away. When they focus on the future, they usually identify the important goals they wish to achieve and, of course, how they intend to achieve them. With this in mind, the Canadian government has identified five national priorities for tourism development:

1. creating products that satisfy market demands
2. providing safe, reasonably priced transportation
3. developing human resource training to improve personal service to visitors
4. creating an integrated, global marketing plan that focuses on all four seasons to increase the number of foreign visitors annually to Canada
5. ensuring that long-term growth and prosperity is balanced between the development of new, and the maintenance of existing, physical and cultural environments.

Most tourism professionals never deal with tourism planning on a national level, but if you decide to become an owner, you will likely get involved at a provincial, regional, or local level of planning. You do not have to be an owner to become involved at these levels, you simply need to be concerned about the direction in which tourism in your area is moving. Involvement may be as simple as planning some form of regional fundraiser or small event, or it may mean getting involved at the political end of the spectrum to help focus your region on positive, achievable tourism goals. Each community, however, should develop goals specific to its interests, but the following goals should be part of a community's tourism plan:

1. a framework for improving residents' quality of life by developing infrastructure and suprastructure for residents and visitors alike
2. improvement of residents' standard of living through the economic benefit of tourism
3. guidelines for appropriate development within the city limits and within a certain radius of the city
4. a tourism program designed to fit residents' economic, cultural, and social views and attitudes
5. a yearly evaluation policy for the tourism plan.

As seen in Figure 3.1, the planning model is cyclical. Once the original cycle is completed, it starts over again. The eight steps in tourism planning are basic to almost any planning process. The process begins with an inventory of what already exists and ends with an evaluation of what has been accomplished. The intermediate steps identify the specifics required in good tourism planning.

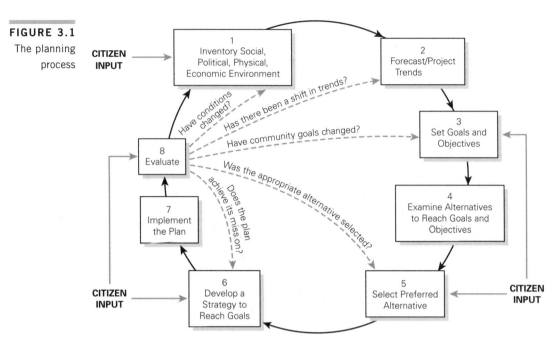

FIGURE 3.1

The planning process

Source: USTTA, *Tourism USA* (Washington, DC: Department of Commerce, 1986), p. 20.

PUTTING PLANS INTO ACTION: THE 2010 OLYMPICS

In July 2003, the International Olympic Committee (IOC) announced that British Columbia had been chosen to host the 2010 Winter Olympics and Paralympics. The Vancouver Organizing Committee (VANOC) had been successful! Winning the right to host the Games is an expensive process, requiring a lot of preparation and commitment, but British Columbia has always led the way in Canada in developing its tourism industry. The province has had strong tourism leadership for many years, and, as always, a plan. The following discussion attempts to illustrate how the eight steps of the planning process might have been used by the VANOC for the 2010 Olympic Games to help ensure their ability to create a strong and profitable event.

Step 1—Inventory

The first step is to conduct a thorough inventory of the community's social and political atmosphere and its physical and economic environment.

a) **Political atmosphere.** Assess the political atmosphere of the community, indicating attitudes of local politicians and community leaders toward tourism that need changing or reinforcing. How does the community feel about the tourism industry, and do they understand the benefits it will bring to their residents?

b) **Social atmosphere.** Outline the political and cultural history of the region. Note festivals and special cultural events. Assess community awareness of the value and benefits of tourism. If the region is found to be tourism illiterate, it is important to inform residents of the tourism planning process and the value of the industry to their region. This can be done in a variety of ways: town meetings, television or radio talk shows, newspaper articles or editorials, and a general education campaign. It is also important to identify the "people resources" in the area: individuals with artistic abilities, those with knowledge of local cultures, and those with training in the industry who are willing to get involved. Using local talents during the development process helps to eliminate opposition and encourages a sense of pride and commitment in the community as the plan proceeds.

c) **Physical environment.** Consider the region's geography: its location, natural resources, climate, and natural history.

d) **Infrastructure and suprastructure. The product capacity**—the number of guests your infrastructure and suprastructure can accommodate—must be examined. Will transportation systems to and around your destination support an influx of visitors? What improvements are needed? Will additional infrastructure be required and who will be responsible for its development and cost?

List the accommodations, restaurants, attractions, and conference facilities available for the tourist. Can a tourist play a round of golf? Take a swim? Go canoeing or biking? Are any facilities geared toward the adventure tourist?

e) **Economic environment.** If a community has a strong economy, then it may not see a need for tourism development. If this is the case, it might be useful to focus on the fact that tourism diversifies the economy by providing employment for students, those returning to the workforce, and new immigrants. If a community is economically depressed, then it may lack the financial resources to invest in tourism. Finding the capital to help fund tourism development can provide a much-needed infusion of money and jobs and can help solve the region's economic woes.

Before beginning the process of putting together a bid, British Columbia had to assess its readiness to go after the Olympics. Politically speaking, the province has long recognized the value of the tourism sector to the overall well-being of the province. Their tourism workforce is large and they have good training programs in place. They have the economic base to actually build the new facilities required to run the Games—and who could ask for a more beautiful spot than our westernmost province? Vancouver already has a good urban transportation system, a wide variety of hotels and restaurants, and good shopping areas. While the snow-sport competitions will be held in the mountains, indoor sports like ice and speed skating will be featured in urban areas to facilitate access for the many visitors who love to watch these events.

Step 2—Forecast Trends

Forecasting trends is important in our industry because it identifies opportunities for regions or developers and helps keep a destination and its tourist activities on the cutting edge of what is popular. A **trend** is "a current style or preference." However, people are fickle and what is trendy one year may not be so the next year.

Quick change is difficult for tourism because most infrastructure and suprastructure is expensive to build—and permanent. Tourism entrepreneurs must be able to recognize trends that will last for a long time.

Forecasting means looking to the future. Edward Inskeep states that planning, in a broad sense of the word, is simply "organizing the future to achieve certain goals."[2] While no one can predict the future with certainty, there are two general methods that help foresee it. They allow us to look at the potential growth of the community and the surrounding region, and to see how that growth will enhance or hinder tourism in the future. The two basic methods used in forecasting are:

1. **Qualitative methods.** The use of experts and their accumulated experience and knowledge to predict the likely outcome of events.
2. **Quantitative methods.** The analysis of numerical data (current and historical) to help determine the future.[3]

One form of **qualitative forecasting** is the Delphi technique, a systematic survey of tourism industry experts who are asked a series of questions developed by a panel of community members. The experts' collective opinions are sent back to the panel, which reviews the answers until a consensus on the timing of future events is reached. This structured method is particularly useful for analyzing medium- and long-term changes in demand and in weighing less tangible factors such as motivation. Qualitative approaches usually require less data and money than quantitative approaches.

Quantitative forecasting employs rigorous mathematical and statistical models. The results are generally more accurate and useful. Quantitative forecasting requires an adequate database to which a range of numerical techniques can be applied. **Trend analysis** plots historical data over a number of cycles. For example, tourist arrivals at some future date are estimated by analyzing past arrivals and projecting these numbers into the future.

One difficulty is the scarcity of reliable data. Although hotels and restaurants have for some time been collecting and using information such as occupancy percentages and average guest cheques, only recently has the tourism industry as a whole been concerned with such data. Timely and reliable data are needed to make tourism strategies more effective and less risky.

Looking at the past, it is clear that the value of hosting the Olympic Games has increased. For example, between 1972 and 1985, the growth rate of international visitors to Alberta was 0.25% annually. However, by the time the 1988 Olympics were held in Calgary, international tourism had jumped 15%. Of course, this growth was due to the huge draw of the Olympics, but in the years following, the province maintained a steady annual growth rate of 3.25%—a nice increase from 1985. In 1994, Norway hosted the Games in the small town of Lillehammer. Tourism to Norway during 1994 jumped by 43%, and the Olympics put Lillehammer on the map. It is estimated that more than two billion people watched the Salt Lake City Olympics on television in 2000. These numbers show that interest in the Olympic Games is big and that international awareness of a region and country grows when it hosts such a global event. B.C. experts forecast that the Games will generate $10 billion in tourism revenues, provide over 228 000 jobs, and bring in an additional $2.5 billion in tax revenues.[4]

Step 3—Develop a Vision, Mission Statement, Objectives, and Goals

A mission statement should provide an overall vision for the destination, site, or activity. A good mission statement not only reflects the purpose of the development, but also provides specific objectives on how the project will improve the quality of life in the region.

After the mission statement and objectives have been written, specific goals should be identified. Goals should be clearly stated and measurable, helping to determine if the plan was a success. Most important of all, goals must be realistic and achievable.

VANOC has developed both a vision and a mission statement, and a set of objectives with goals reflecting the International Olympic Committee's recent addition of a third pillar of Olympism—environmental conservation—*to the first two pillars*, sport *and* culture.

The vision: *A stronger Canada whose spirit is raised by its passion for sport, culture, and sustainability.*

The mission: *To touch the soul of the nation and inspire the world by creating and delivering an extraordinary Olympic and Paralympic experience with lasting legacies.*

The objectives aim to*:*

- *ensure we consider citizens' needs of today and tomorrow*
- *integrate and optimize sport, environmental, social, and economic considerations*
- *help build community, domestic, and international support*
- *ensure we create sustainable legacies*
- *enable the Games to become a showcase of sustainability to the citizens of Canada and the world*
- *increase understanding of sustainability through the Olympic medium.*[5]

www.vancouver2010.com

Step 4—Study Alternative Plans of Action

Rather than identifying only one method to achieve a set of goals, it is important to brainstorm as many alternatives as possible. Sometimes a suggestion may seem outrageous, but might be manipulated into an innovation that has not been used before. At this point, public discussion or the use of experts may again become important. Each alternative should be looked at from both a positive and negative point of view.

This huge event requires that many different venues be developed, including additional infrastructure and suprastructure. As a result, the building of Olympic sites must be handled by a wide variety of businesses. For each of the Olympic development sites, VANOC has considered all bids, carefully examining each for the specifics that the committee has identified as essential to the process.

Step 5—Select Preferred Alternative

Once all possible ways of building or achieving goals have been thoroughly examined, decisions must be made.

VANOC has chosen companies that best reflect and can attain the desire for quality and sustainability in the final product, considering each business's ability to create the product in an environmentally sound way.

It is important to build rest areas into the design. Butchart Gardens, now a national historic site, is not only one of Victoria's main attractions, but also a great spot for relaxation.
(Photo courtesy Canadian Tourism Commission.)

Step 6—Develop a Strategy to Reach Goals

At this point, an outline is needed of specific objectives that must be met in order to reach the goal, as well as a detailed plan that allows community members to see exactly how the goals will be achieved. Plans should consider all community components, address the varying levels of services provided, and identify when, where, and how each objective will be met. A timeline showing deadlines for each objective helps individuals focus.

From the beginning VANOC has had a timeline in place, and most of the target dates have been met so far.

Step 7—Implement Plan

During this construction stage of development, setbacks will likely occur; weather and other unexpected developments may require a change in thinking and possibly in planning.

Community support through local chambers of commerce, city councils, and other businesses is a prerequisite for success in a community-planned business. The grand opening of the event or attraction should be a gala affair with many community members present.

The development of competition sites and the expansion of the new Sea to Sky Highway leading from Vancouver to Whistler have begun. In April 2005, VANOC unveiled ILANAAQ (the Inuit word for "friend"), the 2010 Olympic emblem.[6] The emblem is based on the traditional inuksuk, a navigational landmark used by the Inuit. Over the years, the inuksuk has come to characterize friendship, hope, and hospitality. As part of the continuing Olympic promotions, a soft cuddly ILANAAQ was released for the 2007 Christmas season and the biggest problem it created was that demand far outweighed supply! Many different Canadian corporations have become sponsors of the Games, and stores are now carrying other articles bearing the Games' official emblem.

Step 8—Review, Evaluate, Revise, and Continue with Plans

Everything in tourism needs to be evaluated continually, from Step 1 right through to operation. What factors contribute to success? What factors inhibit success? Are goals and timelines being met? Ongoing evaluation is essential because early detection of problems allows for changes to be implemented while they are still feasible.

Will VANOC be able to meet its own goals and the goal of the International Olympic Committee to hold a profitable Winter Olympics that meets new requirements for sustainability? The answer will be found after the 2010 Olympic and Paralympic Games have been held.

In Practice

Choose a community in your area that could benefit from a tourism plan. Write a brief description of the social, political, physical, and economic environment in that community. Based on this information and your knowledge of the area, design a mission statement with goals and objectives for tourism planning for the community. Write strategies for two of the goals.

TOURISM DEVELOPMENT

Tourism development ranges from well organized (areas that are ultimately pleasant to visit) to haphazard (areas where past and current upheaval in the community is obvious).

One classification of tourist development, defined by Douglas Pearce,[7] is based on the division of responsibility in the development process. **Integrated development** comprises development by a single promoter or developer. **Catalytic development** occurs when a major promoter encourages complementary development by other companies or individuals. **Coattail development** occurs when visitors are enticed to an area of natural or unique qualities, and development takes place to provide the facilities and amenities they desire.

Integrated Development

Walt Disney World is a classic example of *integrated development*, which occurs when an individual or company acquires a large parcel of land and develops the property to the exclusion of all other developers. The resort can usually stand alone, with all the necessary amenities.

The following factors are characteristic of integrated development:

1. **One developer.** The entire resort is built by a single developer who has all the financial and technical resources. As a result, local participation is largely excluded from the development process.

2. **Balanced development.** Because the entire property is under the same ownership, one portion of the resort can operate at a deficit that is offset by a more lucrative portion. For example, at a ski resort, the sale of ski tickets and the operation of chairlifts may not be very profitable, but these low margins may be offset by large margins from condominium sales and rentals, creating a **balanced development**.

3. **Rapid development.** Once approvals are given to build, one entity generally will not encounter roadblocks caused by other groups or the community. Because it is private, the company can move quickly in the building phase, resulting in **rapid development.**

4. **Functional form.** An individual developer has the power to build an entire resort community based on a cohesive theme. This theme requires all buildings to adhere to a **functional form**: to look a certain way, to be located in the most convenient spot, and to enhance the recreational activities of the tourists.

5. **Isolation.** Complete freedom is necessary to develop such resorts. As a result, these resorts are commonly located away from existing settlements. Eventually, community development may occur nearby, but generally, this type of development remains in **isolation.**

6. **High prices.** This type of resort is generally first class in all respects and attracts those who can afford the high prices. The increased costs of developing an integrated resort are usually offset by the high cost of staying at the resort. In fact, the isolation of the resort may enhance its status.

Catalytic Development

Whistler, British Columbia; Banff, Alberta; and Mont Tremblant, Quebec, are examples of *catalytic development*, in which initial development stimulates other projects. The catalytic development process is characterized by the following steps:

1. **Centralized development.** Initiating **centralized development** is a single, large promoter who provides the basic facilities such as ski lifts, major accommodation units, and promotion. Again, the developer usually has a large parcel of land to develop, but is basing the success of the resort on the added facilities others can provide. In a general sense, the developer is providing the infrastructure for the other facilities.

2. **Secondary developers.** Based on success in the initial years of the resort, **secondary developers** build complementary facilities such as nightclubs, movie theatres, restaurants, shops, accommodations, and additional recreational activities such as miniature golf or swimming. These developments require less capital investment, which permits active participation by local companies and individuals.

3. **Interdependency.** The success and increased expansion of this type of resort depend on the entrepreneurial activities of others, creating a condition of **interdependency.** If the initial resort development does not succeed, other developers will not proceed with their projects. Conversely, if the other developers do not succeed, it could lead to the demise of the initial resort. In some cases, the principal promoter will pressure municipalities to block secondary developments considered incompatible. Additionally, the local government may intervene to control growth.

Coattail Development

Niagara Falls is a good example of *coattail development*, which tends to occur around national parks, historic sites, and unique natural attractions. People are so drawn to these areas that entrepreneurs jump at the opportunity to ride on the coattails of the original site. Some of the characteristics of coattail development follow:

1. **No common theme.** Without a central organizer, there is no effort to have a common theme. Businesses develop because the tourist is readily available in the area. Initially, the nearby community sees little or no reason for a common theme. As tourism evolves, however, a community may develop a theme to fill a niche or create a sense of uniqueness in order to compete with other coattail communities in the area.

2. **Duplication and redundancy.** Because no single promoter dominates this area, no guidelines or regulations are established stating what type of business is needed. Many entrepreneurs build similar businesses. Consequently, the variety of motels, restaurants, and shops is limited.

3. **Greater competition.** An offshoot of duplicated effort is increased competition in the area. If tourists have four T-shirt shops from which to choose, they are more likely to compare prices and variety before making a purchase. This competition among retailers produces a healthier business atmosphere.

4. **Late community involvement.** Most coattail development is piecemeal, which means development occurs as the need arises, without an organized plan. Many communities are now seeing the need to create consistency in the look and atmosphere of the town. But, because most of the tourism businesses were established years ago, it is difficult to convince the business leaders of the need for change. Communities are starting with business improvement district (BID) approval, which encourages the improvement of downtown areas. Through a BID or other form of regulatory process, the community can influence the types and appearances of new businesses and

Natural attractions like Niagara Falls are an important part of Canada's tourism product.
(Photo courtesy Canadian Tourism Commission.)

promote the area as a unified group of shops, restaurants, and motels. The Niagara Region, for example, has worked hard to redevelop the destination, and today Niagara serves as a model of tourism planning.

SIX KEY FACTORS TO A TDA'S SUCCESS

What makes a destination "tourist friendly"? Why is one destination so much easier to navigate for a tourist than another? Why is one attraction in the centre of town and another in the suburbs? Smith and Reid[8] have identified six factors that are keys to helping a destination provide tourists with the least amount of discomfort and the maximum amount of enjoyment during their stay:

1. identifying a sense of place
2. ensuring the product/market match fits
3. clustering facilities (e.g., sites, restaurants, accommodations)
4. creating good transportation systems
5. creating positive partnerships within the community
6. maintaining/restoring the environment

Unique towns and villages such as Saint-Jean-Port-Joli, Quebec, provide tourists with the opportunity to purchase local crafts and to snap a few photographs.
(Photo: Paula Kerr.)

Identifying a Sense of Place The first selling point of a TDA is its ability to define itself, to identify something that is unique about the city, something no other city can claim. This **sense of place** may arise from a natural resource or may be created by people through historical perspectives or design. A destination marketing organization (DMO) would call sense of place the destination's unique selling proposition **(USP)**. For Niagara, of course, it is their magnificent waterfalls. For Edmonton, it is likely the West Edmonton Mall. For smaller towns, deciding on a USP can be difficult. A USP for Brantford, Ontario, could be that it is the birthplace of Wayne

Gretzky. Another element that impresses visitors to a TDA right from the start is the effective use of a **city gateway**—an access point that signals to visitors that they have arrived. An effective gateway may be just a noticeable and attractive sign, or it may include an information booth or other method of offering tourists accessible information upon their arrival.

The capital city of a country should be one of the best examples of a tourist-friendly destination, but are they? Washington, D.C., is an excellent example of the use of the six key factors. Is London, England? Nairobi, Kenya? Melbourne, Australia? Is it possible for a city, already defined by growth factors, to create a friendlier, more accessible tourist experience? Using Ottawa, Canada's capital, as our example, you will be able to see that a well-developed city can still, if it decides to do so, become more tourist-friendly by adjusting a number of these factors.

Ottawa is a good example of how these "six key factors" can make a stay more (or less) enjoyable. Ottawa was a logging town with no apparent destiny until Queen Victoria chose the city to be the capital of Canada. Other cities were unhappy because their positions were far better—they were bigger, had money, and already had a presence in the country. However, as mentioned in Chapter 2, Ottawa was a distance from the U.S. border, making it harder for the Americans to invade, and the possibility of a safe water route to the large port of Kingston (Toronto was just another short sail away) were two factors that influenced the monarch's decision. Of course, the rapids on the connecting Rideau River meant a canal and a series of locks would have to be built between Ottawa and Kingston. This incredible feat was accomplished in just six years. Thus, Queen Victoria handed Ottawa, that grubby, wild, logging town, its USP—that of capital of Canada—and in the process, created the latest UNESCO Heritage Site, the Rideau Canal. How does Ottawa deal with the gateway aspect of a sense of place? It doesn't. Signs announcing you are in the capital are almost invisible—the same size as any other sign along Ontario's highway. The "scenic routes" suggested by one or two of these signs provide poorly marked directions and are likely to lead visitors astray rather than bring them safely into the city core to their accommodations. Finally, the information booth provided for visitors is a beautiful, state-of-the-art facility ready to create marvelous touring plans; however, you must have been able to reach Parliament Hill for it to be of any help.

Product/Market Match When the product a destination is selling meets the target market's needs and expectations, a **market match** is made. For example, if you are targeting the family market, then your destination will feature reasonably priced accommodations, family-style restaurants, and activities that focus on family fun or education. The mature market has very different needs. If you target it, your product will probably reflect the higher income of this market, as well as its desire for cultural and learning experiences, and provide upscale accommodation and dining facilities. Targeting the group market might require special check-in and check-out procedures at a hotel. Since destinations usually attract more than one market, a variety of facilities is needed.

Because of its position as capital of Canada, Ottawa provides for a wide variety of tourist markets, ranging from high-tech business visitors to groups of students from all age categories; "empty nesters" and "boomers" to young families with small children; and foreign visitors to Canada. The one client the city cannot handle well is the convention/ conference market. Many hotels have nice facilities for smaller conferences; however, space is limited for handling large numbers or large trade shows. Conventions and conferences can be one of the most financially rewarding events a city can host. The city simply rents the space, perhaps helps find volunteers and the necessary equipment, and the organization looks after most of the other details. Conventions are good because delegates tend to spend a great deal of money on recreational activities after the sessions. They may bring along their families for a "mini-vacation" or may decide the city is so attractive, they will return with friends and family in the near future.

Clustering Clustering is also important to a visitor, especially one with a limited budget and no personal transportation available. Clustering keeps sites, food services, accommodations, and events in one area, allowing easy walking access to all.

Tourism planning in most Canadian cities has been in the *coattail* category; in other words, it has developed without much forethought, so clustering sites can be difficult once the city has developed.

Clusters can often be created by zoning bylaws. In the historic area of Niagara-on-the-Lake, facilities focus on a more upscale market and adhere to historical designs. The well-known Shaw Festival (featuring the works of the great playwright George Bernard Shaw) is held here annually, and rather than large, modern hotels, accommodations tend to be smaller inns and bed and breakfasts. On the other hand, some of Vancouver's sites are spread among different communities, and while they are not within walking distance of each other, the hosting community can share in the tourist dollar.

Clustering does appear in the downtown area with a wide variety of hotels, eateries, and shops available to the visitor, along with some sites such as the Vancouver Aquarium and the Convention Centre Portside project.

Ottawa has recently turned to clustering its sites, and now most major national museums are within a 30-minute walk of each other. Many events held in Ottawa take place in the large parks that complete the city centre.

Transportation System Even when clustering occurs, the importance of a good **transportation system** cannot be overstated. How do tourists get to and around their TDA? Are signs for sights and attractions clear and are they placed so that the driving tourist has time to move into the correct turning lane? Is the traffic flow simple, or are there many one-way streets, confusing signs, and poor parking facilities? Good, clear, visible road signs accomplish three things: they allow tourist traffic to flow more smoothly through the area, they reduce the risk of accidents, and they make it easier for tourists to find sites, accommodations, or destinations. Niagara has highly visible directional signs. Parking facilities are located at the edge of the city, and a special bus service moves tourists from one cluster to another. Tourists are encouraged to use this system, minimizing traffic congestion and pollution. Toronto's Highway 401 alerts visitors to their exit as far ahead as five km, giving them time to get into the right exit lane. Vancouver has the SkyTrain, SeaBus, and other standard methods of transportation. In some cities, one of the "must do" experiences is using one of their transit systems: San Francisco's cable cars, London's double-decker buses, the TGV in Tokyo, and the Paris Métro, to mention only a few.

Ottawa is a city in crisis when it comes to transportation. For 20 years, the city has been trying to establish an alternate source of transportation to its very old, polluting transportation system, OC Transpo, with no success. Tourists without cars must use taxis to get to some of the outlying attractions, which is costly. While most of the sites are clustered, seasonal bus service, such as the one provided in London, England, would give tourists without cars the chance to see some of the unique attractions located outside the cluster area. If you have a car, there are still problems. A new highway does link tourists coming from the Toronto area to downtown Ottawa, but the highway that crosses Ottawa gives little advance warning for exits (unlike Toronto and Vancouver), and once a tourist is in the downtown area, the city is a poor mix of one-way and dead-end streets and infrastructure projects. All cities need to do road maintenance during the summer, but Ottawa provides little in the way of alternate routes. Add to that mix the fact that each street has a confusing "bus lane" reserved for buses only with large signs warning drivers of the fines for using them, as well as a lack of parking, and you begin to see the difficulties a visitor experiences trying to navigate Ottawa in a car.

Community Partnerships The fifth key to success lies in **partnerships**. In Chapter 2, we discussed the successful partnership between the Canadian Tourism Commission (CTC) and the tourism sector. Partnering with government is essential, as governments provide not only the infrastructure for tourism, but also many social and support services. Historically, tourist regions have vied against one another for customers. The tourism marketplace has changed, however; competition comes not just from our neighbours but also from businesses around the world. Destinations need the strength that is found in alliances and partnerships. Tourism businesses want the same thing— a healthy, economically stable tourist product. Partnerships are hard to forge and can be difficult to maintain. Once created, however, they improve each product's chance of success by linking resources. Partnering also means that the visitor can be supplied with a full, diverse package using one-stop shopping. An example of a tour to Niagara-on-the-Lake might combine the services of the Prince of Wales hotel, dinners at local restaurants, promotional discounts for local shops, tickets to the Shaw Festival, lunch and a tour of Inniskillin Winery, and admissions to local attractions like Fort George. Partnerships are also an integral part of any public festival or event, and without the support of local businesses, some events have been forced to cancel their activities.

Ottawa is a city of festivals. Over 150 festivals, from the Canadian Tulip Festival held in late May to the Labour Day Gatineau Hot Air Balloon Festival, the city celebrates music and heritage from around the world. Finding sponsors/partners can be difficult, with even the widely popular Tulip Festival facing elimination from time to time for lack of support. Providing an event with financial or other forms of support is good both for the company (advertising) and for the economy. Without willing partners, tourism businesses face even harder times.

Environmental Protection The final key to successful tourism is **environmental protection**. The World Tourism Organization has stated that the protection and enhancement of the environment is fundamental to balanced and harmonious tourism. Sustainable tourism development is a primary goal in tourism planning, and it means that a destination fulfills the needs of the tourist with as little damage to the environment as possible. It is unrealistic to expect tourism to bring in revenue and yet cause no added pollution or damage to the environment.

Politicians must not allow indiscriminate or poorly designed construction to destroy the natural environment. Niagara is now struggling with this problem. In the past 10 years, local politicians have been loath to deny building permits for large hotels along the embankment of the Niagara River. There is no question that a view of the falls is a unique selling point, but tall buildings have blocked not only the natural light needed by the ecosystem in that region, but also the spray that has for centuries kept the area's soil moist. As a result, the dry soil cannot sustain the plant life, which in turn endangers the local species that live on the banks of the river. The dry soil itself is eroding as well. Perhaps the most important impact has been the lack of cooling spray given off by the falls, making the air less comfortable for visitors. Several more high-rise hotels are being considered, and there has been an outcry from local citizens to stop all new development along the riverbank.

Every city should claim responsibility for the environment, but as the capital, Ottawa should have that the environment as one of its first concerns. Partnerships are extremely important here, as funding for environmental projects is one area politicians tend to cut first. Ottawa has two groups that oversee maintenance and renewal of the local environment—the National Capital Commission (federal dollars) and the city of Ottawa (municipal tax dollars). Still, in the last several years the city has left grass medians uncut, has reduced recycling, and has not maintain city parks well. Looking after the environment is not only the city's job, it is an individual responsibility. For example, with the ban on smoking in public buildings in place, passersby will find cigarette butts (non-biodegradable) carelessly thrown on the ground when a "butt out" container is just 15 feet away. Tourists also tend to be less concerned about littering on vacation, but this is one area that rapidly earns a negative reputation for a TDA. "Dirty cities" are more difficult to sell and seldom bring a tourist back for a second visit.

In Practice

Do a quick SWOT analysis of one of your regional attractions by identifying its **S**trengths, **W**eaknesses, an **O**pportunity it could take advantage of, and a **T**hreat to its continued success.

WHAT SLOWS TOURISM GROWTH?

The Canadian and provincial governments understand that while growth potential for tourism in Canada is excellent, factors hindering that growth also exist. Throughout this book you will find references to many of these concerns:

1. **Concern for the ecosystem.** Opportunities for new tourism land and resources are declining. Future tourism development in wilderness areas must be sustainable and must minimally affect flora and fauna.
2. **Financial concerns.** Developing new projects is expensive. Where will the money come from? Although financial institutions may lend money to major city-regions, they are often reluctant to provide capital to outlying regions. In addition, financial institutions often have a negative perception of the tourism sector, often basing their decisions on the poor performance of old products without acknowledging the tremendous success of modern tourism products, such as cruise lines.
3. **Tourism illiteracy.** Not all communities see tourism as beneficial. Education may be needed before a community starts any tourism projects.
4. **Seasonality.** Mentioned throughout the text, seasonality will continue to be a concern for Canada. The tourism sector is focusing on making Canada a four-season destination by developing events and activities that can take place year-round.

5. **Lack of trained personnel.** Strong training programs must be readily accessible to tourism workers at a reasonable cost.

6. **Transportation costs.** Many things affect transportation, from the quality of our aging infrastructure (roads, rails, harbours, and runways) to the cost of fuel. Rising gas prices make it expensive for even local drivers to fill up.

7. **Poor product packaging and the lack of an integrated market plan.** Both packaging and marketing must be emphasized in any new tourism plan. Many books have been written on marketing, and most Canadian colleges and universities offer diplomas or degrees in this subject. If you are intrigued by marketing, further education is readily available. What is *marketing* and how can Canada change the way in which we package and market our tourism products? This responsibility actually lies with the Canadian Tourism Commission, our destination marketing organization (DMO), but what problems does it face when setting up a marketing plan? What problems are faced by any marketing company we hire to lay out a marketing plan? To create a successful marketing plan, you should first understand the uniqueness of our products.

UNDERSTANDING AND MARKETING THE UNIQUE TOURISM PRODUCT

According to Morrison, "Marketing is a continuous, sequential process through which management plans, researches, implements, controls, and evaluates activities designed to satisfy both customers' needs and wants and their own organization's objectives."[9] Marketing is the bringing together of products, the seller, and the purchaser. However, tourism is not like manufactured products—we sell service, experiences, and time.

When you purchase a car, you begin by researching different car manufacturers. Then you go to a dealer who sells the kind of car you want and you look at the different types and styles available. You sit in the car, kick the tires, and take it for a drive. If the product suits you, then you make your purchase. If the colour you desire is not available on the lot, the dealer will get it for you. That car is your property and sits in your driveway until you decide to get a new one.

Compare that purchase to the purchase of a two-week holiday in Barbados. Although you do research on your destination, you are unable to physically see or handle any of the components you are purchasing. No one can package it and send it to you—you must physically go to pick it up. Finally, when you finish using the product, you must leave it behind, coming home with only memories and a scrapbook. The product you purchased—Barbados—is still available to be sold to the next customer!

What are some of the other unique characteristics of the tourism product? Let's take a look.

To be able to sell a product well, salespeople must first understand it. The tourism product is complicated not only from the standpoint of its diversity, but also from a marketing perspective. Here are some of the characteristics that make tourism a product that is different from other products that is such as cars, televisions, or shampoo:

1. **Tourism is intangible.** The tourism product is **intangible** in that it cannot be touched or perceived by the senses. It does not sit on a shelf. It cannot be handled, examined, or tried prior to purchase because tourism sells "time," which

becomes experiences and memories. Although most consumers would not purchase a sound system without first testing it out, they willingly spend $1500 on a cruise package without ever having stepped on a ship! Therefore, the person who is marketing and selling the product has been granted a high level of trust by the consumer and must represent the product accurately.

2. **Travel is a costly product.** Vacations are something the working public saves for all year. Although people do not mind spending money on their vacations, they do expect value for their dollar.

3. **Tourism products are highly perishable.** Tourism professionals sell time, and time is fleeting.

   Every day hotel rooms sit vacant, planes leave with empty seats, and attractions are not filled to capacity. Each one of those empty "units" means lost revenue, revenue that can never be "made up" for the business. An airline cannot sell a seat on an aircraft that departed 10 minutes ago. The seat is still there, but the customer with the money is waiting at the airport for the next flight. The tourism industry must sell its products daily or lose the revenue it can generate. Marketers have helped control this situation by putting together seat sales and last-minute discounts, but last-minute purchases of our products are not common. People like to plan their vacations.

4. **The tourism product cannot be stored.** If a business understands the demands of the marketplace, it can often take advantage of periods when demand for its product is high. For example, if Christmas is a time when many people purchase television sets, then the manufacturer can produce and store enough televisions for the Christmas rush. However, as you know, "time" cannot be stored for us at a later date. Even though demand for a product may be high during the summer, businesses cannot store up unused "units" from February to sell in July—so some people who wish to purchase your product may have to go elsewhere.

5. **There is a fixed supply of the product and it cannot be easily altered.** Because of the immense cost of building hotels, aircrafts, cruise ships, and resorts, and because of the length of time construction takes, tourism cannot quickly add to its size. Adding 100 rooms to a 250-room hotel is a long construction process. Even if the hotel increases the number of rooms to 350 in order to handle the high demand in July, it must bear the loss of revenue from those empty rooms in January. Airlines that seat 200 passengers cannot suddenly increase their capacity to 300 during spring break. The demand is there; the capacity is not.

6. **The tourism product is highly seasonal.** Tourism experiences periods of great demand (peak demand) and periods of very low demand. In fact, many Canadian resorts close for the winter. During the tourist season they are full to capacity, but the cost of carrying empty rooms over an extended period of time reduces profit margins. By closing during low season, a company reduces wages, electricity costs, etc. Other businesses prefer to reduce their rates during the off-season. In addition to summer golfing packages, Canadian resorts are now looking at providing winter activities that focus on cross-country skiing, developing a spa (good for both seasons), or going after the lucrative convention business. Creative marketing minds continue to create packages and products that can help build business during thelow season.

7. **The use of the product is curbed by time constraints.** Few people have endless vacations. They are given a week or two once a year. Planning a trip to Australia for a Canada Day long weekend may be possible, but it is impractical. A two-week tour of the Cabot Trail is not possible if a tourist has only one week of vacation.

8. **The quality of the individual product often depends on factors beyond the control of the producer or seller.** Tourism consists of many components, all separate entities run by different businesses. A delayed aircraft could mean that an important business negotiation cannot be completed. A hotel may be wonderful, but a rude reception by a customs official or taxi driver may overshadow the entire stay. A bout of food poisoning from a local restaurant may ruin the memories of the perfect resort. Weather is perhaps the most influential factor determining enjoyment of a vacation. The tsunami in Asia was an enormous natural disaster. In Austria and Germany, floods have ravaged ancient towns, destroying buildings that have stood there for hundreds of years. Travellers depend greatly on the generosity of their host country during such disasters, but when real trouble sets in, like the hurricanes that have pounded the Caribbean, Mexican, and southern U.S. coastlines, they demand help from their homelands. However, Canadian tourists have learned that if you are stuck in a foreign country due to weather disasters—don't depend on the Canadian government to help bring you home.

A good tourism experience depends on so many factors that marketing the product becomes a real challenge. When working with a marketing firm, a professional needs to know the marketing process, to understand the tourism product, and to have an honest and creative approach in order to succeed with this unique product.

Tourism's Elasticity of Demand

Another constraint on the tourism product that marketing agencies must consider is high elasticity of demand. What is *elasticity of demand*? To understand that, it is necessary to understand the terms **supply** and **demand**. Demand (in the marketplace) is created by the need or desire for goods and services—that is, the number of purchasers wanting to buy a product. Supply is the amount of product available. Ideally, supply should equal demand. If a product has an **inelastic demand**, people will purchase it no matter what the price. Gasoline is a good example of a product with an inelastic demand. Car owners must buy gasoline, no matter what it costs per litre. On the other hand, products with an **elastic demand** are price-sensitive. With every price change, there is a corresponding change in demand: the lower the price, the higher the demand and vice versa. The tourism industry learned this lesson with the new millennium celebrations. Overpriced products remained unsold, hotel rooms were left vacant, and huge parties were cancelled due to poor sales.

Why do most tourism products have an elastic demand? Travel is a luxury, not a life-sustaining product. It is bought only when the purchaser has the discretionary income needed. The higher the price of the vacation, the lower the demand. There are a few tourism products that have created inelastic demand, but they usually appeal to an elite clientele and offer a product or service that is unique or unmatched. A destination that is in vogue, and is popular with movie stars, royalty, and millionaires, may enjoy a period when people will pay any price for the chance to mingle with the rich and famous!

The First Four Ps of the Marketing Mix

All products are made up of a **marketing mix**—controllable factors that may help satisfy customer needs or wants. Here we will discuss the basic four: **product, price, place, and promotion.**

1. **Product: What do you sell?** We have already discussed the generic tourism product and its unique characteristics, but *products* also have a physical and service component. Each of these components is developed based on specific market needs—for example, the type of hotel, its rooms and amenities, and the level of services it provides for guests. From a marketing standpoint, these qualities are the most important. How does the location and physical layout of a hotel differ from other hotels in the area? What services does a hotel offer that set it apart from similar ones?

2. **Price: How much do you charge for your product?** Many factors influence the *price* of a product, including location, time of year, and quality of service. Of course, pricing strategy must cover basic costs and expenses and include a profit margin. The elasticity of demand for a tourism product must be considered as well as the competition's pricing structure. Knowledge of clients and their purchasing power is also important.

3. **Place: Where are you going to sell your product?** *Place* is also called the **channel of distribution**. The travel services industry is the packaging and sales force for the tourism sector and can be effectively used by the smart business owner. Many businesses have sales departments that handle marketing and sales.

   The most important channel of distribution today is the internet. Many hotels, restaurants, and attractions have websites that provide clients with pictures or short videos of the location. These websites show package deals and pricing, and make it easy for the client to book. Larger sites such as Expedia.ca or Travelocity.ca offer many destinations, different types of hotels, meal packages, attractions, and airline reservations that can be bundled into a self-made tour package at a reduced price.

   The travel agency is another venue for selling the tourism product. When Cruise Lines International Association (CLIA) first organized the modern cruise industry in 1960, they used travel agencies as their sales force. It was a system that was already in place and it brought the cruise lines immediate success. Ninety-five percent of all cruises are still sold through travel agencies.

4. **Promotion: How will you advertise your product?** What is your advertising budget and how can those dollars be most effectively used? Which media format is most likely to be seen or heard by your target market? The choices are vast and the cost of advertising varies widely. Businesses must know who their clients are and how best to reach them. Large international businesses might opt for national newspapers or TV promotions, but the small business must focus on using community news, radio, brochures, mail-outs, or their own website. (In today's world, a business that does not have a website may be losing customers.) Tourism makes use of two important methods of *promotion.*

The first is the internet. Tourism is made up of a variety of small, often unrelated businesses at a given destination. Individually, these businesses have had very little ability to market themselves effectively before tourists actually arrive at their destination. But, the internet has changed all that! For very low cost, websites can be created to introduce a product to travellers long before they even anticipate their trip. As people become more comfortable with using the internet, this method of promotion will become essential to business survival.

The second important method of promotion in our industry is packaging. With less discretionary time, consumers are looking for one-stop shopping opportunities. Linking tourism products in tour packages, whether these packages are designed for individuals or groups, means that each product enjoys the strength of joint marketing initiatives.

Colourful brochures with beautiful views of destinations help give substance to the intangible tourism product prior to purchase.
(Photo: Paula Kerr.)

Customer-Oriented Marketing

In order to effectively sell tourism products, businesses must create and implement marketing plans. A **marketing plan** is simply a written short-term plan that details how a product will use its marketing mix to achieve its goal (financial or other) over a specified period. How does a business develop a customer-oriented marketing plan? First, the business must understand its products and services. It must also have a clear understanding of the needs and expectations of its customers.

Customers come to a business with specific expectations. They have preconceived ideas about what a product is and how well it will fulfill their expectations. A good marketing plan identifies these expectations and is able to provide value for the customer's dollar. **Perceived value** is the customer's mental estimate of the worth of a product. For some, value is price-sensitive, but for others the total experience is what matters—the friendliness of service and the quality of the experience. It does not matter that different customers have different views of value, because as long as the exchange of dollars matches the perception of what the product is worth, customers will be satisfied.

Can one product fulfill everyone's needs? Will a tourism product that satisfies one traveller's need for hard adventure also satisfy the traveller who wants the comforts of home life? Obviously not. **Market segmentation** is one way to deal with the wide variety of personalities, life stages, and motivations that travel products must satisfy. Market segmentation is simply the division of the overall

CASE STUDY

Vacation Cancellation

Émilie and Jacques Dufresne had travelled little since their wedding 25 years ago—they had been too busy raising five children and putting them through college. Married young, Émilie and Jacques did not have a honeymoon, but they had been dreaming for 25 years of a late but glamorous honeymoon in the sun. Émilie often picked up colourful brochures from the travel agency near her workplace in downtown Saskatoon. She and Jacques would gaze at the incredible pictures of white sandy beaches and beautiful bedrooms with ocean views! Émilie had been saving slowly over the years, and as their 25th anniversary approached, they decided to fly to a resort on the island of Martinique. Émilie used her brochure information to find a similar package on the internet, one that was a little cheaper than the brochure's advertised price, and they

booked their honeymoon—seven days and six nights, all inclusive.

On February 13, the day before their departure, Jacques was rushed to hospital, experiencing chest pains. It was not a heart attack, but he needed to stay in the hospital for at least three days. The doctor absolutely forbade him to fly for the next 30 days. Émilie called the tour company to say that she and Jacques would have to postpone their trip until the doctor had given her husband a clean bill of health. It took her a long time to get the tour company on the phone, and when she did, the callous manner in which she was treated stunned her. Émilie was asked whether she had read the conditions and terms for the trip, which clearly stated their cancellation policies. With less than 24 hours to departure, Émilie was told, it was not possible to postpone the trip and there would be no refund.

1. What is the root cause of the problem the Dufresnes have experienced?
2. Describe three possible solutions for this problem.
3. Each solution you have described will have positive and negative impacts on both the customer and the company. For the three solutions you have described in the previous question, give at least one positive and one negative impact.
4. If you were part of this tour company's management, what would you do to avoid this problem in the future?
5. If you were Émilie, what would you do to avoid this type of problem with your future bookings?

market into groups of people who share common characteristics or have similar needs. Club Med resorts provide a good example of how one company handles a diverse marketplace.

Originally, Club Med was created to provide vacations for single, young adult travellers and offered a full range of recreational activities and social functions, as well as the companionship of other single travellers. After several years of operation, Club Med discovered that its first set of loyal customers had moved on from being single or newly married without children to married with young children. To satisfy this market's changing needs, Club Med designed new child-friendly resorts.

This kind of **niche** or **target marketing** is essential to our industry because of the diversity of clientele and their needs and expectations. The wide variety of tourism products available makes this kind of marketing strategy easy. A career in tourism marketing (see Chapter 11) could be an exciting option. As each destination creates additional attractions, the role of the marketing consultant will be even more important.

Summary

Although planning and development are separate endeavours, they must occur together for tourism to succeed on a local, regional, or national level. Canada has looked carefully at its goals and has developed a series of guidelines for developing and maintaining its tourism product.

Planning is a cyclical, eight-step process. In any situation it is important to begin with an inventory of the social, political, physical, and economic environment of the community or business. This inventory gives direction on what is needed, what can be accomplished, and what should not be attempted. The second step is to look at trends. Forecasting provides a basis for deciding whether to proceed with certain plans. The third step, which creates the guidelines, is to develop a mission statement, goals, and objectives. Steps four, five, and six require the community or business to study alternative plans, to select the preferred plan, and to design strategies to reach the goals. The seventh step is implementation, and the final step includes reviewing, evaluating, and revising the original plan. When a tourism plan is devised as a community document, support for the ideas helps make the plan successful. Without planning, tourism development is a hit-or-miss operation.

Tourism development refers to the type of development that takes place in communities. Integrated development is achieved by a single company or individual, but most communities do not develop tourism this way. Catalytic development occurs when a developer brings a major attraction to an area and encourages other businesses to build nearby, giving local and regional businesses the opportunity to participate and become successful. Coattail development occurs when visitors are drawn to an area because of its scenic beauty or natural qualities. Owners see the potential and start new tourism-related businesses. There is usually little guidance or planning at the initial stages of development. A community must organize itself and put together a planning document to avoid becoming a hodgepodge of buildings without a central theme.

There are some factors that make a destination more visible and more comfortable for a tourist. These factors are developing a sense of place, or a USP—something specific that separates you from other destinations; product/market match—ensuring that the products you are trying to sell meet the needs and expectations of your target markets; clustering—locating your sites, accommodations, and food service establishments in one area (or specific areas for specific clients) for easy access; transportation systems—providing visitors with the ability to move around tourist areas easily; partnerships—providing both help and strength to your event or TDA; and, finally, the environment, which remains a concern for both locals and visitors. Maintaining and renewing the environment should be a top concern. Tourism has specific curbs on its growth that need to be continually addressed.

Marketing tourism products can be challenging. Six unique factors make marketing our products even more difficult and cause the industry to look at developing year-round markets: tourism products are intangible and cannot be tried before purchase; are expensive, are highly perishable, cannot be stored, are in a fixed supply, are seasonal, and must be used within time constraints; and the quality of the product often depends on factors beyond our control. Tourism is also an elastic product; that is, amount of sales can be dependent on price. Marketing is a written short-term plan that details how a product will use product, price, promotion, and place to achieve its financial goals.

Questions

1. Illustrate the effectiveness of your city as a tourism destination by discussing how it meets the five essential components of a generic destination.

2. Discuss the four stages in the life cycle of a destination.

3. Outline five goals that a viable tourism destination should meet in order to enhance the community.

4. a) Briefly explain in your own words the eight steps in tourism planning.

   b) Which of these steps do you feel is most important? Explain.

   c) Identify two factors or situations that VANOC might encounter that could slow the building process of the 2010 Olympic and Paralympic Games. How might these situations be handled to get the process back on its timeline?

5. Define the following terms as they relate to tourism planning: *planning, functional form, product capacity, qualitative forecasting, quantitative forecasting.*

6. a) Illustrate the differences between integrated, catalytic, and coattail development of a tourism destination area.

   b) Which style of development do you feel is best? Explain your answer.

7. List the seven constraints for tourism growth identified by the Canadian and provincial governments.

8. a) List the six key factors of a TDA as described in this chapter.

   b) Looking at your city, which of these factors does it handle best? Why did you make this choice? Which key factor should your city be working to improve?

9. You are working in the marketing department of a large luxury hotel. Define the following marketing terms and provide an example of how you are trying to control or minimize the impact of these situations:

   a) the room you are selling is "intangible"

   b) the room you are selling is very "perishable"

   c) you cannot store leftover rooms to be used next week

   d) you cannot add 25 rooms to be used for a large conference

   e) the quality of your room depends on factors that you cannot control

   f) the room you are selling has a high "seasonal" demand

10. If a product has an elastic demand, what does that mean? If it is inelastic, how does it differ?

Notes

1. *Newfoundland-Labrador* (St. John's: Tourism Newfoundland-Labrador, 1995.)

2. Edward Inskeep, *Tourism Planning: An Integrated and Sustainable Approach* (New York: John Wiley & Sons, 1991), p. 25.

3. Robert W. McIntosh and Charles R. Goeldner, *Tourism Principles, Practices, Philosophies*, 6th ed. (New York: John Wiley & Sons, 1990), pp. 265–267.

4. www.vancouver2010.com.

5. Ibid.

6. Ibid.

7. Douglas Pearce, *Tourism Development*, 2nd ed. (New York: John Wiley & Sons, 1989), pp. 67–70.

8. Smith and Laurel Reid, Six Key Factors to a Destination's Success (Video available fom University of Western Ontario bookstore).

9. Alistair M. Morrison *Hospitality and Tourism Marketing* (Albany, NY: Delmar Publishers Inc., 1998), p. 4.

Transportation

Key terms

airfares
bilateral agreement
BritRail pass
bullet train
bumped
charter
circle trip
corporate rates
direct flight
e-ticket
Eurail Pass
fly/coach tours
Freedoms of the Air

gateway airport
hub and spoke
interline connection
International Air
  Transport Association
  (IATA)
International Civil
  Aviation Organization
  (ICAO)
landing fee
load factor
Maglev
motor coach package

non-stop flight
online connection
open-jaw trip
Open Skies Agreement
Orient Express
overnight/short tours
round trip
scheduled air carrier
sightseeing/day tours
special interest cruise
theme cruise
unlimited kilometres
VIA Rail Canada

Learning objectives

Having read this chapter you will be able to

1. Discuss the emergence of modern transportation systems, explain why travellers choose one mode over another, and identify trends.

2. Summarize the effects of deregulation in Canada on transportation systems and the tourism industry.

3. Describe the Canadian air transportation system, including the impact of global and bilateral air agreements.

4. Compare and contrast the common perceptions of a tour by automobile/ RV versus a motor coach tour.

5. Compare foreign rail with domestic rail in terms of product and services provided.

6. Describe the variety of cruise options available and outline the advantages of vacationing on a cruise.

Some people believe that travel and tourism are synonymous; they are not. The transportation system, along with the infrastructure that supports it, plays the most significant role in tourism: if visitors cannot reach their destinations, then none of the other tourism components are needed. Transporting a visitor to a chosen destination begins the tourism experience.

Part of the joy of travelling is getting to use transportation modes unavailable at home: England's double-decker buses, motor scooters in Rome, camels in the Sahara, the *Maglev* Monorail in China, and jeepneys in the Philippines. If it is unique, travels fast, or does something unusual, you can be sure tourists will want a ride.

While it is important that a travel destination be able to provide methods to carry passengers from one site to another, more important are the modes of transportation travellers use to get to their destination. The choices serve different purposes: to get tourists to their destination fast, to give tourists the chance to see the countryside or, for older travellers, to step back into time and enjoy a method of travel used when they were young. The many different modes of transportation, and why tourists choose one mode over another, is an interesting area of research. How important is transportation to the tourism sector? The sector would not exist without it, and this chapter looks briefly to the past, current, and future of this important industry.

How we travel depends solely on the type of transportation that is currently available to us. Until the Industrial Revolution, in the early 19th century, people had little choice in the speed or the method of transportation. Horses, camels, and donkeys carried you from one place to another, perhaps pulling a cart or caravan in which you stored your goods. Travel by water was faster if the prevailing wind was in your favour, but travel by ship was difficult, uncomfortable for most passengers, and dangerous. Still, the desire to see the world and trade with other nations has existed through all of our history, and adventurers like Marco Polo and Christopher Columbus brought back stories and goods that helped change global perspectives on life. With the invention of the steam engine, transportation suddenly became easier, safer, and more accessible to ordinary folk. Ships and trains were the first to get the "amazing steam engine," and they became major systems of early modern transportation. Now you did not have to be wealthy to travel, and many immigrants to the new world travelled in pest-ridden and filthy ships across the Atlantic Ocean.

However, it was Henry Ford's invention of the automobile that has had the most powerful impact on transportation. It changed not only travel methods, but also travel's accessibility. Cars were not only within the financial reach of the middle class, but they travelled with a minimum of infrastructure—a pitted track and you were off on an adventure! Cars gave people the ability to reach areas of the country that were not accessible by trains or boats. So you could say that it was the invention of the automobile that gave birth to the modern tourism sector because it made travel fun and open to all who wished to try the travel experience. For future travellers, the latest frontier of transportation is within our grasp—space travel.

SELECTING A MODE OF TRANSPORTATION

The availability of the right infrastructure and suprastructure determines the choices a traveller has——harbours and ports, train tracks, and roads and runways must be in place for most methods of transportation. What else helps travellers decide on their mode of travel? Here are some of the obvious factors:

Cost is often one of the first factors an aspiring tourist considers. Transportation is a large portion of a travel budget, so knowing your needs and your financial situation may be the most important consideration. Obviously, the more family members you have travelling together, the more cost impacts your choice.

Service will always be a consideration when choosing a mode of transportation. How well is the customer treated once under the control of the transportation company chosen? Unless an airline trip is over four hours, food is not served. Do you see the flight attendants throughout the flight? Does the porter watch as you struggle up the narrow steps onto a train with your luggage? Are they flexible when your needs change? Or is flexibility a one-way street—"we are delayed, be patient!" Perceptions or knowledge of the quality of service will impact a traveller's decision.

Time is the third factor you are likely to consider. A business traveller will usually choose the fastest method available to allow maximum time for business. Pleasure travellers will often try to condense as much vacation time as possible into their one-week or two-week vacations. However, if travellers live in Halifax and want to visit family in Calgary with only one week of vacation time, travelling by bus, train, or car gives them little time for family reunions. Flying, the most expensive option, becomes necessary.

Convenience of the travel mode is another consideration. Obviously, if you have a car and are transporting your family, it is the most convenient mode of transportation available to you. Other things to the consider regarding convenience are the location of the departure/arrival terminals, the case of check-in procedures, the ability to travel with equipment you will need at your destination, and how the mode of transportation handles travelling with babies or family pets.

Safety issues will also be a concern. How carefully does the mode of transportation deal with your comfort and safety? What is their safety record? (In 2007, the airline industry still maintained its "safest mode" status, and in the last 10 years has reduced the number of accidents from 1.74 per million flights to just 0.75 accidents per million.)[1]

Route structure is another concern. In 1976, train travel in Canada changed with the creation of one passenger line, VIA Rail. Many smaller towns with track accessibility were no longer serviced by the train. During the winter, some areas of Canada have no air service. Keeping a global perspective, smaller countries may have only one airport and the balance of transportation must be done by car or bus. The longer it takes you to reach your destination and the more complicated the route structure you are using, the less time you will have for fun and relaxation.

Frequency of departures may also be a problem. Many smaller towns in our north may have air service, but only on Wednesdays and Saturdays. It is likely that major destinations will have much more frequent service. Travelling from Vancouver to Vancouver Island forces tourists to adhere to a limited schedule with ferry crossings that take several hours. Going to and from the island in one day would likely best be handled by air. If Ottawa is your point of departure, buses and planes leave hourly, but the train leaves only three times a day. With a snowy day, however, passengers may realize the better option is to take the train!

Personality and psychology also factor into choosing a mode of transportation. In his research, Dr. Jagdish Sheth has identified several *psychological factors* that influence the decision-making process.

1. *Fears and prejudices* formed during childhood will affect a person's choice of transportation. A child who grew up with a fear of water will likely not choose to travel by ship as an adult. Fear of flying for a businessperson may make travel so difficult it impairs his or her ability to perform on the job effectively.

2. *Stereotypes and perceptions* are also difficult to overcome. Perceptions are often based on a lack of knowledge and similar to fears, perceptions, however erroneous, may impede our ability to make informed choices.

   The perception of performance of a mode of transportation may influence a traveller's choice. Does it consistently depart and arrive on time? Are the service personnel friendly and professional? Is the seating comfortable? These factors create a positive or negative perception in clients' minds that may change their travel decisions. As an example, it is common knowledge that the demand for air travel slows for a brief period after a major airline crash.

3. Finally, our *self-image and our desire for status* may eliminate a method of travel that would otherwise serve us well. A person wishing to travel from Calgary to Vancouver may choose an airline over a bus, despite cost factors, simply because travel by air reinforces a personal image of success.

Transportation operators are aware of these many emotions, needs, and constraints, and their marketing programs address each in detail. Tour bus companies focus on the quality of their equipment, the ease of seeing the countryside without having to drive, and the friendliness and knowledge of their staff. Airlines promote fast, friendly, and safe travel, using images of qualified pilots and crewmembers, and caring, concerned mechanics and ground personnel. Providing high-quality service is an integral part of any transportation promotion. In the end, the choice of how we travel is a personal one. We use all of our experiences and knowledge to choose the mode best suited to our needs at a given time.

TRAVEL BY AIR

The airline industry has the most significant impact on global development of any other global industry. From a financial aspect, it provides 31.9 million jobs globally that range from airline distribution personnel (pilots, flight attendants, and ground support personnel such as baggage handlers and people who refuel and clean the airplanes and other airport facilities) to sales and marketing forces. Air is the major carrier of goods and, in 2008, the industry handled $3.557 billion USD (that figure equates to 7.5% of the world's GDP). There were 27.8 million scheduled departures in 2007, and the industry continues to grow. But a more important factor is the actual economic and social benefits the industry brings to citizens around the world:

- It is the driving force behind the growth of international tourism and trade.
- It connects people, countries, and cultures in a fast, safe, and mostly convenient manner.
- It provides the world's goods with access to global markets.
- It is a force that drives both economic and social progress.
- It forges links between developed nations and those struggling to improve their economic standing globally.[2]

Air Travel from a Historical Point of View

How quickly this industry has developed from its tiny flight in Kitty Hawk, North Carolina, in 1903. Sixty-three years later, the first men walked on the moon! The *SST Concorde*, which flew in the 1970s–1990s, travelled faster than the speed of sound, picking passengers up in London at 11:30 a.m. and depositing them in Miami by 8:30 a.m. of the same day! And now people are booking seats for space travel with Richard Branson's Virgin Galactic company.

www.aircanada.ca

Air service did not arrive in Canada for 27 years after its initial flight, but in the 1930s, the federal government began its airline known as Trans Canada Airlines (TCA—now Air Canada). Canadian Pacific Airways (CP Airways), privately owned, was given international routes to Pacific Rim countries and struggled for many years to gain equality with the government-owned TCA. In 1966, the first important *Canadian Transportation Act* was passed, and while it also dealt with other forms of transportation in Canada, it finally gave CP Airways rights to 25 percent of Canada's domestic air routes. In the 1970s, "regulated competition" was introduced, which liberalized the strict rules of charter regulations. This change saw the emergence and growth of new, small charter airlines. While Ward Air, a charter airline based in Edmonton, Alberta, had been fighting for scheduled routes, regulations were opened further allowing privately owned companies like Ward Air and Pacific Western, based in Vancouver, to enter the tough air marketplace.

In 1978, the United States government made a daring move and deregulated the American airline industry. Prior to deregulation, travel by air had been viewed as a service industry, which should provide fast, efficient transportation to all parts of America. The politicians who opposed the strict government regulations sought to free the airlines and felt market force and competition should determine the price of a ticket, not the government. It was a challenging time for airlines south of the border with many smaller and several larger airlines going bankrupt or being bought out.

Also recognizing the need for change in the airline industry, Canada passed a new *National Transportation Act* in 1987, which replaced the *Passenger Ticket Act* and the *Government Railways Act*, and this new legislation was far-reaching. It affirmed that a safe, economic, efficient transportation network was necessary to meet the needs of Canadian businesses and travellers. It replaced the Canadian Transportation Commission with a new agency, the National Transportation

Agency (NTA), and privatized Air Canada. Pricing regulations were eliminated and entrance into the scheduled airline business was opened to all Canadian airlines. Canada's *National Transportation Act* did not go as far as the U.S. legislation in deregulating the airline industry. Recognizing the difficulties of serving vast, thinly populated areas, especially in the north, the government continued to regulate northern routes. However, it soon became clear that the same chaos the United States was living through was now at our door. Smaller airlines attempting to compete with larger ones failed, and many airlines merged rather than leave the business entirely. For example, Pacific Western Airlines (PWA) and Ward Air merged with Canadian Pacific Airways to become Canadian Airlines International (CAI). Entering the difficult years of the late 1990s, Canadian Airlines International was forced to seek bankruptcy protection. In 1999, with a foreign company in the bidding, the federal government stepped in and gave purchase rights to Air Canada, leaving the country with only one major carrier.

Small airline companies—like Bearskin Airlines and Calm Air—lived through the turmoil by not expanding into the larger markets and continuing to operate as regional or "feeder" airlines, servicing destinations like London and Sudbury, in Ontario, and Yellowknife, Northwest Territories. These small airlines have been able to survive because they use smaller, more fuel-efficient aircraft, carry fewer passengers, and require fewer personnel.

One benefit of deregulation has been the emergence of no-frills or discount airlines, which focus on shorter flights with limited services or charters. Discount airlines such as the following can be strong competition for the major carriers because they control their costs so efficiently: CanJet, based in Halifax, WestJet, based in Calgary, Porter and Jazz in Toronto, and Air PEI in Charlottetown. WestJet, established in 1996, has been the most successful by keeping its eye on service and lower fares. How has it kept its costs low? Clive Beddoe, WestJet's CEO, acknowledges that it has been difficult with the rising cost of fuel, but says "you succeed in business because you provide quality service for a good price."[3] WestJet's simplified fare structure, with low ticket pricing based on the day of the week or time of the year, does just that.

Route structures also changed with deregulation. During the early years of the airlines, routes were linear. In other words, they flew in "straight lines" on one flight, like from Toronto to Vancouver. They returned via the same route. Linear routes are still common in international flight structures. However, with deregulation, the **hub and spoke** system emerged. Airlines concentrated their services at major airports, reducing costs by consolidating staff in one or two major centres. The larger aircraft (*Airbus* and *Boeing 747*s), which are more expensive to operate, carry passengers between major cities, then transfer them to smaller planes (more cost-efficient) for the flight to their final destination. Feeder or regional airlines are the link between the hub city and the smaller, final destination. In Canada, our major hub cities are Montreal, Toronto, and Vancouver. Regional or feeder airlines such as Air Nova, Air BC, and Air Ontario are affiliated with Air Canada.

No history of air travel will ever be complete without addressing the far-reaching implications of September 11, 2001, on the airline system and other modes of travel. In the late 1960s and 1970s, airlines had been forced to deal with a rising number of hijackers who used passengers and planes as bargaining chips for their causes. But the events of September 11, 2001, painted a whole different picture of terrorism, as jumbo jets became moving incendiary bombs. American Airlines Flight 11 was flown into the north tower of the World Trade Center at 8:46 a.m. At 9:03 a.m., United Airlines Flight 175 slammed into the south tower. In Washington, D.C., the Pentagon was the target for the hijackers of American Airlines Flight 77. At around the same time, passengers on another hijacked plane, United Flight 93, heard of the other attacks, realized their aircraft was heading toward Washington, and forced their plane into a field near Shanksville, Pennsylvania. Once officials determined this was a terrorist operation, the Federal Aviation Administration (FAA) closed U.S. airspace. In two and a half hours, over 4500 aircraft nationwide were forced to land or were diverted. International flights destined for the U.S. landed in Canada, flooding small and large airports with stranded, frightened passengers. U.S. airspace stayed closed for three days, and by the time operations began again, America's faith in its airline system had been badly shaken.

Airlines suffered extreme financial losses. United Airlines, the world's second largest carrier, lost over $5 million daily. Some governments provided one-time bail-out grants; Air Canada received $5 million. Several airlines declared bankruptcy, including Scandinavian Airlines (SAS) in Europe, and Canada 3000 in Canada. Air travel has never recovered fully.

In January of 2003, the Canadian Air Transport Security Authority (CATSA) began operations at most Canadian airports. CATSA's mandate is to ensure the safety of passengers, with improved screening processes for both airport workers and airline passengers, thus decreasing the risk of terrorist acts. This increase in security has meant an additional security surcharge is added to each airline ticket to cover costs. Critics say airport security is still too lax. While passengers undergo close scrutiny, airport workers and their access points do not.

By April 1, 2003, Air Canada was finally forced to file for bankruptcy protection. The company emerged from bankruptcy protection in 2004 by reducing costs through layoffs, restructuring union contracts, cutting services, decreasing the weight limits of baggage, and increasing the cost of overweight items.[4]

On March 10, 2005, one of Canada's deep discount airlines, Jetsgo, grounded its fleet and declared bankruptcy. In June of 2008, Zoom airlines did the same thing. Bankrupt! Passengers in both cases were stranded across Canada and in resort destinations, inconveniencing them and costing them money. This event prompted provinces without legislation to consider consumer protection laws. British Columbia, Quebec, and Ontario already have protective legislation in place. The Travel Industry Council of Ontario (TICO) is taking an aggressive stand to ensure that travel agencies and tour operators meet higher standards of performance. TICO has fought Bill C-44 (legislation tabled in Parliament in 2005, aimed at creating a more efficient transportation system), asking that the legislation provide more protection for the travelling public and that the position of airline travel commissioner (ombudsman for the airline industry) be retained, not eliminated.

In a speech delivered at the Aviation Forecasting Conference in October of 2005, James May of the Air Transport Association of America identified five major issues facing airlines today:

- Airlines are being taxed to death by governments; taxes often add as much as 50% to the cost of a ticket.
- Politicians and airline executives need to rethink the way airlines are structured and operated.

- Resources must be provided to allow the antiquated air traffic management systems around the world to move to a satellite-based system.
- Current soaring fuel prices leave little prospect of making a profit this year.
- Bankruptcy of one major airline has a direct impact on feeder airlines who depend on the transfer of passengers from the majors.[5]

Understanding Canada's Air System

The federal department responsible for all of Canada's transportation systems is called Transport Canada. It sets the rules and regulations for licensing pilots, flight engineers, and airplane mechanics. It provides licences for each commercial aircraft and determines the number of hours a plane can fly between maintenance checks. It sets the appropriate weight loads allowable for each type of aircraft. It also sets the maximum number of hours a pilot may remain on duty. Many airlines choose to set pilot hours at eight hours of flight time with an additional four hours "on ground." Flights with over eight hours of scheduled flying time will have what is termed a "double cockpit," with two extra pilots on board to relieve those flying. Recently, one of our investigative channels did research on this subject and discovered Canadian pilots do not have the 12-hour limit, but may actually be on duty for as long as 19 hours without relief. The program was concerned for passenger safety, pointing out that the last few runway mishaps have been blamed on pilot fatigue.

For more than 60 years, Transport Canada also operated the country's air navigation system. In November of 1996, NAV CANADA (NAVCAN), a non-share, capital, private-sector corporation was given ownership and control over the country's air navigation system. By putting the safety of airline passengers under one private corporation, the government hoped to save money and provide Canadians with a more efficient, safer air system. NAVCAN currently provides aircraft with air navigation, air traffic control, flight information, weather briefings, airport advisory services, electronics, and services such as training and electronic maintenance. NAVCAN charges users (primarily commercial airlines) service fees, which are, of course, passed on to the consumer.

www.tc.gc.ca

Understanding Air Terminology

Air travel is best described in terms of *scheduled* and *non-scheduled service*. In addition to scheduled commercial flights, air travel includes fleets for use by private corporations, small private planes for business and pleasure, and planes for special services such as fire prevention and law enforcement.

Scheduled air carriers operate with published timetables on defined domestic or international routes for which licences have been granted by the government or governments. Air Canada and WestJet are both scheduled carriers.

Charter airlines or charter air services arrange to fly wherever and whenever a group plans to travel. A group of travellers may charter any form of transportation, usually at lower rates than those of regularly scheduled service.

Charter operators have much more flexibility than operators of scheduled flights; they can fly on their own time, even cancelling the flight if necessary. Using cheaper chartered service does have its problems from a passenger standpoint as

Some of our finest wilderness experiences can be reached only with float planes.
(Photo courtesy Canadian Tourism Commission.)

these aircraft fly only on the dates, times, and departure points pre-set by the charter company. Tour operators with large groups often choose to charter an aircraft to help keep costs lower.

Airports

Airports fall into two major categories: *air carrier* airports and *general aviation* airports. Most of Canada's major airports are now leased from the government to a private company or airport authority. Since these companies are in business for profit, service charges have gone up. Increased landing fees, which of course must be passed on to passengers, have been a major concern to airlines. Cities with airports currently under private management include Halifax, Montreal, Ottawa, Toronto, Winnipeg, Calgary, Edmonton, and Vancouver. Some airports are owned and operated by provincial authorities, and a few remain under the control of Transport Canada.

Many of our airports require extensive remodelling, new and longer runways, and improved services to stay competitive and handle expected higher passenger volume. To cover these costs, most airports charge passengers departure taxes called Air Improvement Fees (AIFs), which may be added to the ticket at the time of purchase or collected when passengers go through security. Airports also make additional revenue from rental spaces, parking facilities, and other services. The year 2007 was one of the worst travel years for customers in the United States, with major airports so badly congested that heavy delays and flight cancellations became the status quo. As a result, the United States is considering adding a "congestion fee" to encourage passengers to use other airports. Many major airports such as Heathrow (England) and Kennedy Airport (USA) are equally challenged.

Airport Components Airports consist of many different components: passenger terminals, parking lots, control towers, hangars, runways, taxiways, loading aprons, chapels, customs and immigration facilities, restaurants and bars, lounges reserved for first-class travellers, souvenir shops, car rental agencies, banks or money exchange services, administration offices, and any other service that the airport feels is needed by a traveller. Some airports have hotels as an integral part of the terminal, and others have direct access to subways or a train station. Many major airports around the world can provide passengers with a unique experience and enjoyable stopover. A new addition to the airport experience is the Common-Use Self-Service (CUSS) kiosks being set up in all major airports.[6] They allow passengers to check themselves in no matter which airline they are flying on. These kiosks may be conveniently placed around the airport, in the parking area, or near rental car returns or shops, and allow airports and airlines a number of cost-saving benefits like the need for less check-in counter space and fewer employees, and expedited check-in for customers. IATA is hoping to have over 130 airports around the world set up using these kiosks, and Toronto has already begun the process. Another change bound to decrease boarding time is the introduction of bar-coded tickets. This means passengers may check in at home and print a computerized document valid for their entire round trip. When travellers are boarding with this document, computers will scan and check-in each traveller. Over one hundred airlines around the world now offer this convenience.[7] Recently, a concerned group of airlines, travel agents, and passengers concerned about the cost of this program have begun the legal process of having the bar code system for all airlines adjusted as it was felt the cost factors of introducing the system could be an impediment to an airline struggling already with debt.

Airline Terminology You Should Know

landing fee	fee charged to an aircraft each time it lands at an airport; passed on to the consumer in the ticket price
gateway airport	an airport that receives a high volume of international flights
e-ticket	ticket-less travel where a code is your check-in document. Since May 2008, all IATA airlines should be using only the e-ticket.
bumped	term used for when a flight is oversold and confirmed passengers are denied boarding
round trip	trip that originates in one city, takes passengers to their destination, and returns them to the originating city using the same airline
circle trip	a type of round trip in which the route taken to the destination differs from the route taken from the destination
open-jaw trip	trip that takes passengers to one destination, allows them to use another mode of travel to a second destination, and flies them home from there
non-stop flight	a flight that travels from one destination to another without a stop
direct flight	a flight that travels from one destination to another, making at least one stop, then continuing on the same plane
online connection	a flight that requires travellers to change aircraft to get to their destination
interline connection	a flight that requires travellers to change airlines to get to their destination

Airfares and Reservations

Deregulation and more efficient operations have dramatically reduced airfares, and as suggested earlier, when airfares drop, more people take to the skies. The airline industry is, however, greatly affected by changes in oil prices. The dramatic rise of gas prices since 2004 has caused hardship for the already struggling airlines. Most airlines have now added a fuel surcharge, allowing them to quickly adjust ticket prices to cover these rising costs.

Airfares are set according to two very broad markets: the business traveller and the discretionary traveller. Business travellers usually want to adhere to a relatively strict schedule, so they have fewer options on flight times. Because of this inflexibility, they pay the standard fare or even the higher business or first-class fare. Discretionary travellers, who can shop around for more convenient flights at the best price, are usually able to get discount fares because they are not locked into a specific schedule.

Airline strategies in discount fares have led to multi-tiered pricing, with as many as 100 different prices for the same route. The difference in price between a standard fare, a discount fare, and the last-minute sale price made over the internet can be considerable, but selling these unoccupied seats at the last minute can bring the airlines at least a minimal fare to cover costs. (In Chapter 3, we looked at the perishability of the tourism product—and here is an example of how an industry tries to sell its products in a timely fashion.) For passengers able to travel at the last minute, these fares can be an added bonus to a trip. This arrangement also allows airlines to increase their **load factor**—the average percentage of seats filled by paying (revenue-producing) passengers. Generally, the major costs of the flight, such as crew salaries, aircraft depreciation, and maintenance, are fixed, and incremental costs to carry one more passenger are minimal. Therefore, revenue is maximized by pricing some seats at a lower rate to encourage additional passenger travel.

The International Air Transport System: How It Works

Bilateral agreements are international agreements made between two countries. Every country with air service will have signed bilateral agreements. These agreements cover a number of issues, including the number of flights permitted from each country into a specific airport, the size and capacity of the airplanes, and special fares. The **Open Skies Agreement** of 1995 is an example of a bilateral agreement between Canada and the United States. It has "opened the skies" above North America, providing tourists with more options for carrier, destination, and type of flight. This agreement has benefited cross-border tourism, allowing Air Canada to serve many new U.S. destinations and U.S. airlines to provide some cross-border competition for Air Canada. In 2005, Canada and the United States updated this agreement, giving greater access for Canadian and U.S. passenger and cargo flights and providing more flexibility in pricing structures, which should bring lower prices for consumers.[8]

Most countries claim ownership not only of their land but also of their shorelines, waters, and skies. In the early years of aviation, this ownership caused some concern for aviators. To ensure the right of safe flight, the nations of the world sat down to write some very basic rules. The rules regulating air activity have been developed at worldwide conferences, through bilateral agreements, and by organizations like the International Civil Aviation Organization (ICAO) and the International Air Transport Association (IATA).

Airline Associations

www.iata.org

IATA The **International Air Transport Association (IATA)** was formed in 1919 and reorganized in 1945. Its members currently include more than 200 of the world's scheduled airlines, with major flag carriers taking a leadership role. The principal function of IATA is to facilitate the movement of persons and goods from and to any point on the world air network by any combination of routes. Some of IATA's mandates are to

- provide a forum for airlines to meet and discuss mutual concerns
- promote air safety
- represent the airlines in travel agency affairs
- encourage global air travel

Each country has absolute right to its airspace and can set any conditions it likes with regard to air travel, so to be effective, rules or tariffs formulated by IATA must also receive approval from the appropriate government.

By 1940, IATA had overseen a series of world conferences that had set up parameters for controlling a variety of flight issues, including aircraft registry, issuing airline tickets, setting liability of the airline with regard to lost luggage, and setting liability in the event of passenger injury or death.

One of the more important accomplishments of these world conferences has been the development of rights called **Freedoms of the Air**. The first two freedoms deal with the rights of passage for an airplane. After the Bay of Pigs incident in 1963, in which the United States encouraged an unsuccessful invasion of Cuba by Cuban expatriates, Fidel Castro rescinded all Freedoms of the Air for U.S. airlines. Because Canada still has these rights, Canadian airlines may fly across the island, but U.S. airlines are forced to fly around it.

The next four freedoms are called *traffic rights*. They deal with the dropping off and picking up of passengers. The last two freedoms are the newest. They give special rights to certain airlines under specific circumstances. The eighth freedom, called *cabotage*, gives a foreign airline the right to carry passengers from one destination within a country to another, allowing Delta Airlines, for example, to pick up passengers in Toronto and let them disembark in Vancouver. Canada does not currently give U.S. airlines the right of cabotage. Some believe that granting this right to foreign airlines would prevent Canada's flight system from becoming monopolistic. However, this proposal has not been met with much support because our Open Skies Agreement already gives considerable freedom to North American airlines to form partnerships and to share routes and fare structures. Here are five of the most important freedoms:

First Freedom: right of transit (e.g., Air Canada departs Toronto and flies over the United States to reach Mexico City)

Second Freedom: right of technical stop (e.g., Cathay Pacific departs Toronto and lands in Anchorage to refuel en route to Hong Kong)

Third Freedom: right to discharge passengers in a foreign country (e.g., Air Canada boards passengers in Halifax and they disembark in London, England)

Fourth Freedom: right to pick up foreign passengers in another country and transport them to the airline's country of registration (e.g., Air Canada boards passengers in Miami, Florida, and allows them to disembark in Montreal)

Eighth Freedom: right of an airline registered in one country to fly passengers between two points within another country (e.g., United Airlines picks up passengers in Montreal and flies them to Calgary. This is an example of *cabotage*.) If Canada were to lose one of its airlines and Canadians had just one choice of carrier, the impact such a monopoly might have on the price of a ticket could be high. As an alternative, the Canadian government could give a U.S. airline (e.g., American Airlines) cabotage rights in Canada, providing some competition and taking away monopoly rights.

ICAO The **International Civil Aviation Organization** is an agency of the United Nations, and its members are representatives from UN member countries. ICAO was formed to ensure that the development of the airline system is both safe and orderly. ICAO is responsible for organizing world conferences, mediating disputes between members, and setting standards for aviation equipment and operations. Canada has played an active role in ICAO and promoted an international no-smoking policy that it hopes will be observed by all international air carriers, making international flight a smoke-free experience.

Air rage—when passengers abuse cabin crew or other passengers—has become another security problem that airlines must deal with. In the United States, stiff penalties and jail terms can be given to any person disturbing the normal activities of the cabin crew. Canadian law is not as tough; however, crews today are more cognizant of their passengers, and pilots are quick to

FOOTPRINT

IATA is stepping forward to urge both airlines and countries to invest in critical areas of need concerning global warming. Their aim is to get companies to reinvest in modern, fuel-efficient aircraft that eliminate most of the carbon waste currently emitted by those in use such as the *B747*, *A310*, and the *B737*. It asks that stop-gap measures such as fuel surcharges and new charges being levied to offset the rising cost of fuel (like checked baggage charges) be eliminated; that management and unions recognize the need to control labour costs (reducing salaries and management bonuses) so that investment in newer aircraft is possible; and that airlines be freed from national ties and eliminate bilateral agreements that strip the companies of the ability to create route structures that benefit the needs of passengers. CEO Giovanni Bisignani states that "governments must drive progress by taking the politics out of air traffic management, acting globally on emissions trading, and supporting positive economic measures to drive innovation." In 2007, IATA Green Teams created savings of 10.5 million tonnes of CO_2 and shortened 395 routes, but governments still think punishment for emissions rather than investment in carbon-neutral flights is the answer. Fuel efficiency in the past decade has improved by 19% and non-fuel costs have dropped by 18%. However, average air margins for the industry are just 0.3%. Fuel-efficient aircraft, better equipped airports, and more efficient route structures would be a big step toward eliminating most of the negative impact of aircraft emissions.

(*Canadian Travel Press*, June 9, 2008, p. 3)

In Practice

With Canada moving closer to giving Air Canada a monopoly in the sky, how will this impact air passengers? The United States is the only country to have more than one major airline. Australia, Great Britain, France, and Germany are examples of countries with just one national airline. In groups of four to six, take a piece of paper and divide it into two sections. On one side, list the advantages of having just one major airline. On the other side of the paper, list the problems you see arising if Air Canada were to gain complete control of our skies. Now, make a decision: should Canada protect smaller airlines like WestJet to insure competition, should we follow other nations and move to a single carrier, or should we look at giving cabotage rights (eighth freedom) to one U.S. airline? Defend your choice.

respond when given an alert by the flight attendants. If trouble begins in the cabin, the aircraft will land at the nearest airport and the perpetrator will be turned over to local police. Despite the problems air travel has experienced over the past decade, it remains the safest and most viable method of transportation for the long-distance traveller.

SNAPSHOT

Maxwell William Ward

Maxwell William Ward was born to fly! "Max," as he is affectionately known in the tourism sector, lived and slept with dreams of flying throughout his childhood. Those dreams became a reality in 1940 when, at the age of 18, he enlisted in the Royal Canadian Air Force (RCAF) as a pilot. His first flight was marked by "poise, courage, and breakfast," as Max quickly found out that he was prone to airsickness! But dreams overcome many of our weaknesses, and Max went on to get his wings and graduate at the top of his class. As did many young fighter pilots, Max itched to get into World War II. But it was not to be, and instead he spent his years in the RCAF training other pilots for action. At the end of the war, Max left the air force to work for Northern Flights Limited, but he soon discovered that he was not interested in flying for someone else—he wanted to be his own boss. The trials and tribulations Max Ward faced

over the next 43 years clearly reflect how the federal government "hog-tied" Canada's commercial airline industry until deregulation. In June of 1946, Max began his first airline, called Polaris Charter Company Limited, and with the help of family and friends, he bought his first aircraft, a single-engine biplane called a *Fox Moth*. His career as an airline owner/operator did not start off auspiciously. His first commercial flight ended with a crash! Then his company was forced to fold when the Air Transport Board (ATB) discovered Max had not applied for a commercial licence.

By 1949, after a series of mishaps and a broken partnership, Max decided to give up his airline dream, and he returned to Alberta to build houses. Within three years, he realized that life without flight would be no life at all, and he applied to the ATB for a commercial charter licence. He was turned down the first time, but his persistence finally paid off, and

Ward Air was officially launched. He chose a de Havilland Otter as the company's first aircraft, and he flew gold miners and equipment into the northern territories. It was tough going for the little airline, as the purchase of every new plane required that Max cut through the mass of red tape needed for government approval to fly commercially. Every new route it applied for was initially turned down. However, despite the negative, restrictive government climate, Ward Air beat the odds and survived. By 1961, Ward Air was making a profit and Max changed the name to Ward Air Canada Ltd. Within a year, Ward Air had flown its first passenger charter from Calgary to Ottawa and its first international charter to Denmark. In 1966, Ward Air took delivery of its first jet, a *Boeing 727*, the first one of its kind in Canada. It looked as if the little airline that Max had built finally had its wings.

Trouble followed hard on the heels of his first success. Back in the early days of charter flights, only groups or associations could charter an aircraft, and the rules defining a group were very restrictive. Max tended to define his clients in the loosest sense of the word "association," and soon the Air Transport Board of Canada had expelled him for breaking the rules of charter flights. To add to his difficulties, the government set new, tougher guidelines for charter companies, called the "charter affinity rule." This made it even harder for private airline companies to compete with the newly renamed national carrier, Air Canada. Max Ward refused to give up. Lobbying Ottawa against its restrictive, unfair air transport policies, Max succeeded in having the affinity rule abolished. Max was invited back into the Air Transport Association of Canada, given a lifetime membership, and named Transport Man of the Year.

By 1975, Max Ward had been awarded the Order of Canada and was running Canada's third-largest airline. In 1978, after the United States deregulated their airline industry, Max went back to Ottawa to demand more freedom in the charter airlines

business. He was successful, and Ward Air was finally given permission to fly domestic charters. He booked his first advanced booking charter. Ward Air International expanded aggressively, and its high-quality service earned it the title of "world's best charter airline." As the Canadian government began to consider deregulation, Ward Air was granted its first scheduled route between Canada and the United Kingdom. Max had achieved the success he had strived so hard for, and his little airline entered the big leagues.

In 1988, deregulation in Canada went into effect; to meet the demands of the marketplace, Ward bought 12 *Airbuses* and 16 *McDonnell Douglas MD-88*s. Not only was Ward Air recognized as one of the best airlines in the world, but its aggressive, creative marketing placed the airline in a favourable position against the two big carriers—Air Canada and Canadian International.

In the real world, however, Jack seldom beats the giant, and so it was with Ward Air. Max Ward had not invested wisely in computer reservation systems, and he had overextended the company in purchasing new equipment. Unable to compete effectively with Canada's two major carriers, Max sold his beloved company to Pacific Western Airlines Corporation, and Ward Air merged with Canadian Airlines International.

Max Ward is one of tourism's most beloved pioneers: he created a fine airline, he fought to reduce government red tape and overregulation, and, in the end, rather than see his employees out of work, he made the hard decision to sell his company before its competition, Air Canada, bankrupted it. "I don't think he would consider himself totally a success in business," his son, Blake, once said. "He didn't beat them." Those who knew Max saw him for what he was—a giant in the Canadian airline industry, a fighter who never quit, and a man who stood for excellence in service and helped create the Canadian air system as it exists today.

Space Travel—Is It the Future?

Deep in the Mojave Desert, Richard Branson's company Virgin Galactic is hard at work developing a private sub-orbital space module that will allow travellers the same magnificent view of the earth that astronauts see. With three days of pre-flight preparation in a simulator called the *White Knight* carrier, passengers learn how to deal with things like zero gravity.

A specially designed jet transports your capsule to 50 000 feet, the capsule is then released, and you begin to circle the earth at 2500 km/hr, which is just over three times the speed of sound. To return to the landing area, the pilot simply throttles back, the pull of gravity begins to increase, and you are quietly returned to earth, transformed by the visions you have seen of space and the earth. Astronauts say the view is life changing. Interested? Reservations can be made for $2000 USD and the final cost of the ticket will be $200 000, which is money well spent, according to Richard Branson.

TRAVEL BY LAND

AUTOMOBILE AND RECREATIONAL VEHICLE TRAVEL

Transportation's transition from horse-drawn carriage to private automobile changed domestic travel habits and, more than any other factor in tourism, gave the average family more freedom of movement. Before the automobile, travel patterns were very predictable, and resorts and hotels were built along rail lines and in ports. The automobile introduced a more random, unstructured pattern of travel movements. Hotels, motels, and attractions sprang up along the highways and enjoyed success.

The automobile continues to be the most popular mode of travel for the tourist. People choose to travel by car for the following reasons:

1. low cost, especially for three or more people
2. convenience of having the car at your doorstep
3. flexibility in departure and arrival times, routes, and stops
4. enhanced trip experience
5. easier luggage transport with less restriction
6. assured transportation on arrival at the destination
7. the enjoyment of having your "own space" with your own comforts

Recreational vehicle (RV) travel, of course, has all the advantages of the automobile plus the convenience of carrying one's home along on the trip. RV travel eliminates the hassles and the expense of hotels and restaurants. The traveller can experience the great outdoors without really leaving the comforts of modern-day life, thus enjoying the best of both worlds. The style of an RV varies dramatically from simple pop-up tents to very luxurious ones, fully equipped with every

RVing is an inexpensive way to tour with the family and is gaining in popularity. Many RVs now provide the luxuries found at home.
(Photo: Canadian Tourism Commission.)

convenience including big living rooms, fireplaces, and full bathrooms with Jacuzzi tubs. Upscale RVs may be bigger than your house and often are not used for travelling vacations, but are pulled to a specific RV park and placed semi-permanently on their own pad. Nearly 13% of all Canadian households own some type of RV. It is interesting to note that when travelling in their RVs, most tend to stay in province, 8% say they prefer to travel to other provinces, and 7% choose to go south, into the United States or Mexico.[9]

The family vacation market accounts for about 80% of all vacation travel in both the United States and Canada, and much of this travel is done using the family's car or RV. Concerns about the rise in fuel costs and about the impact the price will have on tourism have been raised across North America. RVers are hit the hardest as their vehicles demand more fuel, but it is interesting to note that 48% of RV owners say they are unconcerned about the price of gas. Fifty-two percent show concern for oil prices, but they will deal with it by shortening their trips, staying in their own provinces to vacation, and looking at spending longer in one spot. Owners agree that travelling by RV is such a cost-saving way to vacation, they will be able to offset the price of gas by changing spending habits on the road. Some RVs are now winterized, allowing travel to continue throughout the year. Those who do choose to travel during the winter say the campsites are very quiet and the outdoor experience is healthy for their children.

The Car Rental Industry

The car rental business can be traced back to the early 20th century. Recognizing that not everyone could afford a car but might need one for a day or two, a wise entrepreneur decided to offer them for rent. Hertz started renting his cars in 1918, and his company is now the largest and oldest car rental agency in the

www.hertz.com

Top Five Reasons RVers Stay on the Road[10]

- The cost of a new RV can be as reasonable as $6000
- Studies show RVers can save as much as 70% of vacation costs over a traditional vacation
- Full-service campsites are reasonably priced, from as low as $25 to $45 per night

- Most new RVs can now be used all year long
- Travelling by RV is a great family vacation and gives RVers the chance to see their own country

world. Car rental agencies did not see a real boom in business until the age of jet travel. Expansion was rapid once business travellers found that, although they could travel long distances by air in a short period of time, they needed a car at their destination.

Business travellers still make up the greatest percentage of renters, but in recent years the leisure market has expanded dramatically. Combining a car rental with another mode of transportation provides a leisure traveller with the freedom to get around at the destination, a convenience that is becoming increasingly more popular. Fly/drive packages are a good example of how the industry has learned to package products. Each car rental company has its own requirements for the age of the driver, the number of drivers permitted, and insurance policies.

Some car rental agencies provide customers with a wide variety of cars and SUVs, others choose one brand name like Ford, while still others may go for niche

With rising concern for global ecosystems, some tourists choose their mode of transportation based on its carbon footprint.
(Photo: Canadian Tourism Commission.)

markets——low-cost rentals or high-end car rentals with vehicles such as Cadillac, Porsche, and Mercedes Benz. As in any tourism business, you must know your market's needs and be able to fulfill them if you are to be successful.

Car rental companies glean additional revenues from a variety of sources besides the rental fee. Add-on charges include insurance, gas, drop-off, and lost-key charges. Insurance covers the collision damage waiver and personal accident. When renting a car, customers should be aware of the personal insurance they carry on rented vehicles. A gas charge is added if the car is dropped off with less than a full tank. If the vehicle is dropped off at a location other than where the driver picked it up, substantial drop-off charges may apply. Charges are also imposed for lost keys.

Although these extra fees may be irksome to consumers, they do represent costs incurred by the car rental business. One reason add-on fees are itemized apart from the standard rental fee is so companies can advertise more competitive prices. To remain competitive with larger firms, small agencies may not charge some of these fees.

Marketing Strategies Marketing strategies in the car rental business are coveted information. Because demand can change so quickly, most companies are not willing to provide information on fleet size, structure, or marketing ideas. However, basic product, price, and location strategies are visible to everyone.

Pricing in car rentals has been creative and very competitive. A program called **unlimited kilometres** allows the traveller to drive as many kilometres as desired for a flat fee. Even though the major car rental companies began this program, they are now trying to ease themselves out of it because of the substantial difference it makes in revenues. **Corporate rates** are reduced rates given to companies with a high rental volume. In addition to the corporate rate, some rental companies have separate check-in areas for their corporate customers. The major car companies have frequent-driver programs (similar to airlines' frequent-flyer programs) to encourage customers to stay with the same company each time they rent a car.

RAIL TRAVEL

It's being awed by mountains towering above the train's glass dome. It's suburban gardens and the glow of the approaching city lighting up the sky. It's fishing shacks and a shoreline so close you could throw out a line. Or feeling you could lean out and touch the passing maple trees.

This is not 35 000 feet. It's not highway hassles. It's huge windows, wide seats, and walk-about aisles. It's quick snacks and fine dining. It's unwinding over a drink on your way home between cities. Or curling up in bed, in your own cozy cabin.

And all the while, up close, the world moves silently by. Just as you, spellbound at the window, move just as surely towards your own destination . . . . [11]

This is the image of train travel that railways wish to impart to visitors considering this mode of travel. Whether you are crossing the Siberian landscape or seeing the beauties of South Africa or the Canadian Rockies, train travel has always had a comfortable image in the eyes of many travellers and is often the chosen method of transportation.

History of Train Travel in Canada

For baby boomers and others, the words "All aboard!" evoke the romantic thrill of travel by train. In 1836, when Canada's first train roared over the tracks between La Prairie and Saint Jean sur Richelieu at a breathtaking speed of up to 48 kilometres per hour, a love affair began between Canadians and the train. Not only was the new form of transportation fast (a trip of 23 km could be made in just 43 minutes), it soon became the most convenient form of transportation for Canadian travellers. By 1856, all the major centres in Upper and Lower Canada were connected by this new mode of transportation.

As the United States promoted settlement of its western territories with the offer of free land, British politicians worried about maintaining control over their North American colony, and construction of the Canadian Pacific Railway from Montreal to Vancouver began. The line was completed in November 1885, and as the last spike driven into the ground at Craigellachie in British Columbia, and Canada was united from sea to sea. In June 1886, the first transcontinental train, called the *Pacific Express*, left Montreal and arrived in Port Moody, just east of Vancouver, a remarkable six days later. Canada had moved into the golden age of rail.

Over the next 20 years, many small entrepreneurial railroad companies emerged and prospered. Trains not only linked the Canadian provinces, but also extended their services into the United States. Two of the more famous international routes were the Allouette (Montreal to Boston) and the Maple Leaf (Toronto to New York). Because this method of travel was safe, efficient, and comfortable, it continued to be the major form of land travel until the 1930s.[12]

The first glimpse of trouble for Canadian railroads emerged as immigration and settlement of Canada slowed during World War I. By 1923, many of the smaller railroads were financially unable to continue operations, so their companies were united under the government-owned Canadian National Railways, providing direct competition for Canadian Pacific Railway. The Great Depression of the early 1930s caused financial ruin for many, and the railways suffered along with the rest of North America. There was a brief resurgence of popularity for rail transportation during the war efforts of the 1940s, but the golden age of rail was over.

www.viarail.ca

In 1976, the Canadian government reviewed the future of rail transportation. It concluded that Canada could not support two passenger railroad companies and called for the merging of the passenger services of Canadian National Railways and Canadian Pacific Railway. This new Crown corporation, **VIA Rail Canada**, was to be responsible for all passenger traffic. At first, there were few changes to the system, but in 1981, VIA Rail downsized, eliminating 20% of Canada's rail system. By 1990, VIA Rail operated only one transcontinental train, *The Canadian*, from Toronto to Vancouver, through Edmonton and Jasper, and it abandoned the southern route through Calgary and Banff. Seizing the opportunity, a team led by former motor coach operator Peter Armstrong established a luxury rail company, Rocky Mountaineer Vacations. Leaving Vancouver for Banff and Calgary, with an overnight stay in Kamloops, B.C., passengers can experience the best of the Rockies during daylight hours and in complete luxury. When winter arrives, guests enjoy the glittering beauty of snowfalls in the Rockies and can participate in a variety of winter sports on their arrival in Banff. By 2002, the Rocky Mountaineer had welcomed half a million passengers.

Three factors have contributed to the decline in rail travel in Canada. First, the automobile provided travellers with more freedom to choose time and place, so as more people bought cars, the need for train travel diminished. Second, the convenience and speed of airline travel, its relatively low cost, and the easy connections between cities have made flying a desirable way to travel long distances. Finally, the cost of maintenance, equipment, and labour was high for train travel compared with other types of surface travel.

Over the past few years, VIA Rail service has focused on the Quebec/Montreal/ Toronto/Windsor corridor. Both VIA first-class service and economy service are provided on these routes, giving travellers a choice of service level and price. For very simple reasons, many business travellers choose the train over the plane when travelling in this corridor. First, the train from Ottawa to Toronto takes only four hours, and passengers arrive at Union Station, right in the heart of Toronto. Seats on the train are comfortable, meals are available, and there is time to get some work done. Weather has little effect on the trip or the arrival time. At first glance, a four-hour train ride seems long compared to a one-hour flight. However, passenger check-in is now required one hour prior to departure at the Ottawa airport, and the trip from Pearson International Airport to a downtown Toronto destination will often take an additional 60 minutes. Those three hours of travel time easily increase with traffic or weather delays. The price of the trip by train has no surcharges and is competitive with the cost of air. With new, faster locomotives coming on line, it seems that the train may be a good option after all.

In 2000, the transport minister persuaded the federal government to earmark $400 million over the next five years to rebuild, refurbish, and renew VIA Rail. By the end of 2003, VIA Rail was expected to have 139 plush new cars and 21 new locomotives. (Seasonal rail travel has risen dramatically, and after the September 11 attacks, the train experienced a 63% gain in ridership. Unlike its American counterpart, Amtrak, VIA Rail has been relatively free of fatal accidents. Although the number of passengers has declined over the past year as faith in the air system is renewed, many travellers still view the train as a safer method of transportation.

VIA Rail Accommodations Each standard coach found on VIA Rail trains has up to 76 reclining, turn-around seats fitted with adjustable footrests, overhead luggage racks, and tables. There are washroom facilities located in each car. VIA's *The Canadian* offers dome cars that feature skylights for better viewing, dining cars with table service and gourmet meals, and four types of sleeping accommodations: double

VIA Rail's The Canadian *provides tourists with a spectacular transcontinental ride from Vancouver through the Rockies, across the Prairies, and around the tip of Lake Superior to Toronto.*
(Photo courtesy Canadian Tourism Commission.)

berths, single bedrooms, double bedrooms, and drawing rooms. Double berths have both upper and lower berths, and privacy is obtained by simply pulling a curtain around the bed. Washroom facilities are found at the end of the car. Single bedrooms or roomettes accommodate one passenger and contain a fixed seat, private toilet, and folding bed. Double bedrooms sleep two and have a variety of seating and sleeping layouts. Two bedrooms can easily be combined to sleep a family of four by removing the partition between them. Each room has its own set of controls for air conditioning and lighting, and can be adapted in the day to a private living space with large, comfortable armchairs that swivel to face a picture window. Drawing rooms are approximately 25% larger than the bedroom layout and can sleep three passengers. Bedrooms and drawings rooms are provided with the appropriate amenities and have private bathroom facilities. Not all trains have these sleeping configurations available, and surcharges are added to the larger bedroom/living quarters.[13]

VIA has recently been studying a plan to create a "cruise-like" all first-class product using *The Canadian* and providing elegant meals, activities, and multiple available stops. VIA fares continue to be competitive with other forms of transportation. Here are some examples of their discounted fares:[14]

- North American rail pass allows 30 days of travel within Canada and the U.S. using VIA or Amtrak
- 10 round-trip commuter pass allows travel anywhere within selected zones
- discount student fares for students of any age / children's fares
- special discount passes, such as the monthly commuter pass and the Biz Pak
- discounts for children between the ages of 2 and 17, free for children not occupying a seat
- seniors' discounts for 60+ years
- outdoor adventure pass allowing passengers to disembark along special routes, even if there is no scheduled stop

Foreign Railways

Although travel by train in North America has declined, in Europe it is one of the most widely used modes of travel. Here are some of the reasons travel by rail is so popular there:

1. Rails crisscross most of Europe. As countries built their own railroads, they also connected their systems to neighbouring countries'. This network of railroads is now called the international intercity network.
2. Train terminals are usually conveniently located in the heart of the city.
3. Although many Europeans own cars, the cost of gasoline has made driving an expensive way to travel.
4. The proximity of one country to another and the short distances between major towns and capitals make travel by train an efficient way to move from one destination to another.
5. Trains in Europe are noted for their on-time arrivals and departures.
6. Many railroads are still owned and operated by European governments.
7. European countries co-operate by marketing their trains as one rail system.

The **Eurail Pass** is a good example of a marketing strategy that has proved highly successful. This pass is available only to inbound European tourists and cannot be purchased in Europe. It provides unlimited first-class travel in 17 countries and is also valid on some ferries, intercity bus routes, and rental cars. The pass has a range of validity periods, from 15 days to three months. (Note: Great Britain does not participate in the European network but offers a similar discounted fare for the British Isles—the **BritRail pass**.) Many tourists travelling in Europe feel that the train is the only way to go. It is a relaxing, comfortable travel experience that allows the tourist to fully enjoy the scenery while mingling with local residents. With the completion of the Channel Tunnel (nicknamed the Chunnel), England was linked by rail to the rest of Europe. Travelling below the surface of the English Channel for almost 50 kilometres, tourists now make the trip from London to Paris in a short time and without seasickness! Many critics have noted the tunnel's outrageous construction costs and high toll, and some environmentalists would prefer that the link had never been finished, but for the tourist it provides a convenient, fast, comfortable and unusual way to cross the English channel.

Trains of the World

Bullet Train Japan, on the leading edge of train technology, has one of the most advanced rail systems in the world. The Japanese created the high-speed train and built the first **bullet train** in 1964. This train, known as the *Shinkansen*, connects major Japanese cities at speeds of up to 200 kilometres per hour. Russia lays claim to the longest train ride in the world with the *Siberian Express*, which travels from Moscow to Mongolia during a leisurely 19-day trip. The *Blue Train* of South Africa provides a luxurious trip from Cape Town to Pretoria. The *Royal Scotsman*, staffed by servers in kilts, gives tourists a slow, comfortable trip through the Scottish Highlands in the true elegance of days long past.

Orient Express But the *grande dame* of the rails is the famous ***Orient Express***. In 1833, the *Orient Express* began service from Paris to Istanbul, carrying queens and kings, political leaders, the very rich, and the very powerful. The route was spectacular and the service fit for royalty. The train was also the setting for many famous stories, including Agatha Christie's *Murder on the Orient Express*. But fame, in the end, could not save it: in 1977, tired, worn, and forgotten, the *Orient Express* made its last run. But one of the values of the tourism sector is its vision, which often leads to the restoration and renewal of disappearing cultures and history. Five years later, under the direction of James Sherwood, founder of Orient-Express Hotels, many 1920 vintage railcars were restored to their original splendour and a shorter version of the *Orient Express* was inaugurated. The Venice–Simplon Orient Express tour travels from Paris to Venice, passing through some of the most spectacular scenery in Europe. This tour has allowed many tourists a chance to travel back in time and ride the magnificent *Orient Express*. Sherwood has since added several luxury vintage train excursions in Asia and Australia, as well as a luxury train in the Andes Mountains, to complement his three new Peruvian luxury hotels.[15]

The *Maglev* Fifteen years ago it was just a dream and now it is reality. But what is its future in the business of tourism? The Superconducting **Mag**netic **Lev**itating Vehicle (***Maglev***) is a train that runs on a monorail using highly powerful magnets that allow the train to run with an air pocket between the rail and the body of the train. In 2001, the Chinese government signed a contract for the first ever commercial *Maglev* system. Produced in Germany, the train has undergone intensive mechanical trials and checks. Two concerns were what the top speed attainable would be, and whether two trains could pass each other at top speed without incident. In November of 2003, one train travelling at 501 km/hr (world record) passed a second train travelling at 430 km/hr without incident. With the last obstacles set to rest, the Shanghai train began commercial operation in 2004. This sleek train runs on 30 kilometres of track between Shanghai International Airport and the Shanghai Luijiazui financial district with the trip taking just under eight minutes. The costs are currently huge, as with any new invention, but safety factors have been proven and China is considering other areas for adopting this mode of transportation. Perhaps not for the next 20 years, but a *Maglev* between Ottawa and Toronto could make the trip in about 60 minutes. Along with space travel, the environmentally friendly *Maglev* system is likely to be the new mode of transportation for 2050![16]

In Practice

Knowing why people travel by train and why they do not, what methods could VIA Rail use to increase ridership? In light of the aging population of North America, what future do you see for train travel? Why?

MOTOR COACH TRAVEL

Travel by bus has long been an alternative for tourists for whom travel by car was not readily accessible. In 1949, scheduled intercity bus service peaked at 208 million passenger-kilometres. By 1996, a steady decline had reduced that number to just 18 million passenger-kilometres. Buses play an important part in many lives, beginning with the first step onto a yellow school bus. They provide transportation for class trips or to various sporting events, and for those without cars, they provide transportation around cities and regions, and between city centres as well. Most tourists are comfortable using a bus, but surprisingly, people often have a negative perception of bus services. They believe that travel by bus necessarily means riding in an old, uncomfortable, dirty vehicle.

However, the new tour bus design includes more comfort, with a larger, reclining seat, footrests, and more leg space. Wraparound windows now provide a full view for passengers. Services on the bus include overhead storage bins, modern washroom facilities, video monitors, and CD/cassette stereo systems. Some executive coaches provide refrigerators, microwaves, and lounges with sofa-style seating. Experts predict that travel by bus will be an increasingly popular mode of transportation for the baby boomers as they retire.

www.omca.com

The Canadian bus industry is still regulated in terms of entry and exit requirements, but both federal and provincial governments have indicated that they intend to deregulate it. As with many other tourism businesses, consolidation of the industry is inevitable. There will be fewer family-owned and -operated bus operations.

www.brewster.ca

Today the key players in Canada's bus industry are Coach USA (which operates in 25 states and two Canadian provinces), Greyhound, Laidlaw, Brewsters, and Trailways. Most of these larger companies are focusing on the lucrative tour market rather than on scheduled, intercity services.

The Advantages of Motor Coach Travel

There are many reasons a person may choose to travel by bus. It is the least expensive of the travel modes, except for personal automobiles, so cost is often cited as a prime factor. Scheduled intercity bus service is particularly price-sensitive. However, for small towns that have no infrastructure to handle rail and air, bus service is the only commercial transportation that links them to larger cities. A driver who chooses to travel by car must concentrate on driving and may miss most of the sights along the route. A driver must also know the route, have parking available at the destination, and, if moving from province to province, know how traffic laws differ.

Fly/motor couch tours allow tourists to fly to their destination and then climb aboard a luxury bus for the ground portion of their tour. Buses are the most environmentally friendly and fuel-efficient form of travel, and according to the Ontario Motor Coach Association (OMCA), the safest as well.

Charters versus Tours

With most chartered services, a pre-existing group secures the services of the bus at a reduced price. Group members may belong to a particular club or organization, or may simply form through the common interest of travelling to a destination at a reduced cost. A bus tour, on the other hand, has very specific components. Depending on the duration of the tour and the level of service the operator wishes to provide, bus tours will contain one or more of these components: (a) transportation; (b) accommodations; (c) attractions; (d) sightseeing; and (e) meals. These factors help determine the price and the grade of the tour. The higher the quality of the components used, the higher the grade of tour. Bus tours are currently graded as budget, first class, and deluxe.

Categories of Tours

Bus tours are categorized as sightseeing/day tours, overnight/short tours, longer tours, and fly/coach. **Sightseeing/day tours** may be limited to an urban area such as Vancouver, or they may be a day excursion to a special event or festival. For example, a tourist might travel from Edmonton to see the Calgary Stampede, or from Toronto to see a theatrical performance at the Shaw Festival in Niagara-on-the-Lake. With day tours, the price of admission is usually included in the tour price.

The second category is **overnight/short tours**, and these tours will include accommodations. Tourists who must travel more than three hours to get to their destination are more likely to choose a short tour. Both day tours and overnight/short tours offer groups affordable short getaways, provide a restful drive to and from the destination, and eliminate parking problems.

The third category, *longer tours*, varies from three to thirty days and are usually referred to as a **motor coach package**. In this type of tour, a tour director accompanies the group to ensure that all goes well. Longer tours will include several major city destinations and may include some interesting off-the-beaten-track local sights. Tours focus on a region—perhaps Calgary or Vancouver, with Banff and Jasper National Parks; Nova Scotia and Cape Breton; the wine region of Niagara; or a combined Ontario–Quebec visit with stops at Quebec City, Montreal, Ottawa, and Toronto.

Fly/coach tours combine airfare with an escorted bus tour. This type of tour is essential when the visitor is travelling a long distance, and it is particularly popular with Japanese tourists, who often fly into Vancouver, travel by motor coach through Banff and Jasper National Parks, and then fly out of Calgary. The tour company will then often greet a second group in Calgary, reverse the trip, and end in Vancouver.

In choosing a tour, travel agents and clients should carefully research the company and its past performance. The old adage that you get what you pay for has particular meaning when booking a bus tour.

Marketing Bus Tours

Marketing a bus tour is similar to marketing any other tourism product. Product, price, place, and promotion all play an important role. Niche or target marketing, however, is becoming increasingly important. The OMCA has identified several special markets. Focusing on education and learning experiences, the *youth market* provides an important and growing opportunity for tour bus operators. During the school year, school groups may travel to historic sites such as the forts of the Niagara Peninsula to learn about history; they may visit a special museum to gain knowledge about a specific branch of science; or they may travel to participate in outdoor activities such as winter skiing. During the summer, exchange tours allow students to visit and learn about a new culture.

Most destinations have some form of unique transportation. In Banff, gondolas carry tourists to the top of Banff's Sulphur Mountain.
(Photo: Canadian Tourism Commission.)

The *mature market* (55 and over) has been a cornerstone for the bus industry in the past and it will continue to be a big market as boomers retire. How will boomers change the tour product? They are looking for a more active tour product, for soft adventure and learning activities that allow them hands-on experience. They are more sophisticated than their predecessors, have a higher level of education and more disposable income, and demand good service. These characteristics will influence their choice of accommodations and food services included in a tour package. This market enjoys the companionship of a touring experience, likes a mix of ages—and prefers not to be called the "seniors market."

Finally, the growth of specialty markets over the past 10 years has been strong. Special interest tours include trips to Stratford, Ontario, attendance at special events such as the Stanley Cup playoffs, and visits to the wineries in the Niagara region.

In Practice

Assume you want to start your own tour bus company in your hometown. To be successful, you will need to identify the potential markets in your region. List local clubs, groups, associations, businesses, and churches that might be interested in a group tour. How would you increase your likelihood of success? What marketing strategies would you use to gain business?

TRAVEL BY WATER

CRUISE INDUSTRY

The History of Cruising

Although people have travelled by water from earliest times, it was not until the invention of the steam engine that travel for pleasure began in earnest. Ships in those days carried passengers from one destination to another and were called ocean liners or passenger ships, not cruise ships. Ocean liners in the early 1900s focused their product on wealthy patrons who enjoyed travelling in high style and living in luxurious surroundings. However, hidden beneath the luxury on the lower decks was another, very different cargo—immigrants trying to reach America to start a new life. This below-decks class of service was called "steerage," and the conditions were squalid. In 1907, the Cunard Line developed and installed improved engines on their two newest ships—the *Mauritania* and the *Lusitania*. These ships still had luxurious interiors, but more important, they provided passengers with a faster, smoother ride, reducing the Atlantic crossing from 10 days to 4 1/2.

Not to be outdone, the Cunard Line's rival, the White Star Line, launched its new boats in 1911 and 1912. The *Olympic* and the *Titanic* were slower than Cunard's ships, but what they lacked in speed they made up for in grandeur. The builders of the *Titanic* had provided the ship with new, innovative safety features and claimed that it was "practically unsinkable." Looking for a marketing edge, however, White Star eliminated the word "practically" from its advertising and proclaimed the ship "unsinkable." As such, *Titanic* did not provide enough life jackets or lifeboats to accommodate the passenger load. But, on April 14, 1912, *Titanic* struck an iceberg and did sink, losing 1601 passengers and crew. The sinking of *Titanic* was the single worst disaster in the history of the industry.

One of the passengers who died that day was the manager of Canadian Pacific's newest hotel, the Château Laurier, located in Ottawa; lost with him was the furniture that was being imported for the hotel. Despite the tragedy, ocean liners thrived until the end of World War I.

With the outbreak of World War II, ocean travel became dangerous, and many ocean liners were refitted as troop carriers. At the end of the war, tourism entered a boom era and so did the ocean liner business. People wanted to experience foreign destinations; with increased disposable time and wages to spend, they flocked to the passenger ships.

In October 1958, the world of tourism changed forever. Pan American World Airways flew the first non-stop passenger flight from New York to Paris in just 7 1/2 hours. Within six months, ocean liners had lost two-thirds of their business, and, by 1960, they carried a mere 5% of the trans-Atlantic traffic. To survive, passenger lines were forced to redesign their product. Cunard's slogan changed from "Getting there is half the fun," to "Being here is all the fun." Cruise lines repositioned themselves as "resorts on water," not as a mode of travel.

In 1971, cruise lines carried half a million passengers. In 2008, they are projected to carry over 12 million passengers, and the industry is growing at a rate of more than 7 percent yearly. Estimated use in 1998 was at 91.6% capacity, an amazing statistic for any tourism product. After September 11, 2001, the cruise lines saw a flurry of cancellations and a drop in bookings, as many passengers were afraid to fly to their departure point. As these fears have subsided, reservations have returned to near-normal numbers.

The Cruise Lines International Association (CLIA) announced in the late 1990s that between 1999 and 2004, more than 60 new ships would be launched. Some are mega-ships like Cunard's *Queen Mary 2*, launched in January of 2004. This ship is the longest, tallest, and grandest cruise ship, and carries a passenger load of 2620.[17]

www.cruising.org

Other smaller ships, like those being built for the Crystal Cruise line, will focus on high-end travellers who want a more intimate, luxurious setting. Some will be yacht-like, and cater to more adventurous travellers. Most new ships will fall in between these categories. Surprisingly, only 16% of the North American population has taken a cruise, leaving an enormous untouched market available to the cruise lines.[18]

The growth trends in cruises are a positive sign for the tourism sector. When cruise line passenger volumes increase, revenues increase for airlines, hotels, and restaurants. This positive correlation has encouraged co-operative arrangements between cruise lines and airlines, railways, resorts, and attractions.

In Canada, the port of Vancouver has seen dramatic growth over the past 10 years. It is now ranked as one of the busiest ports in the world, serving more than 500 000 passengers a year. Most cruise companies are based in the United States, but an increasing demand for small-vessel cruising favours the Canadian cruise industry. Canadian cruise ships carry between 15 and 250 passengers on short trips ranging from 3 to 10 days. The Canadian cruising experience often focuses on historical sites, wilderness themes, or adventure, and pampers the tourist with gourmet food and a professional, knowledgeable crew.

Cruise Types

The image of sailing on a large luxury liner like the *Love Boat* characterizes only one aspect of the cruise line industry. Cruise lines are certainly the largest component of the industry, but smaller cruises on rivers, coastal areas, and lakes are also common.

Sea Cruises Sea cruises range from one-day "see nothing" trips to three-month around-the-world trips. One-day trips may cost as little as $70 per person, whereas a three-month world trip may cost more than $24 000 for two people. The typical sea cruise is three to seven days with stops at various ports.

A sea cruise is now promoted as a vacation in itself. The stops are an added luxury to an aboard-ship vacation of sun and relaxation, whether cruising in the Caribbean or Mediterranean, or viewing mountains and glaciers along the Alaskan and Canadian coasts.

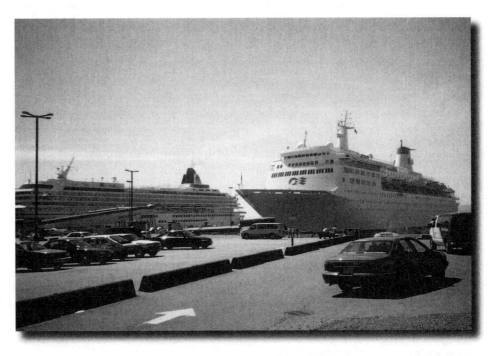

Victoria is a favourite port of call on the Inside Passage cruise.
(Photo: John Kerr.)

The Caribbean and Mediterranean are the most popular destinations for warm-weather cruises. Other warm-weather destinations are Mexico and the Mexican Riviera, the Bahamas, Hawaii, and the Pacific Rim islands. North American trips include cruises along the Pacific coast from Los Angeles to Vancouver, or from Vancouver to Skagway or Prince William Sound, Alaska. Northern Europe is also popular for its scenery in and around Norway and Sweden, and Mediterranean cruises provide travellers with a sense of history enjoyed in the comforts of a cruise ship.

Cruise lines have been very creative in marketing their product to new target groups. **Theme** and **special interest cruises** are gaining in popularity—for example, country and western cruises, which book top country and western singers to perform nightly. The entire cruise offers a unique opportunity for fans to enjoy their favourite performers. Special-interest cruises fall into six distinct categories:

- recreation (sports, bridge, backgammon)
- culture (opera, theatre, music)
- education (conferencing, history, religion, wildlife, financial planning)
- health (diet and exercise)
- hobbies (stamp collecting, gourmet cuisine, murder mystery)
- adventure (a trip up the Amazon, to the Galapagos, to Alaska)

The final type of sea cruise available to tourists is called the *repositioning* cruise. Ships that cruise the Alaskan routes or sail northern European waters have a limited season in those areas. As the weather grows colder and ice becomes a threat, these ships must relocate—change their home ports and destinations. For a tourist who loves to cruise, this kind of trip offers an interesting set of ports, perhaps combined with an ocean crossing, often at a reduced cost.

Why take a sea cruise? One of the most important factors is the level of satisfaction cruisers have with the product. Forty-five percent of all passengers rate the experience as "extremely satisfying." The top five reasons a person decides on a cruise over another type of vacation are

- the destinations visited (no packing and unpacking!)
- the all-inclusive price and service levels
- best opportunity to relax and unwind
- convenience of booking (one-stop shopping) and having all activities so close
- sightseeing and activities off the ship

River Cruises The river cruise, like the sea cruise, can be short or long. A short trip may be two to three hours, whereas longer river cruises may last 12 days. One of the most historic and romantic cruises is down the Rhine River in Germany. All sizes of boats with differing service offerings are available, and passengers may often get on and off the ship at any point in the trip to view the historical area they are passing. In North America, the Delta Queen Steamboat Co. carries passengers on luxurious paddlewheel boats back in time to relive life on the mighty Mississippi in the 1880s with its riverboat gamblers and lush living.

Many riverboats are used for company retreats, wedding receptions, and other group parties. The seasonal aspect of the business is a disadvantage, as many northern rivers freeze during winter months. Unlike a cruise ship that can head south to another season of tourist traffic, the riverboat must close down for the season.

In Canada, many rivers have short cruises available, and each province has its own cruise experience. Winnipeg offers a variety of cruise options along both the Red River and the Assiniboine, including the MS *Paddlewheel Queen*, Canada's largest riverboat, which sails through the heart of the city offering an afternoon of sightseeing or an evening of dinner and dancing. The St. Lawrence Seaway offers cruises that have gained worldwide recognition, such as the whale-watching cruise that departs from Tadoussac, Quebec, and sails up the Saguenay River. In the Northwest Territories, tourists cruise Great Slave Lake, live on board the MS *Norweta*, and hike the rugged terrain to learn about the wildlife habitat of this beautiful region.

Lake Cruises and Ferries Lake cruises are common in some of the Great Lakes. Combined as a ferry and a cruise, the ship travels to a destination across the lake, then turns around for the return trip. Many vacationers take their vehicles across Lake Superior on these ferries to experience the cruising life, as well as to avoid the long journey around the lake, through Chicago. Ferries travel day or night across the lakes.

Ferries that carry passengers, and often their vehicles, onboard are common around Seattle and New York, between Alaskan and Canadian islands and the mainland, across the English Channel, and around other spots where people need to get across a body of water with their cars to work or play on the opposite shore. Ferries have managed to maintain ridership throughout the increased popularity of the plane and automobile because they go to areas where plane service is expensive or non-existent and automobile access is limited or non-existent. Ferries that travel short distances usually have informal seating and deck space. Long-distance ferries may have cabins, food service, and even recreation rooms.

Most ferry service in Canada is found along the coasts. On the east coast, ferry routes connect Saint John, New Brunswick, to Digby, Nova Scotia; North Sydney, Nova Scotia, to Port aux Basques, Newfoundland; and Yarmouth, Nova Scotia, to Portland, Maine. In British Columbia, ferries connect Vancouver Island to the mainland and Victoria to Seattle. It is often a surprise to Canadians from the east who plan to use the ferry crossing that the trip takes about four hours. Vancouver Island looks so close on a map, and, as is the case in many of our destinations, is much farther than the tourist anticipated. To go from Vancouver to Victoria, travellers can choose a large, comfortable catamaran. Aisles are wide, seats are comfortable, and no cars are allowed.

Charter Yachts, Sailboats, and Houseboats In the past, chartering a yacht, sailboat, or houseboat was an activity for the very rich. Now it is within the reach of people with middle incomes. Charters can be arranged for a few hours or an entire

Tourists and B.C. residents may opt to use the high-speed catamaran that connects Victoria and Vancouver.
(Photo: John Kerr.)

vacation. A charter can be rented with the sailor included, or to people experienced enough to sail on their own. Many private owners are willing to charter their boats to keep up with maintenance costs. Houseboats provide family-style living on the water, and the chance to get away from the hassles of travel while still enjoying different port calls.

Cruise Line Marketing Strategies

The cruise industry knows it has a great untapped market and is using a variety of strategies to win potential cruisers. Creative marketing is required to secure the business of the return passenger and to encourage new passengers.

Product The product a ship has to sell depends on the target market it has chosen. Many ships will look at both families and singles, like the Carnival Fun Ships. Others are developed for the mature market and some ships do not allow children at all. Ships try to reach their markets with specific products like the amenities and services on board, and the route. Each part of the product is provided with quality and service in mind. A big sea cruise liner is physically laid out to accommodate a large number of passengers without feeling crowded. Accommodations may come with or without balconies or may be inside cabins with no view of the sea. If you are claustrophobic, you will need an outside cabin and porthole.

The rest of the ship is the resort centre for the vacationing guest. The cruise liner may be equipped with large multi-purpose rooms for meetings, conferences, or dancing. Most ships have health spas, fully equipped gyms, and swimming pools. Newer ships have ice rinks, rock climbing walls, and wedding chapels. The deck is laid out so that passengers can sunbathe next to the swimming pool, play board games in the sun, or simply lie back on a lounge chair and read a book. Since the price of a cruise includes meals, food becomes a major source of entertainment. Elegant dining rooms serve a wide variety of North American and ethnic foods. Some dinners have a theme—for example an Italian night, with fine Italian dishes and wines and perhaps strolling musicians. Some cruise ships have ventured beyond the more formal dining setting and are providing specialty restaurants like pizza and burger parlours, salad bars, and Italian bistros for customers wishing more casual dining. The midnight buffet and the captain's cocktail party are two of the favourite events. Food is available 24 hours a day and passengers can indulge in their favourite foods at no extra cost. Beverages, both alcoholic and non-alcoholic, are not included in the cost of a cruise and are an important method of increasing onboard revenues while keeping the cost of a ticket low.

To maintain quality service, cruises need a high ratio of crew to passengers. Labour costs are offset with the onboard revenues generated from a ship's casino, souvenir and clothing sales, duty-free shops, and added services that help make the ship a total resort experience. These services usually include a spa facility, an exercise room with all the latest equipment, virtual reality centres, and special sports opportunities such as golfing and skeet shooting. A full medical staff with state-of-the-art equipment is available on board.

Shore tours also add to the expense of a cruise and may cost upwards of $60 to $100 USD. A number of free activities often complement these services. For example, a seminar on how perfume is made encourages passengers to pick up a new scent at the duty-free shop; a seminar on skin care may encourage passengers to try the spa. The conference and meeting market is the latest target for cruise ships; the *Queen Mary 2* has a 500-seat auditorium with all the latest technical equipment.

The actual route and stops en route are also part of a key marketing strategy. These cruises usually stop for several hours in one or more ports to allow passengers to shop and to experience another culture.

Pricing cruises, like resorts and hotels, varies according to cruise by season and length of the trip. Other considerations used when calculating price are the ship's age or profile, and cabin choice. A ship's profile includes factors such as the number of outside cabins with balconies; the variety of recreational activities; the number and quality of restaurants and lounges; the size and placement of the cabins; and the ports and entertainment during the cruise. Most cruises are popular because the passenger pays one price and receives the same service as everyone else on board. There is a cruise that will satisfy even the most unusual interests or hobbies and a price that will suit any wallet.

Cruise ships depend on their travel agents to sell bookings and often offer free trips. They want to be sure agents understand (and have tried) the facilities and amenities aboard their different ships, and know how to effectively close the sale. Travel agents sell about 90% of all cruises, as compared to 47% for resort holidays. With the techniques now offered by the internet, including videos showing all areas of a ship, the number of people booking via the internet is growing steadily. Niche or target marketing will become even more important as the number of ships increases. Ships are partnering with the airlines, rail companies, and rental car agencies to provide packages that meet all of the consumers' transportation needs.

Promotion directly to the consumer is usually through newspaper advertisements, individual mass mailings, or through trade shows that focus on vacation choices. Some of the larger cruise lines, such as Royal Caribbean, advertise extensively on television.

In Practice

Are travel agents the best means of selling cruise vacations to the consumer? Why or why not? How is selling a cruise line ticket different from selling an airline ticket through a travel agent? In groups of four, try to design a new method of ticket selling for a cruise line.

T R A V E L   A T   D E S T I N A T I O N

PUBLIC TRANSPORTATION

Once you get to your destination, you need to know how to get around it. Having a car and a good map is great, but many tourists don't have cars at their disposal. Public transportation is any organized passenger service available to the general public within a small geographic area. Visitors commonly use these transportation systems to see the city sights.

Most cities have some form of bus transit system, but the bright red double-decker buses in London, England, are a particularly popular choice among tourists. London and Edinburgh, Scotland, have special inexpensive and easy-to-use buses that carry passengers from one site to another with onboard guides who provide a description of the route. These services run all day long, and for the cost of a day pass, passengers may make as many stops as they want.

In the Philippines, visitors can ride the brightly decorated Jeepneys. The modern subway systems of Washington, D.C., and Paris have gained worldwide reputations for their user friendliness. In San Francisco, the cable cars are not to be missed. Travellers between Victoria and Vancouver must use a ferry or an airplane. The list of public transportation methods is as varied as the number of cities a tourist can visit.

Travellers need to understand how an individual public transportation system works. For example, if you ride the GO Train in the Toronto region, you are responsible for validating your own ticket; if you fail to do so, you may be fined. In Tokyo, *white glove pushers* will literally push you onboard the transit trains during rush hour. They are not being rude—simply doing their job by putting as many people on the train as possible. Calgary has light rail transit (LRT) systems that run on their own tracks, circumventing traffic. LRT systems are not only quick, but also environmentally friendlier. Cab drivers in Halifax have all had special training developed by the Tourism Industry Association of Nova Scotia and other provincial TECs. Their knowledge of the city and their friendly, helpful attitude make a taxi ride in Halifax pure pleasure.

Airports offer limousines, buses, and taxis as options for the traveller. At Kennedy Airport in New York City, an alternative to the bus service is the AirTrain JFK, or "train to the plane." This special subway takes passengers into the heart of the city, avoiding traffic delays on the expressways.

Information about the public transportation system in any destination city is available from many sources, but travel agents or a good guidebook will provide you with the travel tips you need. Public transportation is usually the least expensive way to move around a town and provides the tourist with a bit of local colour that may otherwise be missed.

Sightseers enjoy a leisurely tour of Victoria in a horse-drawn carriage.
(Photo: John Kerr.)

CASE STUDY

An Untimely Death

Marc had been working with Cool Travel as a counsellor for four years. He had developed good profiles on all his regular clients, which had helped make him successful. One day in late March, one of his regular business clients paid a surprising visit—surprising, because for the first time, the client wanted a vacation trip. Mr. Bennett stated plainly that he wanted lots of sun, good margaritas, to gamble into the night—and he wanted the total package to be inexpensive. Marc had just received a promotional brochure for a new resort casino in the Caribbean. Together they looked at the brochure, read the fine points, and discussed the problems sometimes encountered when booking a resort right after it opens. But the price was right, the time was available, and Marc booked the trip. Wednesday evening, just before the Easter holidays, a very happy Mr. Bennett headed to the Caribbean. As Marc closed shop on Saturday of the long weekend, he got a call from the distraught casino manager. Mr. Bennett had been found dead on his bed, a half-finished beer on the bedside table.

The police were summoned, but the only contact information they could find in the room was for Cool Travel. The resort doctor confirmed that the guest had died of a heart attack.

The manager had called Marc to ask how to get in touch with Mr. Bennett's family. Mr. Bennett had referred Marc to his, Mr. Bennett's, secretary in the event of an emergency. Mr. Bennett's office was closed, his secretary was gone for the Easter weekend, and Marc had no idea where to start.

1. If you were Marc, would you feel responsible for the care of Mr. Bennett? Why or why not?
2. If you were the manager, and the police left saying the situation was not within their jurisdiction, what would you do?
3. What steps should you take in trying to get Mr. Bennett's body home? Which step would be the hardest to accomplish? Why did you choose this step?
4. Does Cool Travel have any liability in this case? Does the resort? Why?
5. If you owned a travel agency and had profiles on all of your clients, list six items you would be sure to include in each profile.

Summary

Choosing a mode of transportation is complicated by many factors, both practical and psychological. Time, cost, ease of access, route structure, and frequency are often the deciding factors. However, self-image and stereotypic views of transportation modes can complicate decision making. In the end, the method of travel chosen will often depend on the circumstances of the moment.

Trends and changes in the airline industry have increased the volume of traffic as well as the choice of destinations. Deregulation in the airline industry has opened the doors to more carriers, brought about a hub and spoke airport concept, and produced price wars and other marketing strategies beneficial to consumers. Deregulation left many medium-sized communities with very limited or no commercial air service.

Since September 11, 2001, travel by air has declined, putting even large airlines like United and Air Canada on the verge of bankruptcy.

The airline industry is divided into scheduled air carriers and charter air service. Airfares for flights change daily. Computerized reservation systems allow airlines to respond immediately to a competitor's fare change. Discount tickets with restrictions have become a standard pricing technique to increase the load factor on the plane.

Airports are the backbone of the airline industry. NAVCAN now operates the air traffic system, and many larger airports are run by private companies. Airlines lease space from an airport to board and unboard passengers and park aircraft overnight.

Automobile and RV users represent the largest group of travellers. More kilometres are logged by private automobiles than by airlines, and family vacations by car account for 80% of all vacation travel in the United States. The trend is toward more mini-vacations for families with two working adults.

The car rental industry is volatile and competitive because of its ability to change fleet size and structure rapidly. Most major car rental agencies get more of their reservations through travel agents than as walk-ins. Marketing strategies in the car rental industry include specialized vehicles, fly-and-drive programs, and pricing strategies such as unlimited kilometres for a flat fee. Car rentals from airport locations make up nearly 80% of all the rental business, making location a prime concern in the industry.

The RV industry expects to see an intense growth period as baby boomers move into the prime RV-buying age bracket. RV caravans and rallies are becoming popular ways to spend pre-packaged vacations with others.

Trains in North America have had their ups and downs in ridership. Amtrak and VIA Rail were born from the near-collapse of the railways in North America. These government-subsidized trains have slowly rebuilt the system by providing more comfortable seating and sleeping arrangements, convenient stops, speed, and package vacations at prices competitive with other means of transportation. Since September 11, North American railroads have seen a growth in passenger revenues, as increased numbers of travellers choose the train over the plane.

The bus industry comprises scheduled bus service, charter service, and tour service, and also uses a hub and spoke model. Convenience and price are often cited as reasons people travel by bus. Charter service is provided by bus companies that simply rent the bus and sometimes the driver to the interested group. The popularity of the charter business is growing with student, church, and social groups because it provides an opportunity for members of a club or organization to travel with friends and acquaintances with common interests. Motor coach packages are becoming more popular and will continue to grow as the baby boom segment of the population ages.

The cruise line industry is the fastest-growing segment of the travel industry. Cruise lines began billing themselves as floating resorts in the 1960s and 1970s, after airlines took over the mass transportation market. Passenger numbers have increased 7% annually for the past few years and are expected to continue at that rate of growth. The future looks promising for cruise lines as they band together to promote cruising as an alternative type of vacation. Themed cruises and business and convention cruises are the latest trends. Other methods of water transportation include ferries, lake cruises, freight liners, riverboats, and charter yachts and sailboats. Proximity to water and the desire of many travellers to see the countryside from a different perspective have transformed many communities into attractions. Casino riverboats on the Mississippi are the fastest-growing form of river transportation.

Public transportation is an important means of moving tourists from one site in a city to another. Many cities have their own system, providing the tourist with a unique cultural experience.

Questions

1. Many factors help determine the mode of transportation a traveller chooses.

   a) What three factors would most likely influence a business traveller?

   b) What three factors influence your choice of transportation? Explain your answers.

2. Summarize briefly the impact of deregulation on Canada's transportation systems.

3. a) How does the role of IATA differ from the role of ICAO? Explain your answer.

   b) Why were the Freedoms of the Air developed and how do they affect Canada's air industry?

   c) What is the name of Canada's latest bilateral agreement regarding air travel, who is the agreement with, and how has it affected our air transportation system? What does the new article, added in 2005, do to change this agreement?

   d) Why has Canada privatized its air transportation system? Who runs it? How has privatization affected airlines?

4. Compare and contrast three advantages and three disadvantages of travel by automobile and travel by motor coach.

5. a) Using the four Ps of the marketing mix discussed in Chapter 2, discuss the following tourism products: motor coaches, railways, and cruise lines.

   b) What is the greatest challenge faced by each of these tourism products? Explain how you, as a marketing consultant, might deal with each challenge.

6. Compare and contrast the following terms as they relate to the transportation industry (use examples where possible): *direct/non-stop flight*; *online/interline connection*; *scheduled/charter trip*; *open-jaw trip/circle trip*; *theme/special interest* cruise; *day/overnight tour.*

Notes

1. "Industry sees fewer fatalities," www.iata.org/pressroom, May 8, 2008.

2. www.iata.org/pressroom/facts_figures.

3. *Maclean's* magazine, interview with Clive Beddoe of WestJet, October 3, 2005.

4. "Changes to checked baggage allowance," www.aircanada.com, August 23, 2005.

5. "James C. May at the annual aviation forecasting conference, October 5, 2005," www.airlines.org/news, December 7, 2005.

6. www.iata.org/pressroom/facts_figures.

7. Ibid.

8. *Skies Set to Open, Maybe*, News and Events, www.canadatourism.com, November 25, 2005.

9. www.gorving.ca/media.

10. www.gorving.ca/media/facts.

11. *Canada Up Close As Only the Train Can Show You: A Traveller's Guide to VIA Rail Services* (Montreal: VIA Rail, 1995).

12. David Wright, *Professional Travel Counselling,* 2nd ed. (Toronto: Canadian Institute of Travel Counsellors of Ontario, 1994), p. 208.

13. www.viarail.ca/planner

14. Ibid.

15. www.orient-expresstrains.com.

16. www.maglev.com

17. www.cunard.com/QueenMary

18. www.cruising.org.

Accommodations

Key terms

American plan (AP)
back of the house
bed and breakfast
  (B & B)
Bermuda plan (BP)
boutique hotel
campgrounds
cannibalization
cash bar
chain ownership
condominium
conference hotel
confirmed reservation
continental plan (CP)
corporate rate
day rate
double
double double
dude or guest ranch

European plan (EP)
family plan
franchise
franchise advisory
  council (FAC)
franchisee
franchiser
front of the house
Green Key rating
guaranteed reservation
hospitality suite
hostel
hotel
inn
joint venture
management contract
modified American plan
  (MAP)
motel

open bar
overbook
rack rate
referral system
REITs
resort
resort hotel
run-of-the-house rate
single
spa
suite
time-sharing
tourist courts
turn-down service
twin
walking
weekend rate

Learning objectives

Having read this chapter you will be able to

1. Explain trends in the lodging industry.

2. Compare and contrast the four basic management systems within the lodging industry.

3. List the advantages and disadvantages of being a franchisee.

4. Identify the needs of specific travellers: business people, families, the disabled, and those from different cultures.

5. List and discuss the interaction between the nine major departments in a large hotel.

6. Discuss the growing niche market of disabled travellers and their needs.

7. Explain eight factors that affect the pricing structure of a hotel room.

8. Analyze the Green Key system and its advantages for the owner of a lodging facility.

9. Identify 10 different types of lodging facilities available for tourists globally.

Accommodation, one of the oldest components of the tourism sector, operates under many of the same principles today as it did hundreds of years ago. Providing lodging and offering other services with the room to enhance guests' stays began as soon as people began to travel. There are a wide variety of hotels and experiences to be had in Canada, and the lodging industry has remained in a slow but steady growth pattern.

Canada provides guests with more than 439 818 rooms found in over 8287 hotels[1] and other types of accommodations. These rooms offer a variety of living experiences ranging from deluxe accommodations to classical, heritage inns or rustic cabins with no indoor facilities. Accommodations earned $17.9 billion in 2005 and employs over 378 000 people in Canada. The occupancy rate has remained in the 65% range for several years with the average room rate increasing slightly to $123 per night.[2]

This chapter discusses history and trends in accommodation, lodging management systems, the departments within a hotel and their responsibilities, the variety of lodging choices available in today's market, factors that affect the pricing of this product, and career opportunities within this industry.

LODGING HISTORY AND TRENDS

For as long as people have travelled, they have needed lodging and food along the way. The history of the accommodation component of tourism began long ago, and the earliest known "hotel" system belonged to the Roman Empire. The early Romans were great road builders, and along their roads they built lodgings to house travellers—Roman soldiers who journeyed to distant provinces to keep peace and order in the empire, as well as Roman citizens who travelled for business purposes, education, or relaxation. The different needs of these Roman travellers required that the lodging system provide a variety of accommodations ranging from simple huts to more elaborate dwellings with all the amenities of the day. In the city of Pompeii, frozen in time by the eruption of Mt. Vesuvius, two examples of ancient hotels—the *hospitium* (full-service inn) and *caupona* (budget inn)—are still visible. With the breakdown of the Roman Empire, around 400 CE, travel became a rare and dangerous undertaking and this early system of lodgings disappeared.

By the year 1000 CE, the crusades into the Holy Lands had begun. Religion, for a brief period, was the cornerstone of the accommodations industry. Monasteries and other religious institutions provided lodging, believing it was their holy duty to offer shelter to weary travellers. Soon, however, the flow of soldiers and pilgrims to Jerusalem became greater than these religious institutions could handle. To meet the growing demand for lodging, people along the route began to offer rooms and meals in their homes. In 1282, in order to protect their interests, the merchants of Florence, Italy, formed a guild that controlled the licensing of the city's innkeepers and ensured that each inn received its fair share of business. During this period of time in Europe, travellers would find beds in rustic inns, local homes, and sometimes in castles. Luxury was a bed free of bugs and a pint of ale.

In North America, growth of the lodging business was imperative, and early inns were established along water routes and in seaport towns. The first inn was built in Jamestown on the Virginia coast in 1607.[3] These inns typically provided family-style meals, a large common room (known today as a lobby), a number of private bedrooms, and a stable for guests' horses. The inn also became a meeting place for local politicians, clergy, and other citizens' groups.

Roadside inns began to appear throughout the eastern states, as horse-drawn coaches became a familiar sight. Early city hotels were much grander and had many more amenities for guests, including single and double rooms, locks on doors, soap, towels, bellhops, and room service.

In Canada, the first building specifically designed as a hotel opened in 1831 in Aylmer, Quebec. Upper Canada Village, a living-history museum located near Morrisburg, Ontario, invites tourists to wander through an exhibit of two of Canada's earliest inns.

The hotel era boomed in the days of the railroads' expansion and domination of transportation. Towns sprang up along the railroad routes, with hotels to accommodate the rail passengers. With the completion of Canadian Pacific's trans-Canada railroad, tourists began flocking to the Fairmont Banff Springs region to enjoy the hot sulphur baths. The Fairmont Banff Springs is Canada's first and best-known example of lodging built in a national park specifically for the pleasure tourist market.

www.Fairmont.com

The Great Depression of the 1930s saw a collapse of the industry with money as scarce as travellers, but the industry rebounded during and after World War II. In the 1950s, there was a period of rapid expansion, as automobiles became part of family life and the ability to travel became easier. Helping the growth of the industry was a new method for financing properties—a method called *franchising* (discussed later in the chapter).

Technological advancements have had the greatest impact on the development of the hotel industry, beginning with those that emerged from the Industrial Revolution in the early 19th century. Besides providing accommodations with innovations such as the elevator, this bloodless revolution dramatically changed both the modes of travel and the tools used to conduct a hotel's business.

Accommodations have evolved over the years, based on the needs of both the transportation system and the traveller. For example, prior to the early 19th century, courtyards with stables for a guest's horse were an integral part of any inn or hotel. When railroads became a major form of transportation, hotels were built along the rail routes. Many hotels were constructed directly beside or over the train station. The Fairmont Château Laurier in Ottawa and the Fairmont Royal York in

Toronto, each linked to train stations by underground tunnels, are excellent examples of old railroad hotels.

With the emergence of the automobile as a major form of transportation, the design of a hotel changed. Mom-and-pop **tourist courts** provided the customer with a small cabin and a parking space. Soon the tourist court evolved into the motel. Motels differ from hotels because they provide not only free parking, but also access to a guest's room directly from the parking lot, eliminating the need for large lobbies.

In the 1960s, the jet age of travel saw new hotel development clustered around the local airport. Airport hotels have evolved into highly specialized facilities that provide unique services to fulfill the needs of their transient guests. As these hotels are not located in the heart of a city's business district, they must be able to provide many services that might otherwise be supplied by merchants in the downtown core.

No new modes of transportation have evolved since the jet age, but hotels have continued to evolve, moulded not by new transportation systems but by new technology, global economies, and changing consumer needs. In the 1970s, when economic difficulties arose because of a gas shortage, hotels focused on an inexpensive, no-frills product. In the 1980s, as global business boomed, city hotels were built in the downtown core and older hotels in this area underwent massive restorations. In the 1990s, convention and conference facilities became the focus of new hotel product offerings. This decade also saw the emergence of the all-suite hotel. Rooms in these facilities resemble an apartment, and guests may choose to make their own meals or eat out.

In the first decade of the 21st century, the focus is on the total person—with wellness of both body and spirit. Depending on the property, spas may be simple or they may have all of the latest equipment. Small hotels can even participate in the spa experience by hiring a masseuse or renting out space for a therapeutic practitioner.

Over the past 30 years, resort hotels have emerged—multi-purpose lodgings built with a wilderness setting are good at changing with the times. Because of the variety of entertainment and recreation offered at a resort, total vacation packages meet the needs of a wide variety of target markets. Resorts are particularly popular with families as facilities are geared toward different age groupings.

New technology has significantly altered the way most properties do business. Using the internet to determine which hotel will suit a traveller best is common now. Even conference-goers have held back from using the "special conference group rate" because they feel they can find a less expensive rate on the internet. Check-in and check-out are streamlined with the use of computer systems. Daily reports are available to managers, summarizing the day's activities. Heating and cooling systems are computerized, functioning only when a guest is actually registered in the room. Even the keys used in many major hotels have changed—the big, old brass keys of the past are collectors' items now, replaced by electronic cards that open the door. Today, a high-speed internet connection in the room is a "must have," not just an added advantage.

The start of the 21st century was full of promise for tourism, and the accommodation industry experienced steady growth. But 2000 proved to be a difficult year as sales in the high-tech industry slowed and profits fell. Falling profits hurt investments and stock markets around the world. Investors lost billions on falling stock prices, the industry laid off thousands of high-tech workers, and business travel declined. Over the past decade, a series of terrorist attacks have slowed growth. In the wake of September 11, 2001, business travel fell by almost 60% as firms struggled to deal with both the decline in the high-tech industry and the fear of more terrorist attacks.

Fortunately, the 2010 Olympics promises to hand the industry the boost it needs. The Vancouver Olympic Committee is getting ready and is on budget, and other provinces are hoping that Olympic visitors will want to see more of the country during their stay.

MAKING GUESTS WITH DISABILITIES COMFORTABLE

Travelling as a disabled person is often more of a challenge than it needs to be. The United Stated has tough legislation in place that forces business establishments to provide adequate facilities for the disabled traveller. Unfortunately, Canada has been slow to follow suit. What are some of the more important features a hotel room should have to properly serve this growing market? Rooms need to be large enough to manoeuvre a wheelchair around. Levers instead of doorknobs and doors that open outwards are also important for easy manoeuvring. Wheelchair-accessible bathrooms with roll-in shower stalls or tubs are scarce in Canadian hotels, but even a shower bench and grab bars improve a bathroom facility. Grab bars should be available not only in bathrooms, but also in areas of the room where guests cannot navigate a wheelchair. For example, a grab bar near the bed makes getting into and out of bed much easier.

For the visually impaired, good lighting is essential, and important information should be provided in a large, bold print. Instructions in Braille are a very basic feature that should be available in all hotels today. For the hearing impaired, a bed shaker for wake-up calls and alarms, closed-captioned television, and lights that flicker when the phone rings or someone is at the door are all important features. Making guests with disabilities feel comfortable and welcome makes good economic sense for the hotel business.[4]

Beautiful, historic hotels like the Fairmont Algonquin in St. Andrews by-the-sea, New Brunswick, form part of the area's pull factors.
(Photo: Canadian Tourism Commission.)

LODGING OWNERSHIP AND ORGANIZATION

The terms *owner* and *manager* do not necessarily refer to the same person. In smaller, independently owned properties, the owner often acts as the manager; however, in larger hotels and within chains, different people normally carry these titles. Up to the time when chain motels became prevalent, ownership by individuals was common. Today, with the diversity of the lodging industry, establishments are managed in four ways: by an individual (private ownership), by a corporate chain, by a franchise chain, or by a management contract. A description of these methods of management follows, along with a brief discussion of referral systems and hotel real estate investment trusts (REITs) in the lodging industry.

Ownership

Nearly half of all lodging establishments in North America are operated as individual proprietorships. These small hotels, including mom-and-pop motels, inns, and bed and breakfasts, are an important component of the accommodations industry. The chief advantage of individual ownership is that the owner has full control over policies and operating procedures. Add to that the potential for individual profitability and a decision-making process free of bureaucratic red tape and it is clear why people enjoy owning their own property. The major disadvantage is that the owner/manager assumes full risk for the property. In bad times, the owner lacks the financial resources of a big company. Furthermore, the individual owner does not have the advantage of national advertising and reservation systems—a serious shortcoming when competing with national chains and franchises. A good website is essential for privately owned hotels. Finally, independents have trouble raising capital to expand, or add new, properties.

www.all-hotels.com

Sometimes hoteliers may opt to form partnerships with investors. These **joint ventures** work because one partner supplies the expertise in the hotel business and the other partner provides the financial investment needed for a new property.

It is probably safe to say that individually owned hotels and motels exist in most communities that have lodging facilities. To compete with large, familiar, franchised or chain properties, these privately owned hotels become affiliated with organizations such as the American Automobile Association (AAA), the Canadian Automobile Association (CAA), Independent Motel Association (IMA), or the Hotel Association of Canada (HAC). AAA and CAA approval gives small businesses credibility; travellers generally feel more comfortable staying in a lodging facility that has met certain standards. In addition, both the CAA and the AAA recommend their approved hotels and motels when designing itineraries for members.

Referral Systems How does a property owned by an individual compete with the large franchise chains? They use a marketing strategy called a **referral system**. The largest hotel chain in the world is, in fact, a system of independently owned hotels represented by a referral company known as Best Western. The most important aspect of becoming a member of Best Western is the use of its brand name. Travellers look to a brand name facility because they know it is a quality product. The independent owner also has immediate access to a worldwide reservation system, as well as national and global advertising campaigns. As an example, when a family-owned hotel in Ottawa wanted to expand its clientele, its owners chose to join Best Western. The move allowed them to operate their hotel as they liked, while instantly linking them to a global market. A large percentage of their market had been visiting friends and relatives (VFR), but within a year of becoming a referral system member, the owners saw an increase in their business of more than 15%, directly attributable to their new affiliation. Service fees charged by companies such as Best Western are similar to those charged by a franchise operation, and the quality of the hotel is monitored.

www.hotels.ca

Corporate Chains

The term *chain* is used to describe a group of facilities that use the same name. Four Seasons hotels is a good example of **chain ownership**. The company operates a number of properties, all reporting to corporate headquarters. All major management decisions are generated from headquarters, making changes to management, services, and decor much simpler to implement. Four Seasons has created a niche in luxury accommodation, yet—although the level of service does not vary—each Four Seasons hotel has its own unique ambiance, capturing the local culture. For example, the property in Bali is not a hotel building but cottages with private pools, porches, and fans. Although ownership is centralized, hotels in a chain have more operational independence than franchises; while customers are seldom aware of ownership structures, they can sense the distinctive feel of a hotel.

Franchise Chains

The third type of operation is the **franchise**. The franchise relationship consists of two parties: a name brand company, called a **franchiser**, and the property owner, called the **franchisee**. Those who opt to purchase a franchised business are usually buying a proven business formula. Franchising offers the advantages of a brand name product, while leaving ownership and most management control in the owner's (franchisee's) hands. The franchisee agrees to follow all of the franchiser's management policies, to pay an initial development fee, and to pay a monthly franchise fee. This fee usually falls between 3% and 6% of the total gross room sales. All the hotels in a franchise have the same decor and image; unlike the varied Four Seasons properties, a Holiday Inn in Halifax is very similar to a Holiday Inn in Regina. The advantages of the franchise system include the following:

1. Use of a nationally known brand name and a known product
2. National and international advertising and reservation systems
3. Lower borrowing costs because lending institutions are more willing to lend to a mortgagee affiliated with a nationally recognized franchise organization
4. Professional managerial assistance provided by the franchiser
5. Group buying power and a central purchasing office that provides supplies at much lower costs (franchisers provide architectural plans, layout, decoration, and other critical development components at substantial savings)
6. Employee training available at little or no cost to the franchisee
7. Common decor and a familiar atmosphere for travellers

However, a franchise does come with a number of disadvantages:

1. Initial franchise fees that are generally quite high
2. Franchise fees that usually include a percentage of the monthly gross revenues
3. Adverse effects when other franchise owners do not live up to customers' expectations
4. Financial consequences for the franchisee if the franchiser becomes financially insolvent or does not provide the management assistance required
5. Little or no flexibility for the individual owner regarding policies and procedures that are set by the main office and require strict adherence
6. A clause in the franchise agreement that allows the franchiser to buy back or cancel the franchise if the franchisee does not follow the rules set by the franchiser

Franchise companies often agree to keep all their properties far enough apart to avoid **cannibalization**, or competition within the franchise.

Franchising does not always result in a happy partnership. It is important to research the company with which you are investing to ensure that they manage a quality product in an ethical manner. In the 1950s and 1960s, when hotel franchising mushroomed, many disputes about interpretation of franchise agreements arose between franchisers and franchisees. To create a better working relationship, **franchise advisory councils (FACs)** were started. These bodies represent the franchisee and provide a forum through which to address concerns and solve problems. Individuals thinking about investing in a franchise must find out whether the company has a working FAC. Most large franchise companies work well with their FACs, recognizing that their success is dependent on the success of their franchisees.

Management Contract

The fourth type of management system is the **management contract**, which separates hotel ownership and operation and can be made with individual properties or with hotel chains. The Delta Hotel chain, owned by Fairmont Hotels, is a good example of a management contract company. The owners (the investors in this relationship) contract with a professional management team to operate the property (the investment) for a fee or a percentage of gross revenue. It is the preferred method of management when the owner has limited knowledge of the hospitality business. Furthermore, lending institutions are more likely to step forward with financing if they know a professional team is managing the investment. International hotel chains use the management contract system to establish a hotel in a foreign country, especially if the country does not permit outside ownership or is politically unstable. When a chain takes on the role of the manager, it often places its name on the property, allowing the hotel to access the brand name, international reservations system, and professional marketing plans. However, the contract chain may also operate as a silent management team, with only employees aware of who pays their salaries.

The disadvantages of a management contract are similar to those of being part of any large company, especially if communication between upper management (owners) and lower management (management contractor) is not good. Some owners believe that they are not kept adequately informed about the managers' business activities. Owners may disagree with some of the operational decisions made by the property's management, but generally owners do not have control over those decisions. In addition, the owner must pay a guaranteed management fee of between 1 and 3.5% of gross revenues. Finally, as with franchises, management contract companies may lack an understanding of the local culture when operating a foreign property. To be successful, any business must have a good knowledge of and working relationship with local cultural traditions.

These are the four basic styles of ownership, but it should be noted that variations are common, and today most major hotel chains are associated with other chains through franchises and management contracts. Employees need a clear understanding of their property's ownership and management structure to follow company policies.

Hotel Real Estate Investment Trusts (REITs)

Many traditional hotel companies, such as Fairmont, are using **REITs** as a new form of ownership. REITs emerged as hotel companies searched for new ways to fund development, using sources other than financial institutions. Hotel REITs are companies that buy hotels and hotel resort properties worldwide. They then sell shares in their company, trading them on the stock market like any stock. From an ownership perspective, REITs are used to gain funding for acquisitions, new construction, and renovations. The remarkable success of REITs is generally attributed to their terrific performance for investors. They provide hotels with liquidity in the capital marketplace and the financial support they need to expand in this growing industry.

Organization and Functions

The organization of a hotel or motel depends on its size and ownership. Owners of small, individually owned motels might hire only maids, performing most of the other work themselves. They do not usually have any kind of food service, with the exception of vending machines. Most hotels, however, require a fairly large staff to function properly. The hotel staff is divided into those who work in the **front of the house** and have direct contact with customers: front office, food and beverage, housekeeping, and customer services; and those who have little contact with the guests and work in the **back of the house**: administration, sales and marketing, accounting, engineering, and security.

Administration The administrative staff includes the general manager, assistant manager, and all the department heads. The general and assistant managers are responsible for the overall operation of the hotel. They assist and direct the other managers and keep all departments informed on the day-to-day business of the hotel. The department managers are responsible for their departments' success and the direct supervision of their employees. They must all work together, normally meeting weekly to report on their progress and share information. For example, all managers need to be aware of the needs of any arriving group that has been booked by the sales managers, as well as specific promises made by the sales managers.

Sales and Marketing This department is responsible for four different areas: sales, advertising, research, and public relations. Sales include both group and convention sales—promotions, rate setting, and travel trade sales (group bookings from travel agencies and tour operators). The sales staff spends most of its time bidding for conventions, corporate meetings, and other multiple reservations.

Public relations involves creating a favourable image for the property by cultivating contacts with travel writers and editors or becoming involved as a sponsor with a major event such as the Festival of Fire, held each summer in Victoria. News releases, press kits, and promotions are part of public relations.

The marketing component includes learning about the competition, researching customers' wants and needs, and designing a product and service that meets those needs. Marketing is a relatively new concept in the tourism industry, one introduced within the past 50 years. The term itself carries a double meaning—one naming the specific department and the other describing the actual functions of the marketing staff in dealing with customers, sales, and promotions. A company that seeks first to satisfy the wants and needs of its clientele is one that has a marketing management style.

Front Office and Guest Services These are the people who have direct contact with guests. They are normally both the first and the last people to be in touch with the guest. The image, attitude, and professional standards they convey set the tone for the guest's total experience. The responsibilities of front-office personnel include check-in and check-out, providing information, answering telephones, and cashiering. The service staff includes the concierge, bellhops, bell captain, lobby porter, and doorperson. Although most of these positions are entry level, the guest will judge the hotel through encounters with these people.

Accounting The accounting staff is responsible for tracking all financial information. In some instances, the control function is separated from other management functions by having the comptroller or financial officer report directly to the home office rather than to the general manager of the hotel. This method decreases the possibility of perpetuating ineffective accounting procedures and allows the general manager to concentrate on guest relations rather than on financial issues. Under this arrangement, the comptroller becomes a key financial advisor for the hotel. Other positions within this department may include auditors, accounts receivable supervisor, payroll supervisor, cashier, and purchasing agent.

Food and Beverage (F&B) Department Most hotel food service areas are owned and operated by the hotel, although some hotels opt to rent out space to franchised companies or independent restaurant owners, with a percentage of gross food and beverage sales going to the hotel. Hotel food and beverage service comes in many forms: fine dining, fast food, coffee shop service, room service, buffets, banquets, poolside bars, snack bars, and lounges, and can provide up to half of the hotel's overall revenue. The food and beverage department needs to be aware of hotel reservations in order to forecast food and beverage and staff requirements. For example, a large conference will require extra servers for banquets and socials; a full house of independent travellers will require extra workers in the restaurant and lounge. Open communication with other departments ensures effective cost management, resulting in increased profitability. In addition to serving guests, many hotel restaurants and lounges offer incentives for community residents to eat and relax at their property. This service requires knowledge of the community and good marketing or promotional schemes to encourage local use.

Food preparation may be part of the food and beverage department, or it may be a department on its own. The executive chef and assistants are responsible for maintaining an enticing menu, experimenting with new recipes, and supervising all kitchen staff. Chef positions are often held by people with culinary talent but no experience in personnel management. Havoc may ensue when the chef is good at food preparation but delinquent in hiring, motivating, and maintaining a staff. A good chef provides the meals, works on budgets and menu planning, supervises staff, and maintains working relationships with other departments in the hotel.

Room Service Room service is a travel luxury that pampers the guest by delivering meals directly to the room. Many people get this type of pampering only on vacation. All first-class hotels are expected to provide this service to their guests even if it is not a profit-making venture. Room service is expensive to operate and requires a great deal of organization to be successful. Equipment must keep hot food hot and cold food cold, and meals must be delivered as quickly as possible to satisfy the guest. Some hotels have special service elevators, which help staff provide fast service without disrupting other guests.

Breakfasts account for 70 to 90% of room service orders, with continental breakfasts topping the list.[5] Some hotels provide a doorknob program, which allows guests to select their desired meal and delivery time on a small menu that is then placed on the outside doorknob. During the night, the menu is collected, and breakfast is served at the requested time. To help cover additional costs, room service meals are generally more expensive than the same meals served in the restaurant. Some hotels also add a service charge. Room service may be limited to certain hours of the day or may be offered on a 24-hour basis. The type and size of the hotel will determine the extent of room service available.

Many Canadian hotels are known for their superb cuisine, but The Fairmont Jasper Park Lodge Hotel goes one step further with outstanding views.
(Source: Canadian Tourism Commission.)

Banquets and Catering Banquets and catering are the responsibility of the catering director or banquet manager. Catering is usually set up as a separate function within a hotel's food and beverage department because it requires different services and meals from a hotel restaurant. Although banquets can be hosted by other restaurants, most do not have the capacity to compete with the hotel's banquet capabilities. Banquets range in size from small business meetings of perhaps 15 people to groups of more than a thousand convention-goers. Weddings, conventions, Bar and Bat Mitzvahs, anniversary dinners, reunions, and business meetings account for the majority of banquets. All convention hotels have catering services.

Catering services can be profitable if well organized, because the group holding the event must provide the catering manager with the total number of guests expected, and agrees ahead of time on a set menu at a set price. Even if some people do not show up for the meal, the group must pay for the number it guaranteed. Revenue from the sale of alcohol, either through a **cash bar** or an **open bar** (where the host pays for the alcohol), makes banquets even more profitable. In addition, servers are staffed only for the time needed, food quantities are known ahead of time, and the speed with which a banquet can be served ensures economies of time and expense.

Housekeeping This department ensures the guests' comfort by keeping individual rooms and public areas clean and neat. In most hotels, a head or executive housekeeper is responsible for supervising all room attendants, floor supervisors, serving specialists, and housekeepers. When a guest needs an extra towel or an iron and ironing board, housekeeping delivers. This one-on-one interaction with the guest requires well-trained and pleasant employees.

Unfortunately, housekeeping jobs are low paying and provide employees with little incentive to excel. Most hotels now pay housekeepers on a per room basis, encouraging speed and efficiency and allowing workers to set their own pace. (This method puts an additional burden on room checkers, who must ensure that each room is cleaned to the hotel standard.) Hotels are constantly challenged to hire and keep good employees for the housekeeping department.

Engineering This department, sometimes called maintenance and operations, focuses on the physical structure of the hotel. All problems with air conditioning, sound systems, electricity, equipment, and outside maintenance are sent to the engineering department. A director of engineering must have considerable knowledge of building maintenance and equipment. Although guests have little contact with them, the importance of engineering personnel cannot be overemphasized, because any problems with the physical structure of the hotel will mean inconvenienced or uncomfortable guests.

Security In many larger hotels, especially in downtown areas, a security department is essential. This department is responsible for protecting guests and property. Some, but not all, security officer positions may require police training. Generally, the presence of a security officer at the entrance to a hotel makes a statement that the property is safe for the guest. Hotels usually prefer to have security personnel in street dress rather than uniforms because the presence of uniformed security guards can upset guests, who wonder whether there are security issues of which they are not aware. Because security officers need an understanding of law enforcement rather than of hotel operations, these positions are not usually stepping stones to hotel management.

In Practice

How do a Comfort Inn, an independent motel, and a Sheraton differ in terms of management and ownership? Which would you prefer to work with and why?

CLASSIFICATIONS WITHIN THE ACCOMMODATIONS INDUSTRY

The two main categories in the accommodation industry are the hotel and the motel, and the two differ in several ways. A **hotel** has a central lobby, its rooms are accessible from the hotel lobby, and guest parking may or may not be provided. Hotels can also be classified by their location, the purpose and duration of guest visits, and the room rates and level of service provided. Table 5.1 shows the world's largest hotels.

Location

Hotels may be classified as downtown, suburban, airport, town, highway, or resort (located in a natural setting such as near the seaside, a mountain, or a lake).

Downtown Travellers who choose to stay in a *downtown* location are willing to pay for the convenience of being near attractions or their place of business. These visitors often fly into a city and prefer to use public transportation rather than rent a car. One new hotel product in the marketplace is the bistro hotel, which caters to the upscale business traveller. The atmosphere at a bistro hotel is one of old-world wealth, with a quiet understatement of lavish luxury. Guests receive highly personalized treatment, from the greeting at the door to individualized amenities.

www.hiltonhotels.ca

TABLE 5.1   *World's Largest Hotels"*[6]

First World Hotel	Genting Highlands of Malaysia	6118 rooms
MGM Grand	Las Vegas	5044 rooms
Mandalay Bay Hotel	Las Vegas	4752 rooms
Luxor	Las Vegas	4408 rooms
Ambassador City Jomtien	Thailand	4210 rooms
The Venetian Palazza	Las Vegas	4049 rooms
Excalibur	Las Vegas	4008 rooms
Bellagio	Las Vegas	3993 rooms
Circus Circus	Las Vegas	3774 rooms
Flamingo	Las Vegas	3565 rooms

The largest hotel in the world is currently being built in Dubai. As part of a $27 billion complex, the Asia-Asia will have 6500 rooms.

Suburban On the other hand, a family taking a touring vacation could very well prefer a *suburban* location. They might want to be near family who live in the suburbs, or they may be concerned with cost. These visitors often drive their own car and look for inexpensive lodging with free parking. It does not matter how far they are from the attractions because they have the convenience of their own transportation.

Airport These hotels generally target the air traveller. Stays are short, often only overnight, and many hotels offer day rates for travellers forced to spend a full day waiting for a specific airline connection. Many airport hotels offer 24-hour valet and food service. Quick check-in and check-out are particularly important for weary travellers who must catch a plane. Some hotels offer television channels that provide travellers with information on the weather at their next destination or provide updated departure and arrival times for local airline companies.

Small Town/Country Hotels Even small towns require some type of accommodation for the traveller. Many of the smaller towns located near major tourist destinations provide lodging at a more reasonable cost and happily accept the tourist who has been unable to book a hotel room near an attraction or event. Some towns have converted historic buildings into inns or hotels, providing the opportunity for entrepreneurs to use the local culture and history to their advantage.

Guests staying in Num-Ti-Jah Lodge, located on the Icefields Parkway, enjoy a quiet drink after exploring the Columbia Icefield in the Canadian Rockies.

(Source: Canadian Tourism Commission.)

Highway Highway motels are familiar to truckers and travellers on the Trans-Canada Highway or to those driving north to the Yukon on the Alaska Highway. This kind of lodging is essential in the middle of a highway wilderness, and is a welcome stopping place for the long-distance driver.

Resort Finally, **resort hotels** usually promote a specific destination. Even in ancient times people needed to escape the cities, the summer heat, or the winter blues, and they travelled to the seaside, health spas, or mountain resorts for relaxation, recreation, and entertainment. Summer resorts offer golf, tennis, swimming, horseback riding, boating, fishing, and canoeing. Winter resorts add skiing, snowboarding, snowmobiling, skating, and sleigh rides. Thanks to Canada's many beautiful natural sites and destinations, our resorts have gained fame

Hotel Terminology You Should Know

single	one person staying in the room, no matter how many beds
twin	room with two twin beds
double	two people staying in one room
double double	room with two double beds
suite	accommodation with two or more rooms combined—one set up as a living room
hospitality suite	room that has a bar and sitting area, often provided to the executive of a conference to be used for informal meetings
rack rate	standard daily rate
weekend rate	discount rate charged for weekend stays
run-of-the-house rate	discount rate for block bookings
corporate rate	discount rate given to members of an organization, usually negotiated ahead of time, based on anticipated volume of business
family plan	special family rate that allows children to stay with parents at no additional charge
day rate	rate charged for short stays during the day, often at airport hotel locations—usually 9:00 a.m. to 9:00 p.m.

around the world. Jasper Park Lodge, Château Whistler, Château Montebello, and Fairmont Algonquinin St. Andrews by-the-Sea are just a few of the spectacular resorts from the Fairmont Hotel and Resort chain.

A resort may stand alone as a destination or, like The Fairmont Château Whistler in British Columbia, it may support additional businesses. Nestled in the coastal mountains of British Columbia, this carefully planned resort community offers shopping, a variety of dining options and evening entertainment, as well as other amenities such as babysitting and daycare, church services, fitness centres, laundry and dry cleaning, medical and dental clinics, a public library and museum, video rentals, and movie theatres.

Every province has a variety of resorts to fulfill the needs of vacationers—from luxury travellers to those seeking a more rustic vacation. However, in today's world of tourism, seasonal resorts are having a difficult time remaining profitable and are looking to expand their businesses throughout Canada's four seasons.

Purpose of Visit

Another way we classify hotels is based on the *motivation* or *purpose* of a visitor's trip. *Business guests* stay at business hotels, usually found in downtown areas or near major airports, which provide specific services for the business traveller, such as airport limousine service, computer hook-ups with working space, room service and mini-bars, valet services, and easy check-in and check-out. Many business hotels provide a check-out system that may be accessed from the room using the TV screen as a monitor. Business travellers are important because they use non-discretionary money and are thus less concerned with cost and more concerned with service. A strong business clientele provides revenue for a hotel even during the off-season and recessions.

Conference-goers stay at **conference hotels**, usually found in larger cities with strong pull power, or in resort-like settings. These hotels must provide large meeting spaces and smaller meeting rooms, and have portable food service available. Many are turning into high-tech conference centres that house audio and video recording facilities with equipment such as slide projectors, overhead projection units, and portable computer systems. Group meetings can now be held in special audio-visual rooms designed to record the meeting from a variety of angles, with up to 10 different video cameras! Also available are in-house TV channels that broadcast to guests' rooms and meeting facilities, along with satellite uplink and downlink capabilities for people who cannot attend the conference in person. Large convention hotels may have an audio-visual staff and even in-house experts to help conference presenters, all on short notice. All these services are needed for hotels to succeed in the very competitive convention market.

The final grouping by motivation or purpose is the *pleasure/vacation guest*. These guests are often more concerned with price and location than with valet and room service. They do, however, appreciate information from a concierge desk, knowledgeable front-desk staff, or a brochure rack.

Level of Service

Hotels may also be classified by *level of service,* which is determined by the needs of the hotel's target market (Figure 5.1). *Budget hotels* are designed to provide clean, safe, low-cost rooms. They offer very few services and may not have in-house food service. Instead, budget hotels may choose a location near a restaurant strip or provide a menu in each room from a local restaurant that is willing to deliver. A Comfort Inn is a good example of a budget hotel.

A *mid-scale hotel* will have a coffee shop on its premises, may have a swimming pool or exercise room, and may or may not provide airport service. A Ramada Inn is a good example of a mid-scale hotel.

Upscale hotels are far more service-oriented, providing a wide variety of benefits such as room service, concierge, dining and lounge areas, pool and exercise areas, and gift shop or mini-mall. *Luxury properties* take service to an even higher level. Located in a prestigious area of the city or countryside, a luxury hotel's lobby is often large and spectacular (for example, it might include a waterfall or an indoor garden), with elegant furniture and lighting. Service is discreet and efficient. Luxury hotel chains such as the Four Seasons cater to travellers who can afford the expense and expect their every want and need to be fulfilled.

Duration of Visit

Length of stay is the final category for classifying hotels. Not all hotels cater to *transient guests*—that is, those who spend only a short period of time at the hotel. *Residential hotels* provide guests with long-term accommodations, sometimes for a year or more. Most of these hotels are mid- to upscale, and all their services are available to the resident guest. A transient hotel may also opt to provide residential rates. In Ottawa, where a great many politicians spend six months of the year representing their hometown constituents, hotels providing residential rates are more common than in Calgary, for example.

Clearly hotels can fit into several classifications. For example, an upscale hotel might be located downtown and cater to business clientele and the conference market.

FIGURE 5.1

Marriott
Corporation's hotel
operations

Price Segment	A Product in Every Lodging Segment
Luxury/ Quality	Marriott Suites Marriott HOTELS + RESORTS
Moderate	THE RESIDENCE INN COURTYARD
Economy	FAIRFIELD INN

Source: Marriott Corporation.

Motels As previously mentioned, motels and motel chains first appeared in the 1950s with the establishment of interstate and interprovincial highway systems. A **motel** is a lodging property that offers free parking to travellers. Most motels have doors to the parking lot from each room, and, as a result, generally have little use for large lobbies. A motel that is located in a downtown area, however, may have a lobby and more of a hotel atmosphere.

Motels offer simple, clean, and inexpensive accommodations to tourists travelling by car. Chains and franchises choose simple room plans that translate into savings in design and construction costs. Rooms are usually limited to one or two double beds, and cots are available when needed. Many motels look to the family or seniors market, both of which look for a clean, safe, and comfortable room with few amenities.

A traveller usually chooses a motel over a hotel based on two factors: cost and location. Canada's largest motel chain, Choice Hotels Canada, owns Comfort Inns, Sleep Inns, Econo Lodges, Quality Inns, Rodeway Inns, and Clarion Hotels.

Other Lodging Options

Inns Modern inns are usually found in smaller towns that have a tourist base. Often the building is historic, renovated to meet the expectations of travellers looking for an upscale but quiet vacation. Most **inns** have excellent dining rooms that attract local patrons as well as guests. They create a "homey" feel by providing fireplaces in guest rooms or small libraries for guest use. Many are now adding features such as spas. Some hotel chains, such as Holiday Inn, use the term "inn" because they wish to create the perception of a homey, intimate lodging facility.

Spas The ancient Romans knew the value of rejuvenation. Their **spas**, which were frequently located by the sea, offered many of the services that modern spas offer: mud baths, massage, exercise programs, and healthy food. In fact, spas have thrived in many cultures throughout the ages. Focusing on the body and mind as one, spas pamper and work the human body back to health. Spas are found all across the accommodations industry. Resorts and hotels may offer a spa weekend; inns have joined the trend, and even cruise ships promote spa cruises. Their staff include certified professionals who deliver the spa program, and chefs with a solid knowledge of nutrition who prepare healthy gourmet food. Facilities allow the client to achieve complete relaxation. Hydrotherapy tubs, massages, and exercise rooms become a necessary component of the lodging facilities. Now you can also enjoy hot rock massages, mineral pools, yoga, Pilates, and different beauty treatments. The price tag for a week at a spa may be higher than for other vacations, but for those who want to feel rejuvenated, spa vacations provide a healthful alternative. Most spas also have beautiful, relaxing restaurants that serve both the spa-goer with healthy, inviting, calorie-reduced meals, as well as the outdoor enthusiast with meals that provide the nourishment they will need to get up and golf for one more day.

Boutique Hotels These belong to the upscale/luxury market. **Boutique hotels** have all of the convenience of a modern hotel, but bring back an era of luxury and uniqueness. Each room has its own décor, its own subtle luxury. They are smaller, more intimate hotels where the doorman actually does remember your name and housekeeping puts the type of bottled water that you prefer in your room along with a plate of home-baked cookies. These hotels appeal to the business traveller who spends a great deal of time on the road and is looking for a more familial, less sterile setting.

Condominiums and Time-Shares Condominium and time-share units are also resort accommodations. The word **condominium** means "joint domain" in Latin. Condominiums allow an individual to have full ownership over one unit in a complex. In many cases, the owner uses the condominium for only a few weeks each year and rents it out through an independent management agency for the remainder of the year. The management agency maintains the grounds, roads, and recreational facilities, and provides security and cleaning services for a percentage of the rental fee. Resort condominiums in places like Florida, Hawaii, and Colorado allow the traveller to have apartment-style accommodations in an area filled with recreational amenities. As the baby boomers begin to retire, this type of investment and holiday is coming back into vogue.

Time-sharing involves buying a vacation segment for a specific period of time, usually two weeks, in a condominium unit. The purchaser owns only the two-week segment, not the entire unit. The segment is scheduled so that only one owner

Memorable vacations do not need a five-star hotel. For some visitors, it is just a tent for two with a view.
(Photo: Canadian Tourism Commission.)

may use it at a time. Some time-share companies encourage their owners to swap segments, allowing them to go to a new resort each year.

Dude Ranches Another type of resort is the **dude** or **guest ranch**, which is usually family-owned and -operated and offers the guest a western experience. The dude ranch is becoming a popular choice for city dwellers with a desire to get back to basics.

A dude ranch may be a working ranch where guests assist the owners in day-to-day operations, or it may be a luxury resort with swimming pools, horseback-riding lessons, and rodeo shows. Dude ranches include guest ranches, resort ranches, working cattle ranches, fly-fishing ranches, hunting ranches, and cross-country skiing ranches. Most ranches are located in the western United States, British Columbia, and Alberta. The movie *City Slickers* encouraged demand for working ranch vacations.

Foreign and domestic tourists are also opting to spend a week working on a farm in rural Ontario, helping out an egg farmer in Nova Scotia, or joining the harvest on a wheat farm in Saskatchewan. Guests pay for their lodging and meals, and enjoy some of Canada's agricultural tourism products.

www.bbcanada.com

Bed and Breakfasts (B & Bs) Nearly every city and country around the world is home to **bed and breakfasts**. B & Bs provide foreign travellers with a cultural experience and the opportunity to live with a family in a new city or town, enjoying the daily life of the local people. Domestic travellers may decide to explore their own backyards and hidden communities by searching out B & Bs. Guests are usually pampered by owners who enjoy sharing local folklore and recommending points of interest and good places to eat. B & Bs are often restored older homes in rural settings, scenic waterfront estates, cozy Gothic cottages, train stations, converted schoolhouses, or old mills or plantations.

Because these lodgings have been converted from single-family homes, many do not have private washroom facilities for each guest, so the communal bathroom down the hall must be an acceptable alternative for vacation and business travellers. Guests can mingle and meet new people in the parlour. Most B & Bs serve family-style breakfasts; some offer dinner as well.

At the Train Station Inn at Tatamagouche, Nova Scotia, old railroad cars have been renovated as bedrooms, providing unique sleeping accommodations.
(Photo: Paula Kerr.)

A B & B is usually family-owned and -operated. In a small B & B, the staff may be strictly family members; larger properties may hire extra help. Checking in guests, cooking, baking snacks, cleaning, accounting, designing advertising campaigns, and acting as tour guide could all become part of a daily routine at a B & B. Owning and running a B & B is a unique and fun way to learn about the accomodations business on a small but comprehensive scale.

Hostels Generally known as a youth hostel, a **hostel** is a lodge with communal washrooms and bedrooms designed for four to twenty people. Hostels may be found in specially constructed buildings or in older homes, YMCAs, and even churches. In most cases, guests prepare their own meals or assist in meal preparation and cleanup. The low cost makes travel feasible for students and others on limited budgets. The hostel has been popular in Europe and many other countries for decades.

www.hihostels.ca

Hostelling International-Canada (HI-Canada) provides services such as discounts on already inexpensive accommodations and on different types of organized tours, including hiking, bicycling, canoeing, and skiing. HI-Canada represents more than 80 different hostels across the country. At a hostel, the guest reserves a bed rather than a room.

One of the more interesting hostels in Canada is the Ottawa Jail Hostel. This historic stone building, located on Nicholas Street in downtown Ottawa, served as the Carleton County Gaol from 1862 to 1971. In 1972, it opened its doors to the public as a youth hostel called Nicholas Gaol. The colourful history of this building attracts many travellers. The prison was the site of Canada's last public hanging and—allegedly—of many evil deeds. During the building's renovation, a mass grave was discovered in the courtyard. A few visitors have claimed over the years that they hear ghostly voices moan stories of cruelty and mistreatment. Today the cozy surroundings show few traces of the past, and the hostel has been renamed the Ottawa Jail Hostel.

Travelling in Europe and elsewhere can provide the tourist with interesting accommodation options. Travellers may decide to rent a room in an English castle, a château in Burgundy, or a quiet monastery. In Greenland, travellers can rent an igloo; Quebec City builds an ice hotel every winter. In Switzerland, farmers take their cows to alpine meadows for the summer, clean out their barns, and replace the old straw with fresh hay. For a very reasonable price, you can rent a stall! The variety of lodging facilities is limited only by the ingenuity of the owner and the tourist's desire to try something new.

Campgrounds As a form of accommodation, **campgrounds** have always been popular with cost-conscious travellers, outdoor enthusiasts, and RV owners who simply want to enjoy an area surrounded by the comforts of their own belongings. In the past, campgrounds offered a piece of grass to set up a tent, and possibly a lake for fishing and swimming. Such campgrounds still exist in North America, but many people are demanding more than a spot to set up camp. Camping has increasingly become a sophisticated art, with first-class RV hook-ups, and campground programs for all ages. Many campgrounds have hot showers, coin-operated laundries, electrical and sewer systems to accommodate RVs, playgrounds, swimming pools, and recreation rooms. Campgrounds may also have small grocery stores, and some even have gift shops.

In Practice

How do campgrounds and dude ranches fit into the hospitality industry? What differentiates an economy hotel from a luxury hotel? Name three different hotels for each service level: economy, moderate, upscale, and luxury.

MARKETING THE ACCOMMODATIONS INDUSTRY

Marketing a nationally known chain or franchised hotel differs greatly from marketing a small, family-owned inn or bed and breakfast. Larger hotels have the resources to hire prominent advertising firms to create high-profile ad campaigns that present their messages in a full range of media: television, radio, newspapers, and magazines. But for both the major hotel chains and the small, privately owned lodgings, skill and knowledge of advertising and promotional techniques are becoming more and more essential. How can any lodging facility best use the four Ps of marketing: product, place, price, and promotion?

Product

Is there more to being a hotel than simply being a place to sleep? The answer to this question is yes and no. Some no-frills hotels pride themselves on simply providing an inexpensive, clean, comfortable place to sleep. Other luxury properties have a wide variety of facilities, provide special services such as **turn-down service** (folding down the bedspread, and placing a chocolate on the pillow at night), and take great pride in the friendly expertise of their staff.

Although the hotel room is intangible to the customer at the time of purchase, very tangible elements of a property need to be properly conveyed. Decor, ambience, facilities, and services may be illustrated through colourful pictures and written words. This may be done in a brochure format and mailed to prospective clients, but the most important new technological development in sales and marketing is a *website*.

For a small investment, any business can promote its facilities to a global marketplace. Some websites simply show a picture of the hotel and provide basic information. But many businesses are creating interactive sites that allow the visitor to look at the rooms, the dining facilities and menus, and special features such as their indoor pool and hot tub. In addition, they link their site to the websites of local attractions, providing even more incentive for a customer to visit. Reservations are easily made over the internet; the site may also list phone numbers for those who wish to speak to a representative in person.

How do prospective clients determine the quality of a product? As mentioned earlier in this chapter, organizations such as CAA provide a rating scale for lodging properties, and nine of our provinces share a common rating system developed by Canada Select Accommodations rating program (Table 5.2). In addition, some provinces, such as Alberta, go further and provide information on an accommodation's ability to provide services for people with disabilities. The Green Key program now alerts customers to the quality of a lodging and the concern it has for the ecosystem.

TABLE 5.2   *Canada Select Accommodations Rating Program Categories*

★	clean, comfortable accommodations
★★	clean, comfortable accommodations with some amenities
★★★	very comfortable accommodations with a greater range of facilities, guest amenities, and services
★★★★	the highest standard of accommodations with an extensive range of facilities, guest amenities, and services
★★★★★	exceptional properties that are among the best in the country in terms of their outstanding facilities, guest services, and quality provided

Source: Canada Select Accommodations Program.

Price

Very few hotels have a single fixed price for a room. Prices depend on a number of factors:

- location (of the hotel and the room)
- the room size and its amenities
- the pricing expectations of target markets
- competitors' pricing strategies
- seasonality
- group purchase discounts (e.g., conference, tour, or corporate)
- discounts given to special market segments (e.g., travel agents or seniors)
- available meal plans (Table 5.3)

www.marriott.com

Reservation agents need to be fully aware of all pricing options and should provide the guest with the best possible price available. It is important to remember that the tourism product has a very elastic demand—the higher the price, the more difficult it is to sell. For example, at the turn of the millennium, many hotels were surprised to find they had overestimated what the public was willing to pay and were left with empty rooms and lost revenue.

Place

What are the channels of distribution for the accommodations industry? The internet has become one of the most important sales tools for the industry, allowing travellers to log onto a website to see rooms, facilities, menus and dining room,

TABLE 5.3   *Meal Plans*

European Plan (EP)	room only with no meals
Continental Plan (CP)	room rate that includes a continental breakfast: juice, coffee, and roll or pastry
Bermuda Plan (BP)	room rate that includes a full American breakfast: juice, coffee, eggs, sausage/bacon, toast
American Plan (AP)	rate that includes three full meals: breakfast, lunch, dinner
Modified American Plan (MAP)	rate that includes two meals, usually breakfast and dinner

and other services. Many websites now provide mini-tours of the property. Websites do not have to be that interactive to attract customers, but a good website is a sales tool no lodging should be without. Hotel rooms are also sold through websites such as Expedia.ca, which provide tourists not only with a broad selection of properties but with an entire vacation package.

Hotels also sell directly to the public using their own reservation systems. Large chains may use a single 1-800 number for all properties, allowing clients to access reservations from anywhere within the country. Individual properties may choose to join a referral system.

One final channel of distribution is the travel agency and its resource materials, such as the Official Hotel Guide. Travel counsellors can often suggest the hotel best suited to the customer's needs, as well as activities to suit the customer's interests.

Promotion

Advertising is important but not critical during high season. Low season, however, can be a challenge for any hotelier. Large hotels have sales and marketing staff that create packages best suited to the needs of a specific target market. For example, a hotel in a downtown location with a large business clientele may be booked during the week but have rooms available on the weekends. Creating a package that provides local residents with "romantic getaways" or "stress relief weekends" may be part of the answer. Included in this type of package might be an overnight stay, use of the pool and exercise facilities, dinner for two in the hotel's elegant restaurant, and a champagne breakfast. For the higher-value tourist, some hotels provide special floors that offer limited access, open bars in a comfortable lounge, and free breakfasts. Still others may provide frequent-guest cards, airport limousine service, and instant check-in/check-out for corporate guests.

Public relations are also an important part of promotion. Supporting a special festival or event, raising money for local charities, and supporting local town improvements in association with a chamber of commerce or convention and visitors bureau all enhance a hotel's image in a very competitive business. Promotions can be as creative as the promoter, and understanding marketing principles and the needs and wants of the clientele is the best way to ensure that promotions are effective.

A **confirmed reservation** means that a hotel has a room waiting for a client—but the hotel can sell the room to a waiting guest if the client does not show up by a specified time (usually 4:00–6:00 p.m.). Disney properties have a special desk that deals solely with confirmed but unclaimed room reservations! A **guaranteed reservation** means the client has supplied a credit card number and must pay for the room with or without using it, unless the reservation is cancelled by a certain time and a cancellation number obtained.

Most hotels have a high season and a low season. Because their product is so perishable, it must be sold daily—a room that goes unsold represents lost revenue. Sometimes a hotel will **overbook**, or sell more rooms than it has, anticipating that not all guests will show up. Occasionally, the hotel is then left with too few rooms for the guests holding confirmed or guaranteed reservations. This is an unpleasant position for any hotel to be in, and it is the responsibility of the hotel to find the guests rooms at another property. Doing so is called **walking** or *farming out*. Usually the hotel will cover the guest's room charge and offer some additional compensation.

SNAPSHOT

Cesar Ritz

Ritzy and *putting on the ritz* are just two phrases that bear witness to the master of graciousness and quality—Cesar Ritz. He was born into a family with no wealth, yet the mere mention of his name conjures up visions of glamour, prestige, and elegance. Who is Cesar Ritz and why is he an important part of tourism's past?

He began work as an apprentice at age 15 in Brig, Switzerland. At 19, he moved to Paris, and by the late 1860s, he had become a restaurant manager—not an easy feat for one so young. Realizing that his education was far from complete, he left his managerial position to become an assistant waiter at the most famous restaurant of the day, Le Voisin. Here he learned everything he could about service, including the correct and genteel fashion in which the wealthy enjoyed dining. It was not long before he had developed such a knack for pleasing his customers that they insisted on having him as their waiter. He knew their likes and dislikes, their vanities and their habits. Cesar Ritz learned the finer points of service by understanding one of the basic needs of people: to be recognized and made to feel special.

At 27, he became manager of one of Europe's most elegant hotels, the Grand National in Lucerne, Switzerland. It was here he partnered with the great Auguste Escoffier and together they not only returned the hotel to profit but continued to work successfully together for many years.

In 1887, Ritz was asked to take over the management of London, England's grand new hotel, the Savoy London. Barely open six months, it was losing money at an enormous rate. Ritz was given carte blanche to operate the hotel. Soon he had created a dining room that boasted fine culinary treats and live bands playing Strauss. He designed lighting that would flatter the complexion, and he instituted a dress code, making evening wear mandatory. In 1898, he and Escoffier opened the first Ritz hotel, with Escoffier preparing some of the world's best food while Ritz ensured each detail in the hotel was perfect, and each guest taken care of with equal concern.

While he went on to develop his own chain of hotels, the difficulties of the early 1920s and 30s proved too great, and he sold his share so that his hotels became the Ritz Carleton, long revered as a deluxe hotel chain.

Cesar Ritz was a man who believed in excellence. He felt that his customers' wants, needs, and expectations should be fulfilled in a prompt, courteous, and quiet manner, and that their surroundings should be elegantly comfortable. He believed that service was the key to satisfied, repeat business. It is a testament to his steadfast devotion to beauty and charm that a new word became part of the English language. *Ritzy* means elegant, luxurious, and grand; *putting on the ritz* means living, behaving, or dressing in a refined and fashionable manner.

The Green Key Eco-rating Program This program is designed to be as all-inclusive as possible, welcoming all lodging facilities. Its simple, online approach makes becoming a partner easy. The graduated **Green Key rating** system helps owners determine how well they are doing when it comes to recycling, reusing, and reducing. The program illustrates how owners can save money by reducing operating costs while helping

At the Inverary Resort, Baddeck, Nova Scotia, guests have a choice of bedrooms in the main lodge, in two-room cabins, or in outlying buildings.
(Photo: Paula Kerr.)

"green" the planet. It includes all major departments of an accommodation and is adjusted for those who do not have full services available. The multiple choice quiz is done online, and results are given within minutes of finishing the quiz. It covers energy conservation, water conservation, solid waste management, hazardous waste

FOOTPRINT

TABLE 5.4   *Accommodations: The Green Key Program*

A hotel has taken steps to reduce environmental impacts by analyzing its operations and identifying opportunities for improvement. An action plan focusing on resource conservation and waste minimization has been established and is supported by a firm commitment to continual improvement.

A hotel has taken considerable strides to identify environmental impacts and implement policies, (i.e., best management programs to minimize ecological footprints). A firm commitment to continual improvement has resulted in programs and actions that have shown effective results.

A hotel has taken significant steps to protect the environment. Strong environmental programs, best management practices, training programs, and engineering solutions have been implemented that have benefited the environment and the local community.

A hotel has shown national industry leadership and commitment to protecting the environment through a wide range of policies and practices. Hotel has mature programs in place that involve management, employees, guests, and the public that have shown substantial measurable results.

A hotel exemplifies the highest standards of environmental and social responsibility throughout all areas of operations. The hotel employs cutting edge technologies, policies, and programs that set the international standard for sustainable hotel operations.

management, indoor air quality, community outreach, building infrastructure, land use, and environmental management. Points are scored based on the impact on the environment and social structure of a community. The Footprint on page 149 includes Table 5.4 showing the level of concern ownership has for our ecosystem based on how they operate their establishment.

In Practice

Write the names of 10 hotels or motels in your community. Identify their locations and what else is in the vicinity. Does the location dictate the type of clientele of each motel or hotel? What type of marketing strategies does each use? Why does one facility do better than another in the same community?

CASE STUDY

Killing the Golden Goose

Arnold Jackson owned a large sheep farm in New Zealand. After listening to a presentation by a Canadian trade delegation regarding business possibilities in Canada, he decided to travel there to check out business opportunities for his family's beautiful handmade woollen products and his organically raised lamb. His first stop was in a large Canadian city, and he chose to stay in a large hotel in the downtown area because he was an inexperienced traveller and nervous about being in a foreign country. He quickly discovered that Canada was like home—the Canadians he met were friendly and enjoyed entertaining him. He made some excellent business connections and enough sales to pay for the trip. However, when he checked out of the hotel, he was shocked to find that his total bill was approximately $400 more than the $1720.55 he had anticipated. Fully expecting additional charges for tax, he was still surprised to find a "promotion tax," and surcharges for housekeeping and room service, for restocking the mini-bar (which he had not opened), and for a high-speed internet connection charge. When he went to the assistant manager to question these items, he was told that every hotel in the city added these charges and nothing could be done to eliminate them. Not wanting to make a scene or miss his flight, Mr. Jackson paid the bill and left, taking with him a very poor memory of what should have been a positive trip.

1. What was the main cause of Arnold's dissatisfaction?
2. Was there any course of action the assistant manager might have taken immediately to reduce Arnold's distress?
3. What might the hotel do to ensure that other customers do not have the same experience?
4. What might be the long-term negative impact of the taxes and surcharges Canadians are adding on to tourism products, especially hotels, restaurants, and air travel? Is there any way the negative spin might be contained?

Summary

The hotel business has been around for centuries and continues to grow and change. From small roadside inns to time-shares, this industry provides a wide range of career opportunities.

Hotels are operated under four basic types of management. The individual owner usually has a small property and single-handedly manages the business, operating it in any manner desired. Outside staff may or may not be needed. A company chain operates its own hotels from a single, corporate headquarters. Franchise properties are owned by an individual (or sometimes a company) but fall under the guidelines of the franchise. (A referral system provides privately owned hotels with a nationally known name and reservation system.) Under a management contract, one company owns the property, but another company (usually a chain) manages it. This method is ideal in countries where foreigners are not allowed to buy property—a local company owns the building, but a hotel company runs the business as if it is part of a chain.

Properties should make good use of the internet and have an easily accessed website with pertinent information for prospective guests. The more knowledge the guest has about the establishment, the easier it is to make a decision. Lodging facilities must also adapt their rooms to suit the growing number of travellers with disabilities.

Hotels are classified as either economy/budget, mid-scale, upscale, or luxury. In addition to the various price ranges for accommodations, there are also motels, convention hotels, resort hotels, inns, condominiums, time-shares, dude ranches, hostels, campgrounds, and bed and breakfasts. Customers can now see a lodging's rating on how well the establishment adheres to a reduce, reuse, recycle commitment by the number of Green Keys it has been awarded. Each type of accommodation uses a different strategy for attracting guests. Location is important to determining who will stay where.

Questions

1. a) Explain the differences in the way a hotel or motel is operated based on: i) individual ownership; ii) chains; iii) franchises; iv) referral systems; and v) REITs.

   b) Which types of management are represented in your region? Provide examples.

2. Briefly describe the duties performed by three front of the house departments within a hotel and three back of the house departments.

3. Many Canadian lodging establishments have not designed their rooms to suit the growing number of travellers with disabilities.

   a) Why is this market growing?

   b) What types of adjustments should a hotel consider to make the disabled more comfortable?

4. How do the following hotel classifications determine the scope and quality of the hotel product? Back up your answer using examples.

   a) location

   b) room rate

c) purpose of visitors' trip

d) level of service

e) length of stay

5. The text discusses a wide variety of lodging facilities that might be used by a traveller. Choose five types of accommodation, and briefly describe—and explain why you would like to stay in—each one of your choices.

6. a) What does the term "highly perishable" mean in the context of tourism products? (See Chapter 3 – Understanding and marketing the unique tourism product.)

   b) How does an upscale hotel attempt to handle the highly perishable nature of tourism products?

7. Using a hotel advertisement taken from a newspaper, magazine, or hotel, show how the property has used product, price, and place in its promotion.

8. Define the following terms as they relate to the accommodations industry: *AP*, *MAP*, *EP*, *walking*, *back of the house*, *cannibalization*, *guaranteed reservation*, *time-sharing*, and *hospitality suite*.

Notes

1. Hotel Association of Canada, *Hotel Industry Fact Sheet*, March 19, 2007.

2. Ibid.

3. David W. Howell, *Passport* (Cincinnati, OH: South Western Publishing Co., 1989), p. 141.

4. *Ask Right Questions When Booking a Hotel*, www.icanonline.net.

5. *Ontario Restaurant News*, May 2002, p. 9.

6. www.executivetravelmagazine.com/page/ world's+largest+hotel.

Food and Beverage

Key terms

200 km menu
allergy awareness
bistro
buffet house
cafeteria
coffee house
commercial food service
contract caterers
contract food service
corkage fee

current trends
ethnic restaurant
destination restaurant
family-style restaurant
fast food restaurant
fine dining
haute cuisine
menu
multi-unit corporate
    restaurant

non-commercial food
    service
organically grown
    foods
pub
signature item
social caterers
specialty restaurant
theme restaurant
upselling

Learning objectives

Having read this chapter you will be able to

1. Explain briefly the history of the food service industry and its current trends.

2. Differentiate between the two major divisions of food service: commercial and non-commercial.

3. Explain the difference between the fast food and full-service dining styles.

4. Describe and identify different styles of full-service and fast food restaurants.

5. Explain the importance to the tourism sector of non-commercial food service.

6. Discuss the impact the food service industry has on tourism and the tourist.

Food means life. Without food, even the tiniest organism cannot survive. As human beings, we use food not only for survival but as part of our recreational life. Early human beings would light the fire, roast the great beast they had just killed, dance, and sing of their great fortune. We celebrate with food the birth of a child; birthdays; graduation from college/university; and marriage; finally, when we die, we hold a "wake"—a party that celebrates our life. The movies have long used food scenes to create suspense or amusement. Some use food as their main focus: *Babette's Feast, Eat Drink Man Woman, Vatel* (a glimpse into 17th century feasting), *Chocolat,* and *Sideways*, a movie that focuses not only on relationships but on the wines and wineries of California. Soap operas use food as their main background drop with many important moments taking place while actors are sitting in restaurants, bars, or cocktail lounges. Books that focus on foods and eating are highly popular and may be written by a well-known singer or movie star, a doctor, a real chef, or simply someone choosing to capitalize on this trend. These books often focus on diet, entertaining, specific foods or cultures and, sometimes, simple, old-fashioned home cooking. Actors, in particular, seem to have a strong affiliation with foods, creating their own product lines or opening restaurants. A restaurant associated with a famous person has helped develop the term "destination restaurant." A **destination restaurant** is a restaurant that people will travel a good distance out of their way to visit. Often the lure is a famous chef, a celebrity owner, or simply an outstanding location.

Windows on the World, located on the top floor of the North Tower of the World Trade Center, gained its reputation because of its dramatic view and good food. It was one of the most sought-after restaurants in New York City, and was full to capacity with patrons enjoying "breakfast with a view" on September 11, 2001. Not one customer or worker survived that catastrophe. On a lighter note, Rita MacNeil's teahouse in Nova Scotia is an example of a celebrity dining spot. It is open only during seasonal months, and lines of guests curl down the road with everyone hoping for, and often getting, a brief conversation with the famous Canadian songstress. If you are interested in visiting a destination restaurant, reservations, if available, should be made well in advance, and expect the bill to be a major expenditure. Most vacationers, however, are simply looking for good food and some local ambience with a chance to try new dishes and local products. Yes, food plays a very important part in any vacation.

The food and beverage industry is the largest of all components of tourism and one of the hardest to track for revenues, as not everyone who dines out is a tourist. NAICS reports that this industry employs over 650 000 people[1] and it is the only tourism industry that would likely survive, though in a very different state, the total collapse of the tourism sector. Due to the high labour, utility expenses, and low profit margins, new statistics indicate full-service restaurants have a 65% failure rate. This sector contains more independently owned businesses than any of the others, so if being your own boss is a goal, and you have the education and love to cook, then you may have found your niche in food and beverage.

The food and beverage industry is divided into two distinct divisions: commercial and non-commercial food service. **Commercial food service** includes restaurants and fast food outlets, private clubs, bars, and pubs. **Non-commercial food service**, often referred to as **social** and **contract caterers**, includes food and beverage services found on airlines and railways, in stadiums, museums, and department stores, and at recreational events and recreational camps. The contract catering division of food service enjoyed a growth of 6% in 2007, while commercial food services showed very little growth.[2]

Tourism accounts for about 21% of commercial food sales. The year 2006 was a good one for the industry, with sales increasing by 3% even in a slowing economy. According to the Canadian Restaurant and Foodservices Association (CRFA), the rising value of the Canadian dollar, the rising price of gas, the rising cost of food, and the loss of 4.2% of our largest foreign tourist market, the United States, will continue to hurt food and beverage sales, but experts do forecast an increase, although very small, of 0.2% in 2008. Revenues in 2009 are projected to gain slightly and should reach 0.5%.[3]

This chapter deals with both commercial food services and non-commercial food services as well as **current trends**, ownership styles, and the importance of food service in the tourism sector.

TOURISM AND THE FOOD SERVICE INDUSTRY

Other than the cost of airline tickets, the average traveller spends more money on food and beverages than on any other vacation expenditure. Determining the number of restaurants dependent on tourism dollars is difficult. In some communities, 40% of all restaurant sales are to tourists, but the total percentage in Canada and the United States is unknown. However, smart managers generally know what percentage of their customers is made up of tourists.

Restaurants can be divided into three types: tourism sales dependent, tourism profit dependent, and resident sales dependent.[4]

Tourism Sales Dependent Restaurants Tourism sales dependent restaurants earn more than half of their sales revenues by making tourists their primary market. In communities that prosper from tourism, nearly all restaurants depend on tourist sales. Ski resorts are a classic example. Without Banff National Park, Banff Township in Alberta might not exist, nor would all the restaurants located in Banff. Dependence is determined by location, not type of ownership. A McDonald's located across the street from a train depot may be tourism sales dependent, whereas another McDonald's just three miles east may be resident sales dependent.

Tourism Profit Dependent Restaurants These restaurants make 20% to 50% of their sales from tourists. Most restaurants fit into this category. Even though residents make up half or more of their market, these restaurants could not maintain profitability without tourists. Location is key. The restaurant must be close enough to a major highway, an attraction, a high-traffic shopping area, or lodging establishment to attract tourists and yet be easily accessible to the community. When a restaurant starts attracting more tourists than residents, the manager must be careful not to offend local people. Especially when tourism is seasonal, local traffic must be maintained to keep the restaurant open during slow tourism periods. During the hockey strike of 2005, restaurants near stadiums struggled to make ends meet. A few went bankrupt but clearly the loss of hockey night ticket holders was devastating to these restaurants.

Resident Sales Dependent Restaurants A restaurant that derives less than 20% of its sales from tourists is in the resident sales dependent category. These restaurants

---

How to Build a "Destination Restaurant"[5]

- create and prepare quality food using fresh local products whenever possible
- create an ambience in your establishment that is fresh, unique and always puts the guest first
- provide guests with foods and service that go way beyond their expectations
- be sure your servers are familiar with your menu and recommend your signature items to guests—those items you do best
- keep guests comfortable at all times, especially if you do not take reservations and the wait is long

- better yet, take reservations; know your turnover times; book accordingly; if you are 15 minutes late on the reservation, give the meal for "free" or some other "apology gift" like a bottle of wine
- understand that your guests come a long way to enjoy your food; train your servers to find the time to talk about local sights and events of interest; make guests feel comfortable both with you and your city/town or area

---

may profit from tourist dollars but could operate without them. In metropolitan areas, resident sales dependent restaurants can succeed easily, but in smaller communities with some tourist traffic they tend to be less successful.

Although the food and beverage industry is not totally dependent on tourist dollars, tourists are dependent on food service. Many commercial operations in the downtown core of a city rely heavily on tourist traffic for their profit margins. For tourists, one of the great pleasures is leaving behind the grunt work in their own kitchen to dine out, trying different restaurants and food service options. Depending on the method of transportation and type of accommodation, tourists will use food service establishments that best suit their needs at the time of a meal. If tourists are staying in a hotel, they can order breakfast in the room (if the hotel offers room service), they can buy muffins from the corner store and make coffee in the room (many hotels now provide coffee makers for guests' convenience), or they can eat in a coffee shop or restaurant in the hotel or local area.

Tourists need information about local eateries, but where can they find it? Many tourists choose to do research on the internet prior to arrival at a destination, so restaurateurs not advertising on the internet may be losing customers. Restaurants that have good reviews, provide a unique dining experience, or reflect the culture and cuisine of the region are most popular with tourists. Travel packages that are booked using online services such as Expedia.ca often include dining packages that are available for each destination. Each city, through its convention and visitors bureau, may provide an information booklet that includes information on local restaurants. Hotels will often leave this type of information in each room. Visitors might also ask the front-desk attendant or concierge for advice on where to eat, and many restaurants will put menus in their windows to entice customers into their establishments. Zagat.com has for some time offered a service for tourists that researches their vacation destination searching out restaurants that meet their style and pocketbook. Recently, a small company emerged in Vancouver that will also provide similar information, for the allocentric eater (the risk taker), the midcentric eater, or the psychocentric eater, who simply wants foods "just like Mom makes."

HISTORY OF THE FOOD SERVICE INDUSTRY

Food has always been a necessity, but from the early days of civilization it has also been associated with celebration, cultural rituals, and friendship. Dining out has a long history. As early as 1700 BCE, the Egyptians were meeting in public places to share simple meals of fish or fowl, olives, grains, fruits, and vegetables. However, it was the ancient Romans who were the first to create truly lavish banquets with live entertainment and portable food services for their troops, as well as fast food outlets and snack bars. In the ruins of Pompeii are the remains of tabernae (bars), thermopolia (snack bars), and popinae (the world's first fast food restaurants).[6]

By 1100 CE, the world had emerged from the Dark Ages. Travel became safer, and public entertainment and food services were again part of community living. Peasants ate simple foods made from grains, but seldom had meat, fish, or fruit to put on their tables. The diet of the aristocracy was slightly more varied and included roast meats; fresh salads made from bitter, leafy greens and onions, accompanied by a strong vinaigrette dressing; and sweet puddings. Utensils for eating were not common, even in the large courts of England and France. The fork was introduced to the French court when Catherine de Medici was betrothed to King Henry II of France in 1533. Desolate at having to leave the comforts of the Italian court for the more barbaric ways of France, she agreed to the marriage only when her father promised to send his chef and kitchen staff with her. (So it was in the roots of Italian cuisine that the world-renowned French culinary tradition arose.)

As travel increased, so did the number and the variety of food service establishments. The tradition of elegant French dining out began with the French Revolution in 1789. As the royals rode to the guillotine, their talented chefs suddenly found they were out of jobs. Many of them became entrepreneurs and opened small, fine-dining establishments that catered to the new upper class.

In the United States, the first true full-service restaurant opened in New York City in 1827. It was called Delmonico's and was operated by three brothers—John, Peter, and Lorenzo. Delmonico's closed during the depression of the 1930s. Tourists visiting New Orleans today often make a point of dining at Antoine's, which opened its doors in 1840. A restaurant with an excellent reputation for fine dining, Antoine's holds the record for the longest continuous restaurant service in North America. While many other restaurants in New Orleans were destroyed by Hurricane Katrina, Antoine's sits on higher ground in the historic district and was spared. It kept its doors open during the crisis that followed, and for 10 days fed the people working on that disaster for free.

As North Americans fell in love with the automobile and took to the roads, a new kind of restaurant emerged—the franchised fast food establishment. Companies such as A&W, Kentucky Fried Chicken, and McDonald's sprang up on many neighbourhood corners. A&W developed the "drive-up" restaurant, which allowed the occupants to stay seated while servers on roller skates took their orders and delivered the food to the car window. In the 1970s, fast food operators cashed in on their

SNAPSHOT

Portrait of a Pioneer: Georges Escoffier—"King of Chefs and Chef to Kings."

Did you know that the way we lay out our kitchens, using standardized recipes, working in professionally styled uniforms, and using menus that explain to guests what they are ordering is the legacy of just one man? His name, Georges Auguste Escoffier, is perhaps one of the most recognized names in the culinary world. Escoffier was the creator of the modern kitchen. He moved it from a medieval, cluttered collection of people cooking to space that was organized by food products and preparation methods. He recognized that cooking is really a science and so created standardized measures to ensure uniformity of his food products. His recorded recipes included descriptions of each ingredient and the method used to create the product. He laid out his kitchen keeping hot and cold preparations separate; he kept food products apart—beef, chicken, vegetables, sauces, etc., giving each product (and chef) its own work space (which of course reduced the risk of cross-contamination); he made cooks into professionals by giving them the tools they needed and responsibility for their product. Escoffier created the clean, white uniforms and it is only recently that colours have been accepted back as part of a uniform. The position of expeditor, so important to smooth service, was another Escoffier advancement. He insisted that his dining room servers carry triplicate order pads—for the kitchen, themselves, and the guest. He created the modern, classical French menu with specific courses served when the taste buds and tongue were ready for a new flavour and texture. He added descriptions on his menus so the guests might know in advance what they were ordering. No single person, at any time before or since, has had the impact that Escoffier had on the culinary world. He lived to be 91 and won many honours including France's highest, the Legion of Honour, but nothing fits his achievements better than the title he earned from his peers—that of "king of chefs."

customers' more mobile, busier lifestyles and began opening for breakfast, thereby taking advantage of a time period during which the restaurant had previously been closed. By the 1980s, competition in the fast food industry had become extremely fierce, and the era of the elegant and pricey "haute cuisine" restaurants was coming to a close. Profits in these sumptuous restaurants were undermined by the cost of highly skilled servers, equipment costs and maintenance, higher insurance premiums due to liability for tableside flambées, a faster lifestyle, and a clientele with changing needs. As a result, many haute cuisine establishments evolved into fine dining establishments, allowing these restaurateurs to maintain quality of service and eclectic, gourmet cuisine while eliminating equipment costs and lowering labour costs. While flambées are still part of elegant dining, due to liability with the open flame, fewer and fewer restaurants are offering this service style. Every major TDA has a myriad of restaurants ranging from fast food/ "mom and pop" style to fine dining, giving to our tourists tremendous choice and often memorable dining experiences.

In the late 1980s, fast food franchises began linking their product with children's television programs like *Sesame Street* or with newly released children's movies—and toys, not food, became a drawing card for kids. In the 1990s, family-style restaurants such as East Side Mario's and Red Lobster flourished as they catered to busy families and parents looking for friendly, quick service and reasonably priced food served in a more relaxing atmosphere than fast food could provide. But toys remain a big drawing card. Today much of the hype for movies for children comes from the promotion of toys available at major restaurant chains.

The food service industry in North America has experienced lower revenues as the number of business and pleasure travellers has dropped. The forecast of a decelerating economy over 2008 and 2009 will continue to challenge all restaurants, especially the fast food genre, to keep food products acceptable in the eyes of the client. Staying in business means keeping a sharp eye on controlling costs and being able to implement quick, cost-saving changes.

TRENDS IN THE FOOD AND BEVERAGE INDUSTRY

New items are always appearing on menus to intrigue and invite the curious to enter and try! It is important to understand the difference between a food fad and a food trend. Fads have a short life. They may be in the marketplace for just six months or they may last as long as several years, but fads come and go. Trends, on the other hand, stay on the menu in one form or another for a period of five to ten years; if they stay popular, they become "mainstream items," those items consistently found on menus. An example of a recent fad (circa 2000) might be the "tasting menu." Started in New York City, customers would come to a well-known restaurant. For a fixed price, the chefs would choose and present samplings of their most exotic, tempting menu items. Instead of one appetizer, the client might receive small portions of carpaccio of fresh sturgeon along with a tiny heart-shaped pastry full of wild exotic mushrooms, and a serving of Mexican shrimp with confit of tomatillo. It was an interesting concept. Fun when it first started, it was time-consuming for the kitchen to prepare, not all guests enjoyed the choices, and the cost was usually high; so, while still on menus, samplings are not as popular as they once were. Wraps, on the other hand, are examples of fads that became trends and are now mainstream items on most menus because their flavour and low carbohydrate/ caloric content have kept them popular with clients.

Concern for the environment has meant changes in the food service industry. Coffee cups are now biodegradable, as are the napkins and paper wraps. Newer products made from sugar cane are appearing as takeout/take home food containers. These new containers could replace plastic ones, reducing decomposition time from over 50 years to just under a year.[7] Knowing the clientele is even more important today. If you are located in a region that strongly supports recycling of all types, adding a few cents to the cost of a product because you are using new biodegradable containers could be a strategic marketing tool. People in other areas that are less concerned may balk at higher prices even when the item is proven to be "green."

One of the newer trends is the 200 km menu (the distance can change depending on where you are located). These "**200 km menus**" use products raised and grown in the local area. Chefs realize the value of having fresh, local food products whenever possible, and a menu item identified as "200 km" indicates that all the major ingredients have been grown within 200 km of the restaurant. Canadian seasonal changes make this more difficult in December, but it is still possible to create some dishes that meet this criteria in the dead of winter by buying from local beef, poultry and dairy farms. Many consumers today are also looking for **organically grown food**—homegrown foods raised without the use of chemicals or foreign substances. These customers prefer meat and poultry to be raised "free range" in local pastures with vegetables and fruits pesticide-free. The 200 km menu meets two criteria at once. First, it provides customers with the freshest possible foods, and second, it brings the tourist dollar directly into the hands of community farmers.

With the influx of new Canadians, more and more cultural diversity is being developed beyond the ethnic restaurant. New spices are on the market and there is a growing desire to use pure spices over the blended type found in a grocery store. These "vintage" spices are far superior with truer flavours and scents. Blending these herbs and spices with the wide variety of global cooking methods provides chefs with new ideas with which to design their **signature items**, those menu items that have been carefully created just for that particular restaurant by the chef.

Service The most important reason for consumers to return to a particular restaurant remains service. In the past there has been a large discrepancy between management's perceptions of customer satisfaction and the actual level of satisfaction customers express. This gap indicates that restaurants need to look more closely at their customers' expectations and satisfaction. Restaurant surveys and customer contact are the easiest ways to appraise customer satisfaction, but these methods require extra time and money and are often overlooked until the restaurant is desperate to find out what is wrong. By that time, it may be too late for the restaurant to recover its losses. Hiring people certified as food and beverage handlers helps to ensure the quality of table service, and giving them the ability to make quick decisions once a customer is dissatisfied allows for smooth handling of situations before they get out of control.

Takeout Delivery and takeout are an important driving force behind the restaurant industry's growth, with takeaway traffic representing nearly 50% of the industry's total. This is expected to increase by 7 to 9% over the next several years.[8] As lives become busier and more stressful, with both parents in a household often working, takeout food offers a family the chance to sit and eat together in the comfort of their home. Grocery stores are finding that less of the food dollar budgeted by a family is being spent on groceries and more is being spent on takeout foods. To recapture this lost revenue, grocery stores are offering more ready-to-eat foods. Fried or roasted chicken, chicken wings, ready-made pastas, salads, even sushi are all part of their product lines. To meet this paradoxical challenge from grocery stores, smart restaurateurs have their own menu items readily available as takeout. If it's takeout, why not delivered? Swiss Chalet has added delivery to their meal options, and providing this service for a client, while more expensive, serves a need—fast meals and no waiting in line.

Casual Dining As more people stretch their financial resources to make ends meet, the luxury of fine dining is being replaced by a more casual dining atmosphere. Plants, natural woods, and earth tones have replaced the formal look of cut glass chandeliers, crystal goblets, and sterling silverware. Restaurants are becoming smaller and more intimate. Menu choices have an ethnic flair to them, and unless a restaurant is using frozen food products, there are fewer menu items from which to choose. Value-driven consumers are setting the trend for restaurants to provide lower-priced menu items. Pasta, pizza, and bistro fare are still popular with a focus on whole grains and fresh, lower-fat sauces. Larger franchise restaurants focus on family dining with children's menus and props like crayons (with paper or a picture to colour) or a toy of some sort.

A recent fad, that likely piggy backs on the public's desire for "natural" cooking, is called *slow cooking*. This style of food preparation uses products purchased from local farmers, but it differs from the upscale restaurant as each dish is prepared using old-fashioned techniques that reflect homestyle cooking and a slower pace of life. "Personal chefs" have gained some ground as families hire a chef to come in and prepare one or two weeks's worth of frozen dinners during the course of one day. This can be expensive, and grocery stores have responded by packaging fully cooked, then chilled roasts, turkey breasts and ribs with sauces, allowing for a busy family to make hot, delicious meals in minutes. These alternatives to the frozen "TV" dinner are tasty and may leave leftovers for sandwiches the following day. In 2005, no Canadian companies were creating this type of prefabricated meals, but today, there are over 600 meal assembly facilities.[9]

Canadian restaurants face a particular financial challenge because of legislated wage levels. Canadians working in the food and beverage industry are paid better wages with better benefits than are their counterparts in the United States. In Ontario, minimum wage was increased from $8.00/hr to $10.25/hr by 2010. The wage for students aged 18 or younger, working under 28 hours per week, will increase by $2.10/hr and liquor servers's wages will go from $6.95 to $8.90 by 2010. Alberta has also raised its minimum wage and other provinces are sure to follow. Although this is good for workers, it puts additional financial strain on a fragile industry. With real profits before tax around 3% of total revenues, to survive, restaurateurs will have to be able to do more with less.[10] That means tighter control of food and labour costs, simplifying menus, being innovative in production methods, training wait staff, and providing customers with the products and services they demand.

Nutrition For more than a decade, nutrition and health have been national issues, reflecting both governmental and consumer desire to reduce intake of foods high in saturated fat and cholesterol in an effort to stem the quickly rising obesity rate among its citizens. Fat-free, carb-free, and low-fat foods dominate grocery store shelves and restaurant menus. Fast food and family restaurants have responded by using all-vegetable oil or shortening for frying, and have expanded their menus to include pita sandwiches, wraps, and interesting salads. Fast food establishments are also giving customers choices for side dishes—for example, a salad instead of fries. However, research shows that less than 5% of sales are derived from these nutritionally sound choices. Although good nutrition remains a top concern for diners, it does not entirely translate into menu choices. Many people who watch their diets at home choose to "treat themselves" when dining out. People who are dieting are likely to choose what they want and return to their diet the next day. This behaviour changes, however, if they (for example, business people) eat out on a regular basis. They tend to stick to dietary concerns.

In Ontario, a private members bill provided little concern in the industry as it passed its first reading in parliament. Bill C-283 would have forced restaurants with annual sales of over $10 million to list, alongside every menu item, its calorie count, sodium level, and sum of saturated and trans fat as a percentage of the recommended daily intake. Fortunately Bill C-283 was defeated. But other states, provinces, and cities are also looking at methods to trim down their constituents. New York City has passed legislation that bans foods containing trans fat as of July 1, 2008.[11] Trans fats are not highly prevalent in most foods, but they are in the oils used for deep frying. This is an inconvenience for New York restaurateurs (KFC has already eliminated trans fat from their chicken and Taco Bell units) but it is not a devastating decision. May other cities are watching the success New York has with similar legislation waiting to be passed. Along with this ban, however, comes an addendum that requires restaurants to label foods on menus with their caloric content, sodium, and fat content. The theory behind this legislation follows the labelling of packaged foods in a grocery store. New York politicians note that many consumers now check the information posted on foods purchased in a grocery store, helping them to make healthier choices. Oddly, this information is already available in most restaurants, and fast food units hang a large poster with this information on it, but few people make their restaurant food choices based on this information. How does a restaurant, making menu items fresh daily, ensure that the calorie or sodium content is accurate? A touch more cream to thin a sauce changes everything. With a product that comes in many different flavours, the calorie content will change. So, if ice cream is listed as a dessert, the chef must use the average calorie count based on flavours served. Bill C-283 may have been defeated in Ontario, but how long will it take before this type of control over an individual restaurant crosses the border? Be aware of what is occurring politically in your region and province!

Allergy Awareness The issue of **allergy awareness** continues to concern the food and beverage industry. The growing use of ready-to-cook and ready-to-eat foods means that, because kitchen staff do not prepare these foods from raw ingredients, they often do not know the ingredients. But consumers have begun asking for a list of the ingredients that have gone into creating the dishes they order, and they have a legal right to know. Monosodium glutamate (MSG), peanuts, nut oils, preservatives—all of these products must be identified for a customer on request, and it is the responsibility of restaurant staff to identify all ingredients in a dish, whether or not that dish has been prepared on the premises. Health Canada requires that all food items sold in Canada have a full listing of their ingredients, which makes the server's task much easier. Concern for customers may help prevent legal action—and a tragedy.

Legal Issues Legal issues have become a great concern to Canadian restaurateurs. New laws enacted over the past 20 years dealing with alcohol consumption and smoking have changed revenue generation and owner liability. Prior to current drinking-and-driving legislation, many full-service restaurants could expect beverage sales to be at least 50% of the total dinner bill. Today alcohol consumption accounts for less than 25% of the revenue generated. Restaurants and alcoholic beverage producers are addressing this problem in a number of ways. First, many restaurants now sell all their wines by the glass, allowing customers to enjoy their favourite wine with the meal. The cost of the bottle is usually recovered with just two glasses of wine. All servers are then made aware of recently opened wines so they can promote them to other customers. Second, half bottles of wine are sold whenever they are available. For champagne lovers, Piper-Heidsieck has introduced the Baby Piper, a 200 mL bottle. In British Columbia, patrons who don't finish a bottle of wine are now being permitted to carry the open, partial bottle home in a doggie bag. Ontario is allowing restaurants to purchase a licence that allows guests to provide their own bottle of wine. Restaurants can then charge a **corkage fee** for opening the bottle. Patrons in Quebec have been doing this for years.

To make up for the loss of alcohol revenues, restaurants must generate more money from the sale of food. This is difficult because the number of seats is static and cannot easily be changed. Servers are trained to use **upselling** techniques, such as suggesting a soup or salad before the meal, or a dessert with coffee. Upselling should never be aggressive, but should consist of helpful suggestions. Of concern to customers is the amount of tax added to a bill; often more than 15% of the total cheque consists of goods and services tax (GST) and provincial food and beverage taxes.

Smoking has been the biggest legal issue facing restaurants today. Restaurants and bars in British Columbia may dedicate 45% of their floor space to a *designated smoking room* (DSR). The air must be redirected outside or cleaned through a ventilation system; employee workstations may not be located in the smoking area; and workers cannot spend more than 20% of their shift in the smoking room. B.C. municipalities have the option of passing their own, stricter smoking legislation.

Ontario initially allowed restaurants and bars to build costly DSRs, and restaurants invested in these facilities in good faith that their investment dollars would eventually be retrieved. However, in the spring of 2005, the provincial government passed strict no-smoking legislation that forced public places to eliminate all smoking by May 31, 2006. This ban includes any public area, including restaurants, bars, bingo halls, and Legion halls. Alberta, Saskatchewan, Newfoundland and Labrador, PEI, and New Brunswick all either have less restrictive smoking bans or are struggling to come up with legislation that balances the needs of both residents and restaurants.

Canada is not the only country to put an end to smoking in public places. Other countries like the United States, Australia, Britain, Sweden and even France, to mention a few, all have similar legislation in place. For the French, there has been a loud outcry with no result, and Britain has currently exempted bona fide pubs.

RESTAURANT OWNERSHIP

Restaurants may be owned or managed in three ways: as independents, under a single corporate structure, or under a franchise agreement. Unlike hotels, the majority of restaurants are owned independently, but brand names from large corporations are gaining ground.

Independents

The majority of restaurants are owned by one or two individuals. These are flexible businesses that allow the owners to change menu items at will, or redecorate to tailor their establishments to the changing needs of the community. However, such independence can be risky because it requires a huge personal investment of time and money. Bankruptcy rates have fallen dramatically over the last 10 years, but opening a restaurant is still a very risky business.

Multi-Unit Corporate Restaurants

Just as in the hotel business, a single corporate headquarters often runs a series of restaurants in one city or across Canada. For a **multi-unit corporate restaurant**, corporate headquarters provides the leadership, control, and planning for each

*Quality food begins
with fresh products.
Granville Island,
near Vancouver,
provides tourists with
delicacies prepared in
front of them.*
(Photo courtesy Canadian
Tourism Commission.)

restaurant. Managers are trained by the corporation and given freedom to operate independently—as long as company policies are adhered to and the profit quota is met. Companies may own and operate restaurants that are very similar, such as Lone Star, based in Ottawa, or Boston Pizza International, a chain from Vancouver. In this case, their expansion will usually be provincial, or perhaps national. Boston Pizza does franchise.

Still other corporations own and operate restaurants that are very different. These corporations will focus on a region or a city, keeping their locus of operational control small and easily handled. An example of the latter model is SIR Corp., based in Burlington, Ontario. One of Canada's fastest-growing restaurant companies, SIR Corp. operates Jack Astor's Bar and Grill, Alice Fazooli's Italian Grill, and Canyon Creek Chophouse as their restaurants, then branches out with several specialty restaurants: Reds (an award winning bistro wine bar); Petit Four (a high-end bakery and café); the Loose Moose Tap and Grill, Four (their high-end eatery focusing on dishes all under 650 calories); and Far Niente (their award-winning, upscale restaurant).

Larger corporations will often purchase a successful corporate chain, adding a new but established product to their business. CARA Operations, which operates Swiss Chalet, Harvey's, and the Cara Airline Solutions group, have added Milestones from the Spectra Group and from Kelsey's Inc. of Oakville have added Kelsey's, Montana's, and Canadian franchise rights to the Outback. The rights to the Outback were sold back to the U.S. group, citing high food costs, and in 2004, CARA Operations bought back its shares and returned to private status.

www.cara.com

Franchises

Are you interested in owning your own restaurant but feel you need more training and experience? Then you may want to look at a franchised restaurant. Franchising is one of the major forms of ownership in the commercial food service business. Franchises may fall under a corporate chain or may be held by a parent company. The same pros and cons apply to restaurant franchising as to accommodations franchising (Chapter 5). Two important benefits are national advertising and the heft of a brand name such as McDonald's, Swiss Chalet, Boston Pizza, or Tim Hortons. Banks and lending institutions are also more willing to lend money to a brand name restaurant whose success is more likely. Other advantages include assistance in finding the right location; a proven layout and design; training procedures for all levels of staff; group purchasing power; food and beverage labour cost control systems; and managerial support. Of course there are disadvantages as well. It is costly to purchase a good franchise restaurant, and a given percentage (usually around 15% of gross revenue) must be paid yearly to the franchiser. The franchisee has no say in how the business is run and cannot adapt to serve local needs (for example, to use local food products), or to take advantage of trends in the restaurant business. For tourists, a franchised restaurant means a familiar menu and decor no matter which province, state, or country they are visiting. Brand names and familiar foods in a foreign country provide a level of homestyle comfort that is often a treat for a traveller.

THE MAJOR DIVISIONS OF THE FOOD SERVICE INDUSTRY

As discussed at the beginning of the chapter, the food service industry is split into two distinct divisions: commercial food service (78% of the market share) and non-commercial food service (22% of the market share). As mentioned previously, commercial food service comprises any food service establishment whose primary business is food and beverage service. It includes

a) full-service restaurants: licensed and unlicensed fine dining, casual, and family restaurants, including restaurant-bars

b) limited service restaurants: fast food, **cafeterias**, food courts, and takeout and delivery systems

c) drinking establishments: bars, taverns, pubs, cocktail lounges, and night-clubs (with limited food service available)

Non-commercial food service establishments are those whose primary business is something other than food and beverage service. (Branded restaurants in any of these settings are considered commercial food services.)

a) social and contract caterers: supplying food to airlines, railways, institutions, recreational facilities, and special events

b) institutional food service: hospitals, residential care facilities, schools, prisons, offices, and factories

c) retail food services: department store cafeterias and restaurants

d) other food services: stadiums, sports and private clubs, movie theatres, special events, vending machines, and other seasonal or entertainment operations.

Commercial Food Service

Commercial food service covers a wide variety of eating establishment styles.

A *full-service* restaurant allows customers to sit down and have their orders taken by a server, who then serves the meal. How their food is prepared, presented, and served depends greatly on the style of restaurant and the philosophy of the owners. Full-service restaurants comprise a range of styles, although differences may be somewhat blurred as many restaurants combine aspects of more than one style.

The Midas Touch—Fibre in Your Diet!

A new franchise is about to enter the Canadian foodservice market called the Magic Oven. This high-end takeout pizzeria boasts many qualities not found currently in most pizzas. Called "Pizzaceuticals," each pizza contains a number of antioxidants, and the crusts are made with an ancient, extremely healthy grain called "spelt." A grain grown by farmers as early as 5000 BCE, spelt is high in fibre and B-complex vitamins, contains significantly more protein than wheat, and has, of course, both simple and complex carbohydrates. Most people dealing with gluten sensitivities have been able to eat products made from spelt, allowing those who have this allergy the opportunity to enjoy a tasty pizza crust. Spelt's heavy husk allows it to be grown without the use of pesticides, also making it an organic food substance. Tony Sabherwal developed the pizzas to meet the needs of a niche market that looks for "vegan," "dairy free," or "organic"

food products, and he insists all their products be organic and locally grown. But that is not the only difference in the Magic Oven's pizza offerings: for $108 you can purchase the "uber-Sustenance" pizza, making the person you are treating feel like a king. It glitters with gold! Gold is edible, and ancients used it to cure a wide variety of medical problems including bronchitis and arthritis. Tony is not the first to revitalize interest in gold as a garnish, and you will find it in liquors, on cakes, and in marmalade.

In 2006, F. Durrer and Sons made its 125th anniversary marmalade with aged whiskey, champagne, and gold flakes, selling it in a beautiful crystal jar for just $10 000 each. It sold out quickly! But really, who buys a pizza worth $108? Fifteen-plus "uber-Sustenance pizzas" are sold weekly to corporations wishing to honour an employee with a product that is not only healthy but sparkles with the Midas touch.

Haute Cuisine This very elegant and expensive style of restaurant is noted for its opulent decor, highly trained staff, exemplary service, beautiful table settings, and exclusive clientele. The **haute cuisine** restaurant has beautiful silverware, crystal goblets, fine linen tablecloths and napkins, and fresh exotic flowers. Wait staff are exceptionally well trained and include positions such as commis (junior waiter), chef de rang (chief server), maître d' (head waiter), and sommelier (wine steward). The food is fresh, cooked daily by the chef and sous-chef, and the menu often includes signature items—dishes that have been created specifically for the restaurant. The food is frequently prepared tableside on a guéridon (cart) and may be flambéed in front of the guest by the chef de rang. The wine cellar is stocked with a wide variety of excellent vintage wines. The entire dining experience is elegant, a true adventure into the world of gastronomy. These restaurants were popular at the turn of the century, when those who dined out were wealthy. In order to survive in a very competitive world, many of these restaurants have had to reduce their costs by eliminating the finer touches, such as the sterling silver place settings and the crystal goblets; the quality of service, wine list, and foods have not been changed. The George V Hotel in Paris boasts one of the finest haute cuisine restaurants left in the world.

Fine Dining Many restaurants still provide elegant service, but have dispensed with the many levels of wait staff and the costly table settings. The food remains unique and exciting, and the staff still require a high level of skills. Few of these **fine dining**

restaurants continue to flambé food because of high liability costs. Food is prepared from fresh, raw ingredients and is "plated" in the kitchen, and great care is taken to ensure that presentation is a wonderful collage of exciting colours and tastes. These fine dining restaurants boast extensive wine cellars stocked with wine that is well chosen to suit a variety of clientele tastes and price ranges.

Dining This category includes a wide variety of dining experiences and is the largest group of full-service restaurants. Ranging from a good local eatery to the greasy spoon around the corner, this style of restaurant is distinguished from the fine dining/haute cuisine experience by its more casual approach to the guest, the menu, and the price. (Remember that all restaurateurs bring their own philosophy of food and service to the marketplace, but successful restaurateurs understand their clientele's needs and are able to fulfill expectations.)

Bistros, cafés, and trattorias show how the restaurant industry has responded to the demand for more casual dining combined with the fresh, eclectic food served by fine dining establishments. Although decor in these establishments is simple and the restaurant is usually small, the food from the kitchen may feature unusual pasta dishes, pizza from a wood-burning stove, exotic lettuces, oils and vinegars, home-made desserts, and specialty coffees. The **family-style restaurant** is often found in the suburbs or near tourist attractions. This type of restaurant designs its service to be fast, its food to be "comfortable," and its decor to be suitable to the younger diner. As customers walk through the door, they will see highchairs and booster seats along the wall. Children's menus are provided, and the decor can handle spills and messes. Servers are not required to handle complicated menu items, but they need to be friendly, fun loving, and ready to serve young customers. These restaurants attract families by using many different marketing techniques such as activities for children, a "kids eat free" policy, or family specials.

Another style of restaurant that often caters to the family market is the **specialty restaurant**. This restaurant differs from the family style because it serves one kind of food. For example, Red Lobster is known for its seafood, St. Hubert and Swiss Chalet for chicken, and Tony Roma's for ribs.

With the tremendous immigration Canada has seen over the past 40 years and the numerous cultures that have become part of the Canadian way of life, **ethnic restaurants** specializing in national dishes have sprung up across the country. French, British, and American foods have always been available in Canada, but today, customers can choose from a global marketplace of restaurants. There are three main reasons for the growing desire for foods with a foreign flair. First, Canadians are travelling to more exotic places or learning more about foreign foods by watching television. Second, the population of Canada has become more diverse, and immigrants have brought their own culinary cultures. Finally, grocery chains and frozen-food packagers are responding to these trends with sauces such as Memories of Singapore (from Loblaws), dishes like moussaka, and products such as arborio rice, fresh figs, and papaya. More Canadians are now willing to try something new in the dining experience, making ethnic restaurants a viable alternative to standard Canadian fare.

With the emergence of theme parks came **theme restaurants**. These restaurants transport a customer to a time and place, often providing entertainment before, during, and after the meal. The theme is carried through the choice of foods served and their description—with the theme often becoming more important than the food. Theme restaurants do not have to be big, but because of the expense involved in creating the theme, many are quite large. They are

Canada boasts many fine restaurants with chefs who stand on the world stage as winners of gold in a variety of gourmet eating options.
(Photo courtesy Canadian Tourism Commission.)

usually located in major cities with good tourist traffic, appealing to the conference and convention market as well as the general public. Medieval Times, located in Toronto in Exhibition Place, is a good example of a theme restaurant. This U.S.-based company opened its first restaurant in Orlando, Florida. It owns the largest breeding farm in the world, raising and training Andalusian stallions for its shows. The Toronto site was developed in 1990. During their meal, the audience watches a program that includes an illustration of how the Andalusian stallions are trained, and a spectacular drama re-creating a battle between the Knights of the Kingdom and their archrivals, the Visigoths. Servers are dressed in costumes that reflect medieval times, and the menu items are appropriately named. Medieval Times has the capacity to serve 2500 customers at a time, focusing on large groups that come to the Toronto area for conferences and conventions.

During the 1980s, North America saw the re-emergence of the **buffet house**, a concept that is centuries old. A buffet is a wide assortment of food, both hot and cold, held in a serving line. Customers help themselves to the foods they want in portions they desire. These all-you-can-eat restaurants provide a customer with some table service, such as removal of empty dishes and service of drinks, coffee, or tea. They combine the speed of a fast food restaurant with the attention of table service—a nice combination in a busy world.

Limited Service Restaurants The serving style of a **fast food restaurant** is to let the customer share the work. Once the food has been received, the customer must locate the napkins, condiments, straws, and a place to sit, and must often clean up afterwards. This serving style decreases the cost of the meal, since servers and buspeople are unnecessary. The drive-through concept has contributed to lower costs and maximized revenues by increasing the output of food without adding seating. Fast food franchises include McDonald's, Wendy's, Burger King, Kentucky Fried Chicken, Harvey's, A&W, Dairy Queen, Pizza Pizza, Taco Bell, Extreme Pita, Tim

---

How to run a successful restaurant

- Begin with a strong business plan with enough cash reserve to take you through the first few difficult years.
- Understand and implement tight cost and portion control methods, food specifications, and proper receiving and storage of food products.
- Keep labour costs in line.

- Keep up with trends and have a good vision of your customers' likes, dislikes, and needs.
- Hire and train those willing to invest time in your establishment, then treat them as well as you want them to treat your customers.
- Keep everyone's focus on quality foods and on service beyond customer expectations.

Hortons, and Made in Japan Teriyaki Experience. Fast food franchises have learned the secret of success by locating along busy highways, and near resorts, theme parks, recreation areas, and malls—locations that provide convenient stopping places for the traveller. It is very common to see several fast food restaurants located within a few blocks of one another along a major travel route, on the theory that people are more likely to stop if they see a choice of restaurants.

Not all fast food restaurants are franchised; many are independently owned. Every country around the world has its own variety of single, often mobile restaurants with fast food menus that serve products popular in their specific region. Many Canadian restaurants will serve the standard hamburger fare, but in Quebec, tourists will also want to try poutine—French fries topped with cheddar cheese curds and smothered in gravy. This dish is so popular in Quebec that some McDonald's restaurants now offer it. Many regions have developed specialty treats, although tourists are sometimes reluctant to try these new foods. In Ottawa, Hooker's Beavertails serves a must-try treat that is popular all year round, but particularly in the winter. A Beavertail is a deep-fried French pastry shaped like a beaver's tail, served with a variety of toppings such as maple syrup, cinnamon sugar, or strawberry jam. Despite the name, tourists soon give in to the desire to sample this tasty treat. In 1996, Hooker's Beavertails made the move south to Walt Disney World and can be found at the Canadian Pavilion at EPCOT.

Coffee houses are popular once again, serving coffees from faraway places such as Kenya, Jamaica, and Hawaii, and providing a full range of specialty drinks such as cappuccinos and lattes, as well as specialty teas like Japanese green. Tim Hortons, Second Cup, and Starbucks are the leaders of this trend. Coffee houses traditionally sold snacks like donuts and muffins, but due to consumer demand now serve a full meal concept adding soups, sandwiches, wraps, salads, etc.

Drinking Establishments Bars, pubs, taverns, cocktail lounges, and nightclubs comprise the final group in commercial food service. **Pubs** and *taverns* try to recreate the ambience, menu items, and types of beer and whiskey typical of an English, Irish, or Scottish bar. Prime Restaurants, based in Mississauga, has developed not

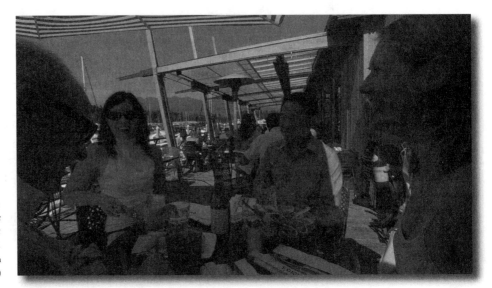

Summer, high season for tourists, makes patio dining a pleasant change.
(Photo courtesy Canadian Tourism Commission.)

only the Irish pub concept (for example, D'Arcy McGee's and Sláinte) but has also added a new concept with Esplanade Bier Markt in downtown Toronto, which boasts of having Canada's longest beer list. Cocktail lounges are often found in casinos or upscale hotels, and nightclubs bring in local and name talent for guests' entertainment pleasure.

In Practice

Divide a piece of paper into eight columns and put one of the following food service types at the top of each: independent fast food, hotel restaurants, theme restaurants, family-style, cafeteria, coffee house, specialty, and ethnic. Write the names of restaurants you have patronized in each of the appropriate categories (no more than five in a column). Compare and contrast the restaurants within each column and among columns on food quality, quantity, service, and price. Do you notice any significant trends in your data?

Non-commercial Food Service

Non-commercial food service includes any food service located in a business whose main reason for existence is not to serve food; for example, in airports and museums and at events.

Social and **contract caterers** are important to the tourism sector because they are the major suppliers to the airlines and rail systems. They also run the food service at recreational camps, in museums and at historic sites, at sports arenas like the Rogers Centre in Toronto, and at many major special events. These host venues choose not to run their own food service because they have no expertise and no desire to be in the food business. Using professional food providers relieves them of many headaches and provides their staff and customers with a better product. The airlines recognized years ago that their business was transportation, not food service. They use Canada's largest contract food service company—CARA Operations. CARA's in-flight kitchens provide on-board food and beverage service for airlines that use Canadian airports.

Train, bus, and air terminals offer meals to their travellers either through contract services or by leasing space to franchises. It is becoming more common for terminals to use nationally known restaurants. CARA Operations and McDonald's are just a few of the big corporations that understand the valuable link between food service and transportation. Restaurants in a terminal have a valuable captive audience. The restaurant's brand name offers travellers comfort from the stress of travel. The terminal avoids worries about feeding the traveller, yet still makes money from the rented space. It seems to be a win-win situation for everyone!

The Compass Group is the world's largest food service contractor and recently purchased CARA's Health Services Division. It is best known for its ability to handle food service for large events, such as the 2002 Winter Olympics in Salt Lake City and World Youth Day, July 2002. Compass served more than 3.5 million meals at each event, facing the challenging logistics of making, holding, and serving such quantities safely and quickly at a reasonable price. World Youth Day was held during one of Toronto's hottest summers on record, and 700 Compass managers along with 5000 volunteers served 250 000 young pilgrims three meals a day. Canada's next biggest challenge in this area of food service is the Winter Olympics of 2010 which will be operated by CARA Operations.

www.restaurant.org

Institutional food services are not directly tied to tourism as a sector, but the industry is growing and it happily embraces those students who have hospitality training. Hospitals, retirement homes, schools, and offices make good use of students with hospitality and culinary training, and the working conditions, including the hours, are very different from commercial food service.

Retail food service is often found in department stores. While Zellers has simple cafeteria-style food, eating at Holt Renfrew can be an elegant experience. Tourists out for a day of shopping often choose to eat where they shop.

Non-commercial food services also include private clubs, festivals and other seasonal events, and stadiums. Scotiabank Place in Ottawa is home to the NHL's Ottawa Senators, and during "dollar dog hockey night," more than 15 000 hotdogs are sold in just three hours. As well as fast food outlets, Scotiabank Place has a fine dining restaurant called the Club Scotiabank, and casual dining experiences like Frank Finnegan's and Marshy's. In addition, for $45, guests can book a seat in the Penalty Box, watch the hockey game, and enjoy an all-you-can-eat sandwich buffet.

SNAPSHOT

In Canada, **contract food service** has not yet reached the size and scope of its U.S. counterpart. However, some colleges and universities that offer "board plans" have moved to professional food providers, such as ARAMARK, Sodexo, Compass Group, and CARA. With changing demographics, such as an increase in the number of seniors looking for upscale retirement homes, many new opportunities will arise in this area of food service.

Schools often contract out their food service, and some, like the University of Alberta, choose well-known fast food chains like Pizza Pizza, Tim Hortons, and Taco Bell.
(Photo: Paula Kerr.)

MARKETING THE RESTAURANT BUSINESS

Branding has become the most important aspect for restaurant success in the past few years. How does a single-unit, no-name restaurant survive in the highly competitive marketplace of food and beverage? Many do not, and research shows that 80% of owner-operated businesses go bankrupt in their first five years of operation. Yet the single-unit restaurant continues to exist, and new establishments quickly open in the spaces vacated by failed ventures. The challenge of the restaurant business is often underestimated by new owners, but the dream of success drives them to try to succeed where others have failed.

How does a restaurant sell the products it creates? With its most effective in-house marketing and sales tool—the **menu**. The menu defines a restaurant and how it will satisfy a customer's needs. Food descriptions must be well written and well designed to intrigue and tantalize customers into ordering that special soup, salad, or dessert—and to come back again to try a different entrée. Pricing should reflect the quality and value of the selections, as well as the customer's pocketbook. Menus may rely on colour, design, material, or shape to create uniqueness. The menu should be displayed so that passing pedestrians can easily read it and be enticed into stopping to dine.

Restaurants advertise and promote their business in a variety of ways, including through local radio stations and newspapers. But for a restaurant, the best advertising is word of mouth, and with the internet so accessible, word of mouth from a wide variety of customers can make or break your publicizing campaign. It costs nothing and says a lot—hopefully, what you do, you do well.

Learning how to partner with the community and with other tourism products is becoming more important in today's competitive world. Local restaurants

www.crfa.ca

will sponsor sports teams and take part in community activities such as food drives and charity fundraisers. Restaurants located in the tourist area of town often partner with accommodations, tourist attractions, festivals, or events, join the convention and visitors bureau, and ensure the restaurant is listed in its local information guide. Providing "order-in" service for a hotel with limited food services adds value to the hotel product and brings more customers to the partnering restaurant. Linking the restaurant product with tour operators reaches an additional source of revenue, as does becoming an active participant in a festival or special event and setting up food booths for the event. This kind of strategy allows both the local resident and the tourist to taste your product and experience your hospitality.

Understanding tourism and the needs of the tourist can provide opportunities that other establishments miss, and can mean that a restaurant is one of the 20% that learn how to thrive in this highly competitive industry.

In Practice

Flip through any edition of your local newspaper and list the various promotional techniques used by restaurants. What types of restaurants are advertising? How are they drawing the value-driven customer? What restaurants are not advertising? Do you believe they are doing better, worse, or the same as those that advertise? In your experience, which restaurant in your community has best responded to current trends in dining out?

Getting the Most from the Tourism Sector

Have you given any thought to how your establishment might encourage visitors to drop in for lunch or supper? According to surveys, people are more likely to treat themselves to a mid-scale or upscale restaurant when on vacation.

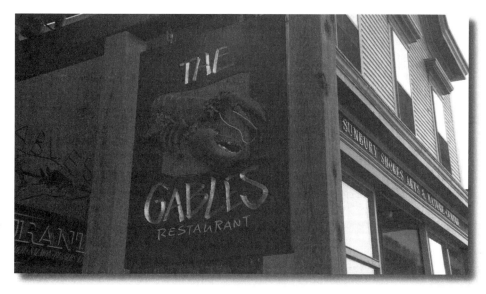

Your town does not have to be big to have fine dining available for the tourist. St. Andrews, New Brunswick, hosts a variety of eating options.
(Photo courtesy Canadian Tourism Commission.)

Fourteen percent of all vacationers choose full-service, fine dining restaurants, 32% choose mid-scale restaurants, and 53% eat at fast food establishments. Compare that to resident choices: 8% of local clientele choose fine dining establishments, 23% opt for family-style/mid-scale restaurants, and 69% choose fast food. Vacationers tend to choose fast food for breakfast and lunch to get a quick start on the day's activities. At night they are ready to relax and enjoy their meal and tend to choose a full-service restaurant. Some restaurateurs have discovered the advantages of group tours. Many tours offer meal services, and tour operators are willing to schedule dinner a little earlier than normal if the price is right. Partnering with tour operators by providing quality food and service at a discounted price may mean additional revenue during the early, slower dining period. Since the meal is usually a set menu and the number of

CASE STUDY

Making Ends Meet

When Dan was hired by the owner of a small bistro, the job sounded like a good deal. Along with his salary as manager, he would receive a 20% incentive pay bonus. Dan was good at inventory control and he worked well with people. He made sure that waste was kept to a minimum, and after the first year, he had received the bonus pay every single month. But the amount kept getting smaller as prices on little things began to increase. The import tax increased on the unique products the bistro bought from Caribbean suppliers. Even the cost of rice had risen. Dan convinced his owners to buy a proofing oven, and he began making his own bread and hamburger buns. To the owner's satisfaction, the fresh quality of these products brought in new customers and increased sales. Then the value of the loonie began to rise against the U.S. dollar, fuel prices doubled, and the cost of food increased again. For two months Dan struggled to keep within the budget. His bonus pay disappeared. Finally, he made a decision. He chose three items listed on the menu for consideration: a 1 1/4-lb. lobster that sold for $39, the 6-oz. hamburger that began at $8, and the 16-oz. sirloin steak which sold for $24. Dan adjusted these products thusly: the lobster went to a pound, the burger dropped to 5 ounces, and the sirloin dropped to 14 ounces. He did not reflect these minor changes on the menu. As he expected, his bonus pay was restored and no one was the wiser!

1. What caused Dan's problems?
2. Which of the two solutions Dan came up with is ethical? Why?
3. "No one was the wiser"—what emotions and thoughts might the owner have when he learns the truth? the customer?
4. If you were the owner, how would you handle this problem? What would be the positive and negative impacts the other staff might feel? the customers?

guests is known in advance, profit margins should be good. As we enter the next decade, with a growing boomer market, partnering with other tourism businesses may mean the difference between success and failure for the independent restaurateur.

In Practice

Identify 12 restaurants in your community and classify them as tourism sales dependent, tourism profit dependent, or resident sales dependent. If possible, talk to some of the restaurant managers to confirm your guess. Next, identify which factor discussed in the previous section has the greatest effect on the sales status of the restaurants.

Summary

The food and beverage industry is the largest of all eight tourism components. It has two divisions: commercial and non-commercial food service. Commercial food service is further divided into two distinct categories: full-service and fast food. Restaurants can be owned by an individual, as part of a multi-unit corporate group, or as a franchise. There are many different kinds of restaurants available to the public, each serving a different need. Non-commercial food service is found in establishments whose primary purpose is not the service of food. Contract food services are found in museums, sports arenas, schools, hospitals and retirement homes, at festivals and special events, and within the transportation system. Non-commercial food service is growing fast. Canada's largest contract food server is CARA Operations.

Trends and concerns in the industry include the 2 km menu, use of organic foods, quality of service, fast food and takeout, nutrition, concern for the environment, allergy awareness, and legislation affecting alcohol consumption and smoking.

Restaurant advertising and promotion entice the local crowd to eat in the restaurant. Public relations promotions tend to produce more loyal local traffic than any other type of promotion. Unless the tourist is camping or staying at the home of friends or relatives, dining out is part of the vacation experience. Breakfast and lunch are more likely to be eaten at a fast food restaurant, whereas the evening meal, with time to relax, is spent at a mid-scale or upscale restaurant. Restaurants that depend on tourist dollars for their existence, such as lodging restaurants, are tourism sales dependent. Restaurants that are tourism profit dependent need both the tourist dollar and the local dollar to maintain profits. Most restaurants, however, depend on local residents, and many restaurateurs miss the opportunity to appeal to visitors who are looking for good places to eat. Tourism is a financial boost for the food service industry that has often been overlooked.

Questions

1. Restaurants, like hotels, may be owned and operated in several different ways. Briefly explain the differences between and the pros and cons of owning i) an independent restaurant unit; ii) a multi-unit restaurant chain; and iii) a franchise.

2. Commercial restaurants are categorized by level of service, style of the restaurant, and menu. Briefly describe eight different types of restaurants found in your area and give at least two examples of each.

3. a) Looking over the trends in food service, list them in the order of importance you feel is most appropriate and provide a brief explanation of each.

   b) Justify your ranking of the top three trends and the bottom trend on your list.

   c) Which of these trends do you feel is most prominent in the industry today? Why?

4. a) Agree or disagree with the statement "Non-commercial food services will continue to play an increasing role in the tourism sector." Support your answer with examples.

   b) If you were to choose contract food services as your career, design your career ladder and discuss the benefits you would enjoy working in this industry.

5. Differentiate between a tourism sales dependent restaurant, a tourism profit dependent restaurant, and a resident sales dependent restaurant, and provide an example of each from your area.

6. Define the following terms as they relate to the food and beverage industry: *200 km menu. organically grown food, menu, bistro, contract and commercial food services.*

Notes

1. *Year-in-review 2006 facts & figures,* www.canada.travel/research.

2. www.crfa.ca/research.

3. Ibid.

4. Uel Blank, *The Community Tourism Industry Imperative* (State College, PA: Venture Publishing, 1989), p. 17.

5. Eric Hahn, "What makes a destination restaurant," *Chef 2 Chef News Desk*, no date, http://chef2chef.net/news/foodservice/ Editorial-Chefs_Corner/What_Makes_A_Destination_Restaurant.htm.

6. Harold McGee, *On Food and Cooking* (New York: Collier Macmillan, 1984), p. 131.

7. *New York Times*, September 12, 2001, p. 4.

8. *New York Times*, September 12, 2001, p. 1.

9. www.crfa.ca/issues.

10. *Ontario Restaurant News*, May 2002, p. 9.

11. www.yaleruddcenter.org, May 24, 2008.

Attractions

Key terms

amusement park
aquarium
art museum
casino gambling
children's museum
heritage or cultural
  tourism

historic site
historical museum
living history museum
mega-mall
museums
oceanarium
parimutuel gambling

scientific museum
site-specific
theme park
UNESCO World
  Heritage Site

Learning objectives

Having read this chapter you will be able to

1. Define the scope and variety of tourist attractions.

2. Discuss UNESCO's criteria for designating World Heritage Sites, using Canadian examples.

3. Discuss how public, private, and non-profit attractions differ.

4. Provide examples of public attractions and compare them with private or commercial attractions.

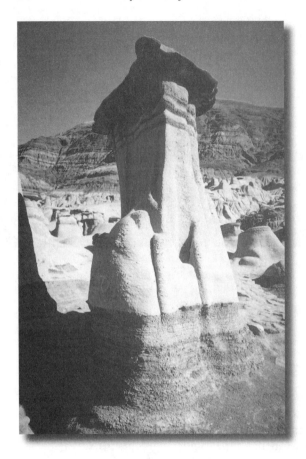

Visitors from across Canada and around the world come to Drumheller, Alberta, to visit the Royal Tyrrell Museum, take day trips to dig for dinosaur bones, and gaze at nature's spectacle, the hoodoos.
(Photo: Tom Hadley.)

When you think of a particular country, what is the first vision that comes to mind? A building? A mountain or beach? A historical encounter? If you are like most people, there will likely be at least one specific attraction that comes to mind. If your interest in that attraction is high enough, you will add the country to a list of destinations you would like to visit. Choosing where to spend your vacation depends on many things, but the entertainment value of a destination is critical in the decision-making process. Ask foreigners what picture the country "Canada" brings to mind, and their answer usually has to do with our spectacular landscapes or our weather—snow! They are right. Much of Canada's attraction for tourists does lie in its natural resources (mountains, lakes, rivers, oceans, and forests and wildlife), but tourism also depends on artificial attractions that have been created to entertain and educate visitors and residents alike. If we look at tourism as a single platform upon which to build an industry, the first three supports would be transportation, accommodations, and food services. A traveller must have all three to survive. The fourth support would be entertainment.

Chapters 7–9 consider the entertaining of our guests—or, if you prefer, the main reason people choose to travel in the first place. These industries generated an overall income of $16.2 billion in 2006 for the tourism sector.[1]

When determining our gross domestic product in tourism, NAICS bundles three activities into one grouping called "entertainment." In fact, under this heading there are three separate and equally important areas of tourist activity: attractions, events, and adventure tourism/outdoor recreation. For a clearer understanding of the components, they are best studied separately because each component is very different, attracting different target markets. *Attractions*, the first component, consists of permanent sites/facilities that are always available to a tourist. In the middle of January, when most tourists head to sunnier climates, tourists can come and enjoy the Museum of Civilization in Ottawa, or shop at the West Edmonton Mall, or visit the Vancouver Aquarium. One of the values of permanent facilities is that tourists do not have to book vacations around specific times. In fact, many people prefer to see the Eiffel Tower in October when the weather is still good but the hordes of tourists in Paris have gone home. *Events*, on the other hand, are created by a destination in order to attract specific target markets at specific times. Every summer Toronto hosts Caribana, the largest festival of its kind. In its 41st year, this festival attracts those who wish to enjoy "island heritage" without leaving Canada. It is held in July and lasts for only three days. *Adventure tourism and outdoor recreation* provide a totally different style of vacation. These tourists want to be physically active, enjoying the great Canadian outdoors. They would be thoroughly dissatisfied with a vacation that focused strictly on attractions and events.

The large grouping of attractions may be further subdivided into *natural attractions*, *cultural attractions*, and *attractions that entertain*. No matter the type of attraction, there are some important criteria to include when designing (or redesigning) an attraction:

- **Determining the sustainability of the attraction.** How many people can you bring through on a daily/yearly basis without doing irreparable damage to the area? At what point does the number of visitors simply overwhelm the facility, making it less enjoyable?

- **Identifying the target markets.** Facilities to accommodate visitors must reflect the needs and expectations of visitors. Are those with disabilities considered when the site is designed? When dealing with foreign visitors it is important to ensure that rest facilities, food service, and welcoming facilities can meet the differing needs. In addition, tourists often look for a souvenir of their visit, and setting up a gift shop may benefit both the attraction and the visitor. The items you choose to sell must also reflect your market—people are willing to pay a great deal more when choosing a souvenir if the item is authentic and handmade.

- **Determining visitor flow patterns.** No matter the size of the attraction, determining where patrons enter and pay (if applicable), identifying the areas where they tend to spend more time, and providing good signage to guide people through your site are extremely important. Strategically placed rest stations and easy access to parking should be provided. Also important are signs on local streets showing how to reach the facility. If parking is set at a distance from the site, what is the system for transporting people to the attraction? Buses are an easy answer, but concern for the environment should be part of the final decision.

- **Training of workers and management of the facility.** Whether your attraction is natural or cultural in nature, do you use workers who have an understanding of the site and its background? Are your workers sensitive to the differing needs of the ethnicities who visit? How does management track current and future success?

CANADA'S ATTRACTIONS

Natural attractions depend solely on what the country's landscape offers to the visitor. In Canada, people look to our glorious mountains, oceans, rivers, miles of untouched wilderness, and animals that are found in our national and provincial parks and Crown land. While a tourist would not look forward to meeting a grizzly bear face to face, watching and photographing a herd of deer on the mountain slopes or capturing the splash of a killer whale's tail from the safety of a boat are considered part of Canada's attractions. So it is of utmost importance that areas being developed recognize this and build toward sustaining the natural environment.

Forty years ago, many prospective visitors viewed the history of Canada, at merely 400 years old, as new, and felt that, compared to the incredible sites in ancient Orient or Europe, we had little culture to promote. Now the world is taking notice of the original in habitants of this country, our First Nations and Inuit people. This has helped promote a keen interest in their arts, history, and religions. Particularly interested in our Aboriginal cultures are those from Pacific Rim countries, areas from which it is believed First Nations may have migrated.

In many cases, attractions are the reason people travel. Attractions may be the primary destination or only one component of a larger vacation. The attractions a country has to offer, however, provide increased incentives for foreign travellers to visit.

OWNERSHIP

Theme parks, museums, zoos, casinos, and Broadway-style theatres are only a few of the different types of attractions found around the world. Attractions come in so many shapes, sizes, and types of ownership that throwing them all into a single category called "attractions" seems incongruous. Comparing Walt Disney World to Niagara Falls, or the CN Tower to the Mayan ruins of Mexico, is inappropriate, yet each is classified as an attraction.

Attractions differ not only in type but also in ownership; they may be privately owned and operated, non-profit, or publicly owned. Table 7.1 identifies the type of ownership, sources of funding, and the different types of attractions found in each category.

www.attractionscanada. com

In Practice

In groups of 5–10, take 10 minutes to brainstorm sites and attractions you have visited or have heard about in Canada. List every suggestion. Then review your list, eliminating the sites you think are least attractive to visitors, until you have your own list of top 10 sites. Write your list on a large sheet of paper supplied by your instructor and post it in the classroom. Review your classmates' lists. Have you chosen any similar sites? Using these lists, create a final list with your class's idea of Canada's top 10 sites. What criteria do you think were most commonly used to choose these sites? What new attraction do you think will be popular in 10 years?

TABLE 7.1   *Sources of Funding in the Attractions Industry*

	Public	*Non-profit*	*Private*
Funding	Taxes	Admission Fees	Admission Fees
	Admission Fees	Donations	Food & Beverage
	Donations	Grants	Merchandise
	Grants	Memberships	Entertainment
			Parking
Types	Museums	Museums	Theme Parks
	Zoos/Aquariums	Zoos/Aquariums	Amusement Parks
	Historic Sites	Historic Sites	Carnivals/Circuses
	Casinos		Theatres
			Shopping Malls

CULTURAL ATTRACTIONS: PUBLIC AND NON-PROFIT

As provincial and federal governments cut budgets, money for the upkeep and enhancement of public and non-profit attractions has dwindled. Many Canadians fear that funding cuts will undermine institutions that support heritage, culture, and the arts.

Governments own and operate public attractions. Taxes are often the prime source of funding; however, government cutbacks have forced public institutions to become more creative in raising funds. In addition, some taxpayers are less tolerant of the idea of fully supporting a public attraction. As a result, public attractions are now charging entrance fees and are bringing in exciting special events or shows to boost ticket sales and provide added revenues. Additional money is made from parking fees and the sale of souvenirs and gifts.

Many attractions raise additional revenue through their food and beverage service. After hours, space may be rented for private functions. For example, the Vancouver Aquarium provides a fascinating setting for people attending a conference in the city. It provides guests with the opportunity to view the attraction at their leisure and to enjoy a meal away from the hotel setting.

Non-profit attractions are just that—they are not in the business of making a profit, and any revenue they earn is funnelled back into the attraction. Some began as public attractions and are no longer funded by government. The Log Farm in the Ottawa region is a perfect example. One of the area's earliest farms, it was used as a living history site, showing tourists and local residents the farming methods of the early 19th century. When the government of Canada ended its funding, a group of concerned citizens took over the operation. It now exists on revenue received from grants, donations, membership fees, and special events such as the sugaring festival. In the early spring, visitors come to watch maple syrup being made in huge cauldrons. Volunteers boil the maple sap to make fresh syrup and maple taffy, which is sold to the public.

The Diefenbunker in Carp, Ontario, is another example of how non-profit attractions begin. Between 1959 and 1961, at the height of the Cold War, this huge four-storey bunker was built into the Carp Escarpment to protect government officials in the event of nuclear war. In 1994, the bunker was abandoned. It was later purchased by the citizens of the town of Carp. Prior to sealing its entrance forever, final tours for interested area residents were conducted and it became apparent that this unique site provided a glimpse into the Cold War era in Canada. The bunker has been restored and operates as the only Cold War museum of its kind in the world. Funding comes from admissions, grants provided by the Ontario government and the Regional Municipality of Ottawa-Carleton, as well as donations.

Some non-profit attractions are started by wealthy philanthropists who amass a collection on the subject of their passion (for example, art or history) and who then provide funds to house and maintain the collection.

Admission fees and the sale of souvenir items often bring in revenue for non-profit attractions. Additional revenues are generated from the sale of memberships, donation boxes at the entrance, benefit dinners, and special events. What benefits would a membership in a non-profit organization bring? Members receive monthly newsletters, get free admissions, and have the satisfaction of knowing they are contributing to a cause in which they believe. It is sometimes hard to distinguish between a public and non-profit attraction but, in the end, the tourist doesn't care as long as the staff is knowledgeable and the experience enjoyable.

Museums

Visiting museums is an important part of many itineraries and is sometimes the main focus of a trip. A **museum** can display just about anything, from trains and motorcycles to books and letters. Museums are historical, scientific, or artistic. Although they are usually sponsored by government or non-profit organizations, some are commercial for-profit enterprises, and a rare few are privately owned.

Most museums have a permanent area on the property that displays the same exhibit at all times. Another section usually houses a succession of travelling shows. These special events keep local people coming to the museum, so changes in artists, new historical displays, or recent scientific discoveries are promoted to local residents as well as tourists.

A museum has a director, various assistants, and volunteers, depending on the size of the museum. Volunteers often outnumber paid staff. The director is responsible for searching for new displays, scheduling travelling shows, obtaining permanent displays for the museum, and completing paperwork such as budgeting and payroll. A board of directors is responsible for hiring and guiding the director, and is often elected from the membership of the museum. The board and the director decide on themes for the upcoming year, special events, and marketing ideas.

Art galleries and museums were once primarily cultural centres in metropolitan areas, where people of sophisticated tastes gathered to express their opinions about the works of a particular artist. Canadians have long had the opportunity to visit both nationally and provincially funded art museums. **Art museums** can be found in communities throughout North America. Young artists usually get their start by displaying their work in smaller galleries, which in turn support the local art museum. Support is garnered by displaying and advertising the work of local artists. By starting with the young, the art museum is able to maintain citizens' lifelong support. The artist may also autograph a limited number of prints during a showing, giving tourists and locals alike an opportunity to rub elbows with the artist. Open houses, dignitary social hours, and other small events are held to reach more people and to show off what the museum has to offer. Art museums both large and small strive for variety, providing all types of artwork, including sculptures, oils, watercolours, and carvings.

www.national.gallery.ca

Historical museums are more likely than art or scientific museums to be in small communities. These museums usually present relics, along with a written explanation of the pieces, and sometimes struggle to maintain an uncluttered look as they receive more and more items that donors expect to see displayed.

Living history, which uses people in period costumes to portray historical figures and times, is a popular trend for historical museums. **Living history museums** are popular among all age groups. Upper Canada Village, located just outside Morrisburg, Ontario, and Fortress Louisbourg in Cape Breton, Nova Scotia, provide visitors with an early Canadian experience. Living history museums are successful because they are both fun and educational; they also provide jobs to local people and bring tourist dollars into the area.

Modern museums have replaced the old "do not touch" mentality with displays that can be touched, eliminating the need to keep young hands off artifacts like a horseless carriage or an old-time rocking horse. Video presentations and interactive computers are replacing the more expensive museum interpreters and engaging the user with the communication so vital in today's educational style. The designers of the new Canadian War Museum, which opened in Ottawa in May 2005, used this strategy to create a "real life" experience for all visitors. The museum is laid out in historical avenues so that visitors may choose to know more about the War of 1812, or move to the corridor that explains the events of World War I. The Canadian War Museum does not glorify war, but instead illustrates its dreadful conditions and pays homage to its casualties. Throughout the museum, various interactive activities bring war to life for visitors by allowing them to hear the control tower clear a bomber heading to Germany, try on the helmet worn by soldiers on the ground, or move into a dark, smelly trench like the soldiers of WWI used. In the trench, visitors listen to the silence, and hear the "soldier" next to them whisper, "Here they come."[2] The night sky then lights up, the platform shakes with the explosions, and gunfire is heard all around. Intermingled with these sounds are the cries of frightened and wounded soldiers. Providing a balance of "real life" and simulated experience is vital to the overall mission of educating the visitor.

Perhaps the most memorable element of the new museum is the Memorial Hall, which houses the headstone of the tomb of the Unknown Soldier from World War I. Light from a single window reaches the headstone only once a year—on November 11 at 11:00 a.m. In its first 30 days of operation, the new Canadian War Museum attracted more visitors than the old war museum attracted during an entire year.

With environmental concerns in mind, the designers of this museum made good use of its location. From a distance, the museum almost melts into the landscape with its "green roof," which is planted with native grasses. A green roof helps insulate the museum from both cold and hot weather. The Ottawa River, which

One of Canada's finest, the Royal B.C. Museum in Victoria is noted for its First Nations displays and its focus on the environmental issues facing Canada.
(Photo courtesy Canadian Tourism Commission.)

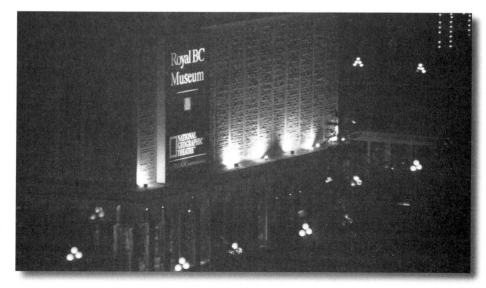

flows past the building, provides water for the modern cooling system. With research and innovation, museum designers have created a unique Canadian museum.[3] For their next phase of updating, it would serve the museum well to include better signage to the museum and its parking lot. It can be surprising how the clarity of directions can affect a visitor's impression of a site.

Scientific museums showcase items ranging from dinosaur bones to spaceships. These museums tend to show a process, whether it is the existence and extinction of dinosaurs as at the Royal Tyrrell Museum in Drumheller, Alberta, or the history of the space age as at the Kennedy Space Center in Florida. The Royal Tyrrell Museum is located near Dinosaur Provincial Park, one of the world's most extensive dinosaur graveyards. Tourists from all over the world visit the museum, which houses one of the world's largest collections of dinosaur bones. Climbing onto the back of a *Tyrannosaurus rex* could be the highlight of a child's visit to the museum. Interested tourists may also book a daylong tour to help search for dinosaur bones.

One of Canada's most respected museums, the Royal British Columbia Museum, is located in Victoria, British Columbia. It is typical of a large museum in that it blends both science and art; the museum houses the best collection of totem poles and Aboriginal art in North America. One floor is dedicated to dioramas of West Coast forests and seashores, and another floor presents the human history of the province. The Royal B.C. Museum is also noted for its programs on ecology.

www.royalbcmuseum.
bc.ca

Many scientific museums, such as the Royal Tyrrell Museum, are **site-specific**—that is, they are located where the scientific event took place. Small communities that claim a scientific history can easily create a museum in honour of the person, animal, or event. The latest trend in scientific museums is the **children's museum**, which allows young children to experiment with various scientific discoveries. These scientific museums, such as the Ontario Science Centre in Toronto, provide hands-on experience for visitors; it is impossible to simply stroll through without getting involved. As in a living history museum, visitors are encouraged to learn while having fun.

Overall, museums endeavour to involve the young, understanding that if youngsters become interested, the museum will have their support for life. Museums are becoming more family oriented and more visible in community events and tourist advertisements for the area. In the off-season, museums become classrooms. Local support is increased through school events at the museum—a smart use for a tourist attraction.

Historic Sites

Historic sites are located in every country that has taken the initiative to commemorate them, and Canada has thousands of special interest sites. Some are commemorated with just a marker that explains the historic importance of the site, but many have interpretive centres or small museums. The United Nations Educational, Scientific, and Cultural Organization (UNESCO) has placed several of Canada's national parks and historic sites on their list of World Heritage Sites in recognition of the outstanding universal value of the area. Nominees for UNESCO heritage-site designation are carefully reviewed by an international panel before being given this designation (see Table 7.2). L'Anse aux Meadows, on the northwestern tip of Newfoundland, is a **UNESCO World Heritage Site**

TABLE 7.2   *Canada World Heritage Sites*

Name	Province/Territory	Year Designated
Nahanni National Park Reserve	Northwest Territories	1978
L'Anse aux Meadows Archeological Site	Newfoundland and Labrador	1978
Kluane National Park • Wrangell—St Elias • Glacier Bay/Tatshenshini-Alsek Park	Canada & USA	1979 added in 1994
Dinosaur Provincial Park	Alberta	1979
Head-Smashed-In Buffalo Jump	Alberta	1982
SGaang Gwaii	British Columbia	1981
Wood Buffalo National Park	Alberta/Northwest Territories	1983
Canadian Rocky Mountain Parks • Banff National Park • Jasper National Park • Yoho National Park • Mount Robson Provincial Park • Mount Assiniboine Provincial Park • Hamber Provincial Park	Alberta/British Columbia	1984 and 1990
The Historic District of Old Québec • Fortifications of Quebec • Artillery Park	Quebec	1985
Gros Morne National Park	Newfoundland	1987
Waterton Glacier International Peace Park	Canada & USA	1995
Old Town Lunenburg	Nova Scotia	1995
Miguasha National Park	Quebec	1999
Rideau Canal	Ontario	2007
Joggins Fossil Cliffs	Nova Scotia	2008

Source: Courtesy of Parks Canada.

that commemorates the arrival of the first Europeans in North America a thousand years ago. This site is the only authenticated Norse settlement in North America. Nearby at L'Anse-Amour, tourists visit the 7500-year-old burial mound of the first residents of Newfoundland and Labrador, the Maritime Archaic people.

Prince Edward Island's Province House is considered the birthplace of Confederation. The first meeting to discuss federal union was held here in 1864. Several rooms, including the Confederation Room, have been restored to their 19th-century appearance. This building also houses the provincial legislature. In New Brunswick, tourists may visit the Acadian Historical Village, which chronicles the Acadians' struggle for survival after their expulsion from Nova Scotia in 1755. In Nova Scotia, the town of Lunenburg, which was recently declared a UNESCO World Heritage Site, can trace its ancestry back to 1753, when the first settlers arrived. Lunenburg is famous for its shipbuilding and, in particular, for the *Bluenose*, the sailing ship that was champion of the seas from 1921 to 1946.

Quebec City is Canada's oldest city. The original section is walled, with narrow cobblestone streets and ancient greystone houses, churches, and the old stone fort, still complete with its massive gates and cannons. Montreal, unlike Quebec City, was first established as a mission whose goal was to convert the Iroquois to Christianity. It is not surprising that Montreal has been known for its magnificent churches. Many tourists walk up Mont-Royal, following the path to the summit to see the modern cross, placed on the spot where Maisonneuve placed a cross in 1643.

In Manitoba, tourists visit the site of the last rebellion in Canada, led by Louis Riel and his band of Métis. In Saskatchewan, which has more museums per capita than any other province, the history of Canada's red-coated Royal Canadian Mounted Police comes alive at training headquarters. Alberta is home to another World Heritage Site, Head-Smashed-In Buffalo Jump, where Aboriginal tribes of the Northwest killed buffalo by driving them off high cliffs.

The Aboriginal people of British Columbia, working with cultural ecologists, have reconstructed much of their history. Both the Haida and Gitksan peoples are famous for their arts and crafts, especially their magnificent totem poles. The villages of Kitwanga and Kitwancool have some of the finest totem stands in North America.[4] 'Ksan, a Gitksan village designed to teach its history to visitors, has replicas of ancient cedar log houses and a salmon smokehouse. Tourists can watch Gitksan carve their dugout canoes, or may be guided around the museum by Gitksan women who vividly describe their ancient culture. The Frog House of the Stone Age presents Gitksan life before the arrival of Europeans, and presentations of "Breath of our Grandfathers" illustrate the songs and dances of the Gitksan people.

Tourists who visit Alberta make it a point to visit the world's largest mall, West Ed, with its Fantasy hotel, wave pool, ice rink, and fun park.
(Photo courtesy Canadian Tourism Commission.)

Heritage Tourism

Heritage tourism is to a culture what ecotourism is to nature. Prominent tourism specialists argue that ecology and culture are so intertwined that the term "cultural ecotourism" should be used instead. The World Tourism Organization defines **heritage** (sometimes called **cultural**) **tourism** as "immersion in the natural history, human heritage, arts, philosophy, and institutions of another region or country."[5] Heritage is our past—what we have received from our ancestors and what we pass on to future generations. By showing people how and why cultures differ, heritage tourism becomes a strong link to world peace, teaching the value of art, traditions, culture, and history. Because both ecotourism and heritage tourism are part of a learning process, they require experienced, knowledgeable guides. The number of visitors and guides involved in these activities continues to grow.

According to Statistics Canada, typical heritage tourists are between the ages of 45 and 64; they are better educated and have higher incomes than the average visitor. They are also willing to spend more money on their vacations than the average tourist. It is estimated that 40% of the overseas market, 37% of the U.S. market, and 33% of the domestic tourist market include some form of heritage-related activities on a Canadian vacation.

FOOTPRINT

Rebuilding National Heritage

In the 1880s, a small railroad company, the Kettle Valley Railroad (KVR), built a 525 km set of tracks through rough terrain in southern B.C. in order to transport silver, mined in the region, to the coast. It was a difficult project as the tracks were forced to hug the hard rock cliffs and sharp curves and to span deep gorges, but a cleverly designed set of 18 tall, graceful, sturdy wooden trestles completed the run. Unused for nearly a quarter of a century, these tracks became part of the ambitious millennium plan to build a trail from the East Coast to the West Coast called the Trans Canada Trail (TCT). With the tracks removed, the bedding created a smooth, easy trail that reached into wilderness untouched by modern society's roads. For backpackers and bicyclers, this 525 km run found in the Myra Canyon is one of the safest and easiest

in Canada. But, in 2003, during one of the driest seasons on record, lightning struck dry timber and unleashed a firestorm that destroyed more than 25 000 acres of land, 239 homes, and 12 of the 18 trestles found in Myra Canyon. Just seven months earlier, the Myra Canyon had been awarded national historic site status. After the fires, the federal government stepped in with a one-time grant to have them rebuilt. Today, this section of the TCT has reopened, and small businesses like B & Bs and local wineries are enjoying a rebirth. Backpackers and cyclists are back, enjoying spectacular scenery. More important, a piece of Canadian history lives on to tell visitors the story of our ancestors and their amazing feats, feats that helped open up a passageway across our beautiful wilderness to the coast.

Zoos and Aquariums

While the majority of museums are publicly funded, zoos and aquariums are a mix of both public and private operation. Large zoological parks and gardens are significant tourist attractions. These attractions exhibit animals in enclosed areas or in a natural habitat where they can roam free, as in the Toronto Zoo. Zoos are no longer old, smelly places with bars and wires, but comfortable natural settings for breeding rare and endangered species. One of the newest animal parks is located at Walt Disney World and features a fully developed natural African setting that allows the animals a free and healthy life. The late Marlin Perkins, the famous curator and host of television's *Wild Kingdom*, insisted that zoos are a necessity; several species have escaped extinction because of zoos, and most zoo animals are healthier than they would be in their wild state.

A zoo, like a museum, is and should be an educational experience for the visitor. But because the displays are alive, the visitor learns without noticeable effort. The trend in zoos is to keep people involved.

Aquariums and oceanariums are both aquatic zoos. **Aquariums** are usually found inland and exhibit fresh and saltwater fish. **Oceanariums** are located on the ocean coast and may include large fish such as sharks, as well as seals, otters, dolphins, and other aquatic life. Canada's best-known aquarium, in Vancouver, is renowned worldwide for its educational programs and creative displays. This facility also houses one of Canada's largest Imax theatres, which brings visitors back for special film events.

Many oceanariums present special shows with trained dolphins, sea lions, or seals. These shows provide entertainment and allow the trainer to explain the habits of the animal. Zoos also sometimes host hourly shows with elephants, monkeys, or other animals. Elephant or camel rides are popular with youngsters and produce a small amount of revenue. Petting farms allow the visitor to feel, smell, and touch the animals. Generally, the more people get involved with the animals in a zoo, the longer the people will stay, the more they will learn, and—with luck—the more they will spend.

ATTRACTIONS THAT ENTERTAIN: PRIVATE/COMMERCIAL

Theme and amusement parks, carnivals and circuses, live entertainment, spectator sports, gaming, and shopping constitute the majority of private or commercial attractions. A fast-growing commercial attraction area is the family fun park. Private attractions rely on admission fees, food and beverage sales, merchandising, parking charges, and special event fees (see Table 7.1). Admission fees are often higher than those of public-sponsored attractions, which can rely on grants. Private attractions, free of the bureaucratic red tape and committee structure of public enterprises, can make quick decisions and therefore adapt faster to markets. Other than great attractions like Walt Disney World and Disneyland, most private attractions are regional tourist draws at best and are considered one component of a larger vacation trip. However, each province now offers a wide variety of family fun parks that range from water activities to carnival rides, historic adventure to wildlife viewing. And, except for the actual visit, most everything, including "tickets to ride," can be arranged in advance over the internet.

Theme Parks

The **theme park** concept is most widely attributed to Walt Disney. Theme parks are oriented to a particular subject or historical area and combine costuming and architecture with entertainment and merchandise to create an evocative fantasy atmosphere.[6] Theme parks trace their roots back to the amusement park business. With the opening of Disneyland in California in 1955, Walt Disney transformed the amusement park from a run-down hangout for teenagers to wholesome family entertainment with a full day's worth of thrills and fantasy. Disneyland showed that theme parks could experience great success.

It is the powerful scenic beauty of our landscape that makes Canada a sought-after destination. Rapids in Sambaa Deh Falls Park, NWT.
(Photo courtesy Canadian Tourism Commission.)

In creating Disneyland, Walt Disney wanted to realize a perfect vision of his own childhood, right down to a smaller version of the main streets found in the midwestern towns of his youth. This theme park was to have all the virtues of an amusement park with none of the vices. And it was to offer the Disney fantasy as a means of escape. It should be noted, as with many of our products, tourism tends to combine categories or activities to increase the number of target markets it attracts. So a theme park, meant to resemble a huge space centre with workers dressed up in spacesuits, may also include an amusement park with rides and an aquarium with all sorts of colourful undersea aquatic creatures to view.

Attractions, especially large theme parks, are among the first businesses to feel the downturn of the economy. Past experience tells us that vacation travel bounces back quickly from economic slowdowns, but will it this time? Disney has faced these problems head on and continues to entice its customers by adding new attractions and making good use of special events such as the year-long celebration in 2005 commemorating the 50th anniversary of their first theme park, Disneyland.

SNAPSHOT

Walt Disney

He created a world of magic and laughter—theme parks, a new tourism product: entertainment that was family oriented, clean, safe, and well executed. Walter Elias Disney was born in 1901, fourth son in a family of five. His childhood was spent following the dreams of a father who never achieved the success he had hoped for, and after World War I, Disney returned to the States determined to make his living drawing cartoons. The early years were very poor, and often Disney had only a crust of bread and a little cheese to survive on—but he also had a friendly mouse that came by to nibble crumbs. This little mouse became the most famous mouse in history as Mickey Mouse. His animated self, Mickey, is the world's second most recognized figure next to Santa. The turning point in Disney's life was when he joined forces with another cartoonist named Ub Iwerks. Ub became his best friend, and although the fame followed Disney, Ub was *the* renowned Disney cartoonist. Steamboat Willie was the first major success for the pair and the first talking cartoon film ever produced. In the next three years, they added the other members to Mickey's family, including Minnie, Pluto, and Donald Duck.

In 1937, Disney produced the first full-colour animated film, *Snow White and the Seven Dwarfs*. It was a smashing success. Not all of his films went on to be successful but many, like *Pinocchio* and *Bambi*, remain top sellers even today. In the late 1940s, bored with the film world of cartoons, Disney began to envision a family-style park where kids could come, meet all of his cartoon characters, and ride the river with Tom Sawyer or swirl around in the Mad Hatter's teacups. Unable to get funding from his own company, Disney sold the new TV network ABC on his idea for a weekly "Wonderful World of Disney." Disney took the profits from his TV series and funnelled them into his new project, the family park named Disneyland. It opened in 1954, "a success facing failure," as he had neglected to foresee that not only children loved Disney, but parents did, too. The area had no possibility of expansion! Disneyland was far too small from the day it opened. Walt immediately began the hunt for new space and quietly began buying land in central Florida. Although Walt Disney died in 1966 of lung cancer, in 1972, Disney World opened in Orlando, Florida, to an equally huge audience. Now that there was land in which to expand, his company slowly added new areas to the park every few years—to keep customers coming back. In 1995, recognizing the need for "hands-on" fun, the Walt Disney Company opened Disney University, where visitors learn new skills during the day (like drawing cartoons, rock climbing, or learning how to cook the Disney way) and play in the park at night. Disney's company has now opened theme parks in France, Japan, and China.

Walt Disney left a legacy of magic—and of firsts. He was a man of action who believed in himself when others did not, and he showed the world that dreams do come true. Without his creative genius and dedication to excellence, tourism would be missing a little of the magic we all know as Disney parks.

In 1991, Disney Corporation was selected to join in the Dow Jones Industrial Average, a group of 30 large American corporations whose business health and shareholder acceptance are used as measures of the United States' economic strength. Disney replaced USX (formerly U.S. Steel) and became the only representative of the tourism sector, signifying that recreation and travel had become a staple in the American economy. Disney's Dow Jones status also reflects the shift in focus from an industrial society to a leisure society.

disneyland.disney.go.com

Other theme parks have emulated the Disney model. Canada's Wonderland, just outside Toronto, for example, has themed areas such as International Street, with restaurants, stores, and boutiques in the style of Mediterranean, Alpine, and Scandinavian countries; the Medieval Faire, with live theatre, rides, restaurants, and boutiques in the style of medieval Europe; and Hanna-Barbera Land, with Taft cartoon characters in their well-known environs.[7]

Theme parks have developed into large-scale operations that have sophisticated computers controlling rides and animated entertainment. Details are carefully operated at a central point within the park. Obviously, these types of parks are billion-dollar operations.

The development of large-scale theme parks in North America has come to a virtual standstill. Perhaps because of the huge capital outlay required for large theme parks, smaller parks are becoming the trend. Sesame Place in Langhorne, Pennsylvania, is an excellent example. This park has live entertainment, water attractions, computer and educational exhibits, dozens of "kid-powered" play elements, and storefronts representing Sesame Street and the surrounding Sesame neighbourhood.

Water theme parks are becoming more attractive to all ages as well, and small wading pools and slides are being built for the under-five crowd. Even miniature golf courses are turning "theme," with putting greens often built around a time period or scenic wonder. The success of theme parks is built on the "permission" granted to children and adults to forget the trials and tribulations of the real world and escape, momentarily, to a land of make-believe and fun.

Amusement Parks

Astroland Amusement Park in Coney Island, New York, Six Flags in several locations, and Canada's Wonderland in Ontario are a few of the larger-scale permanent amusement parks remaining in North America. **Amusement parks** have had to overcome their reputation for being run-down carnivals selling hot dogs and cotton candy, with tattooed ride operators and garbage-cluttered grounds. This image, which plagued amusement parks for many years, is the reason Walt Disney designed his special theme park. Today's amusement parks are touted as family entertainment centres with rides for the brave (stand-up roller coasters) and the not-so-brave (merry-go-rounds). One obvious trend in the computer-oriented youth of today is to provide interactive computer games in a specially designed room that allows parents to sit for a moment and relax or get into the play themselves. Another important trend in amusement parks is to provide new, exciting rides, or a new form of entertainment each year to bring back local clientele. The latest edition to the Disney U.S.A. properties, added in 2008, is an elaborate, interactive ride/game attraction based on *Toy Story*. During the ride experience, *Toy*

FOOTPRINT

Disney Had It Right from the Start

"Conservation isn't just the business of a few people. It is a matter that concerns us all. It is a science whose principles are written in the oldest code in the world, the laws of nature. The natural resources of (the world) are not inexhaustible. But, if we use our riches wisely, if we protect our wildlife and preserve our lakes and forests and streams, these things will last us for generations to come." Those sentiments were spoken by Walt Disney in 1950, before the world had come to the realization that our habits were destroying our ecosystem. Walt was honoured with many awards by early conservation pioneers like the Sierra Club for his work in helping create a more eco-conscious nation. He was one of the first people to use hydroponics to grow vegetables, and his hydroponic gardens at Epcot feed diners in his hotels and educate visitors to the gardens. Disney's Green Standard program has been developed for his cast members to provide suggestions on how to live life, from creating green workspaces to green dining. Following are some of the results of Disney's company's ongoing green program from 2005.

Energy conservation	- creation and use of a new paint for the hull of Disney's Wonder cruise ship that helps prohibit corrosion, minimize surface tension, and increase fuel efficiency - the first year of the "strive for five" program reduced energy use across Disney properties by 3%, the equivalent of 184 000 BTUs, valued at $1.8 million
Waste management	- recycling of compost from Disney's Animal Kingdom of more than 2600 tonnes of "poop" - since 1991, Walt Disney World (WDW) has recycled over 850 000 tonnes of material that would have gone into landfills
Water conservation	- reclaimed water at WDW has provided a savings of $2 million a year - level of drinking water has not increased despite the growth of the park over the past 15 years, because water used to clean the streets and for cooling and irrigation is reclaimed, putting no weight on the ecosystem

Which Disney property is recognized as the strongest participant in the Green Standard program? That would be the Tokyo Disney Resort (TDR). Not only does it meet all of the standards set by the Disney Corporation, but they go one step further: 53% of their waste products are recycled.

Story characters like Buzz and Rex talk back to the audience and help riders play a variety of interactive games, competing for the highest score. The latest addition to Canada's Wonderland is one of the tallest, fastest roller coaster rides in Canada and travels at speeds of 76 mph.

Amusement parks also feature live entertainment throughout the day, showcasing local and regional entertainers who usually come with a fan club of moms, dads, siblings, and friends who pay admission and increase park attendance. Nationally known entertainers are brought in to boost attendance three or four times during the summer season. Some family-style parks also offer interactive rides and activities for all ages, including the popular bumper cars and bumper boats, miniature golf, go carts, and paintball. Petting zoos provide interaction with a variety of small and large animals. The Skytrek Adventure Park, located just outside Revelstoke, B.C., adds light adventure to outdoor activities. Included in the adult activities are zip lines, suspension bridges, canopy walks, and other physically challenging activities.

Special events can be a major draw for amusement parks, and a trained events manager is essential. Event and festival management is one of the new programs available in colleges and universities—and it is one of tourism's fastest growing industries (Chapter 8).

A park's largest expenditure, once it is open for business, is labour, with nearly 33% of total revenue going to the staff.[8] If a park is to stay on the leading edge of entertainment, it must invest in new rides or entertainment yearly. Clients will return if the quality of the experience meets their expectations, the attraction is clean, and the service staff is friendly, helpful, and knowledgeable about the attraction.

Live Entertainment

If live entertainment is supplied by local talent, and promotion of the event remains local, the tourist draw will be minimal. For live entertainment to serve as a major tourist attraction, it must be promoted in tourist brochures and should be a regular, high-quality attraction throughout the tourism season. With competent marketing, word-of-mouth advertising will provide the extra tourist traffic.

Some communities thrive *because* of the live entertainment available to their audiences. For example, Nashville, Tennessee, with the Grand Ole Opry, has become a town somewhat dependent on country singers and dancers.

Larger cities like New York, Boston, and Toronto have their Broadway-style productions, and gambling towns like Las Vegas have also been traditional places to go for live entertainment. Other communities have started their own local theatres, restoring old buildings and recreating the time when community theatre—plays, dancing, and singing—was all the entertainment that was available to the public.

Summer theatres, running from April through October, are found in every province. Canada's most famous summer theatre is the Stratford Festival in Stratford, Ontario. Sitting on the banks of the Avon River, the picturesque small town provides visitors with a peaceful reprieve from the stress of daily living, as well as a wide choice of live theatre, ranging from musicals to Shakespearean drama. The town and surrounding areas are a shopper's paradise and boast some of the finest restaurants in Canada.

Another beautiful town in Ontario is Niagara-on-the-Lake, home to the Shaw Festival—the only theatre in the world to specialize in the plays of George Bernard Shaw and his contemporaries. Nestled in wine country, 20 minutes from spectacular Niagara Falls, Niagara-on-the-Lake is the 1996 winner of the "Prettiest Town in Canada" award.[9]

Gaming

Gaming and gambling have been around for centuries. Today, gambling is a popular and controversial form of recreation. In North America there are four types of gambling: parimutuel wagering, lotteries, non-profit organization gambling (mainly bingo and raffles), and casinos. Ontario's commercial casinos, charity casinos, bingo halls, and racetrack slot operations generated more than $890 million between July 1 and September 30, 2001.[10] Because lotteries, bingos, and raffles have limited clientele, they usually do not increase the flow of tourists into a town. Casinos and parimutuel betting, however, are a different matter. **Casino gambling** includes slot machines, roulette, craps (dice), baccarat, blackjack (twenty-one), and other games of chance. Casino gambling has stimulated such growth in Las Vegas that the city now has nine out of the ten biggest hotels in the world. Casino gambling is also a popular pastime on cruise ships, riverboats, and ferries. The ferry that travels from Yarmouth, Nova Scotia, to Portland, Maine, has long had gambling available to passengers while in international waters.

Casino gambling has been widely available to Canadians only in the past decade, but not all communities welcome gambling. The Casino du Lac-Leamy in Gatineau, Quebec, has raised some concerns: residents have not enjoyed the full benefits of a stronger local economy, and there has been an unusually high rate of personal and small-business bankruptcy in the region. Established bingo halls, whose operations have supported many local charities in the past, have seen a dramatic decline in business and have been forced to shut their doors. As that complex grows, including the new Hilton Hotel, locals hope more jobs and tourism revenues will begin to benefit the local community.

Niagara Fallsview Casino and Casino Windsor, on the other hand, illustrate how communities can benefit from a casino. Both enjoy success due to their proximity to the U.S. border; the Fallsview Casino has the added benefit of overlooking the falls. The resort has over 3000 slot machines, 150 gaming tables, a five-star hotel and spa with 368 rooms, a 1500-seat theatre, and 50 000 square feet of convention space.

In the weeks following September 11, 2001, business dropped 80% at border casinos, as Americans chose to stay close to home. Now casinos again face a loss of revenue with the new U.S. border-crossing restrictions. Approximately 75% of visitors to the casino are from the United States, so the financial losses could be staggering. However, working in partnership with New York State, Canada has somewhat relaxed border regulations, and Americans may cross into Canada using just a birth certificate, citizenship card, naturalization certificate, or green card. To make things even easier, hourly updates on the internet let travellers know which of the three border crossings have the least delay.

Parimutuel gambling is a betting pool in which those who bet on the winners of the first three places also share the stakes of the losers, minus a percentage for management. Parimutuel betting takes place on harness racing in Ontario, Quebec, and the Maritimes. People dine in the fine-food facilities at the track and watch drivers race in two-wheeled carts pulled by horses. Parimutuel betting also occurs across North America on greyhound dog races, quarter- and thoroughbred horse races, trotter and pacer horse races, and jai alai, a court game similar to handball. The Kentucky Derby is the best-known horse race in North America. Part of the excitement of parimutuel betting is the atmosphere at the racetrack. Patrons can dine in exclusive restaurants while watching the event, or munch on nachos and hot dogs in the stands with thousands of other eager bettors. Betting has become a social event that lasts for an evening out on the town, or for a few days, and is an added attraction to visitors.

What effect will long-term legalized gambling have on communities in North America? Some people feel that the social problems caused by gambling, along with the rise in crime linked to gambling, have been downplayed. However, casinos have been proactive in dealing with these concerns, and many will, on request from a self-acknowledged problem gambler, bar the customer from the casino for a given period of time. It seems clear that the economic benefits often vastly outweigh these criticisms. It will be interesting to see whether gambling slowly loses its appeal or whether it proves to be an economic solution for some of our Canadian communities.

Shopping

Shopping as an attraction? Why not? Shopping has always been popular with tourists. Tourists to Edmonton put the West Edmonton Mall on their must-see lists; a trip to Halifax is commemorated with the purchase of a souvenir. With the building of malls, shopping has become regionalized, drawing customers from as far as 500 km away. Mall shopping has become an annual or monthly event for many families. Most cities with regional shopping malls have other forms of entertainment, such as museums, theatres, amusement parks, swimming, or other outdoor recreation. Some malls are becoming the sole attraction by providing entertainment in their corridors and parking lots. Special events have become so important that many malls hire special events coordinators to arrange daily and weekly entertainment, contests, and food festivals.

Increasingly popular are **mega-malls**, huge shopping and entertainment centres with everything from retail stores and restaurants to indoor theme parks, game rooms, and small theatres. To keep people from migrating to warm climates such as Arizona, Florida, and California, cities in Canada and the northern United States are eyeing the mega-mall as a venue for year-round recreation opportunities. The mega-mall could become an enclosed city. The West Edmonton Mall is listed in *The Guinness Book of Records* as the world's largest shopping mall. It is about the size of 85 football fields and has 110 eating places, 900 shops, and 10 feature attractions, including an amusement park, skating rink, swimming pool, miniature golf course, and theme hotel. More than 60 000 people visit the mall every day during the summer—and it draws out-of-town visitors.[11]

Historic marketplaces are another interesting concept. They are often located in the historic part of a city's waterfront, remodelled to suit small boutiques, fresh produce outlets, and food service facilities. Tourists can buy regional crafts and combine a little history with their recreational shopping. Halifax, Saint John, Vancouver, Winnipeg, New York City, Boston, Baltimore, and San Francisco all have well-known historic waterfront marketplaces. Another trend in shopping is the factory outlet store. North Carolina has long been known for the bargains found in its factory outlets, which feature brand-name furniture, clothing, sheets, and towels. Many factory outlets have revitalized the small towns near which they are located.

Charter buses and tours will make it a point to stop at shopping areas such as mega-malls, waterfront shops, or factory outlets. Shopping as an attraction has proven to be a financial boon for the entire region and will continue to provide travellers with an added site to visit.

In Practice

Identify one public, one non-profit, and one private attraction in your area. How do they differ in advertising, price, type of visitors, and service quality? What new attraction would be successful in your community? Why would it succeed? What are the risks?

With its many theatres and restaurants, and the CN Tower highlighting the horizon, Toronto at night keeps many tourists busy.
(Photo courtesy Canadian Tourism Commission.)

One of nature's most intriguing experiences: tide coming in at Hopewell Rocks, NB.
(Photo courtesy Canadian Tourism Commission.)

In Practice

Do a quick SWOT analysis of one of your regional attractions by identifying its **S**trengths, **W**eaknesses, an **O**pportunity it could take advantage of, and a **T**hreat to its continued success.

CASE STUDY

Promoting the "Yap"

In downtown Ottawa, the curious visitor to the Bank of Canada building will find a small, privately owned museum known as one of the capital's "hidden gems." The Currency Museum, located off the lobby of the original building, provides an interesting insight into Canadian currency from early times to present. It also has an impressive collection of foreign currencies dating back to ancient times. Opened in 1980, the museum has so little recognition that a majority of Ottawa's residents do not know of this interesting corner of history. The museum is one of the few remaining that does not charge admission, and guided tours are available. Even *Ripley's Believe It or Not* has taken the time to explore the museum, especially to see its special exhibit—the "Yap Stone." The huge round stone is two metres in diameter and weighs about three tonnes. It was used as currency on Yap, one of the Caroline Islands in the South Pacific, although most of their coinage was "slightly" smaller. The Bank of Canada would like to increase the number of visitors it welcomes on a yearly basis, but this has been difficult as the museum is hard to find and has little recognition.

1. What target market do you think this type of museum might attract?
2. What services should be available to visitors?
3. How would you get tourists to take 30 minutes to check out this museum located directly across from Parliament and with free admission? Describe three different tactics you would design to increase the interest of tourists.
4. If the citizens of Ottawa were more aware of the museum, how do you think that knowledge would improve visitation to the museum?

Summary

An attraction adds to the quality of life in a community and to its economy through tourism revenue. Without attractions, many destinations would not be that desirable to travel to. Attraction trends include the building of mega-malls, a growing number of water parks and miniature golf courses, the renovation of old museums, the building of state-of-the-art modern museums, and the preservation of historic sites. Attractions may be publicly supported, non-profit, or private. Gaming has become popular in the 1990s, as hundreds of casinos have popped up all over the United States and Canada. Each casino must compete to entice the serious or recreational gambler, and time will tell whether gaming is a trend or merely a fad.

Questions

1. Create a table that identifies the following pieces of information:

   a) four public, four non-profit, and four private attractions in your area

   b) a brief description of their products and activities

   c) three ways in which each attraction helps fund its operations

   d) a special event each attraction has used to attract new and repeat visitors

2. a) The gaming industry is growing in all regions of North America. List the gambling options offered in your region and the type of gaming each one represents.

   b) Do you see the gaming industry as a positive influence on tourism? Defend your answer, using examples.

3. Is shopping a true tourist attraction? Defend your answer with examples.

4. Define the following terms as they relate to the attractions industry: *amusement park, theme park, UNESCO World Heritage Site, site-specific museum, children's museum, oceanarium.*

Notes

1. *Year-in-review 2006 facts & figures,* www.canada.travel/research.

2. www.warmuseum.ca.

3. Ibid.

4. www.ksan.org/html/village.htm..

5. www.world-tourism.com.

6. Patricia MacKay, "Theme parks: USA," *Theatre Crafts,* September 1977, p. 56.

7. James M. Cameron and Ronald Bordessa, *Wonderland through the Looking Glass* (Maple, ON: Belsten Publishing, 1982), p. 71.

8. *1990 Amusement Industry Abstract* (Alexandria, VA: International Association of Amusement Parks and Attractions, February, 1991), p. 5.

9. *Maclean's* Magazine, September 1996.

10. *Tourism Canada's Monthly Magazine,* January–February 2002, p. 7.

11. David W. Howell and Robert A. Ellison, *Passport* (Toronto: Nelson Canada, 1995), p. 225.

Events

Key terms

breakout room	fair	seminar
civic event	festival	special event
conference	fundraising event	spectator sporting event
conference centre	hallmark event	summit
convention	Meeting Professionals	trade show
convention centre	International (MPI)	Visit Canada
exhibition	Rendez-Vous Canada	workshop

Learning objectives

Having read this chapter you will be able to

1. Define the terms *special event, festival, fair, fundraising event, hallmark event, civic event, spectator sporting event, conference, convention, summit,* and *trade show.*

2. Discuss the wide variety of special events that might be hosted by a community.

3. Differentiate between a conference, convention, summit meeting, and business meeting.

4. Explain the difference between a conference centre and convention centre.

5. Identify the factors that make Canada a strong competitor for the conference market.

6. Explain both the positive and negative impacts events may have on a community.

The events industry is very important to the tourism sector because it makes good use of the products and services delivered by five of the other tourism components: accommodations, food and beverage, travel services, attractions, and outdoor recreation. This industry also creates jobs for a variety of other businesses, including printers, audiovisual companies, and manufacturers of exhibits. All events are similar in purpose and design but they are developed for different target markets. Special events and some trade shows target the general population, while conferences, conventions, meetings, and trade shows fill the needs of the business market.

Every community, no matter how small, holds **special events**. Rural communities find that hosting a fair, festival, or sporting event brings new visitors to their town and may bring local and sometimes national recognition. Hosting an event can bring a community new full- and part-time jobs, an enhanced image, strengthened community bonds, economic growth, an expanded tourism season, and enhanced diversity of social and cultural activities. Revenues generated by events benefit not only tourism businesses, but also retail businesses and community associations.

As business becomes more global, the need to communicate with people who do not live in the same area becomes essential. Sometimes talking on the telephone is not enough, because people tend to share knowledge and ideas best when they are face to face. Pick up any newspaper and you will find at least one story about a meeting being held in your community or on a national or international stage. Recent reports estimate that more than 50 000 meetings and conventions, involving more than 2 million delegates, are held annually in Canada.[1] Revenue from the events industry, totalling around $4 billion, will likely increase as cities expand both their convention facilities and the promotion of their special events.

Canada is well suited to the events business: the Canadian dollar is fairly stable and Canada provides excellent convention facilities, an international appeal, a familiar lifestyle, and a wide variety of attractions. Unfortunately, many of Canada's best destinations have facilities too small to host large conventions or conferences. In addition, Canada is often overlooked by meeting planners who do not have enough information about our cities and their conference facilities.

People who choose to work in the events industry need outgoing personalities; excellent organizational skills; good management, people, communication, and problem-solving skills; a love of detail; and a flair for public relations and working with the media. For the purpose of discussion, we will separate this industry into two divisions: *events* and *meetings*.

The transportation, events, and conference industries suffered a great deal in the aftermath of the September 11, 2001, terrorist attacks. Major conferences around the world were postponed or cancelled, and business travel took a serious downturn. Conscious of delegate concerns, all major events added security measures.

However, the peaceful conclusion of meetings such as the World Youth Day held in Toronto (2002), the Winter Olympics held in Salt Lake City (2002), and the Summer Olympics in Australia (2004) has helped to reassure worried organizers and delegates. Global summit meetings (such as the G-8 meetings that bring the industrial world's financial leaders together to discuss topics like international trade and globalization) have suffered not from terrorist threats but from activist demonstrations. Violence has erupted during summit meetings in Vancouver, Quebec City, and Rome. The G-8 held in Kananaskis, Alberta, in the summer of 2002 proved to the world that Canada was able to control and contain such demonstrations, and this has helped to promote a stronger global image of Canada as a safe destination.

SPECIAL EVENTS

Festivals and events can be half-day or year-long happenings. They may present new ideas to a new community, or be an event that occurs on a yearly basis. According to Donald Getz, a *special event* is "a onetime or infrequently occurring event outside the normal program or activities of the sponsoring or organizing body. To the customer, a special event is an opportunity for leisure, social, or cultural experience outside the normal range of choices or beyond everyday experience."[2] Getz's definition is the one used by this text.

Special events can be a powerful tool for bringing information and political activism to the forefront in a world that is growing smaller by the day. For example, every two years the Roman Catholic Church brings its youth together to meet and interact and to gain a more personal vision of the church's religious teachings. The Olympics and Paralympics showcase the best athletes from participating countries around the world. One of the best recent examples of a special event sparked by political activism is the Live 8 concerts held around the world in 2005. Inspired and guided by rock musicians Bob Geldof and Bono of U2, musicians in eight countries, including Canada, held concerts to draw attention to the plight of poor African nations. Held just before the G-8 meeting of world leaders in Scotland, Live 8's organizers and participants hoped to pressure G-8 nations to forgive the massive debts owed by the African nations. Unlike Geldof's Live Aid concert held in 1985, which raised $100 million for poverty-stricken Ethiopia, Live 8 concerts were free and were held simply to bring awareness of the plight of poor nations.[3]

Today, special events have become big business for many Canadian municipalities. They are one of the most interesting ways of unifying and enhancing the tourist appeal of permanent structures such as museums, zoos, and arenas. A museum of art

A special event like Canada Day will bring close to 100 000 visitors to Ottawa.
(Photo courtesy Canadian Tourism Commission.)

is an attraction by itself, but add a special event such as a Picasso exhibit and the museum's appeal becomes almost irresistible to locals and tourists alike.

Special events are often initiated by travel destinations in order to lure tourists to the region. Some special events attract domestic tourists and others appeal to the international visitor. Two examples of international events are the Olympics and the World's Fair. In the past 40 years, Canada has hosted two World Fairs (Expo 67 in Montreal, and Expo 86 in Vancouver), and two Olympics (the 1976 Summer Olympics in Montreal, and the 1988 Winter Olympics in Calgary).

Each province has its own special events, and some events, such as the Calgary Stampede and the Royal Nova Scotia International Tattoo, have gained international audiences. Not all special events enjoy such wide recognition, but they remain an important part of a region's draw. The turn of the millennium, on the other hand, was an event recognized and celebrated worldwide. Television transported audiences to different time zones to mark the New Year. Special events play a significant role in entertaining both tourists and local residents.

FOOTPRINT

Toronto Indy Takes on a New Face

On March 5, 2008, Grand Prix of Toronto was finally forced, due to financial problems, to cancel the 23rd running of Toronto's Grand Prix. Even with strong support from the community and its leaders for the event, they were unable to overcome these difficulties. The event attracts about 160 000 people over the weekend who spend $50 million during the two-day event. Visitors to the Toronto area spend an additional $30 million in lodging, food sales, and shopping. In addition, the event has raised $5.75 million for local children's charities. However, on March 18, 2008, Mario Andretti Green Promotions stepped up to purchase the assets of the Grand Prix Association of Toronto, and in 2009, racing in Toronto "goes green." The Indy Racing League has partnered with cleanairpass to: (1) offset over 500 tonnes of emissions; (2) expand its recycling program for Exhibition Place; (3) partner with Turtle Island Recycling by placing food waste bins around the site with hopes of turning the four metric tonnes of food waste into compost and soil; (4) use recycled paper for its promotions and other materials; and (5) encourage visitors to use Toronto transit.

Festivals

Public celebrations centred on themes of local, regional, or national interest are called **festivals**. This broad category of events celebrates jazz, the blues, winter fun, tulips in the spring—and much in between. Many rural cities in Canada use special events to lure tourists and excursionists from their region to their town. Events become an important promotional tool for the area, as festivals will attract both local and national television coverage. Some of the bigger Canadian events include the Symphony of Fire in Vancouver, British Columbia; Folklorama in Winnipeg, Manitoba; and Carnaval de Québec (Quebec Winter Carnival) in Quebec City.

Even small festivals, such as the Port Elgin Pumpkinfest, can be fun to attend. The Pumpkinfest swells the small town of Port Elgin (population 7000) by as many as 50 000 visitors who spend more than $1.4 million dollars in two days. The Pumpkinfest is not only an economic boon to the region, but it also helps to raise much-needed revenue for the area's non-profit groups.[4]

Quebec City's Winter Carnival proves that even in winter, Canada has great activities.
(Photo courtesy Canadian Tourism Commission.)

Fairs

Fairs focus on agriculture or history. Event legacies or historical fairs re-create a certain period by providing the food and entertainment of that time. Medieval and Renaissance fairs are popular examples, and recreations of historical events, such as the final battle between Wolfe and Montcalm on the Plains of Abraham in old Quebec City, are becoming more popular. Agricultural fairs feature livestock, produce, local arts and crafts, carnival rides, and food. Most farming communities have agricultural fairs, where 4-H groups (which teach young people agriculture and animal science) display their goods. Ribbons are given to prize-winning animals of many breeds. Some of Canada's agricultural fairs date back to the early 1840s. They draw regional tourists by featuring nationally known singers and entertainers and are usually held in late summer to allow crops to mature for competition. These fairs are often sponsored by the local government or the community hosting the event, and it is common for a carnival to join a larger event in the community and become a drawing card for non-residents. Two of Canada's biggest and best fairs are held in Toronto. The Canadian National Exhibition (CNE), held at the end of August in Toronto, combines an agricultural fair with a carnival. The CNE is the largest carnival/fair held in Canada. In November, the prestigious Royal Winter Fair brings visitors from across North America. It does not have rides or a midway, but hosts a variety of competitions including horse jumping and a dog show.

www.theex.com

Circuses

Circuses are magic for all ages; however, concern for the welfare of circus animals has caused the decline of this type of event. The only major circus left in North America is Ringling Brothers and Barnum & Bailey's Greatest Show on Earth. Sometimes non-profit organizations such as the Shriners will sponsor a circus in order to raise money for hospitals and children's medical research. Canada's Cirque du Soleil, a circus without animals, has gained worldwide recognition for its unique creativity that uses tumblers, dancers, and acrobats to enthrall its audiences.

Hallmark Events

Major happenings such as the Olympics, the Commonwealth Games, or World Youth Day are called **hallmark events**. These events bring tourists from around the world to a destination and can have a huge economic impact on a community. Participants for World Youth Day in Toronto spent an estimated $110 million on tourism-related souvenirs, restaurants, and hotels.[5] However, the direct costs of staging the event were over budget by $3.5 million, which the Roman Catholic Church, as the organizing body, agreed to cover.

The Summer Olympics of 1976 left its province with a large debt. Montreal's Olympic Games in the summer of 1976 left the city with a debt of $1.4 billion, which was finally paid off in 2006—30 years after the games were held. Events of this size take years of planning, require a substantial investment of tax dollars, and are seldom profitable.

London, England, which was recently awarded the Summer Games of 2012, admits that the cost of the event will likely leave them with a $2 billion debt.[6]

Vancouver has aggressively chased the money for the 2010 Olympics and currently has nearly reached its goal, two years out. They have currently raised, through partners, suppliers, and official supporters, a total of $736 million. An additional pledging of $200 million from foreign sponsors puts the numbers over the top, but VANOC continues to search out new funding opportunities. It has been holding auctions, has launched a new "own the podium" program that hopes to bring in $13.2 million dollars, and has taken part in the Salt Lake City "donor program," which passed some of its revenue dollars on to Vancouver. Calgary reminds Canadians that they made money on their Olympics and are still enjoying financial success through increased tourism 20 years later. Olympic games are not "privately owned" so they are not about making money, they are about sport. For that reason, unlike a private company, profits either go into the community's pocket or are returned to the Olympic committee to be used for future events.[7]

Fundraising Events

Fundraising events have become commonplace in North America. They may be small, like a walk-a-thon to raise money for the local Humane Society, or they may be national, like the Terry Fox Run. (Over the years, the Terry Fox Run has raised more than $30 000 000 for cancer research.) Because of cuts in government funding to hospitals and special disease research facilities, many charities now depend on these events. People have the chance to enjoy a special outdoor activity while helping to support a cause they believe in. Willie Nelson helped create Farm Aid to bring together a group of country and western singers to raise money for cash-strapped, small, independent farms. Hurricanes Katrina and Rita sparked a number of different fundraisers across North America for the evacuees from devastated regions of Louisiana and Mississippi, raising over $3 billion in a matter of weeks.

Civic Events

Civic events may be national, such as the celebration of Canada Day or Remembrance Day. This category also includes the investiture of a new prime minister or governor general, medal presentations, or the opening of a new building. Civic events may also be global, such as a New Year's Eve celebration. Each municipality, region, and country has unique civic events, and tourists often plan their vacations around these events.

Spectator Sporting Events

The largest **spectator sporting event** is the Olympics. However, hockey, tennis, golf, baseball, football, and basketball also draw large crowds. Although most spectators are people who live within a two-hour drive of the event, the regional draw of tourists to sporting events has been growing rapidly. Accommodations, restaurants, and shopping areas have noticed an increase in visitors whose primary reason for coming is to watch their favourite team. Special sporting events such as the Grey Cup, the Super Bowl, the World Series, the Stanley Cup, and the National Basketball Association playoffs bring in thousands of loyal fans who will spend the night and are ready to spend money on food and souvenirs.

Professional sports belong primarily to big cities. Big-name teams like the Toronto Raptors or Vancouver Canucks bring both revenue and recognition to a region, but Canadian cities sometimes have difficulty supporting a professional team because of the influence of the U.S. marketplace. Players often demand large salaries and want to be paid in U.S. dollars, making it very difficult for even a good team to be profitable. The 2004–05 NHL strike did nothing to enhance hockey's image, and lack of business from hockey fans left many small bars and restaurants struggling to stay open, and souvenir shops filing for bankruptcy. ESPN opted not to renew its contract with the NHL, proving that without the broad support of the U.S. television market, major contracts with television corporations disappear. Television rights are one of the big ways in which a professional sport sustains itself. The latest NHL contract now endeavours to ensure the survival of smaller market teams.

Most athletes never make it into the professional arena, but continue to show their love for their sport by forming city leagues. These amateur leagues also bring in tourist revenue as regions host national championships for a variety of sports such as the Canadian National Skating Championship, or the Tim Hortons Brier (Canadian Men's Curling Championship).

Trade Shows

Trade shows and expositions are a marketing and sales tool used by many industries to display and sell their products. Many trade shows are not open to the general public but are designed for specific audiences, small businesses, or entrepreneurs. They usually display the latest developments and products of an industry (such as computers,

With new rules in place creating a faster, higher-scoring game, the NHL is staging a comeback in Canadian cities.
(Photo courtesy Ottawa Senators Hockey Club.)

automobiles, boats, or home care products). Unlike fairs, trade shows are commonly held indoors and require large **convention centres** to display the items. Consequently, trade shows are not generally sponsored by a public or non-profit organization but by the pertinent industry or trade association. Revenues for the use of the facility, however, go to the community. There are approximately 11 000 trade shows held annually in North America. Vendors rent space and set up booths to display their products. Demonstrations are an important part of any trade show, and special trade show prices act as a lure for those thinking of a purchase. In the hospitality industry, there are several large trade shows. The International Restaurant and Foodservice Show in New York City, held every November, and the National Restaurant Association Hotel-Motel show scheduled for the middle of May in Chicago are both noted for their size and for their seminars, which feature top names in the restaurant business as well as high-profile speakers. These shows are important to the food service entrepreneur because they display the latest food products, marketing tools, and equipment for hotels and restaurants.

Many Canadian cities also hold restaurant shows. One example is the Canadian International Food and Beverage Show, held by the Canadian Restaurant and Foodservices Association (CRFA) in Toronto in February. For students, this show provides an educational opportunity that should not be missed, and special student discounts may be available. The International Travel Industry Expo is designed for travel counsellors. It displays the latest travel products, allowing participants to pick up information and make contact with a wide variety of suppliers. The Canadian Tourism Commission and the Tourism Industry Association of Canada sponsor two major trade shows for the tourism sector. **Rendez-Vous Canada**, developed by Tourism Canada in the 1980s, displays Canadian tourism products for the travel trade market—travel agencies and tour operators. The show is now sponsored by TIAC and, in 2007, generated over

$350 million dollars.[8] **Visit Canada**, still operated by the CTC, focuses on the media. Canadian tourism products are made available to travel writers, photographers, and other media representatives, allowing them to do "one-stop shopping" for tourism information.

Trade shows that are open to the general public, such as auto shows, may focus on one product or, like fall and spring home shows, may display a broad range of goods and services. The public pays at exhibits an entrance fee and may spend the day looking and talking to experts. Ottawa's annual Wine and Food Show is an example of this type of show. Here, restaurants, wineries, distilleries, and breweries present samples of their products (for a small charge). **Seminars** are generally free to those who attend. Other examples are craft shows, auto/RV shows, or boating/ sportsman shows. These shows have proven to be highly successful over the past decade. Trade shows generate more than $20 billion of revenue in North America every year. Large trade shows use spacious facilities like the Vancouver Trade and Convention Centre, the Metro Toronto Convention Centre, or the Montreal Convention Centre. All components of tourism benefit. For example, weeks prior to the Chicago Restaurant Show, downtown hotels are completely sold out, and during the show, restaurants are booked to capacity.

CONFERENCES, CONVENTIONS, AND MEETINGS

An association or an organization is created by uniting a group of people with a common interest. Association meetings fall into two categories: conventions and conferences. **Conventions** are large meetings where delegates come together to share ideas and to achieve some form of consensus. Perhaps the best known type of convention occurs when a political party brings together delegates from across the country to elect its leader and create its party platform for the next election. Delegates to a convention usually come from varying backgrounds, so business leaders will mingle with firefighters, mechanics, consultants, and those who choose to work at home. Conventions are also held by large associations such as the Kiwanis Club or Alcoholics Anonymous. There is usually a strong element of recreation in a convention program, to reward those who have spent their time working with the organization.

Conferences are similar to conventions, except that the delegates usually come from a single industry or occupation. The Tourism Industry Association of Canada (TIAC) holds its annual conference in a different Canadian city each year so that attendees may enjoy varied venues and attractions. Delegates come from all areas of the tourism sector to hear about the latest research, to learn more about national certification programs, to exchange ideas, and to listen to leaders in tourism discuss current topics of interest. Many conferences take the time to recognize people who have contributed to the sector in a significant way. Conferences have a more educational tone to their programs than do conventions.

Summits are similar to conferences but tend to be meetings among high-level political leaders, or at least have a political overtone. The G-8 meetings are a good example.

Teleconferencing is the latest trend in meetings. Advances in technology allow businesses and associations to bring together a group of people via a telephone or satellite link. At more advanced sites, videoconferencing enables participants to actually see each other during the discussions. Although this type of meeting does not add to a city's tourism revenue, hotels and convention centres are beginning to provide these services in response to consumer demands.

The Association Meeting Market

Although associations may have very different reasons to exist, as a market they share characteristics:[9]

- Conventions and conferences usually last three to five days.
- Voluntary attendance is the norm, so delegates pay their own way.
- Destination sites must be carefully chosen to entice delegates to attend, and different cities are chosen every year.
- Accessibility is important to delegates.
- Regular meeting dates allow delegates to plan their time well in advance.
- **Exhibitions** displaying the latest goods are important.

There are about 80 000 associations in North America, and many plan annual conventions or conferences. Specific guest needs must be satisfied if the convention or conference is to be a success. The choice of destination is important because delegates often bring their families along, combining business and vacation. Resorts are popular choices, and both The Fairmont Banff Springs Hotel and The Fairmont Jasper Park Lodge Hotel have developed good reputations as conference sites. However, both sites have a major drawback: the closest cities, Calgary and Edmonton, are some distance away. Calgary, for instance, is a 90-minute drive from Banff, forcing the delegate to either rent a car or make the last leg of the trip by bus. As members pay for their travel and accommodations, the cost of the trip is an important factor when booking the destination. Since most delegates like to try different locations every year, the organizing committee is kept busy searching out new sites. Booking a site five years in advance is not uncommon.

Meeting Sites The choice of a meeting location is as varied as the products available. The first concern a meeting planner must address is the size of the facility needed. General meeting space must accommodate the entire delegation, which may be anywhere from a couple of hundred to more than 10 000 people. Smaller **breakout rooms** are needed to handle panel discussions, seminars, and **workshops**, which are an integral part of a conference. The number of rooms available at a destination and the price of accommodations are extremely important to delegates because they pay their own way. Many conferences will choose destinations that offer a wide variety of attractions that families can enjoy during the day, and where delegates can relax together after the meetings.

www.mpiweb.org

Hotels today may generate 20 to 40% of their annual revenues from meetings, conventions, and conferences. Many have designed their properties to accommodate these groups, providing audiovisual support, portable food service, and a staff trained to deal with the logistics of a large meeting. Resorts also attract this market, offering recreational activities and a quiet, undisturbed setting. Older resorts such as the Fairmont Algonquin in St. Andrews by-the-Sea, New Brunswick, have done extensive renovations to accommodate this market. A multimillion-dollar addition to The Fairmont Château Lake Louise's conference space was completed in 2004. The

Conference Terminology You Should Know

seminar	informal meeting in which delegates share information and ideas under the expertise of a seminar leader or presenter; seminars may also be conducted by a panel of experts who provide knowledge from differing sources
workshop	small-group session that focuses on activities in which participants learn new skills or techniques
breakout room	a room in which small groups of delegates participate in seminars or workshops
Meeting Professionals International (MPI)	international professional association of meeting planners

problem with resorts has been high room rates: many conferences are planned during peak season, when resorts are reluctant to reduce their rates.

Conference centres specifically designed for meetings provide a quiet working environment for a conference and its delegates. Because these meetings are of an educational nature, many large universities use their equipment and facilities during the summer months to host small conferences and meetings, thus gaining revenue from rooms and services that might otherwise be unused.

One of Canada's most distinctive conference centres is in Banff, Alberta. The Banff Centre was established over 65 years ago as a retreat for musicians and artists. *Arts* programming is one of three distinct programming areas at The Banff Centre, which also provides conference services year-round. Here, artists come to rejuvenate their spirits and their creativity through professional development offered in a range of programs, which include Music & Sound, Theatre Arts, Media & Visual Arts, Writing & Publishing, and Aboriginal Arts. *Leadership Development* programming is dedicated to relevant professional development for leaders and managers. It offers seminars and workshops designed to develop effective, successful leaders for all areas, including business, government, and Aboriginal communities. *Mountain Culture*, the third programming area, focuses worldwide attention on mountain-related natural and cultural issues. Every year The Banff Centre is host to the internationally acclaimed Banff Mountain Film and Book Festivals, and the Banff Mountain Photography Competition, as well as conferences and summits exploring specific mountain-related themes. The conferences division was opened in the 1960s to provide meeting facilities for the associations market. Net revenues from this area support the centre's arts programming. The centre's multidisciplinary environment and the vast range of opportunities offered to guests are what make this conference centre unique. As well, conference delegates may hike, canoe, ski, or rock climb in the surrounding Rocky Mountains, using professional guide services available in Banff; attend performances and visit exhibits at the centre; and take advantage of a full range of services that include a travel agency and a recreation/fitness centre. Together, all these components add value to The Banff Centre's conference product.

www.banffcentre.ca

Convention centres are specifically built to handle groups of more than 1000 people. They differ from conference centres in several ways: (a) they are larger facilities that do not have recreational opportunities on the premises; (b) they are usually located in big cities; and c) they do not provide guest rooms. Hotels in the area will handle accommodations, and many convention centres are linked to a hotel.

The Banff Centre provides smaller conferences and corporate meetings with unique facilities and beautiful setting.
(Photo courtesy The Banff Centre.)

For example, the Vancouver Trade and Convention Centre (VTCC), located on the waterfront, is linked to the Pan Pacific Hotel.

Because building convention centres is enormously expensive, a unique partnership has developed between the tourism sector and federal, provincial, and municipal governments, which have provided funding as well as special loans. Civic centres also play host to conventions, but their primary function is to host special events such as sporting events or cultural shows and exhibits. Some civic centres work in partnership with smaller convention facilities to help the city handle a larger number of delegates. The Saddledome in Calgary provides seating for an additional 16 700 participants, expanding the convention centre's capacity of 2500; the Halifax Metro Centre (capacity 10 000) is adjacent to the World Trade and Convention Centre, with a capacity of 1300. Many cities in Canada are considering additions to their meeting spaces, and Canadians can look forward to new job opportunities as this expansion becomes a reality.

Canada's top convention centres, from east to west, are as follows:

- Halifax World Trade and Convention Centre
- Quebec Convention Centre
- Montreal Convention Centre
- Ottawa Congress Centre
- Metropolitan Toronto Convention Centre
- Winnipeg Convention Centre
- Edmonton Convention Centre
- Calgary Convention Centre
- Vancouver Trade and Convention Centre
- Victoria Convention Centre

The award-winning Vancouver Trade and Convention Centre has begun a major expansion that will triple its capacity when finished in 2009.
(Photo courtesy Canadian Tourism Commission.)

The Corporate Meeting Market

This segment of the meeting market has slightly different characteristics from the associations market. Businesses will often hold meetings off site in order to avoid distractions and to achieve an atmosphere in which to build a more unified team. Here are the characteristics of the corporate meeting market:

- Attendance is mandatory.
- The cost of the meeting is paid for by the business.
- The number of participants is smaller than that of a conference or convention.
- The meeting is generally shorter.
- Meetings are planned as the need arises and are booked with only a few months' or weeks' notice. Since attendance is mandatory, meetings do not require visible publicity.
- The same destination may be used repeatedly, and it is often near corporate headquarters or factories.
- Exhibits are not generally part of the meeting structure.
- Emphasis is on business, so food service usually provides a working lunch: a simple buffet of cold meats, salads or sandwiches, fresh fruit, and dessert. Beverages are supplied throughout the meeting. Corporate meetings often take place in local hotel facilities. A hotel serious about this business must provide not only quality food service, but also quiet, luxurious surroundings to fit the corporate image.

DIFFICULTIES IN SPONSORING AN EVENT

Clearly, events and festivals are an important component of the tourism sector, benefiting small and large communities alike. However, it would be naive to think that special events have only advantages. Disadvantages do exist, but if they are addressed in the planning stages, they can be overcome or minimized. Potential disadvantages include: (1) difficulty finding volunteers; (2) dissenting community merchants and residents who may block planning; (3) inadequate planning that may result in financial setbacks that jeopardize future events; (4) large numbers of visitors who may tax existing accommodations, visitor services, and restaurants, posing a threat to future events if they go home dissatisfied; (5) damage to the environment; and (6) difficulty attracting visitors until the event becomes widely known.

World-class events like the Calgary Stampede provide summer entertainment for visitors.
(Photo courtesy Canadian Tourism Commission.)

MANAGING EVENTS

What a challenge managing a large event can be! Organizers are doomed to fail if they don't understand the complexities of planning, organizing, and staging a special event. Many colleges and universities in Canada offer excellent training programs. The CTHRC has national certification programs for events coordinator, special event manager, and meeting planner. If events management interests you, here are some of the areas in which you must develop knowledge:

- **Client needs and expectations**. It is important to start with a clear understanding of the purpose of the event, the needs of your client, and the projected outcomes. This means you must develop good communication and people skills.
- **Site selection and inspection**. For regular events such as the Calgary Stampede, the site is pre-selected. Sometimes the client chooses the site. As coordinator,

SNAPSHOT

Isadore Sharp

His company, Four Seasons Hotels Ltd., is one of the top hotel chains in the world. It sits at the pinnacle of the Canadian hospitality business both in quality and revenue generated. Over the past 30 years, Isadore Sharp has become one of the world's leading hoteliers. He did not start out in the hotel business but studied architecture at the Ryerson Institute of Technology in Toronto. Initially he worked for his father's construction company, but by the early 1960s, he had made a decision that would change the course of his life—he founded the Four Seasons Hotel.

Sharp was an innovator, a man with good instincts who focused on quality service long before it became the buzzword in the hospitality business. Having firmly established his first hotel, he designed the Inn on the Park, located in what was then Toronto's northern suburbs. Around the inn, he cultivated beautiful lawns and gardens. Using trees to provide privacy, Sharp created a refuge from the busy city. In 1970, he began to look at international locations for his third hotel. When he chose London, England, his critics felt that he had made his first mistake, for London already had many fine luxury hotels. However, Sharp relied on his instincts, recognizing the need for a premiere property with a modern flair.

As his hotel empire flourished, Sharp never lost sight of his original tenet: quality service is worth paying for. How does he maintain such high standards? He believes that if employees are treated well, they will treat guests in a similar manner. Facilities that serve his employees are as well appointed as those he designs for his guests. Four Seasons Hotels enjoys one of the lowest staff turnover rates in the industry. For his guests, he offers 24-hour room service, a complimentary shoeshine, and luxurious terry cloth bathrobes. His staff is knowledgeable, friendly, and trained to handle even the most difficult situations with dignity. Concierges in Four Seasons Hotels are among the best in the industry. They are required to speak a minimum of two languages; have complete knowledge of the city, its sights, restaurants, theatres, and nightlife; and have the ability to handle any request with courtesy and professionalism under all circumstances.

By the 1980s, Four Seasons Hotels had won many awards for excellence, creating a demand for its management expertise. Sharp took his company successfully into the business of contract management, and in 1992, he moved into the luxury resort business with the purchase of Regent Hotels International of Hong Kong. In 2006, Bill Gates and Prince Al-Waleed bin Talal bought the company, retaining Sharp as chairman and CEO. Today his group owns 37 properties and generates revenues of nearly $2 billion annually. What kind of a man is Isadore Sharp? He is a man who prefers to stay quietly on the sidelines, who trusts his instincts, and who is committed to exceptionally high standards of service. He understands and satisfies the needs of both his guests and his employees, and instills in his staff the belief that anything is possible. "No" and "Can't be done" are not part of staff vocabulary. Isadore Sharp is a Canadian who has led the way in the luxury hotel business for more than 30 years, earning respect and admiration from the hotel industry around the world.

you must become familiar with the site on many levels to ensure you have adequate registration areas, hotel accommodations, food service capabilities, restrooms, and utilities (e.g., electrical power, power distribution, water source).

- **Designing the event environment**. Although this may be the creative side of your planning, your designs must meet your client's needs, the registrants' needs, and the budget.

- **Financial management**. Many events are enormously expensive to run, and keeping tight control of dollars is essential if an event is to be successful. Besides the obvious fixed expenses, a wide variety of vendors, entertainers, caterers, and staff must be paid. Add to these expenses marketing and promotion costs, floral and decor costs, and insurance, and good accounting skills are essential!

- **Training staff and volunteers**. As the event planner, you will be working with full-time and part-time staff as well as many volunteers. Volunteers work for free but often lack specific skills or knowledge. You will need leadership skills to get your people working as a team.

- **Scheduling**. Much of an event is scheduled well in advance, and the client is likely to take an active part. Promotions highlight the schedule of events, and the biggest concern is ensuring that the schedule is followed. A conference speaker who takes just 10 minutes more than scheduled can throw the rest of the day off track, affecting both food service and programmed entertainment.

- **Catering**. Food is often the highlight of any meeting or event, and knowing what your clientele wants is very important. A conference of nutritionists will be looking for freshly prepared, nutritious food while a meeting of high-school students will want pizza or hamburgers. One of the big logistical problems handled by the Compass Group during World Youth Day was ensuring that the 250 000 attendees were fed within meal times. An event planner must also ensure that caterers can handle special dietary needs or allergies.

- **Marketing**. Events are successful only if a smart marketing and promotion plan is in place. Budget will determine where and how you promote the event. The better the promotions, the better the response and the higher the profit margin.

- **Finding sponsorship**. Unless you are dealing with a meeting whose costs are being covered by a specific business, sponsorship is critical to an event's success. The tourism sector can be slow to see the benefits of partnering with a special event, so finding good sponsorship is often challenging. Event organizers must learn persuasive techniques and be ready to show the benefits sponsorship brings to a company.

- **Legal, ethical, and risk management**. As with any business, legal and ethical issues will arise. You need to know how to read contracts and apply risk management techniques to ensure the attendees are safe from harm. Large conventions and conferences have large budgets, and the ethical and professional standards you employ must meet any scrutiny from an outside person.

The conference service manager works at the site of the meeting or convention with the meeting planner to ensure all needs are properly met. The conference service manager understands the hotel or convention centre's functions and the responsibilities of each department. The basic responsibility is to make sure that schedules are maintained and that services are rendered according to the contract. The position involves continual coordination with the various operating departments to make certain that quality service standards are maintained. It also ensures all the elements of a convention or meeting run smoothly and efficiently from the time of the attendees' arrival, through the set-up, to billing and departures. In addition to

CASE STUDY

Credit Refused

Amanda was a new front-desk clerk at a busy country inn. Enrolled in a Hospitality Management program at the local community college, she wanted to put into practice the skills she was learning in school. The fastidious innkeeper, Mrs. Arnheim, kept profiles on each guest to ensure that their next stay at the inn was as good as or better than the last. Amanda was put to the task of inputting guests' credit card numbers and ensuring she had collected information for the profiles. When she got to Mabel and Jane Kennedy, two delightful, grey-haired sisters, Mabel's credit card was refused. Amanda contacted the night manager, John, who made a courteous call to the two sisters, apologizing for the problem and asking if they had an alternate card they wished to use. Jane said she and Mabel planned to pay cash when they left and did not have another credit card. John's next move was to call Mrs. Arnheim to explain the problem. She told him not to worry and promised to handle it first thing in the morning. However, in the morning, the two sisters were even more adamant. Did the inn not trust them to pay their bill? They explained that they were on a package deal and would pay the total amount when they checked out the next morning. Against her better judgment, and not wishing to make a scene in the dining room, Mrs. Arnheim decided to allow the sisters to continue their stay. She informed the front-desk staff that the ladies would settle their bill upon check-out the next day. At noon the next day, Amanda, who had been waiting for the sisters to check out, sent a housekeeper to their room to determine how much longer they would be. Imagine her surprise when the room was found empty, with no sign of the sisters or their baggage.

1. What is the root problem in this scenario?
2. As the manager or innkeeper, how would you have handled this problem? If your method is different from Mrs. Arnheim's, what would the positive and negative impacts of your decision be?
3. Should staff training include tactics for how to avoid situations like this?
4. As the innkeeper, what change to company policy would you make to ensure this did not happen again?

the public relations and service roles, the conference service manager has a sales responsibility to the host facility for rebooking the group by providing the best service and follow-through.

Most conference service managers have worked in the hospitality industry where they may have gained experience in dealing with meetings and meeting planners.

In Practice

Describe 10 special events that might entice tourists to your region. Choose one event from your list and, in your own words, write an advertisement for your local newspaper that would help you promote this event.

Summary

Events and conferences make up an exciting component of the tourism sector. People who choose this field can expect long days, many challenges, and great satisfaction once the job is well done. This industry includes a wide variety of events that range from weddings to fundraising, pumpkin festivals to global events like the Winter Olympics and Paralympics, corporate business meetings to world summits. Events provide a community with jobs and a stronger presence in the region. In the past, many events ended with a revenue deficit, but in today's competitive world, the event must generate revenue or face cancellation. Planning and staging an event require tremendous coordination skills, lots of ingenuity, and patience. To be successful in this field, knowledge, experience, and continuing professional development are essential. If you love planning and problem solving, then this may be the right industry for you!

Questions

1. a) Define the terms *special event, festival, hallmark event, fundraising event, civic event, spectator sporting event*.

    b) Identify one example of each of the above events that has been hosted by your province or region.

    c) Describe five disadvantages to a community that hosts such events.

    d) Explain five benefits to a community that hosts special events.

2. a) Create a table that compares and contrasts a *convention*, a *conference*, and a *meeting* based on the following criteria: i) occupation of attendees; ii) number of attendees; iii) purpose of meeting; iv) location of the event; v) accessibility of the location; vi) payment of fees and costs; vii) duration of the event; viii) timing of the event.

    b) Name a recent conference and a recent convention held in your city or region.

3. Define *trade show* and list 10 different annual trade shows in your region. Tell whether each is open to the public or only to industry members.

4. More and more celebrities like Bob Geldof, Bono, and Willie Nelson are getting involved in politically oriented events like Live 8.

   a) How did the planning of these eight concerts differ from the manner in which a regular event is planned?

   b) Why do you think Canadian politicians might refuse to host an event such as the Live 8 concert in their city? Provide three reasons they might cite to back their position.

   c) What benefits might the concert have brought to your community?

   d) Do you think celebrities have the right to get involved in politics? Defend your answer.

5. Define the following terms as they relate to the events and conferences industry: *conference centre, Rendez-Vous Canada, convention centre, breakout room, seminar, workshop.*

Notes

1. *The Student's Travel Map* (Ottawa, ON: Canadian Tourism Human Resource Council, 1995), p. 11.

2. Donald Getz, *Festivals, Special Events, and Tourism* (New York: Van Nostrand Reinhold, 1991), p. 44.

3. www.live8live.com.

4. Sylvia Densmore, *Staging Successful Small Town Events*, International Festival and Events Association Presentation, February 2001.

5. "Event's tourism boom may echo," *Toronto Star*, July 30, 2002, p. B3.

6. Global News, *6:30 Edition*, September 14, 2005.

7. www.vancouver2010.com.

8. David W. Howell and Robert A. Ellison, *Passport* (Toronto: Nelson Canada, 1995), p. 293.

9. www.tiac-aitc.com.

Adventure Tourism and Outdoor Recreation

Key terms

adventure tourism
carrying capacity
Crown land
ecotourism
ecotourist

Green Plan
hard adventure
low impact camping
national parks system
outdoor recreation

Parks Canada
recreational sports
responsible tourism
soft adventure
sustainable tourism

Learning objectives

Having read this chapter you will be able to

1. Describe adventure tourism, ecotourism, and outdoor recreational activities.

2. Outline the role played by Environment Canada and Parks Canada in this industry.

3. Discuss the key characteristics of ecotourism and the ecotourism market.

4. Define, using examples, *hard adventure*, *soft adventure*, *ecotourism*, *sustainable tourism*, and *low impact camping*.

5. Provide a brief description of 10 seasonal outdoor activities enjoyed by travellers in Canada.

6. Compare the two opposing views of tourism's impact on the environment.

7. Explain how the concept of *carrying capacity* is helpful to both the tourist and the environment.

8. Explain how tourism can damage vegetation, water quality, air quality, wildlife, coastlines, and mountainous terrain.

9. Explain how government and business can implement sustainable tourism.

Globally, Canada already has a strong image in the minds of travellers with its beautiful landscapes and interesting plant and animal life. This image, however, is usually one dominated by ice and snow. Scenes of snow-capped mountains, polar bears, and huge icebergs are all familiar pictures of the Canadian landscape for the outside world. The media attention with 2010 will not dispel the vision of Canada as a cold but interesting place as we host the Winter Olympic Games. Selling Canada as a four-season destination can be difficult.

We are a country that must deal with distinct, often extreme seasons and, whether we like it or not, the arrival of snow cuts tourism figures dramatically. Still, our landscape provides some of the world's best all-season adventure tourism and outdoor experiences, which makes adventure tourism and outdoor recreation (ATOR) a major motivator in attracting tourists. Busy lifestyles and stress make vacations an important part of staying healthy. Our bodies and minds gain strength from relaxation and the chance to unwind. How do people relax? By getting away from work and busy lives and doing something enjoyable. For people to whom fresh air and physical activity are healthy choices for a vacation, ATOR is front and centre when vacation plans are made, and most vacations have at least one outdoor activity. This component of the tourism sector, which includes adventure tourism, ecotourism, and outdoor recreation, is now a trillion dollar industry worldwide.[1]

PARKS AND CROWN LANDS

Canada's National Parks System

We begin this chapter by taking a quick look at **Parks Canada**, an agency that reports to the Minister of the Environment. "National parks are a country wide system of representative natural areas of Canadian significance. By law they are protected for public understanding, appreciation, and enjoyment while being maintained in an unimpaired state for future generations."[2] The national parks system was inaugurated in 1885, when 26 km^2 on the slopes of Sulphur Mountain in Banff were set aside for protection for future generations. Between 1887 and 1915, five more parks were established in the western regions: Yoho, Glacier, Mount Revelstoke, Waterton Lakes, and Jasper. The St. Lawrence Islands National Park was the first in Eastern Canada. Today, Canada has 42 national parks representing 24 out of 39 natural regions, and the Canadian government has set aside an additional 67 natural regions to be held under its protection—39 land-based and 28 marine-based. In addition, 12% of Crown land now falls under the protection of Parks Canada, taking it out of the hands of provincial authorities. The federal government's final goal is to establish national parks in each of the distinct ecosystems found in Canada.

www.pc.gc.ca

Mandates of Parks Canada

Parks Canada does more than just manage the **national parks system**; it manages Canada's 131 national historic sites, historic railway stations, and more than 650 historic sites; it oversees operation of our seven historic canal systems;

it coordinates the federal–provincial co-operative program for the Canadian Heritage River Systems; it directs and implements heritage tourism opportunities and programs; and it provides services to the more than 20 million visitors who use the national parks system every year. Our national parks have been called "Canada's windows to the world."

In 2007, the Minister of the Environment congratulated Parks Canada on updating and amending the Banff National Park Management Plan (1988). His statements reflect not only his vision of Canada, but also the importance tourism places on entertaining and educating visitors:

> From our smallest national park to our most visited national historic site to our largest marine conservation area, each of these places offer Canadians and visitors unique opportunities to experience Canada. These places of beauty, wonder, and learning are valued by Canadians—they are a part of our past, our present, and our future.[3]

In 2007, Parks Canada won two prestigious awards for the consistent quality of its products (our national parks and sites) and for maintaining a high level of praise from visitors by earning an overall 90% satisfaction rate. It was recognized as "Business of the Year" by the Tourism Industry Association of Canada (TIAC); and in London, England, received the World Travel Market Global Award.

Management Plans of Parks Canada

The controversy between use of our national parklands versus protection has flared since the establishment of the first national park in 1888. Today, the emphasis is clearly moving from use to maintenance and protection. This does not eliminate the parks as a destination for visitors, but it does change the way Parks Canada approaches its duties. There are many demands made on our land by big businesses, which range from lumbering and oil/mineral extractions to tourism ventures and environmental protection, so Parks Canada has to do a balancing act to ensure those on all sides of the battle are fairly treated. The agency recognizes that one of its biggest challenges will be maintaining the integrity of the parks' ecosystems. An ecosystem that has integrity is defined as having "their native components intact, including the physical elements (e.g., water, rocks); biodiversity (composition and abundance of species and communities in an ecosystem, e.g., rainforest, grasslands, black bears, brook trout, and black spruce); and ecosystem processes (the engines that make the ecosystem work, e.g., fire, flooding, predation)."[4] Parks Canada must be assured that native species can handle the rates of change forecasted without the significant damages or loss that occurs when we begin to use the area. Conservation of each ecosystem must be based on sound scientific principles, not based on specific demands, and it also recognizes that any use of the land will cause prime environmental damage. Their focus is on a system's ability to regenerate itself.

Stressors

Any event that causes the alteration or demise of a species is called a "stressor," and the intensity is determined by the type and degree of invasion. Easily identified external stressors are the building of roads, establishment of businesses, or increased use of land by people (see box on page 221). But damage is also caused by the invasion of alien species. Some predators are common, such as English ivy, but others, such as the pine beetle currently destroying B.C.'s forests, are truly alien. In the last five years, Canada has been invaded by 185 alien species, all threatening one or more of our native plants or animals.[5] In addition, the overall state of the global ecosystem is causing irreversible damage. Global warming has already changed snow and ice conditions in the far north, causing glaciers to retreat as higher sea levels and stronger storm surges erode shorelines of coastal waters. Other impacts are felt, too—the change in migration habits of both birds and mammals, the loss of grasslands due to drought, and the shifting of plants and animals due to changes in habitat.

How is Parks Canada approaching this problem? If a region has shown an ability to regenerate, it is sometimes just a simple matter of changing usage boundaries for those who use the area. At other times, the region affected may require the reintroduction of native species (e.g., Alberta wolves have been successfully reintroduced to states like Montana and Wyoming) to stabilize it. It may mean attempting to remove a specific alien species such as the zebra mussels that have invaded our Great Lakes, but this is almost impossible once the territory has been invaded. At times it may mean taking drastic steps, such as using fire or flooding to remove an alien species. However, it may be as simple as replacing wheat fields in Grasslands National Park with native prairie grasses. One thing is clear—Canada's *National Parks Act* makes maintenance or restoration of ecological integrity a first priority in park management, and that may mean slowing the use of parklands by tourists.

Provincial Parks Systems

In addition to national parks, each province has created its own protected areas—natural habitats governed by ministries such as British Columbia's

---

Major External and Internal Stressors Facing Canada's Parks

Habitat loss – despite best efforts, land loss for Canadian species of all sorts is inevitable

Habitat fragmentation – large track of lands are bisected by impediments such as a new road, and loss of life due to these changes is inevitable

Large carnivores – are disappearing or have disappeared, destroying the natural predator–prey relationships

Air pollution – impacts all living creatures, especially the smaller at-risk animals

which form an important part of the feeding cycle

Pesticides – high mercury and toxaphene levels continue to be found in many wild species

Alien species – attack local plants and animals unimpeded as they have no local enemies

Overuse – our parks are in such demand, they need careful monitoring to control overuse

Source: Parks Canada

Ministry of Environment, Lands, and Parks. The demands on and damage to their ecosystems are similar to those under federal protection, and each province is responsible for the management of these lands and for the safety of its visitors. National parks have tight restrictions on what a person using the land may or may not do, and many provinces are equally protective of their parks. B.C. limits the number of participants that may trek the West Coast Trail in the Pacific Rim National Park Reserve, and ensures that the strict rules of use for this specific land area are adhered to by hikers. Some of the more popular provincial camps now require advance registration before use. Park attendants patrol on land and water to ensure that users obey the rules and regulations, issue warnings when severe weather is approaching, and determine whether weather conditions make open fires unsafe. Provincial administrations maintain all public access such as roads, bridges, and campgrounds, and often provide rest areas and picnic tables for daytime visitors. Most parks have plans detailing future development in the region, ensuring the preservation and wise use of these protected lands.

Crown Lands

Unlike in many other countries around the world, much of our Canadian wilderness is not privately owned but is designated **Crown land**—that is, land owned by the federal or provincial government. National and provincial parks are Crown land set aside and protected by legislation governing use and development. Much of our Crown land, however, has no legislation covering its use, which makes it attractive to visitors who prefer less restriction on their vacations. Crown land may be leased (under tenure) or purchased by private organizations such as logging companies or tourism businesses. Conflict over the use of Crown land is bound to arise. For example, a clear-cut logging operation, despite reforestation programs, will blight the landscape for many years and conflict with tourism development.

Just how important is Crown land to ATOR? Most adventure tourism occurs on Crown land, and a quick look at statistics shows us why. For example, British Columbia, our third-largest province, covers an area of 94.8 million hectares, of which 92% is provincial Crown land; 1% is federal Crown land; 5% is privately owned; and 2% is covered by fresh water. These proportions are fairly typical. Of B.C.'s Crown land, approximately two-thirds (59 million hectares) is public forest and provides the basis for much of B.C.'s recreational activities. The province has begun a series of initiatives to increase the use of Crown lands for environmentally sound economic development and community uses. Almost 11 million hectares of Crown land already lie within B.C.'s provincial parks system; the goal is to increase parklands by 12% over the next 10 years.

In May 2000, a groundbreaking treaty was signed with the Nisga'a Nation, giving them complete control over 2000 km^2 of Crown land and allowing self-government. British Columbia's citizens include more than 50 First Nations groups, and 70% of these groups are currently in treaty negotiations. Settling a century-old claim of right of ownership, the Nisga'a treaty establishes a basis for future agreements. It is not yet clear how such decisions will affect tourism development.[6]

In all provinces, Crown lands form the basis of much of our outdoor recreational activities, and many hunting and fishing lodges, campsites, and resorts make good use of this land, its rivers, and its lakes. Tourism is seen as a "green" sector, meaning the protection of the land it uses is paramount to the continued quality of the tourism experience. Canada remains active at world conferences on ecology and sustainability and has a growing concern about development when considering our beautiful, untouched lands. In order to be recognized as a world leader in this area, Canada must be proactive in determining proper usage and maintenance of its wilderness areas.

ADVENTURE TOURISM

Adventure tourism is commonly divided into two distinct types, with a sliding scale of intensity between the two: hard adventure and soft adventure.

Hard Adventure

Hard adventure is identified by four criteria:

a) It is usually a strenuous activity requiring training prior to the experience. People who enjoy this type of activity train daily to maintain body strength and flexibility.

b) It often requires some sort of equipment. If the activity is life-threatening, the participant will use their own, trusted equipment.

c) It requires that a person take on, at times, deadly risk. A novice should not only be well prepared but also travel with an experienced guide, at least the first time.

d) Hard adventure usually occurs in a more remote region of the land, where nature is relatively untouched and more challenging as a result.

People who enjoy this type of activity will pay handsomely for the trip, and the greater the challenge, the more satisfaction they gain from the experience. Canada has many hard adventure challenges (see Figure 9.1), but the ones with the most global recognition are found in other areas around the world—climbing Everest, canoeing the Amazon, crossing the Pacific Ocean in a one-person sailboat, and climbing the Colorado Rockies.

Everest may provide us with a fitting example of hard adventure as a number of Canadians have successfully reached the summit. Everest, the highest mountain in the world at 8848 m, was not "conquered" until 1953, with the ascent of Australian climber Sir Edmund Hillary and Tenzing Norgay, a Nepalese climber. Today, as many as 70 people attempt the climb every year, but few are successful in reaching the summit. The first severe risk a team meets is the slowly moving glacier, the Khumbu Falls, and risks increase as the air thins and climbers have less oxygen and become physically exhausted. Still, people try for the top every year. Their reason? "Because it is there."

Of course, not all hard adventure means climbing a mountain. Rivers such as the Nahanni provide challenging, hard adventure activities for the enthusiast. Tourists may be flown into a rustic lodge that acts as home base, but once they are

FIGURE 9.1 Top ten Canadian hard adventure challenges (*Explore* magazine, March 2008)

Top Ten Canadian Hard Adventure Challenges

1. Ellesmere Trek: two weeks backpacking in Quttinirpaaq National Park
2. Kayak Haida Gwaii: eight days kayaking among the Queen Charlotte Islands to view the largest collection of Haida totems
3. Canoe the Nahanni: two weeks of canoeing along one of the last untouched rivers in the world
4. Sail the Great Bear Rainforest: look for the Kermode or Kodiak bear in the world's largest standing temperate rainforest
5. Dive Vancouver Island: explore the "Graveyard of the Pacific " and other sites from the dive boat *Nautilus Explorer*
6. Cruise the Northwest passage: 15-day trip aboard the Russian research vessel *R.V. Akademik lloffe*—follow the path of some of the ill-fated Franklin Expedition
7. Explore the Torngats: by boat and by foot, explore Labrador's only national park—home to Canada's largest polar bear population
8. Ride the best of B.C.: ride the rails at 7000 ft to the Kokanee Glacier and the Chilcotin mountains
9. Kayak with icebergs: eight days of sea kayaking along Newfoundland's northern peninsula with great views of wildlife
10. Hike Baffin Island: backpack along the 100 km Akshayuk pass in Auyuittuq National Park—see Mt. Thor: the "biggest wall on earth"

on the river, their survival depends on how well they can handle their craft, the river, and the wilderness. No soft bed awaits them at the end of the day, and meals are not catered. Accidents and injuries may be life-threatening. The tourist who chooses this type of trip feels a sense of self-discovery and accomplishment once the trip has been completed.

Canada is full of interesting opportunities: heli-skiing, ice climbing, spelunking (caving), sea kayaking, and whitewater rafting. British Columbia abounds with hard adventure experiences and hosts one of Canada's most unusual winter sports—winter surfing. Surfing along the West Coast can be a challenge at any time of the year, but especially when winter storms hit. Canadians first started riding the winter waves in the 1940s, and more than 4000 surfing enthusiasts brave the frigid waves and the cyclonic winds every winter.

Soft Adventure

Soft adventure has some of the thrills of hard adventure but lacks the need to pre-train, has much of the risk factor removed, and has provided facilities to make the "adventurer" more comfortable along the way. Soft adventure may provide vehicles to move the visitor to the activity, comfortable shelter and bedding, and may even bring along a cook. The scale that slides between the two activities subtracts "luxuries" and adds risk.

A climb that might be in the realm of "softer" adventure is the trek up Mt. Kilimanjaro (5895 m) in Tanzania. The path is well trod and maintained and

Chilko River Expeditions provides tourists with a wet and wild ride in Chilkotin, B.C.
(Photo courtesy Canadian Tourism Commission.)

there are stopping stations along the way for rest and refreshment. However, the mountain is high enough to cause pulmonary edema, a deadly reaction of the body to climbing too high too fast, causing the lungs to fill with water and making breathing difficult and causing death. (Note: any high climb presents this risk.) In Canada, our two most difficult mountains to climb are Robson (3954 m) in B.C. and Logan (5959 m) in the Yukon. Mt. Robson's high flat face makes the climb even harder, and the inaccessibility of Mt. Logan adds to its mystique for climbers. Because of its isolation, climbing Mt. Logan means being dropped by helicopter at its base and climbing without any additional resources and no way to get help quickly. Smaller mountains do exist in the Rockies that present less risk: Mt. Rundel (2948 m) in Banff and Mt. Athabasca (3491m) on the border of Banff and Jasper parks.

Soft adventure has much of the risk removed because companies who specialize in soft adventure have studiously worked to control risks to their guests. This doesn't mean that people who participate in these soft adventure activities will never get hurt, but with the proper equipment and trained leaders, soft adventure can be both exciting and safe. The CTC states that 23% of outdoor activities link to soft adventure, and the average age of participants is 18–44.[7] Baby boomers are just discovering soft adventure. Some soft adventures might include cross-country skiing in Austria, visiting the Great Wall of China, swimming with dolphins in the Caribbean, or whitewater rafting with a large raft and guide. The key to planning this type of adventure is to determine the amount of effort and risk demanded from the participant in order to enjoy the activity. Canadian entrepreneurs continue to expand adventure tourism to meet new market demands. Gone is the image of retirees shuffling off to sit in rocking chairs. This market is looking for adventure without the physical demands of hard adventure, so soft adventure looks to be a good source of income for the ATOR industry over the next 25 years.

Ecotourism

www.planeta.com

Ecotourism is defined as "responsible travel designed to educate the traveller about the interrelationships and physiology of organisms and their environment." More simply stated, it teaches the participant the importance of understanding and conserving the world's ecosystems and habitats.

Sustainable tourism is "the informed partnership of all relevant stakeholders constantly assessing impacts and introducing the necessary corrective measures to ensure a meaningful experience to the tourists, raising their awareness and promoting sustainable tourism practices."[8] In other words, sustainable tourism links all of the partners in the ecotourism experience, ensuring that the current visitor enjoys the experience without compromising the ability of future generations to do the same. This is the goal tourism hopes to achieve, and it is one of the three major criteria of the 2010 Olympic Winter Games. Developing a sustainable product that is ecologically sound is called **responsible tourism**. Specific criteria determine whether you are taking part in responsible tourism or not. Both the tourism supplier and consumer have responsibilities, which should include the following:

- minimizing the negative economic and environmental impacts
- generating greater economic benefits for local people and enhancing the well-being of host communities
- improving working conditions and access to the industry
- involving local people in decisions that affect their lives and life changes
- making positive contributions to the conservation of natural and cultural heritage and embracing diversity
- providing a more enjoyable experience for tourists through more meaningful connections with local cultural, social, and environmental issues
- providing access for physically challenged people

Being culturally sensitive encourages respect between tourists and hosts and builds local pride and confidence.

The best tool to ensure sustainability and responsibility, many believe, is through environmental legislation—and enforcement. The Yukon has done just that, putting in place a tough wilderness tourism licensing law that requires companies to have a permit to conduct adventure tours—one that can be revoked if a company does not follow strict **low impact camping** techniques. Low impact camping requires that every item carried into the wilderness be carried out, that every item created during the trip be carried out, that campers use only enclosed fires and biodegradable products, and that campsites be returned to their original state by smoothing out the leaves and replacing any items that have been moved during the stay. Not only is the legislation tough but the fines are large.

www.vancouverislandout doors.com

The Ecotourism Market Segment

www.ecotourism.sk.ca

Surveys have shown that **ecotourists** are generally more mature, have post-secondary education, prefer longer trips (8 to 14 days), and are willing to pay a higher price for this style of tourism.[9]

Concerns for the environment and a love of the outdoors have made biking vacations popular (Yukon Territories).
(Photo courtesy Canadian Tourism Commission.)

Two other growing areas of interest are cultural and heritage tourism. They are almost one and the same thing. Cultural tourism immerses the visitor in the natural history, human heritage, arts, philosophies and institutions of another culture. It also educates the visitor in the architecture, food, and folklore or religion of this culture. About 11% of our visitors can be defined as heritage travellers, and they tend to come from empty nest homes (children are gone). As with the ecotourist market, many of these travellers have diplomas or degrees. Heritage travellers

Wildlife in Canada provides many tourists with both amusing snapshots and more frightening ones. This one shows Newfoundland puffins on parade.
(Photo: Wendy Booth.)

usually combine several activities in their trip, including a visit to historic sites, museums, and events, and families will also include activities appropriate for the age of the children. Most vacations include a component that might be called cultural tourism because it is difficult to travel to another region and not enjoy some of their cultural/historical sites and events.

Risk Management

In this new age of litigation, tourism companies are finding that insurance policies alone do not provide adequate financial or legal coverage if a customer is injured or killed while under their care. We have just been discussing hard and soft adventures, so it is appropriate that we return to the term "risks" and discuss how to try to manage them. A risk management program is not created just for hard core adventure activities, but should be in place for all tourism endeavours. Risk management identifies all potential hazards customers may encounter while under your care, and it reviews the products, services, and processes used in delivering them. Risk management should provide historical data on past accidents or losses, and identify possible risk scenarios in the future. Each risk should then be analyzed carefully, noting frequency, possible loss ratios, the impact of the loss to the customer, and how the incident will affect public perception of the business or activity. At this point, the company should consider each risk and how a staff member should respond if a crisis arises. Included in this list should be the proper safety standards as set out by a manufacturer; also the staff must know the safety standards handbook and be trained to handle situations according to management's directives. Environmental risks must be minimal, and emergency plans tested and in place. Signage identifying all risks must be clear and readily visible, and should alert users to the following:

- the obvious dangers of the activity (e.g., whether not following all safety precautions may result in injury or death)
- any unusual dangers of the activity (e.g., high water levels)
- dangers that apply to specific consumers (e.g., whether a trail requires a high level of expertise, experience, and physical stamina)

Why worry about risk management if it is common knowledge that the activities your company provides have inherent risks (such as swimming with sharks)? A risk management policy can reduce insurance costs by providing an insurance company with documented proof of a high standard of care. Many colleges and universities now offer risk management courses in their programs. Risk management has become a core skill for any tourism business.[10]

OUTDOOR RECREATION

Recreational sports and **outdoor recreation** are a big business in North America. If Canadians are to stay healthy and fit with outdoor exercise throughout the year, then the seasons dictate that they must engage in more than one sport. This benefits both the equipment suppliers and the tourism sector.

A change of season means a tourist may return to enjoy a resort for an entirely different purpose: hiking, playing tennis, or golfing in the summer; skiing, snowboarding, or skating in the winter.

Canada marked the new millennium with the creation of a continuous trail that joins the country from Newfoundland and the Atlantic Ocean to Nunavut and the Arctic, ending at the Pacific Ocean in British Columbia. The project has been designed and built by Canadian associations that represent many outdoor recreational activities such as hiking and cross-country skiing. The Trans Canada Trail (TCT), which is the longest trail of its kind in the world, covers 16 000 km, winds through every province and territory, and provides outdoor enthusiasts with five core activities: walking, cycling, horseback riding, cross-country skiing, and snowmobiling. The Trans Canada Trail Foundation, a non-profit charitable organization, funded the building of the trail with government grants and donations from local businesses and individuals across Canada. The trail is maintained by communities, and the shared experience of building and maintaining the trail has strengthened the tie that binds Canadians—a love of the outdoors.[11]

Winter Sports

Some winter sports enthusiasts claim Canada has the best snow conditions in the world, and that attracts the European, Asian, and Australian ski or snowboard enthusiast. We already have some older (but still state of the art) ski jumps and skating rinks in Alberta and Banff as reminders of the Winter Olympics of 1988. These help train athletes from around the world. The west is also known for its incredible powder skiing. Powder Springs Resort in Revelstoke, B.C., has some of the best big mountain heli-skiing in the world. The lure of virgin powder and a big drop can bring in $1000 per day plus. Move over skiers, the snowboarders are now an official event at the winter Olympics. While skiing has always played an important role in keeping Canadians fit over the winter season, so has skating. Currently Canada has two "rinks" vying for a place in the *Guiness World Records*: the Rideau Canal in Ottawa and Lake Winnipeg in Manitoba. This is a Canadian text book, and hockey does not come first as the main winter sport? The most participated-in winter sport by Canadians from the backyard to the major professional rink, hockey stays an active Canadian sport right through the summer with street hockey. Skidooing, dog sledding, curling, tobogganing, ice sailing and ice climbing—just a partial list of sports available to keep you in shape. Give Canadians a little snow and they'll find a great way to use it! Most of our snow sports are for domestic tourists. We don't get a large number of U.S. visitors to our hills as they have fabulous high mountains too, but Europeans are beginning to discover Canada. With temperatures slowly rising, the ski hills in Austria and Switzerland are finding snow a disappearing commodity. Many Europeans prefer the Canadian ski resorts because of their international flavour and rate them higher than U.S. ski hills for quality of snow and runs.

For the winter athlete, Canada offers some unique events. In January, the Raid International Ukatak takes place. Four-person racing teams from around the globe travel across a 40-km course that tests both their endurance and skills. Over the five-day race, participants will use snowshoes, cross-country skis, mountain bikes, and ice canoes (canoes with blades on the bottom). In February, two major events take place: the Canadian Ski Marathon, and the Yukon Quest International Sled Dog Race. Nearly 2000 skiers take part in the ski marathon, which covers a 160-km trail from Lachute in the Laurentian Mountains to Buckingham, Quebec, just outside the National Capital Region. The Yukon Quest follows the historic gold rush trail from Whitehorse to Fairbanks, Alaska. It is billed as the world's toughest dogsled race, and covers 1600 km of wild winter terrain.

For tourists who might enjoy lying flat on their backs while careening down a mountainside at 50 km per hour, with the only sound the roar of steel runners against compact snow, there is the wonderful world of the natural luge. Dating from the early 19th century, natural luge has been a fringe winter sport in Canada for fewer than 20 years. Unlike the modern luge used at the Winter Olympic Games, the natural luge's steel edges are kept flat on the ground and riders steer with reins and flexible foot-driven wooden levers. North America's first dedicated commercial natural luge course is at Mount Washington Alpine Resort on Vancouver Island. Toronto residents can try Rodle Mountain Luge Training Centre, located near Bancroft.[12]

Spring, Summer, and Fall Sports

Hunting and fishing play an integral part in the lives of Aboriginal Canadians and are major revenue generators for the tourism sector. About 5% of Canadians and 6% of Americans use their vacations enjoying these two sports. Hunters and fishers purchase equipment, lodging, food, and transportation. Freshwater sport fishing alone grosses over $650 million annually for the tourism sector.[13] For the best experience, hunters and fishers know that they must travel into the northern regions of a province. Fly-in fishing camps in the northern regions of all provinces appeal to the true fisher. Deep, pristine lakes, with a wide variety of

Despite warnings, tourists are willing to take chances for that perfect picture.
(Photo courtesy Canadian Tourism Commission.)

SNAPSHOT

Ellsworth Statler

"Life is service. The one who progresses is the one who gives his fellow human being a little more, a little better service." Ellsworth Statler followed his own advice throughout his career. He began as a bellhop, and owned several successful (and unsuccessful) restaurants before he moved into the hotel business. He was a details man, and some of the ideas used successfully in his hotels were full bathrooms with running ice water, telephones, closets with lights, and common colour schemes in each room. From his food service experience he recognized the need for tight cost controls, an auditing system for products, standardized recipes in his kitchens, and local food producers to keep his menu dishes fresh and reasonably priced. Statler started the "service side table" idea, keeping napkins, cutlery, glasses, and condiments easily accessible for servers in the dining room. He also moved his kitchens from the basement of his hotels to the ground floor near the dining room for quicker service. In his hotels, he ordered all guestroom doors to be cut an inch shorter so that staff could slip the morning newspaper under the door. Finally, at a time when no considerations were given to the working class, he introduced health and benefits packages, which included pensions for all Statler personnel. He has left not only his namesake hotels, but also a large endowment called the Statler Foundation. This organization provides students of today with scholarships and hospitality schools with grants so that his idea of "life" service can be continued through education.

fish species, are particularly attractive to the U.S. market. Accessibility of the lake or forest region often determines the quality of the sport fishing or hunting. Hunting and fishing guides with an intimate knowledge of the area may be used to further ensure a good trip. Provinces grant licences for both hunting and fishing, placing limits on the hunting season and the number of animals that may be taken. Park rangers patrol northern highways and randomly stop those leaving the area to check that limits have been respected. Although the popularity of fishing continues to grow in North America, hunting is fast losing its appeal to the younger market; however, hunting plays an important role in maintaining healthy numbers of wildlife, including bears, deer, and ducks. In national parks, hunting and fishing regulations are made at the federal level, and Parks Canada personnel are responsible for selling the appropriate licences and enforcing regulations.

Camping More than 14% of all Canadian vacations are camping trips, and 9.2% of U.S. travellers camp out on vacation.[14] Our parks systems encourages camping by providing a number of different services. In some parks, tourists will find interpretive centres to help them understand the region's ecosystem; small stores that provide environmentally safe soaps, firewood, and other products; and sometimes huts with shower stalls. Advance reservations are advisable for camping in a provincial park, especially at popular parks in the summer. Although camping experiences vary greatly between major campgrounds with facilities and wilderness sites, gaining knowledge of the area and its dangers should be part of any pre-camp planning.

Golf Golf has become the most popular sport in Canada. As baby boomers age, more are choosing to walk the greens of a local golf course or to fashion a winter vacation around one of the golf resorts in the southern United States. About 5% of Canadian travellers and 7% of American travellers pick up their clubs while on vacation.[15] About 2.2 million golfers take to the greens in Canada every season, spending nearly $1 billion annually on equipment, accessories, and fees. Golfers are also likely to spend their tourism dollars on other forms of entertainment, including gambling and spectator sports.[16]

Marine Activities Canada offers a multitude of popular marine experiences and water-based activities. Besides fishing and swimming, coastal waters provide tourists with opportunities to go whale watching, sea kayaking, sailing in tall ships, and deep-sea diving. In Canada's interior, lakes and rivers provide some of the finest fishing and river rafting in the world.[17] The Ottawa River near Pembroke, Ontario, offers excellent whitewater rafting, and rafters come from as far away as Australia and Sweden to train on the river. Sitting on the banks of the Athabasca River in Jasper, Alberta, visitors can watch kayakers on Athabasca's challenging rapids. Swimming, waterskiing, sailing, canoeing, kayaking, and boating are all part of the water experience.

Walking The most popular exercise by far requires no equipment and can be done anywhere at any time. According to the National Sporting Goods Association,

Our northern territories host several world-renowned dog sledding races during peak winter months such as Yukon Quest Dog Sled Race, 1600 km.
(Photo courtesy Canadian Tourism Commission.)

walking far outranks all other forms of exercise. Many cities have walking or bike paths. The large areas of green space that envelop the city of Ottawa, for example, provide safe, easily accessible paths for jogging, biking, and walking. In Vancouver, the path that follows the water's edge in Stanley Park provides residents and tourists with a scenic walk. Even large cities like New York, Boston, and Toronto offer easily accessible walking paths. No matter where you vacation, walking provides you with daily exercise and the chance to meet local residents and perhaps learn more about their city and culture.

Hiking How does hiking differ from walking? Hiking is generally done in a wilderness setting and is the method of transportation used by backpackers as they move into the area, looking for good spots to set up camp. It is cheap, healthy, and always ready for people choosing to use their feet to transport themselves rather than a vehicle. It is also very earth-friendly. Choosing an area for hiking is important. The obvious factor to consider in that choice is the ability of the person. If you are not used to exercise, you can still hike, but you should choose a wilderness path that is not steep or rough. One of the nicest hikes in Alberta is the one to the hilltop teahouse at Chateau Lake Louise. A hike requiring tremendous strength would be the trek along the West Coast Trail. Perhaps a more important issue when choosing the wilderness path is the wildlife. As major predators are squeezed out of their habitats with the expansion of settlements, they become accustomed to humans and their flee instincts are dulled. Every year there are stories of human kills by bears or cougars. These attacks are usually quick and unexpected and even the most experienced hiker can be at risk. Knowing how best to defend yourself under these circumstances and keeping in touch with park authorities are your two best defences. Park authorities can tell you if there have been unusual sightings of large predators even beyond the boundary of the park.

There is no better way to learn than through experience. Here a father explains the markings on a rock found in Sambaa Deh Falls Park, NWT.
(Photo courtesy Canadian Tourism Commission.)

There are many other outdoor activities that can be enjoyed by tourists that offer them the chance to enjoy the climate and the scenery and to exercise at their discretion. Most accommodations that cater to the outdoor enthusiast can provide visitors with supplies and equipment, or can direct them to shops where they can rent whatever they need.

TOURISM'S IMPACT ON THE ENVIRONMENT

Tourism is inherently a user and, in some ways, an abuser of the environment. It is a sector that makes demands on and affects the resources it uses, whether those resources are land, water, air, or any of the inhabitants therein. Tourism around the world is, or at least should be, associated with environmental concerns. Establishing tourism management practices that limit harm to the environment is becoming a top priority for the tourism sector. Some companies have adopted strict recycling policies (Fairmont Hotels is a world-renowned example). There are two opposing views on the relationship between the environment and tourism.

One view holds that tourism provides an incentive for the restoration of historic sites and archaeological treasures, and for the conservation of natural resources. The economic gain from tourism provides the means by which these areas can be restored and preserved. Tourism can also serve as an alternative to more environmentally damaging activities, such as the extraction of minerals or timber. Logging in the world's forests results in the loss of 11 million hectares a year. This deforestation increases soil erosion, landslides, and floods, and reduces the plant population needed to replenish oxygen in the air. Loss of forested land has also caused significant decreases in adventure tourism travel, which depends on forest-based amenities for its drawing power. The Pacific Northwestern areas of Canada and the United States are scarred by clear-cutting, which decreases the scenic value and, therefore, the tourism appeal of the area. From this perspective, tourism is a friend to the environment since preserving this magnificent stands of trees is an integral part of the tourism experience.

The opposing view is that tourism means overcrowding, noise, litter, and disruption or extinction of animal life and vegetation. Tourism results in the dumping of waste materials into rivers and onto beaches. Individuals, groups, and experts who hold this view are adamant that tourism development should be halted or even reversed when it conflicts with the natural environment. The Great Barrier Reef near Australia is a prime example of environmental damage by tourists who knowingly or unknowingly kill the corals by stepping on them. Some may even take the corals home as souvenirs. From this perspective, tourism is an enemy of the environment.

A major problem with environmental damage is that many tourists do not even realize they are the culprits. Planning and education are fundamental to understanding and preserving natural environments. In many cases, the local arm of the federal land-managing agency takes on the responsibility of educating visitors through interpretive programs, brochures, and campfire talks. The education process starts with managers appreciating the relationship between people and the natural environment. An important concept in understanding this relationship is carrying capacity.

FOOTPRINT

"Mother Nature Bounds Back"

The coast of Indonesia has long been a scuba diver's paradise, with coral reefs and a wide variety of exotic, tropical fish. Local fishers catch these colourful specimens and export them for sale in aquariums around the world. Thirty years ago, the fishers were introduced to a "better" and faster way to catch these fish. If a small amount of potassium cyanide was added to the water, the fish became drugged and easier to catch. While about 30% of their catch would die from the dosage, the remaining fish seldom had any injuries and brought in good prices. Nature, however, reacts to the intrusive manipulations of people, and over the years, the cyanide has slowly killed off the living reef. Many fishers were forced to leave the business altogether. Those who stayed in the area returned to their roots, catching fish the old-fashioned way by waiting quietly and then snagging them in their net. It took longer to catch the numbers needed, but death rates dropped dramatically and the fish that were caught seemed to maintain more of their brilliance. In the past few years, these reefs have rebounded, and the beautiful, thriving reef community is once again full and healthy.

(CNN, News at Noon, March 26, 2008.)

Carrying capacity is the maximum number of people who can use a site with only *acceptable alteration* to the physical environment and with only *acceptable decline* in the quality of the experience for subsequent visitors. Determining carrying capacity has become a science that requires setting goals for the area, defining acceptable levels of environmental modification, and

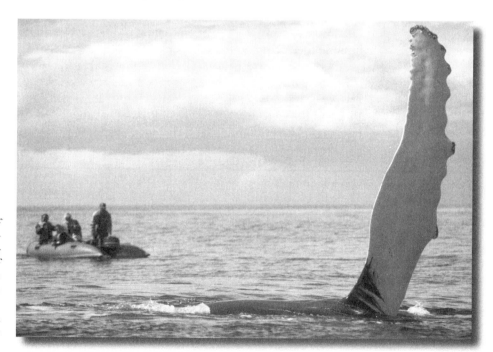

To feel the power of whales playing alongside your boat is a thrill; to learn of their struggle to survive is an education.

(Photo courtesy Canadian Tourism Commission.)

considering the kinds of use. No two areas have the same set of carrying capacity factors. Canada has been attempting to identify carrying capacity in national parks, wilderness areas, camping areas, and front country (that is, the highly developed area consisting of road access, visitor centres, lodging, and retail outlets). There are few available studies, but a recent survey of national parks reported that two-thirds of the regions suffered stress from the ecological impacts of visitors.

One successful approach is to limit privileges or access to more delicate park areas. For example, in order to preserve the Great Bear experience, Klemtu Tourism plans to limit the number of participants to 150 per year.[18]

Tourism's impact on the natural environment can be better understood by studying environmental components separately.

Vegetation Tourism may affect vegetation to the point of destroying the beauty of the area as well as the ability of plants to grow. For example, gathering twigs and branches to light a campfire has been a common practice at most campgrounds; however, stripping a campsite of live branches can permanently damage the trees. Also, fallen branches and twigs decay and become a good source of nutrients for the soil; when they are removed, the soil loses this benefit. To alleviate this problem, land-managing agencies now offer firewood to campers for free or for a minimal fee. Rangers selectively collect this firewood in order to minimize damage to any one area.

Most tourists simply do not think—when they pull up a pretty flower—that the collection of flowers and plants by tourists can cause changes in species distribution. Parks Canada is trying to educate visitors by posting signs along pathways and roads with messages such as "Leave only footprints, take only pictures." Vegetation is often trampled by visitors who do not understand the nature of the plant world. Most people don't consider that their footsteps harm vegetation or prevent it from growing back. The impact on vegetation becomes more serious with intensive traffic in delicate ecosystems and terrain, and can be minimized by building trails and walkways that allow tourists access to controlled areas while limiting their access to more fragile areas.

The careless use of fire has caused long-term damage to many forests and parks. In addition to educating visitors, Parks Canada restricts campfire use during dry periods or in high-use areas. For example, some parks, such as Banff National Park and Rocky Mountain National Park, allow only small stoves in back country. Fires are simply prohibited, and the policy is strictly enforced.

Litter, besides being unsightly, can damage vegetation by changing the composition of the soil, which in turn can change the ecosystem balance. Litter may also kill animals that eat it.

Water Quality Tourism affects water quality in many different ways. Campers using sunscreen, soap, and dishwashing liquid in streams and lakes do not realize that these products leave an unsightly and oily film on water—and introduce chemicals. Low impact camping techniques suggest the use of non-stick pans that require no chemicals to clean or, better yet, soap-free camping. Camping has also increased the level of human waste in water, and mountain lakes are particularly vulnerable to this type of damage. These waste materials carry parasites that can harm the aquatic environment as well as the next visitor who drinks from that water. Using the proper facilities provided by park management services is important, and campers in Canada's less accessible wilderness regions must learn the techniques for safe disposal of human waste. Although dumping refuse is decreasing as citizens become more aware of the damage it can cause, some careless boaters still throw drink cans overboard.

Other concerns relate to oil spills and overbuilding along oceans and lakes. Since 1979, more than 9000 significant oil- and tar-related spills have occurred in the wider Caribbean region, including the Gulf of Mexico, the Straits of Florida, and eastern approaches to the Caribbean Sea.[19] As a result, windward-exposed beaches have tar deposits. Water quality is also affected by activities such as recreational boating, swimming, and camping. Recreational boating on lakes and oceans leaves fuel and oils in the water, causing damage to aquatic plants and wildlife by depleting the oxygen level. The solution is to change tourists' boating habits, restricting the use of motorboats while allowing canoes, rowboats, kayaks, and other small muscle-powered craft.

Wildlife The impact of tourism on wildlife is great, and ranges from causing animals become too comfortable with the presence of humans, to hastening the extinction of a species. Many animals have learned to tolerate the presence of tourists, and in communities like Jasper and Banff, wild animals such as elk and mountain sheep have the right of way on highways and in town. However, the consequences of tourism include disrupted feeding and breeding habits, destruction of habitats, altered food chains, and extinction. Tourism disrupts feeding and breeding habits through resort expansion, overzealous attempts to photograph wildlife, and inappropriate trail development. Tourism development reduces the size of animal habitats, putting greater pressure on the remaining habitat. This condition increases the risk that animals will compete with humans for food and water—or that humans will become a food source. Grizzly bears and cougars scavenge in campgrounds and garbage dumps, and some actually stalk human victims. British Columbia and Alberta have seen an increase in bear and cougar attacks over the past few years and alert people to the dangers whenever possible. Vacationers may believe that because they are spending only a few days in the wilderness, the odds are with them. They are probably right, but being wrong may mean death or injury.

On an international scale, tourist consumption of ivory, fur, animal skins, skulls, and tails has contributed significantly to the illegal killing of many animals. Among those most savagely hunted and nearly eliminated is the African elephant, hunted solely for its ivory tusks, which are made into jewellery, figurines, and piano keys. Importing and selling most ivory products in Canada is now prohibited.

Coastlines Images of sun, surf, and sand have long lured tourists to coastlines around the world. Too often, insufficient planning means that plant and animal habitats are disrupted; geological features are destroyed by excavation; water supplies are contaminated; and the natural beauty of the area is diminished. Lack of planning includes draining swamps or wetland areas for development that is incompatible with the preservation of many species, and failing to properly control sewage and garbage. Littering by tourists has turned many coastline areas into dumping grounds.

Tourism planning in coastal areas needs to consider the effects of structures such as high-rise hotels, and the over-development of beaches. Attention must be given to issues such as unstable ground, water drainage, and eroding cliffs. Regulation of these fragile areas needs to be enforced so that visitors are able to experience coastlines in their natural form.

Mountains The human desire—or need—to leave the pressure of city life behind has put tremendous strains on mountain ecosystems. Mountain terrains are developed as ski areas, hiking and riding trails, campgrounds, and resorts. Accessing the mountains requires roadways that disrupt wildlife habitats. Utility lines are unsightly to area inhabitants and visitors. Roads, ski trails and lifts, hiking trails, and four-wheel-drive trails all contribute to land erosion. In higher elevations where the ecosystem is extremely fragile and the slopes are often steep, the carrying capacity is small.

Deserts Once thought of as places to avoid, desert terrains are now playgrounds for tourists and local residents who travel in dune buggies and four-wheel-drive vehicles and on trail bikes. Many desert areas have been marred by noise, dust, fuel smells, and litter. This fragile environment has lost plant species, animal life, and water holes to the overuse by off-road vehicles. Many people believe the desert is a wasteland anyway, so increasing recreation is the best way to make use of it. The only advantage desert plants and animals have over the tourist is their ability to survive on little water. Fortunately, the lack of this precious resource means that deserts are less likely to become popular for resorts—communities that inevitably endanger the ecosystem.

In Practice

In groups of three to five, design a carrying capacity plan for public land near your school. This land could be a national or provincial park or forest, or any other government-owned land used by visitors. Keep in mind how the area is used and what natural plants, animals, water, or ecosystems exist. Determine the number of people to be allowed at a given time and indicate what criteria you used to set this number. How will you enforce the carrying capacity?

Tourism, while often referred to as "a green industry" because it takes little from a destination, also leaves much pollution behind. In trying to help conserve and save the planet, the UNWTO declared 2002 to be the International Year of Ecotourism (IYE). Many conferences were hosted around the world that began seriously talking about changes in the ecology of the world. That year, Quebec City hosted a Summit meeting to focus on the ecological damages created by the tourism industry.

Over 1100 delegates participated from 132 different countries, showing that global concern is there. The outcome was the "Quebec Declaration on Tourism," a paper that contains specific information on developing a sustainable ecotourism industry. It identified transportation, an essential industry for tourism, as one of the major problems. Scientists have determined that air travel alone is responsible for 3.5% of greenhouse gas emissions. Not figured into that number is the pollution from our cars and buses.

Consumers pay for and expect a beautiful, undisturbed landscape around their vacation "home." However, while we may look like a "green" industry, we are not.

We need roads, infrastructure to support our buildings, hotels, restaurants, airports, and so on. Scientists use the term "carbon footprint" as a measure of the environmental damage incurred by the amount of greenhouse gases produced. Companies or people with concern for the environment try to make their carbon footprint as small as possible. However, if you travel a lot by plane, this is difficult. It is up to the individual purchasing the flight or trip to reduce their impact by purchasing carbon credits. Very simply stated, when you purchase a carbon credit you are buying an emission offset—the money spent could go toward planting a tree or investing in low-emission machinery, for example. Airlines and tour operators are making it easier to maintain your small carbon footprint by purchasing carbon credits online or when you buy your ticket.

Balancing the Negative Environmental Impact

It is certainly important that we begin to deal with climate warming seriously; however, some scholars argue that the purchasing of carbon credits in fact may do as much harm as they do good. By allowing a company to continue to use offending equipment (such as an aircraft or a coal burning furnace) without thought of reducing the carbon dioxide released into the air is not helping to solve the situation, even if their entire output is purchased on a yearly basis. More important is that the company use more fuel-efficient, non-carbon-producing methods of energy. Summing up some of the concerns, Julianna Priskin of Reseau de vielle en tourisme, University of Quebec at Montreal, says that relying solely on this method can cause problems:

- If the trees are destroyed by fire or natural causes, the carbon is released into the atmosphere, thus negating your "purchase."
- It is a complicated procedure to measure how much carbon dioxide a forest can absorb and still very much a subject of debate.
- The effectiveness of a plantation depends on the type of tree species planted. For example, pine trees and non-native trees provide no biodiversity value.
- The establishment of "sink plantations" by developing countries may be displaced or lose access to traditional lands without being properly compensated.
- Planting trees does not move away from using fossilized fuels, nor does it encourage the development of renewable energy or renewable energy projects. It simply makes the person who buys the credits feel better.

She suggests that people who are concerned and travel a lot should try to reduce travel whenever possible and learn to cut their own emissions at home (a positive move for all of the family). If that is not possible, she suggests that making sure the plantation you are investing in is set for a minimum of 100 years, that it is a forest made of hardwood (or the most appropriate local) species, and that the project is one designed for this specific purpose and not simply the reforestation of an already clear area.

The environment's role in tourism—the scenic beauty of mountains, streams, lakes, oceans, and valleys—cannot be overstated. But unless the environment is treated with care and respect, there may soon be no scenic beauty to visit—we may be loving our parks, mountains, and lakes to death.

In Practice

Global warming is a confusing topic. Much of the world is beginning to understand the need for changes in how we live and do business. However, there are still some who deny global warming is taking place. They believe that global warming is a natural progression of climate change that has occurred over the centuries. What are your thoughts on global warming? In teams, take a piece of paper and divide it down the middle. On one side, list the ways in which you think global warming is occurring. On the other side, what arguments have you heard that deny this happening? If your team has concluded that global warming is a reality, what actions have individual team members taken to help slow it?

Canada's Green Plan

The **Green Plan**, created 20 years ago, was a commitment to solve Canada's complex environmental challenges and implement sustainable economic development, identifying tourism as an important partner in the plan.[20] It recommended that 12% of Canada's lands be protected space for parks, historic sites, and wildlife, still a priority for the government. Education of Canadians about the environment and how to protect it was another important piece. However, Canada has never received top grades for implementing positive changes. The Great Lakes is a prime example of the lack of positive movement. A recent report has identified 17 highly contaminated sites, several where raw sewage is being dumped directly into the waters, as an example of lack of effort. The cost of cleaning these sites is estimated at $3.5 billion dollars. The underlying philosophy of the government's sustainable development policy is to change decision making. Changes will only come about, however, if the decision-making process includes environmental considerations. Unfortunately, funding promised by the government for scientific and technical research has not appeared.

www.iisd.ca

Many tourism businesses are getting into the "green" trade as they see the trend toward global warming increase. Some businesses handle the challenge very well while others just pay lip service. Hotels have formed Green Committees and earn "trees" for suggesting environmentally sound practices. Once a year, the teams who have earned the most "trees" win trips to places like Jamaica or Acapulco. Competition can be fierce! The program enlists guests as well as employees in the effort to reduce, reuse, and recycle. Not only does the program benefit the environment, but the company also saves thousands of dollars yearly by

- reducing waste sent to landfill sites by 50%
- redesigning purchasing policies to ensure waste reduction at source
- collecting and recycling all recyclables—cans, glass, paper, etc.
- using environmentally friendly hotel supplies[21]

CASE STUDY

Buyer Beware

A major hotel located near Rio de Janeiro, Brazil, promotes itself as a green luxury resort. It offers a broad variety of activities including golf and tennis, as well as sandy beaches for swimming. However, if you vacation at this hotel, you will soon find that the advertisement did not mention there is only one tennis court. And that sandy beach? It's a five-minute drive from the hotel. The hotel has a shuttle service for the convenience of guests, but that does not change the fact that the pictures are misleading. Once there, guests learn that garbage is being dumped into a site just 10 km inland and that the water used by the hotel is being pumped directly into the river.

Pictures are not always truthful. What can a purchaser do to ensure that what is advertised is what they get?

1. As a guest, would you leave and demand a full refund? Or would you stay and enjoy your holiday and then complain once you got home? Or would you not complain at all?
2. Why would a country allow misleading information to be advertised by one of its hotels?
3. What level of truth is owed to a client? If this experience turns out to be one of your best holidays ever, will this change your actions once you get home?

Summary

The adventure tourism and outdoor recreation component is geared to activity. People who partake of this industry fall into four categories: those who are looking for hard adventure such as mountain climbing; those who prefer a softer adventure such as hiking up a mountain path; those looking for a unique ecotourism experience; and those looking for an outdoor recreational sport such as golfing, fishing, skiing, or boating.

Parks Canada, an independent agency reporting to Environment Canada, maintains our nationally protected wildlife areas and historic sites and canals.

It is important for the student aiming for a career in tourism to remember that tourism is not without its negative effects. Development of any sort will put some form of stress on the area's vegetation, water, and animal life. Establishing goals and minimizing environmental impact through a well-thought-out carrying capacity plan will benefit both the visitor and the natural environment. Some areas should not be developed because of the fragility of the terrain, but in general, if a good plan is implemented, tourists will cause minimal damage to the environment.

Sustainable tourism development encourages tourism while maintaining the natural environment. Canada's Green Plan provides us with a governmental code of ethics. Education is the key to environmental awareness in the tourism sector. Some businesses are already working toward an environmentally safe industry. Examples of environmentally friendly practices include limiting the number of participants, switching to recyclable or reusable materials, using biodegradable soaps, turning down thermostats and lights, and developing a resort or hotel *around* the landscape rather than destroying the landscape itself. As travellers become concerned about the environment, businesses will need to respond to consumer demands.

Questions

1. Parks Canada, an independent agency reporting to Environment Canada, interacts with the tourism sector in two of the eight components of tourism. Identify these two components and show how tourism illiteracy on the part of this agency could undermine the overall Canadian tourism product.

2. Tourists use both federal and provincial parks during outdoor vacation experiences.
   a) Explain the differences and similarities you might see in these parks.
   b) List all of the federal and four of the provincial parks found in your province.

3. Ecotourism is based on what four principles?

4. Is ecotourism an important part of your province's overall tourism product? Justify your answer by referring to the characteristics of ecotourists and how they relate to your province's tourism product.

5. Briefly summarize a minimum of five outdoor recreational experiences available to tourists in your region.

6. Choose four inconsistencies between the needs of the tourist and the need to protect Canadian wilderness. Explain how tourists might enjoy these regions with little or no impact on the environment.

7. Do you believe Canada is doing enough to protect our environment? Defend your answer using examples.

8. Define the following terms as they relate to adventure tourism and outdoor recreation: *hard adventure, soft adventure, sustainable tourism, carrying capacity, Trans Canada Trail.*

Notes

1. ctx_news@ctc.cct.ca, October 18, 2002 article.

2. www.parkscanada.ca.

3. Ibid.

4. Ibid.

5. www.gov.bc.ca.

6. *Heritage Tourism: Discover the Opportunity*, Industry Canada and Canadian Heritage.

7. www.parkscanada.ca.

8. *Canadian Geographic*, Travel Adventure Booklet, Winter 2003.

9. www.ecotourism.org.

10. *Risk Management and Insurance Guide for the Adventure, Ecotourism and Alpine Skiing Industries*, Canadian Tourism Commission.

11. *The Trail Story*, Trans Canada Trail website, www.tctrail.ca.

12. www.tourism.gov.on.ca, Outdoor Segmentation, TAMS 1999.

13. Ibid.

14. Ibid.

15. Ibid.

16. *The Student's Travel Map* (Ottawa: Canadian Tourism Human Resource Council, 1995), p. 62.

17. *Tourism Industry Product Overview*, prepared for Tourism British Columbia and the Council of Tourism Associations of British Columbia, by Price Waterhouse and the ARA Consulting Group Inc., June 1996.

18. Nathalie Southworth, "Under the Great Bear's spell." *The Globe and Mail,* October 2, 2002.

19. Judy Crawford, "Environmental responsibility in the tourism industry," *Tourism: Building Credibility for a Credible Industry* (22nd conference of the Travel and Tourism Research Association, Long Beach, CA, 1991), p. 98.

20. R.W. Slater, "Understanding the relationship between tourism, environment and sustainable development," *Tourism—Environment—Sustainable Development: An Agenda for Research* (proceedings of the conference of the Canadian Chapter of the Travel and Tourism Research Association, Hull, Quebec, 1991), p. 11.

21. Lou Cook, "Shades of green," *Lodging,* October 1999, p. 67.

Travel Services

Key terms

all-inclusive tour
travel counsellor
commission
conference
  appointment
consolidator
consortium
corporate travel agency
customer profile

escorted tour
full-service travel
  agency
gateway city
ground/land package
higher value traveller
hosted tour
inbound tour
incentive travel

outbound tour
override
specialty travel
  agency
step-on guide
tour director
tour operator
tour wholesaler
unescorted tour

Learning objectives

Having read this chapter you will be able to

1. Compare and contrast the roles of tour operator, tour wholesaler, and retail travel agent in the travel services industry.

2. Explain the steps in creating and costing a packaged tour.

3. Define the terms *packaged tour, independent tour, group tour, fully escorted tour, hosted tour, validity dates, gateway city.*

4. Identify 10 distinct types of tours offered in today's travel market.

5. Discuss the advantages and disadvantages of taking a packaged tour.

6. Describe the travel agency by size, clientele, and ownership.

7. Summarize the changes occurring in travel agency operations and describe ways in which agencies are dealing with these changes.

8. Discuss the value and role of incentive travel in today's corporate world.

Selling travel is fun. It is a chance to put together someone's long-awaited dream vacation, to provide a tour of a hard-to-reach country, or to plan the best route at the lowest cost for a business traveller. Travel services comprise a major component of the tourism's sales force. Travel can be sold at the wholesale level by a tour operator or wholesaler, or at the retail level by a travel counsellor. Tour operators sell packages *through* retail travel counsellors, not *to* them. They pay the retail travel counsellor a **commission** and sometimes a volume incentive, often referred to as an **override**. Tour operators, then, are restricted to selling travel arrangements that they have contracted for ahead of time. Travel counsellors can sell all types of travel anywhere, including components offered by tour wholesalers or the pre-packaged tours offered by tour operators. More than 41 000 Canadians work in this industry[1] and, unlike the average tourism worker, travel counsellors are highly educated: 82% have post-secondary schooling.[2] This chapter discusses the business of wholesaling, retailing, and incentive travel.

THE HISTORY OF TOURS

Tours are a relatively new concept in the history of tourism. Their beginnings can be traced back to the early 17th century, when noblemen from England arranged educational tours for their sons and heirs. *Le grand tour* was designed to educate sons in the ways of the civilized world. Upon completion of this tour, these educated, worldly young men returned to the staid life of the British nobleman.

The first recognized packaged tour was developed not by a travel agent (for no such thing existed at that time), but by a minister. Thomas Cook was a firm believer in the evils of liquor, so when the opportunity came to take his parish to a temperance meeting in Leicester, England, he arranged transportation by rail, a small picnic lunch, and entertainment for 570 of his followers. At the end of the day, after all bills had been paid, Mr. Cook discovered he had actually made a profit. The success of this afternoon was repeated many times over, so Mr. Cook left his ministerial calling to form the world's first travel agency.

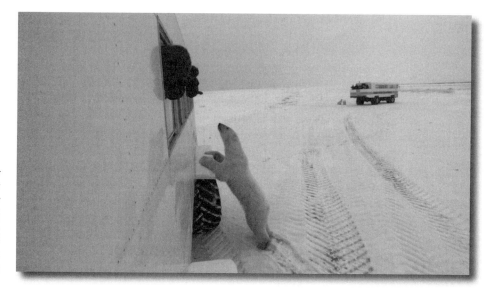

Tour operators have learned that their clientele like it live and close! *(Churchill, Manitoba)*
(Photo courtesy Canadian Tourism Commission.)

Early tours were individually designed and were affordable only to the wealthy, but that situation changed with the new age of jet travel. What had been a costly 18-hour flight or 6-day ocean crossing to Europe now became a 7-hour trip. The new *Boeing 707*s carried a larger passenger load, so the cost of the trip was also substantially reduced. Tours suddenly became affordable for the middle class, and in 1958, more than 700 000 people took tours to Europe. By 1989, this figure had risen to more than 7 million. Taking tours is not only less expensive than booking the transportation, lodging, and attractions separately, but the cost is also a known figure right from the time of booking. Tours are also prepaid, so the traveller need not worry about running out of money. Entrance to sights is guaranteed, because admission fees have been prepaid, and the sights have been chosen for their safety and appeal by a travel professional.

WHOLESALING

People are often confused about the terms **tour wholesaler** and **tour operator**. Traditionally, tour wholesalers went from one travel supplier to another, booking space for their tours. They did not buy the product but acted as intermediaries between the supplier and the travel agency. No money was exchanged until an actual purchase took place. By the mid-1960s, the marketplace had changed. Most of the suppliers requested a pre-purchase of the products to guarantee the low price. Tour operators became those companies willing to invest in advance, purchasing all the components of a tour prior to packaging it. There is still a distinction between these roles, although the lines have become blurred, and the players may overlap. For example, Sunquest acts both as a wholesaler, selling individual products to retail agencies, and as a tour operator, selling complete tour packages, including the services of a destination representative. In contrast, the Toronto-based Holiday House sells only as a wholesaler and does not operate its own tour product.

The latest type of operator to enter the tour business is called a **consolidator**. Consolidators act as wholesalers or intermediaries between the airlines and travel agencies and pay a commission on tickets sold. Most airlines no longer pay commissions to travel agencies, so the consolidator becomes an additional source of agency revenue. Consolidators purchase a large number of airline seats at a bulk price. They then sell these seats at a net price to travel agents, who pass the savings on to their customers. The savings may be as great as 50%—but a word of caution to anyone planning to use one of these tickets. Each ticket has restrictions, which may include advance purchase dates, minimum stay requirements, and no itinerary changes. Furthermore, they are non-endorsable, meaning no other airline will accept them, and flights may not be available every day. Most consolidators are reputable, but an agency must be cautious when dealing with a newer company. One of Canada's largest consolidators is Aventours. As long as international markets are regulated by IATA and deep discounted tickets are not available to the travelling public, you can expect the role of consolidators to continue to expand.

There are five types of tour operators in Canada. The first is an *independent tour* operator, a category that includes large corporations such as American Express or individual operators such as Sunquest. The second type is a travel agency, which packages tours and sells them to its clients. The third is an in-house tour operator, owned and managed by a large company such as Air Canada. The fourth type of tour operator is strictly online. They provide no glossy brochures or sales representatives, but appeal to those travellers looking for savings and comfortable with an online exchange. The last type does not sell to the public, but focuses on clubs, associations, and incentive travel groups. These tour packages must fit the special needs of the group (perhaps seniors or students) and may deal with such concerns as wheelchair accessibility or special medical equipment.

Tours are designated as either **outbound** or **inbound**. An *inbound* tour brings guests from a foreign country to Canada, generating jobs and revenue for Canadians. But when Canadians travel to Santo Domingo, for example, using a packaged tour, they are *outbound*, and their tourism dollars are being spent in a foreign country.

Tour Development

A tour is "the services on a tourist's itinerary, usually consisting of, but not limited to, transportation, accommodation, transfers, and sightseeing in one or more countries, geographical regions, or cities. The services are entirely reserved or contracted for in advance by a travel agent, a tour wholesaler, or a tour operator and are fully prepaid by the tourist."[3]

Tours are divided into two major categories: *independent tours* and *packaged tours*. Individuals or groups who prefer to create their own independent tour may do so using the services of a travel agent and a tour wholesaler. These customers choose between the assorted components offered by the tour wholesaler. Many travellers are opting to bypass the travel agency and do their own tour planning online. Using an online tour operator like Expedia.ca or Travelocity.ca, they can choose flight times, hotels, dining packages, events, and attractions they would like to see. Arrangements can be made at any time of the day or night, and the website guarantees flexibility for the purchaser. A packaged tour, on the other hand, has a set itinerary with all of its components in place. Packaged tours may or may not have an escort and are sold to individuals as well as to groups. Once again, the internet provides customers with fully designed packages that may be booked at any time. The companies that sell this type of tour generally focus on one type of traveller: the single traveller, the economy-minded traveller, or the higher value traveller. The budget-minded traveller would choose from tour operators like Sunquest. A **higher value traveller** is willing to spend more on the trip and looks for quality sites and products to be supplied. An example of a tour operator selling high end, unusual products would be Exodus Tours, a British-based tour operator.

www.exodus.co.uk

There are four steps in the creation of a tour: the tour idea, negotiations, costing and pricing, and promotion (Figure 10.1).

The Tour Idea Every tour has to be new once. After its first venture, the tour can be offered time and time again—if it was initially successful. New ideas, however, require creativity and the ability to listen to what people want. The idea may come from a supplier who provides a super deal for accommodations if the operator books a trip to the supplier's hotel. Or it may be an offshoot of a current trip, such as switching from a whale-watching tour to instead visiting Shediac, New Brunswick, to see the world's largest lobster and enjoy a lobster feast. Market research is needed to determine whether there is a need or a desire for the tour concept. Without

FIGURE 10.1
Tour development
stages

Tour Idea
Creative thinking
Past customers
Competitor's success
Suppliers
Future customers

Negotiation
Who will give you
discounts and how much
will the discounts be?

Costing Based on
1. Meals provided
2. Accommodation type
3. Length of stay in principal cities
4. Sightseeing and admissions included
5. Attractions planned

Promotion
Brochure development
and distribution to
travel counsellors

consumer demand, the tour, no matter how exciting, will not be a success. Most tours are developed around a central theme or destination: for example, learning more about polar bears in their natural habitat on Baffin Island. The theme or destination is the skeletal plan, which the planner must flesh out by providing other interesting or exciting reasons for people to take the tour.

Negotiations Once the destination and other attractions are chosen for inclusion in the tour, the negotiation phase of planning begins. Are there rooms available at the right price? Is there a suitable restaurant in the area for dinner? Will the chosen attractions guarantee entry at a guaranteed group rate? Will a tour guide with specialized skills and knowledge be needed for any part of the tour? What form(s) of transportation will be needed? These questions and others need to be answered before the next phase begins.

Costing and Pricing Costing is the process of determining the total cost of providing the tour for an anticipated number of customers. Pricing is the process of deciding the amount each customer should pay to cover costs, including a markup, operating expenses, and profit. In the costing stage, the direct cost of each component of the tour must be determined, such as transportation, lodging, attendance fees, and exchange rates. Then indirect costs such as promotion, the tour planner's salary, and other overhead items are added. In the pricing stage, a markup or profit on the net cost of the tour must be calculated. Once total cost is determined, assumptions must be made about the volume or number of tour participants in order to work out the price of the tour to the traveller. Correct costing requires an accurate assessment of certain variables, especially sales—usually projected based on past experience and projected load factors. As simple as it may sound, costing is an art and it is the most important step if a company plans to make a profit. Several factors will affect the price to the consumer. In each case, the operator and the travel agent should try to find the balance that best suits the target market.[4]

1. **Meal costs.** The tour operator can significantly lower the cost of the tour if the traveller pays for each meal separately. Advantages include less paperwork for the operator and perhaps greater choice for the traveller. The disadvantage is that tour participants will need to budget and pay for each meal. Many people like to pay one price and not have to worry about other costs during the trip. A tour operator who permits unlimited choice from the menu (à la carte) is offering more than an operator who arranges a set menu (table d'hôte); the tour price will reflect this.

2. **Accommodation type.** The level of accommodation significantly affects the price of the tour. An economy tour books less expensive motels, usually in smaller towns or out-of-the-way locations in larger cities. Deluxe tours are booked with the finest hotels in locations convenient for side trips, shopping, restaurants, and attractions.

3. **Length of stay in principal cities.** Usually deluxe tours spend more time at a principal destination because a good tour should be relaxing. The pacing of a tour (the amount of free or leisure time within a tour's schedule) is an important sales feature. This free time allows individuals to pursue specific interests, explore the destination, shop, or simply relax. Driving long distances every day is not a hallmark of a deluxe tour.

4. **Sightseeing.** On the other hand, itineraries that indicate "the remainder of the day is open to explore . . ." may be tours trying to keep costs down. Built-in sightseeing increases the tour cost. Some people prefer to have every minute accounted for; they want pampering and lots of supervision. Others prefer to make their own decisions and want more open time.

5. **Attractions.** Although the cost of the tour is higher when admission fees are included in the tour price, inclusion saves the traveller money in the long run because group discounts have usually been negotiated with the attraction manager. There is no general rule in costing a tour. Many people do not want to be nickel-and-dimed, whereas others prefer a low-cost tour that requires them to pay for meals and amenities along the way.

Promotion The sale and promotion of tour packages have become very sophisticated. Bright, glossy brochures with pictures featuring the excitement of a rafting experience or the comfort of a hotel are all designed to attract a broad range of clients. Television advertisements, travelogue presentations, and a well-designed home page on the internet also entice tourists. Without good promotional material, even the best tour product may find itself without customers.

Tour Categories

There are two main types of prearranged packaged tours. It is important for the customer as well as the travel counsellor selling the tours to understand the advantages and disadvantages of each type.

Independent Tours Travel counsellors and tour operators can arrange independent tours, but as previously mentioned, customers may create their own vacation packages by using one of the many online tour companies. So why use a travel agency? An agency likely knows the reputation of the chosen tour company, the destination's political or environmental atmosphere, and can accurately provide information regarding the documents and pre-trip medical advice that should be sought. They are also a link to home in case things do not go as planned. The small fee travel agencies charge is well worth it in the end. Single travellers obtain all the benefits of volume discounts and prearranged, guaranteed rates without sacrificing independence and flexibility. Customers can determine departure and return dates as well as budget.

Independent tours vary in flexibility and complexity. Some tours allow the customer to choose accommodations at different hotels listed in the brochure, while others provide car rentals, which increase flexibility for the traveller. Other tours may offer fly/drive, rail/drive, rail/fly, cruise/fly, or other combinations. The keys to independent tour success are flexibility and cost savings for the traveller.

Independent tours may use more than one tour wholesaler in the creation of the package, and a distinct disadvantage of taking an independent tour is that you are on your own. There is no company representative available to help find solutions in case of a problem or difficulty encountered during the trip.

Group Tours The original group tour was based on a true group—a club or a society that wished to take a trip. In order to take part in the tour, a traveller had to be a member of the club. Today, the main difference between a group tour and an independent tour is in the cost. Group tours are usually based on a given number of participants and may be cancelled or delayed if the required number of spaces for that departure date has not been sold. There are two types of group tours: **ground/land package** and **all-inclusive**.

Ground/land package tours include the land arrangements for the purchaser: hotel, attractions, perhaps some meals, and a rental car. They do not include airfare in the price.

Upscale tour operators choose hotels of distinction such as The Fairmont Empress Hotel in Victoria, often including their renowned afternoon English Tea.
(Photo courtesy Canadian Tourism Commission.)

All-inclusive tours have a specific combination of features, usually including transportation, accommodation, meals, attractions, special events, and service charges (such as tips and baggage handling), and may include amenities such as free travel bags and discount coupons. These tours may be fully escorted, partially escorted (hosted), or unescorted (independent).

- Fully **escorted tours** have a **tour director** travelling with the group. The tour director is responsible for the participants' safety and enjoyment, makes sure that the tour operates smoothly, and handles any problems or difficulties. Although the director is usually well prepared to describe the sights of an area, many companies hire **step-on guides** when visiting a city. Step-on guides have special training and a deep knowledge of and love for their city, region, or site. This makes their presentation more responsive to the needs of the group and provides participants with reliable answers to their questions. This type of tour is often preferred by first-time travellers and is most useful when travelling to a country whose culture is very different.

- In a partially escorted, or **hosted tour**, the group travels from destination to destination as a group, without a company representative. At each destination, a tour director from that city greets them and stays with them throughout their stay.

- In an **unescorted tour**, the group has an itinerary and travels without any company representative.

Types of Tours

Tours may be defined by destination and by their focus on a specific country, region, or city. A trip to the Cabot Trail in Nova Scotia is a good example of a regional tour. A two-city tour might bring visitors from Buffalo, New York, to both Montreal and Quebec City, giving them a varied experience of Canada's French culture. Tours defined by purpose are even more varied. Here are some popular examples (some will be familiar from Chapter 9):

- **adventure tours:** whitewater rafting on the Clearwater River through Skull Canyon in Saskatchewan
- **religious tours:** visiting a religious site such as Bethlehem at Christmas
- **ethnic tours:** being immersed in a different culture, or returning to cultural roots
- **educational tours:** travelling to learn something new, whether visiting museums, historical sites, or art galleries, or enjoying a series of lectures on and theatrical productions of George Bernard Shaw's plays
- **soft adventure tours:** enjoying the thrill of adventure while appreciating the comforts of life, an experience provided by most safaris in Africa
- **sports and recreational tours:** golfing or skiing at a resort, or biking along the old highways of France
- **ecotourism tours:** with expert local guides, expeditions to the rainforest or other ecosystems to learn about wildlife, vegetation, and ecology
- **special interest tours:** gambling in Windsor, visiting the wineries of British Columbia, or going to see the Calgary Stampede

www.
crossculturalsolutions.org

Special needs tours are organized for groups of people with special medical problems. For example, a group of senior citizens with emphysema would require not only medication, but also a supply of oxygen and special handling and permits to transport it, especially if crossing borders. People with physical disabilities must have hotel rooms that are fully accessible to them, and attractions and restaurants that can accommodate their needs. *Incentive tours* are created for a company as a reward for employees who have done outstanding work. They are considered gifts and are not taxable.

Tours can also be defined by their duration, such as a seven-day tour or a two-week tour. The newest trend is the three-day weekend tour. This package fits into the changing lifestyle of North Americans who, according to statistics, are taking shorter, more frequent vacations.

The Travel Counsellor's Responsibility for Tours

Although tours can be sold directly to the consumer by the company that designs the tour (provided the company holds a retail licence), many tours are still sold through **travel counsellors**. Tour wholesalers provide a commission to the travel agency for each tour sold. Even though travel counsellors work for the wholesaler, they are responsible for helping potential travellers choose the right tour for them. The counsellor must understand tour requirements and provide accurate details, including those described on the following pages.[5]

FOOTPRINT

As we have explored so far, the relationship between tourism and the environment is a delicate one. On the one hand, tourists bring in money that can go toward environmental programs and recycling initiatives. On the other hand, airplanes, cars, and cruise lines are some of the Earth's biggest polluters. What is a customer to do? Being a smart green shopper extends not only to your rejection of plastic bags and use of sustainable products, but also to the type of vacation and tour you take. Several companies in Canada have created environmentally responsible tours that guests can enjoy guilt-free. Some of these include:

• Tundra Buggy Tours—this tour was created in 1979 to take guests from Churchill, Manitoba, to the frozen tundra 30 km away to witness the polar

bears up close. The tundra buggies travel only on existing trails so they don't upset the fragile ecosystem.

• Boreal Ecology—in Saskatchewan, guests are guided by canoe and kayak to view wildlife and the spectacular boreal forest.

• Earthfoot Trekking—guests travel by horseback into the remote wilderness of the Yukon Territory.

• Discovering Alpine Flowers—tourists hike through forests and alpine meadows to learn more about floral identification and appreciation in the Rockies.

These are just some of the several ecotours available to guests wanting to see more of Canada. As all of us learn more about environmental effects and climate change, making responsible vacation choices will just seem natural.

Validity Dates Tour brochures indicate when a tour is available at the stated price, as well as the dates of departure from the gateway city for international or charter tours. It is important that the counsellor know these dates, as tour prices may change depending on the season.

Gateway City The **gateway city** is the point from which the flight will leave or where the client can join the tour. It is the responsibility of the travel counsellor to get the client to the gateway city on time for departure with the group.

Cultural tourism often includes a show of art or dance, helping to give the tourist better insight into the local heritage. Here an Inuit elder performs a First Nations ritual.
(Photo courtesy Canadian Tourism Commission.)

Itinerary and Amenities Once again, the brochures describing the tour may or may not be explicit. Counsellors need to read all the fine print of the brochure to tell clients what to expect. The number of meals paid for in the tour price may not be obvious. Where sightseeing is "suggested" or "optional," the cost is not included in the tour. If the brochure says the tour will "see" rather than "visit" an attraction, it means travellers will view the attraction from the bus window. If the counsellor does not read the fine print critically, the client will probably be dissatisfied with the tour.

Price Tour prices will vary depending on (a) the season; (b) modes of transportation used; (c) length of stay in principal cities; (d) type of accommodation; (e) number of meals provided; (f) sightseeing and other activities that are pre-booked; and (g) additional service charges, such as tips and baggage handling, that are included. Some brochures quote their low-season price, which sounds like a good deal until the client realizes the tour takes place in the Caribbean during hurricane season! Brochures are often confusing and contain fine print that must be explained to the customer. The travel counsellor must inform the client of items included in the price, items that are optional at an additional charge, surcharges (e.g., for currency fluctuations or fuel costs), and items that must be paid for by the customer.

Name of the Tour Operator Both the client and the travel counsellor need to know the name of the operator or wholesaler for further reference. In some provinces, it is a legal requirement to name the tour operator. When problems occur, the travel counsellor should investigate in order to prevent a recurrence, or should stop recommending this particular operator or wholesaler to clients.

A final concern shared by travel counsellors and travellers alike is safety. For example, disreputable operators may use equipment that has not undergone a thorough safety check, or because of economic concerns, may choose a poorly located hotel, putting the client at risk.

In summary, the travel counsellor is responsible for relaying accurate and reliable information to the prospective traveller. A counsellor who neglects to point out disadvantages as well as additional costs to the client is not providing good service—and dissatisfied customers do not return.

Regulating the Tour Industry

Canadian tour operators are regulated by many different organizations. If the tour contains an air or rail component, the tour operator must obtain approval from the National Transportation Agency prior to promoting and operating the tour. Tour operators are also licensed by the individual province, and the interests of the purchaser are protected by provincial consumer affairs departments. Who protects the purchasers and their deposits when a tour operator goes bankrupt? Tour operators are required to have a special type of insurance policy called a "performance bond," which guarantees payment to all parties (clients, travel agencies, and suppliers) in the case of financial difficulties. British Columbia, Ontario, and Quebec all require that tour operators maintain trust accounts and compensation funds and provide the province with detailed financial statements. The tour brochure and its information are also controlled by some provinces.

IATA plays an important role in the creation of international tours. It requires that every IATA-approved tour have the following components: air transportation on an IATA carrier, accommodations for the duration of the tour, and at least one additional feature (which might be sightseeing, an activity, or transfers). IATA tour brochures will also contain some very specific pieces of information:

- what is and is not included in the package
- deposit and payment schedules
- travel documents needed (passport, visas, health card)
- cancellation and refund policies
- the tour operator's limited responsibilities and liability

SNAPSHOT

Randy Williams

Randy Williams has been president and CEO of the Tourism Industry Association of Canada (TIAC) since January 2002, bringing a strong voice and positive action, supported by more than three decades of travel and tourism experience, to Canada's tourism industry.

Randy studied at the University of Calgary and has a certificate from George Washington University. He began his career in accommodations, managing hotels across Western Canada. He then moved into tourism services, becoming the first president and CEO of Tourism Saskatchewan, Canada's first provincial private–public partnership for tourism marketing. His next executive position brought him into contact with travel services. As president of the Association of Canadian Travel Agencies (ACTA), he transformed the federation into a strong national organization with regional offices across Canada.

Building on TIAC's involvement in cross-border travel issues, which included founding membership in the Coalition for Secure and Trade-Efficient Borders, in 2005 Randy formed the bi-national Passport Coalition to address the Western Hemisphere Travel Initiative (WHTI), which will require all travellers, including U.S. citizens, to present a passport or other accepted document in order to enter the United States. The United States is Canada's second largest tourism market, with over 34 million visits by American residents in 2004, so the potential negative impact of this initiative is a serious concern for the industry. The numbers can be frightening. Between June 2007–2008, same day trips by Americans to Canada were down 22%, overnight stays by 9%[6] and tourism revenue is expected to drop by $1.6 billion.[7]

As president of TIAC, Randy works to ensure that tourism is front and centre in public policy debates. Transportation, infrastructure, human resources, product development, research and marketing, he reminds us, must not be viewed in isolation from issues such as competitive taxation that affect business development in general. He is also a strong advocate of easily accessed visitor information services, and was instrumental in the establishment of .*travel*, a sponsored top-level domain exclusive to the travel and tourism industry that will help internet travel consumers find the information they need to make purchase decisions.

In the four years that Randy Williams has led TIAC, he has taken Canada's national tourism advocate to greater heights and achievements than ever before. His dedication and expertise have benefited the almost 190 000 businesses in Canada, both large and small, that depend on tourism for their livelihood.

The Advantages of Taking a Packaged Tour

Tours are becoming more popular because they offer one-stop shopping. From the colourful brochures, customers can glimpse the facilities available at their destination. If they choose a reputable firm, they can be assured that the tour's components will be of high quality. Everything is prearranged, and the customer knows that tickets and accommodations have been reserved and all the other details of the trip, including transfer of baggage, have been taken care of. Instead of a waiting line for tickets, prepaid tour admission ensures immediate access to sites and events. Volume buying saves money, and travellers need extra money only for shopping.

Most tours use direct flights, and ground transportation is waiting on arrival. In addition, tour companies recognize the need for some individualization and will build preferences into their package. Finally, one of the most important motivators of travel is companionship, and tours ensure a trip with fellow travellers who have similar interests and needs. Many baby boomers enjoy this style of travel, and growth in the tour industry is expected to be strong.

The Disadvantages of Taking a Packaged Tour

There are some drawbacks to taking a tour. Dissatisfaction is sure to occur if the tour operator does not provide what has been promised in the brochure—a quality product. Travel counsellors and clients are dependent on the operator's integrity and financial stability. Because a tour is a prearranged trip, it is inflexible. Your time is not your own. When the tour moves on to the next site, so must you. Do the advantages of taking a packaged tour outweigh the disadvantages? Only the consumer can answer that question.

TRAVEL AGENCIES

The travel agency is a retail business, somewhat like a department store. It has a broad array of items for sale, conveniently located in one area. Customers interested in purchasing something—in this case a trip—will shop at their favourite travel agency. The agency arranges for travel services with suppliers such as airlines, cruise ships, bus companies, railroads, car rental firms, hotels, tour operators, and sightseeing operators, and serves as a vital link between the traveller and the suppliers. The big difference is the amount and quality of personal service provided at a travel agency. Because of the type of business, the travel agency requires a relationship between the customer and the travel professional. Advice has become such an important part of the job, especially with leisure travel, that the more common term *travel agent* has been replaced with *travel counsellor*. Travel counsellors are knowledgeable and persuasive about the products they sell, which makes them invaluable to travel suppliers. Travel agencies are firmly established as the principal distribution system for travel suppliers, and they provide the most efficient way for the consumer to sort out the ever-increasing array of travel options.

www.citc.ca

Types of Travel Agencies

Agencies in Canada are categorized in several ways: by size, by the services they offer, and by ownership.

Small agencies have annual sales of a million dollars or less and generally employ one to three travel counsellors. Much of their business is through word of mouth, and personal service provides them with a small but loyal customer base. Medium-sized agencies employ a staff of eight to ten travel counsellors. They rely on word of mouth too, but also invest in local promotions and advertising. They often focus on both business and pleasure travel. Larger agencies are usually highly diversified. Competition has been so fierce over the past decade that many smaller agencies have sold out to larger, more stable firms or have become part of a merger. These agencies have departments that specialize in travel market segments, such as the corporate market or group tours. They can often compete more effectively because they can afford top-of-the-line equipment and a larger marketing budget.[8] Agencies may be full service (handling both vacation and business travel), corporate (dealing with business travel only), and specialty (handling specific products such as cruises or clients with special needs).

Full-Service Agency Most agencies fit into the full-service category and are equipped to serve all categories of traveller needs, from bus tours to wilderness tours to business trips. The business of a **full-service travel agency** is typically divided 60/40: 60% leisure travel and 40% business travel, or vice versa. The combination provides a more consistent customer base: business travel may be busy when vacation travel is slow. Larger agencies usually have divisions and counsellors that specialize in categories of travel such as business, international, domestic tours, or cruises. As a result, customers feel comfortable going to one full-service agency for all travel needs.

Corporate Agency The **corporate travel agency** specializes in business travel. In an effort to discourage walk-in vacation requests, many corporate agencies do not even identify themselves as travel agencies because the emphasis of their service differs. The nature of the client's business dictates when and where the travel will occur. The counsellor is responsible for finding the best-priced airfare, a convenient hotel, and a car rental. Whereas a vacation counsellor may have time to plan, business travellers often call requesting a flight, accommodations, and a car rental for the next day. Most corporate agencies charge their clients either a management fee or a per-ticket fee and change fee.

Some corporate agencies get so much business from a major client that they establish a branch in the workplace to deal solely with that client's needs. The agency becomes an integral part of the workplace, saving the client time and money, while the agency is assured of a constant customer base. Some large corporations have developed their own travel departments, which not only plan individual business travel for employees but also arrange conventions and meetings. Travel counsellors working directly for a corporation typically get higher salaries and better company benefits than agency employees.

Online travel agencies such as Travelocity, Air Miles, and Expedia have no concrete office space but run huge call centres to handle questions and help with travel problems. Booking online with these companies is very simple for even inexperienced computer users.

Specialty Agency Most agencies cannot deal exclusively with one type of travel because the people needed to fill a tour do not live in one geographic area. However, in large urban centres, some **specialty travel agencies** exist.

Some agencies may be certified cruise specialists. They represent the full line of cruise products, and their agents have had additional training on various cruise ships and on how to sell a cruise package. The wide variety of vacations available from the cruise lines, the different ships and their service styles, and the niche markets that are targeted often complicate the choice of a cruise vacation. A cruise specialist will know if the ship the client is looking at provides a product suitable for families with children, the seniors market, travellers with disabilities, or single passengers looking for fun and romance. These companies will often promote cruises with themes such as country and western or big band music.

A specialty agency deals with a single type of travel product, such as Canadian wilderness adventures.
(Photo courtesy Canadian Tourism Commission.)

As noted in Chapter 9, adventure travel is a fast-growing segment of the travel market. Agencies specialize in arranging exotic trips to places inaccessible to the everyday traveller: a river trip down the Amazon, an African safari, cross-country skiing in the Arctic, or hiking in the Himalayas. With more people looking for the unusual, adventure travel agencies can please the hard to please. Travel can be arranged for both the hard adventurer who prefers primitive accommodations, and the soft adventurer who wants the comforts of a fine hotel and restaurant each evening.

Senior travel is another specialty market. Planning seniors' trips may require knowledge of places with wheelchair accessibility, restaurants that will cater to specific dietary requirements, or motels with handrails in the bathrooms. To be successful with the mature travel market, tours should be designed to spend less time travelling and more time at attractions and destinations.

Clients with disabilities form another specialty market. As discussed earlier in the text, travellers with disabilities make up a huge untapped market, and as baby boomers age, this market will become even more significant. Finding the proper accommodations, the right restaurants, and easily accessible attractions or events is not easy, and an agency specializing in the needs of this market while providing exciting tour opportunities will be on the cutting edge of the marketplace for tours.

Ethnic agencies focus on creating connections between immigrants or the children of immigrants and their countries of origin. Canada has welcomed people of all nations to its shores for centuries, and Canadians of all backgrounds may decide to research and visit their ancestors' homeland. Any ethnic group that has a large representation in Canada is a prime target market for a specialized agency.

Forms of Ownership

Like hotels and restaurants, agencies may be owned privately or as part of a chain, franchise, or consortium/co-operative.

Private Ownership In the early days of the travel agency, private ownership was most common, with many agencies run by families. Today, independently owned agencies must work hard to thrive in the competitive travel world. They serve local clientele and provide a high level of service to meet the needs of their clientele.

Chain Agencies Chain agencies operate under one corporate ownership and one management policy. A larger volume of business allows more vigorous promotion, more buying power, and a higher net profit than what is available to independents. Some brand names, such as American Express and Thomas Cook, have gained worldwide recognition. Employees often receive better fringe benefits and more training, and have greater opportunities to focus on special skills or to rise in the management structure.

Franchises Travel agency franchises were not introduced until the 1980s, but have become popular. The benefits and the drawbacks are similar to those of any franchise system. Most customers don't know whether an agency is an individually owned and operated franchise or part of a chain. Franchises, like chains, are rigidly controlled and thus have difficulty filling the special needs of a local clientele. Employees also receive good training and have good job opportunities. Canada's largest franchised agencies are Uniglobe and Carlson Wagonlit Travel. Carlson Wagonlit operates both a chain and a franchise system.

Consortiums In an attempt to survive the fierce competition of the 1980s and 1990s, smaller travel agencies have formed **consortiums** or co-operatives. In this system, which is similar to hotel referral systems such as Best Western, the agency keeps its independence and personal identity but joins with other independents to get large-scale advertising campaigns, better purchasing power, and a brand name. Each member pays an initial membership fee and a continuing services fee. The central office arranges advertising and promotional activities, negotiates supplier agreements, and administers the affairs of the organization. Canada's best-known co-operatives are Advantage, GIANTS, GEM, and T-Comm.

Agency Operations

How do travel agencies make their money? What do they sell? Who regulates them? Travel agencies form an important distribution channel for all our tourism products. Most suppliers of tourism products pay the agency a commission on every sale. An agency's income used to come from the sale of airline tickets, but major airlines have dropped commissions entirely, forcing travel agencies to charge customers a fee for services that can include a charge for cancelling or changing a trip. Agencies still receive commissions from consolidators, cruise lines, tour operators, car rental agencies, and railways. A smaller portion of revenue is generated from the sale of insurance policies or travel accessories (e.g., guidebooks). Travel agencies may earn additional revenue from "override commissions"—commissions paid at a higher rate once an agency reaches a set sales total over a given period of time. The increase provides an additional incentive to sell the supplier's products. Several factors are changing the way agencies earn revenue.

- After deregulation, major airlines first reduced the amount of commission they would pay on each ticket sold, and then eliminated commissions entirely. To replace this loss of revenues, many agencies now charge customers a service fee of $35 to $100 per ticket.

- The internet has become a competitor for travel agencies, providing interactive sales sites for hotels and attractions, allowing clients to book directly with the supplier. In addition, the latest in discounted last-minute sale prices are quickly put on the internet, providing the surfer with last-minute travel bargains and the supplier with additional revenue on products that might have gone unsold.

- New self-ticketing devices allow travellers to book and ticket themselves on flights, including check-in. These kiosks provide a fast alternative to using a travel counsellor. Airlines may provide this service on their websites.

- Expenses that might have been absorbed by the agency 10 years ago are now being charged to the client. These include services like booking a bed and breakfast, long-distance calls or faxes, or passport applications.

With more and more opportunities for individual travellers to use the internet to research and book their own vacations, agencies must become more creative in bringing in additional revenue.

Is the travel agency business coming to an end? As with any business, technology forces changes that are sometimes difficult to adjust to, and those businesses unwilling or unable to rethink their product and its delivery are eliminated. The travel services industry is facing a challenge over the next decade. Two factors will help it survive. First, businesses are discovering that travel counsellors do save them money. The latest study by Topaz International of Portland found that fares generated by a corporate travel agency saved the company an average of $116 per ticket. Second, purchasers using the internet should be warned that most web fares are non-refundable, non-changeable, and have restrictions. As the large baby boom market begins to retire, travel is expected to flourish. As well, many boomers are uncomfortable with the latest computer technologies, including the internet. They prefer the personal touch of a travel counsellor, and although the way a travel agency earns revenue may change, the professional expertise and friendly service of the travel counsellor will remain an essential element of tourism's channel of distribution—travel services.

Regulating Travel Agencies

Before a travel agency can begin full operations, it must obtain an "appointment"—a form of permission to conduct business. There are two major **conference appointments** required:

1. The Air Transport Association of Canada (ATAC) represents commercial aviation in Canada. The ATAC Traffic Conference handles the Canadian Travel Agency program, as well as all matters dealing with interline standards, ticketing, and passenger and baggage processing. ATAC runs its programs by contract with IATA.
2. The International Air Transport Association (IATA) regulates the sale of international airline tickets.

To apply for ATAC and IATA certification, a travel agency must be open and operating: it must have the cash to purchase tickets directly from the airlines or it must have an agreement with a fully accredited agency to do the ticketing on its behalf. New agencies must have at least two full-time employees—a qualified management person and a qualified ticketing agent. The location must be visible to the public and clearly identified as a travel agency. It must have in place sufficient financial backing to ensure continued operation and must maintain its financial records according to the BSP accounting procedures. Finally, the agency must show that it is actively promoting travel through any method of advertising, including brochures, flyers, direct mail, or newspaper advertisements. In addition to these regulations, British Columbia, Quebec, and Ontario all have legislation to protect the traveller, and new agencies must register with their provincial registrar. Ontario's *Travel Industry Act* includes a specific section to protect the consumer. Agencies must take out special insurance and bonding to protect their customers in case the tour operator files for bankruptcy prior to the completion of the trip.[9] After the bankruptcy of Jetsgo, provinces without this protection are looking at mandatory insurance to cover travellers placed in this position.

In Canada, the Canadian Institute of Travel Counsellors (CITC) works with the travel trade focusing on training and instructional materials, and ensuring professional standards are met. As with all professional organizations, the CITC has created a code of ethics that members agree to follow. Under the auspices of the CITC, the Canadian Tourism Human Resource Council has developed a new program for national certification of travel counsellors and managers based on the required skills, knowledge, and attitudes.

Marketing Travel Trade Products

Travel agencies promote the tourism *products* of other suppliers and are not considered to be a product themselves. However, they are the channel of distribution—that is, the *place* where tourism products are sold. *Pricing* the products is not usually the agency's concern, as many products are already packaged and priced. Retail stores build in their profit margin by setting the difference between their buying and selling price. Since travel agencies cannot set the price of the products they sell, they are trying to restore profits by adding service charges. *Promotion* is an important part of any business's survival strategy. Tour companies help to promote their products by supplying tour operators with colourful brochures and displays. They also have sales representatives drop by to discuss the products and provide sales help to the agents. To remain competitive, travel agencies must promote both the products they represent and their own services. Larger chains and franchises may use television, but as the majority of clients are local residents, most agencies use the travel section of local newspapers or local radio stations.

Marketing efforts should reflect the philosophy of the travel agency. What type of people does it serve? What are their needs and how are those needs fulfilled? To sharpen their focus, travel agencies sometimes undertake formal or informal research on their customers' needs, which may include preparing **customer profiles**. Personal sales are also important. Sales agents must know the product well to describe its advantages and disadvantages to their clients. Finally, a good sales agent must know how to close the sale.

Image is what brings a client through the door—colourful displays and a professional-looking staff. The final success or failure of the travel agency, however, depends on the competence of its travel counsellors and the effectiveness of their personal selling techniques. More than in any other part of tourism, lifelong learning is an essential part of a travel counsellor's job.

In Practice

Many people use a travel agency only for airline ticketing. As a travel counsellor, what techniques would you use to convince the traveller that you can and should arrange the car rental, hotel, or rail ticket? What carefully chosen words would you use to sell more to your client?

INCENTIVE TRAVEL

Incentive travel is another growing area of travel sales. Originally designed as a prize for employee performance, **incentive travel** is now being used in many different ways. Incentive purchase cards such as the Air Miles card are also gaining popularity. From a business's standpoint, incentive travel creates a winning situation for all parties involved: the corporation wins with more sales, increased employee productivity, less absenteeism, and better safety records; the employees win by being treated to an exclusive trip; and the incentive travel company wins by increasing sales and profits.

Incentive travel will grow because it is the ultimate motivator. A trip increases an employee's status among peers and family members and provides the opportunity to go places and experience things never dreamed possible. Not only does the potential trip motivate extra effort, the winning employee returns feeling good and continues to work hard. By using incentive travel, companies show they believe in their people.

At the other end of incentive travel is the destination. Resorts, hotels, and tourism bureaus are starting to see the benefits of bringing in hundreds of people through incentive travel programs. These destinations are actively involved in persuading incentive planners that theirs is the perfect destination, and offer inspection tours to make their point.

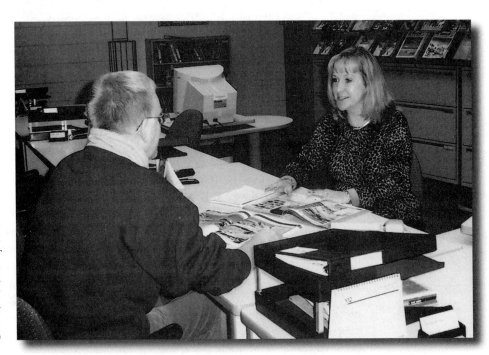

A good travel counsellor must have strong knowledge of many different tourism products, be detail-oriented, and enjoy working with people.
(Photo: Paula Kerr.)

How Incentive Companies Operate

Although it looks simple on paper, developing an incentive travel program is quite complex. Initially, the manager in an incentive house or a specialty incentive travel agency approaches the marketing manager of a company and suggests how incentive travel could help solve the corporation's problem—which could be anything from the need to sell more product to reducing absenteeism.

For example, the incentive travel manager would work out the savings for the company if absenteeism could be reduced by 50%. A portion of these savings would be put toward travel costs. The incentive company would be responsible for setting rules, promotion, program administration, and awards. Accurate records of absenteeism and tardiness over the specified time period would be kept, and letters of encouragement would be sent to participants. To motivate those who had already missed too many days, the incentive company could provide

---

CASE STUDY

Adventure in Spades

Doris had just lost her husband of 26 years and the depression she was experiencing worried her three daughters. They felt she needed to get away; in fact, an exciting trip might lessen the grief they were all feeling. After doing their internet research, the girls chose a well-known company called Tours of a Lifetime, and bought a trip that included exciting experiences and opportunities for each of them, such as bungee jumping and river rafting. Doris agreed reluctantly, and soon found herself hiking 5 km into the mountains from the Jasper Valley. The weather was gorgeous and soon the whole tour group had become friendly. Her daughters bungee-jumped and climbed in the mountains, but Doris declined to take part. Finally, they convinced her to join them for whitewater rafting. Each raft held seven people and an experienced whitewater guide. They each wore life vests, but their guide assured them that falling out of the raft was unlikely, and anyway, the company had guidelines in place that addressed any dangerous situations. Doris began to relax once the trip was underway. The first three sets of rapids were small but exhilarating. As the raft headed for the fourth set of rapids, however, Doris turned to say something to the guide, when the raft bounced in the whitewater. The raft came down and Doris' ankle broke on one of the boulders that lay under the surface. The pain was excruciating. The guide made it safely to the shoreline and her raft mates carried her ashore. The ankle was cleanly broken and swelling fast. The problem they faced was how to get Doris to a medical facility. It was a 10-hour hike over backcountry in order for medics to reach their position. Doris could not even stand.

---

1. What initial three steps should their guide take to begin handling the situation? Why did you choose these steps?
2. Doris will have to be hospitalized. Should she get a refund on the unused portion of her trip?
3. Does Doris have a right to sue the company for negligence? Why or why not?
4. If you were the tour company owner, how would you handle this situation from your office? To avoid future accidents, what could you do?

opportunities for employees to buy in (i.e., people who do not meet the quota or criteria are allowed to pay the difference, enabling them to go with their peers and fill the empty slots on the trip).

www.site-intl.org

The Society of Incentive & Travel Executives (SITE) publishes a newsletter and conducts training programs and seminars on how to succeed in incentive travel. Most important, SITE is the sounding board for problems and opportunities in incentive travel.

In Practice

Make a list of companies in your community that could benefit from an incentive travel program. What problem would you try to solve for those companies? Write down a convincing statement you would use to persuade the company.

Summary

The selling of travel takes three basic forms: wholesale, retail, and incentive travel (which is a combination of the first two). A wholesaler/operator plans and organizes a tour package but gives the retailer (travel counsellor) the challenge of selling it to the customer. The travel counsellor is the retailer for every type of travel. The incentive travel planner organizes a trip for the employees of a company, but only those employees who meet the criteria set up by the planner will win the trip.

Most wholesale travel is in the form of packaged tours. The tour operator decides on an attractive trip, negotiates prices with the suppliers, and sets the consumer price. There are three types of tours. The independent tour allows clients to travel on their own without supervision. The hosted tour is similar to the independent tour but has a host in each city to arrange excursions and to order tickets to attractions. The escorted tour provides a tour guide to accompany the group and to make sure all scheduled activities go as planned. The greatest challenge for travel agencies today is the rapidly increasing use of internet websites for research and bookings.

A travel agency survives on the service and management fees it charges its clients and on commissions from selling various travel products to the general public. Travel counsellors can no longer collect commissions on most airline tickets, but do get commissions from cruise, hotel, and car rental bookings. Four types of agencies exist: the full-service agency provides both vacation and business travel arrangements; a corporate agency works with business travellers; and the solely online agencies and specialty travel agencies work with a single type of product (e.g., cruises or adventure travel) or a single target market (e.g., seniors or travellers with disabilities).

Incentive travel is a growing field because travel is an excellent motivator, encouraging employees to work harder, sell more, or stay with the company longer. The company gains increased productivity or sales, and the employee wins a trip. The destination chosen for the award also wins by hosting a group of people who might not ordinarily be visiting.

Questions

1. Using the steps outlined in developing a tour, create a package tour of your region.

   a) Identify the type of tour and its target market.

   b) Determine whether it will be a fully escorted tour or hosted tour. Justify your choice.

   c) Explain the four individual steps you will follow as you create your tour. Use examples and list the items included in the tour.

   d) Set validity dates, a gateway city, and a suggested price.

   e) Describe four advantages for a traveller taking your tour.

   f) Describe two disadvantages and explain how you will attempt to minimize them.

   g) Identify the regulating agencies you will need to get approval from and how they will affect your final product.

2. Describe the different ownership/management styles found in the travel agency business.

3. Summarize three different changes in the travel agency business and how agencies are dealing with the challenges they pose.

4. What is incentive travel and why is it a growing part of the travel trade industry?

5. Define the following terms as they relate to the travel trade industry: *conference appointment, override, specialty agency, tour operator, tour wholesaler, consolidator, consortium, full-service agency, higher value traveller, inbound tour.*

Notes

1. Canadian Tourism Human Resource Council, *Total Tourism Sector Employment: 2004 Update*, March 2004, p. 16.

2. Dr. Marilyn Mohan, G. Gislason, and B. McGowan, *Tourism Related Employment: 1998 Update* (Ottawa, ON: Canadian Tourism Human Resource Council, 1998), p. 230.

3. David Wright, CTC, *Professional Travel Counselling*, 4th ed. (Toronto, ON: Canadian Institute of Travel Counsellors, 1998), p. 294.

4. Patricia J. Gagnon and Karen Silva, *Travel Career Development*, 5th ed. (Homewood, IL: Irwin, 1990), p. 169.

5. Aryear Gregory, *The Travel Agent*, 2nd ed. (Rapid City, SD: National Publishers of the Black Hills, Inc., 1985), p. 136.

6. Tourism Industry Association of Canada, www.tiac-aitc.ca.

7. Ibid.

8. Wright, *Professional Travel*, p. 33.

9. David W. Howell and Robert A. Ellison, *Passport* (Toronto: Nelson Canada, 1995), p. 323.

Tourism Services

Key terms

chamber of commerce
convention and visitors
  bureau (CVB)

destination marketing
  organization (DMO)
familiarization (fam) tour

front-line training
site inspection

Learning objectives

Having read this chapter you will be able to

1. Describe the five industry components of tourism services.

2. Summarize the activities of the provincial and municipal governments as they relate to tourism.

3. Explain the functions of destination marketing organizations such as convention and visitor bureaus and the role of chambers of commerce.

4. Discuss the membership, mandate, and goals of the Tourism Industry Association of Canada.

5. List the miscellaneous services that ensure the tourism sector in Canada remains competitive, modern, and in a positive state of growth.

The tourism sector is somewhat akin to a stage production: the setting consists of landscape and buildings, and the cast is represented by the entire community—with everyone playing the part of tourism host. Behind the scenes are those who really make the production work. This support group of backstage workers is called tourism services. People in tourism services specialize in serving the needs of the industry rather than the needs of the visitor. A wide variety of organizations, associations, government agencies, and businesses supply these services. Because many tourism businesses are small and privately owned, they rely on this industry for help in dealing with marketing and promotions, taxation, government regulations, safety, education, and staff training. Tourism services is their link to the world of tourists.

Tourism services also includes retail sales and media coverage, and the services of construction companies, financial institutions, and telecommunications and computer industries. Together, the businesses that comprise tourism services ensure that the product offered is modern and competitive and that the tourism sector as a whole runs smoothly. This chapter provides information on the inner workings of the tourism sector—a whole new set of job opportunities!

The tourism services industry can be divided into five components,[1] each handling a different tourism need:

- government agencies
- tourism associations and organizations
- marketing services
- research and consulting
- miscellaneous services

GOVERNMENT AGENCIES

In Chapter 2, we looked at the federal government and the specific departments that play a role in Canadian tourism. The names and roles of each department are subject to change, and this chart is a quick review of the most important roles played by the federal government:

Industry Canada	Responsible for the overall well-being of tourism, including the 2010 Olympic Games and Paralympics
Parks Canada	Responsible for national museums, national parks, national heritage sites, heritage canal systems, and heritage river systems
Canada Border Services Agency (CBSA)	Checks people arriving at the borders for proper documents and illegal goods, or for purchasing more products than allowed while on vacation
Foreign Affairs & International Trade Canada	Provides foreign visitors with visas and Canadians with passports
Transport Canada	Responsible for the development and security of our transportation systems
Canadian Heritage (CH)	With the majority of direct responsibility for the national museums moved to Parks Canada, CH is responsible only for some cultural/heritage events, as well as non-professional sports (does not include the Olympic Games)

As noted in Chapter 2, there are two Crown corporations that also impact the tourism scene in Canada: one is the Canadian Tourism Commission (CTC), the organization responsible for marketing Canadian tourism to the world. The second Crown corporation is called the National Capital Commission (NCC). It is responsible for overseeing the development of Canada's capital region—Ottawa/Gatineau.

www.canadatourism.ca

Provincial Governments and Tourism

Provincial governments have ministries or departments similar to those in the federal government although generally under a different name. The major difference is the scope of their activities. For example, most provinces have a specific department responsible for tourism in their area: Tourism BC; Nova Scotia Department of Tourism, Culture and Heritage; Ontario Tourism. All provinces, however, are hoping to engage in and encourage the following activities:

1. **Promote travel opportunities and increase the number of visitors to the province.** Provinces advertise their tourism products in many ways. Many set up booths at trade fairs across Canada and the United States to promote their resorts, adventure activities, attractions and historical sites, accommodations, food services, and transportation services. Once potential visitors request information from a provincial tourism board, they are amazed at the response. A simple request for information on fishing lodges will result in a deluge of brochures on a wide variety of fishing vacations, equipment rentals, and maps.

2. **Encourage the development of the tourism sector through market research and planning.** All provinces use strategic planning to ensure that they are developing sustainable tourism products with a significant market base. Many programs focus on existing resources: cultural heritage, recreational activities, natural attractions, and historical sites.

3. **Work with the tourism sector in the province to continually improve the product.** Recognizing the need for skilled workers, provincial governments have helped fund tourism education councils (TECs; see Chapter 2), which provide training and certification programs for a wide variety of tourism occupations. Workers dealing directly with tourists may take a short customer service course offered in all provinces under a variety of names, including SuperHost, Alberta Best, and FirstHost. These courses cover quality service and good hospitality practices—in other words, how to handle customers in a friendly, professional, and informed manner. Provinces may also create infomercials to educate residents on the value of tourism as a revenue generator.

4. **Produce literature that promotes the six front-line components of the sector.** Provinces fund television commercials, travel videos, and CD-ROMs that market their regions. The most important time of the year for advertising a province's specialties is around the months of February through April. They tend to focus their advertising in markets close to the province; i.e., Ontario will hear about PEI and Newfoundland, but B.C. audiences

Branding has become an essential element in the marketing of a destination. Our new branding, developed by the CTC, reads: "Canada—keep exploring."
(Photo courtesy Canadian Tourism Commission.)

won't. The cost of sending a CD-ROM is as inexpensive as sending a postcard and has far greater visual appeal and attraction. Newfoundland and Labrador had great success with their advertising efforts in 2006. Provinces have their own webpages and are investing in state-of-the-art tourist information centres. Most provinces also have a toll-free number that provides advice for planning everything from weekend getaways to extended trips.

5. **Liaise with federal and municipal ministries.** Many tourism events require participation from all levels of government. British Columbia would not have been successful in its bid for the 2010 Olympics had it not been able to show strong financial support from all three levels of government.

Municipal Governments and Tourism Associations

Municipal governments have similar needs and perform activities similar to their provincial counterparts. To promote their tourism products (attractions, hotels, restaurants, etc.) some cities have a tourism marketing department. Others turn to private, non-profit associations like convention and visitors bureaus (CVBs) or local chambers of commerce.

Some cities have recently introduced an accommodation tax in order to increase tax revenues. This specific stream of revenue will provide cash-strapped cities with money dedicated solely to promoting and advertising tourism opportunities in the region.

Chambers of Commerce and CVBs Recognizing the financial impact tourism has for its members, **chambers of commerce** become involved in all aspects of tourism. These groups work with the city to promote local events and attract visitors. They advertise in newspapers and magazines, on radio, television, and the internet, and produce booklets, usually in the form of a visitor's guide. These

Reducing the Carbon Footprint of the 2010 Games

World scientists have three basic concerns when they discuss global warming: (1) the impact of human activities; (2) higher surface temperatures; and (3) weather changes that affect local and global social, environmental, and economic patterns. Increased production of carbon byproducts, also known as "greenhouse gases" (GHGs), are the cornerstone identified by scientists for global warming. One of the three components added to the 2010 Games has been "sustainable development and delivery," and VANOC is taking environmental concerns very seriously. They have taken some innovative steps to ensure the carbon footprints created by building and delivering of the 2010 Games are as light as possible. There is little that can be done regarding the number of people anticipated at the games. In fact, VANOC is hoping to attract a larger number than was at Tofino and Beijing. Spectators and participants are the reason we go to the expense of hosting such global events. However, VANOC can and is controlling the GHGs produced by event activities. At Tofino in 2006, 600 temporary generators were used to supply additional energy, and all used diesel fuel. The need for additional energy is such that these temporary backup power generators are essential. For example, while nature is supposed to provide snowy mountain slopes so the daily ski and snowboarding events can proceed, backup snow machines must be available to ensure these slopes are ready, overnight, in an emergency situation. That is an unusual but necessary electrical requirement. For the 2010 Games, B.C.'s electrical provider is using a new system of outlets called "feeders." This innovative system allows VANOC to reduce the total number of temporary generators required from Tofino's 600 to about 100. And, if nature co-operates, there is a good chance some of these generators might never be used. Already the carbon footprint is diminishing.

Transportation is notorious for the carbon emissions it creates, so VANOC is using fuel-efficient vehicles; easily accessible park and rides to provide safe, fast transportation to respective sites; and a geographic information system that will help ensure the best use of vehicles, at all times, using the most efficient routes. This translates into lower fuel use and lower GHGs.

VANOC's offices have been moved to downtown Vancouver to make use of their newer buildings that incorporate LEED Commercial Interior's features like natural lighting and improved ventilation systems (heating and cooling), as well as free bicycle parking privileges and showers and change rooms for employees who commute by bike. VANOC currently has 96 vehicles of which 19 are hybrids, 29 have been equipped with Active Fuel Management technology, and 34 are flex-fuel vehicles using ethanol-based E85 fuel.

guides, which are placed in hotel rooms, offer information on attractions, festivals and events, shops, restaurants and bars, and transportation systems. Some guides are hardcover, and guests are requested to leave them in the room on departure. Other guides resemble magazines, and guests can take them home as souvenirs or to pass along to friends.

The fundamental mission of a **convention and visitors bureau** is to enhances the economic stability of a community by soliciting and servicing conventions and other types of events that generate overnight stays. In addition, a CVB promotes vacation travel to the area. The CVB is the community's liaison between potential visitors and the businesses that will host them. It is a city's information clearing-house, convention management consultant, and promotional agency, and is often the catalyst for urban development and renewal. CVBs have a sensitive and impor-tant role in leading the community's tourism sector. A dynamic and professional CVB creates a favourable image of the community for tour and meeting planners, which can increase tourism volume and profits.

Chambers of commerce and CVBs run on membership fees. Both organiza-tions offer members co-operative advertising programs and trade shows. The CVB usually coordinates these programs and sometimes charges a commission on each convention booking. Destination publications include visitor guides, maps, meet-ing planner guides, and brochures on attractions, hotels and restaurants, activities, and city tours. These may be sent out by direct mail, given to walk-ins, mailed to people inquiring about the destination, and given to meeting planners.

Another way to promote sales is to arrange a **familiarization tour (fam tour)** to show off the city's charms and suitability for conventions. A fam tour, free to the prospective client, is sponsored by city businesses. A **site inspection**, in contrast, is held for a single prospective client (usually an association) at the client's expense and is tailored to its needs and desires. While a fam tour solicits business from associations that have not yet considered the site, a site inspection provides final details to associations that have narrowed the choice to two or three locations.

After all the marketing techniques have been employed and the association or client wants to do business, the CVB puts together a bid presentation. The pres-entation may be given to a single person, a select group, a board of directors, or to the entire association. The bid should answer all the client's questions, so the CVB needs to understand all the client's needs and desires. Many CVBs contact the client's previous convention sites to gather information before the bidding.

Convention Services In most cases, CVBs are not designed to perform the actual convention set-up, although they can provide a wide array of assistance. Some ser-vices are performed for all associations, whereas others are written in as part of the host city's responsibilities. The CVB convention division may provide city and site information to generate interest among association members, or it may host an event at the association's current convention as a welcome to the follow-ing year's meeting. The CVB arranges pre-convention tours to assist the client in planning the convention and may organize programs to encourage spouses to come along. The CVB may also set up a speakers' bureau to book local speakers for the upcoming convention or conference. Finally, if more than one hotel is needed, the CVB may set up a housing bureau to help with hotel reservations and confirmations.

During the convention, services range from the simple—such as a welcome banner strategically placed at the airport and convention centre—to registration and shuttle services. CVBs have a list of trained personnel who can perform many of the tedious convention duties, from typing name badges to collecting registration fees. The CVB may also be asked to provide the speaker for the opening ceremony. When given enough advance notice, it can arrange for the premier, mayor, or other prominent person to welcome the convention delegates. Often the CVB will provide an information desk to give out tourist information. Finally, the convention services department helps the meeting planner with last-minute details: the extra roll of tape, a slide projector, or an adjustment in room temperature. This kind of help takes the stress off the meeting planner, which in turn makes for a successful convention and a happy client.

Tourist Information Centres

Tourist information centres act as gateways and provide visitors with their first impression of a province, region, or town. All levels of government fund information centres to tell tourists about the region: its accommodations, attractions, special events, food service choices, historical sites, and unique environmental experiences. In the Ottawa region, the National Capital Commission has a large information centre on Parliament Hill, open from June to September. Bilingual guides offer visitors tours of the grounds and buildings. Brochures on historical sites are also available. Provinces usually locate tourism information centres along major highways and at border crossings. These centres offer general information on the province as a whole. Information centres all across Canada are easily identified by their question mark symbol (**?**). Because information centres are usually open in the summer, the jobs are often filled by students, who can practise their customer-relations skills and apply their knowledge of the region.

In Practice

List 15 attractions in your region. How would you promote them to tourists at a visitor centre? If you were a CVB, which ones would you emphasize to an association considering a convention? How would you promote them?

Making use of international recognition is also an important sales tool. The Rideau Canal has become the latest UNESCO World Heritage site.
(Photo courtesy Canadian Tourism Commission.)

SNAPSHOT

Ray Kroc

"Find out where your talents lie and then do whatever you are doing better than anybody else. But be willing to pay the price." That is the advice Ray Kroc, owner of McDonald's, offered any student who would listen. Ray did not invent the hamburger and he was not the original owner of McDonald's, but today, his hamburger dream is the largest franchise fast food restaurant in the world. He brought great organizational skills to his new restaurant and simplified the menu. Fewer items meant more care and precision in producing them. Ray believed in many tenets that still drive the food service industry. The QSC&V mandate he established for his restaurants—quality, service, cleanliness, and value—still drives the restaurant chain. He set out to make the best hamburger and fries America had ever tasted, and he succeeded. Standardized recipes and an operating manual that spelled out every little detail of running the business were keys to his success. He developed tools to ensure every hamburger is exactly the same—a 9-inch bun, 4-ounce hamburger, and sauce. Customers soon expected his products to be the best no matter where the restaurant was located. All of the new products McDonald's introduces go through extensive development and exhaustive research to ensure they meet the high standards of the founder. Ray was also a strong believer in giving back to the community, and was the first fast food chain to open living quarters near hospitals for families from out of town whose children were sick. His marketing genius linked toys and movies to kids' meals, and the golden arches are one of the most recognized symbols in the world, telling customers there is a McDonald's nearby. For years, Kroc maintained that he would sell "hamburgers and hamburgers alone," but he began to realize that in a changing world, his menu needed to change, too. So he developed foods that fit the restaurant's neighbourhood. In Germany, they serve beer; in Mexico, quesadillas; and in Nova Scotia, lobster rolls. Ray was the first fast food entrepreneur to offer breakfast—he saw the need and the empty time slot in his restaurants, and soon you could grab an Egg McMuffin on the way to the office. Even the golden arches have, at times, been dramatically changed so, for example, the restaurant fits into the European style of narrow cobblestone streets and 17th-century stone buildings. Ray believed in education, and in Chicago, he built McDonald's University so the company could provide free upgrading and education to those wishing to climb the ladder of success with the company. His dream of providing QSC&V to every customer is still the foundation for his company, and Ray proved that anything is possible if a person has the drive, dedication, persistence, and dream.

TOURISM ASSOCIATIONS AND ORGANIZATIONS

Because of the complex nature of the tourism sector, a variety of industry associations have developed in the past century. They can be divided into two categories: organizations that focus on marketing, and those that focus on advocacy or lobbying. CVBs are examples of marketing-oriented organizations that focus on selling a city and all that it has to offer. Another example of a marketing organization is the Canada Ski Council. Many special interest groups have organizations that help promote their products, and some are linked to international organizations with the same intent. Inns of Canada promotes Canadian accommodations, but it is a member of a global organization called Inns en Route. Going to its website links the searcher to inns around the world. These organizations strive to attract visitors to a destination or to encourage people to participate in a specific pursuit. They develop and execute marketing plans, design special promotions, coordinate publicity, and work with advertising agencies. Tourism advocates and lobbying organizations are more concerned with the welfare of the tourism sector as a whole or with the success of a specific industry such as accommodations, or food and beverage. Many of these associations have already been discussed in previous chapters. Nationally recognized advocacy groups in Canada include

- Tourism Industry Association of Canada (TIAC)
- Hotel Association of Canada
- Association of Canadian Travel Agents (ACTA)
- Canadian Restaurant and Foodservices Association (CRFA)
- Canadian Culinary Federation
- Canadian Association of Foodservice Professionals (CAFP)
- Aboriginal Tourism Canada
- Meeting Professionals International (MPI)
- Association of Tourism Professionals

All of the groups listed above are private, except Aboriginal Tourism Canada, which is quasi-public—that is, it receives some funding from the federal government.

These associations represent their members to governing bodies and the public in general. They put on seminars, sponsor events, conduct research, and keep their members informed about all the activities within their industries. They prepare briefing papers for governments on issues such as taxation and regulations that affect their industries. They have also been instrumental in writing national occupational standards and in providing training and certification (see Chapter 2).

Tourism Industry Association of Canada (TIAC)

TIAC is a good example of a lobbying organization that has made a difference. TIAC is a private organization, founded in 1931, and funded by membership dues. It serves as the tourism sector's national voice. Members come from all areas of the tourism sector: businesses, institutions, associations, and individuals. TIAC's mandate is to strengthen tourism by lobbying the federal government on tax issues, federal tourism initiatives, training programs for tourism workers, and legislation that promotes a proactive tourism sector.

TIAC has been issuing warnings to the federal government regarding the status of tourism for some time. The expansion of the existing and mature global tourism markets as well as exciting new markets has been great, and Canada is being left behind. Tourism impacts the lives of 1.6 million Canadians who make their living working in this industry, and the revenues it has produced yearly are being threatened, not by terrorists, but by Canadian government inaction.

TIAC understands the difficult times tourism has weathered: the terrorist attack on September 11, 2001, the SARS scare, the rise in the cost of fuel, and the rise in the value of the Canadian dollar. To put the dollar's value in perspective, the cost of our tourism products has gone up by 30% solely because of the changing value of the dollar. Prices are sure to rise again as we face the fuel crisis. None of this is our doing, yet all of it hurts our industry. TIAC points out that not only is the government responsible for the well-being of the industry, but in fact it is a major shareholder as it has ownership rights in our national parks, museums, and historic sites. It is responsible for our transportation systems, our border infrastructure, and the global marketing of Canadian tourism. Matters are made worse by its inability to understand the impact new taxes and recently removed tax benefits have on foreign markets. Here are just a few of the real threats TIAC sees for Canadian tourism. They focus on two areas—accessibility and government actions:

1. We need to create the ability to cross our borders with a minimum of effort. Easier access to visitor visas and new cards like the NEXUS card (already approved) and Enhanced Drivers Licences (EDLs), already proposed, would solve the passport/border issue with Americans.

2. Our borders need to be run more efficiently and updated with modern technology. This includes supplying border operations with "real-time traveller information" during a 24-hour period. Other solutions include expansion of the NEXUS program (pre-approved visitors) and increased infrastructure.

3. Our airline system bears unacceptable structural costs, and with the surcharges and taxes passed on to the consumer, creates a ticket that is too expensive. IATA warned Canada of this problem in 2005, but had no response. A recent global review of ticket tax and added airline surcharges ranks Canada among the worst, at 122nd of the 130 nations reviewed. It costs Air Transat $11 000 to land at Pearson in Toronto and $3 500 to land in Paris.

4. The Open Skies Agreement needs to be signed with the Chinese. Negotiations need to be actively moved toward a Memorandum of Understanding (MOU) with the Chinese government to give Canada Approved Destination Status (ADS). Over 134 countries have already signed this MOU, including the United States, and Canada still refuses to sign. The Chinese market has huge potential for us, with many Chinese tourists actually preferring Canada over the United States.

5. There is a need to create a smoother intermodal system of transportation to make it easier for a tourist to travel around the region or country. High speed rail (HSR) between major cities is an option that has been under discussion for many years. Costs are high but TIAC argues that if cost were amortized over a 25-year period, it would make the project financially feasible. In its favour, HSR is also a green mode of transportation. The last modern technology added to Canadian transportation systems was the airplane!

6. We need to use our destination marketing organizations (DMOs) more effectively, including the CTC. Proper CTC funding would allow it to show the variety and excitement of the activities we can provide for tourists. From $100 million in 2004, the CTC received only $58 million for 2007. Visiting Canada must become a higher priority in the eyes of our foreign markets.[2]

It is short-sighted that the government dismisses tourism so easily, especially now that many large corporations are closing shops and moving workers to less expensive countries. That won't happen with tourism—we need Canadian workers doing their job right here in Canada. The collective weight of association membership influences government policies and legislation, and can create a healthy environment for workers and visitors alike. Without the strong voice of TIAC and associations that have joined with it in demanding that politicians take action now, it may be too little too late. Most businesses know it is much easier to keep a consumer than to try to find new ones, but without substantial help from the government, tourism may be facing a cataclysmic disaster.

MARKETING SERVICES

For the most part, travel is not an activity essential to our survival. Consequently, advertising and promotion need to entice the traveller. Canadian destinations compete not only in the global tourism marketplace, but also between provinces and cities. The tourism sector as a whole is competing not only against mature marketplaces like the United States and new marketplaces like Nicaragua and Peru, but also against other discretionary purchases, such as home renovation and consumer goods.

Canada's National DMO—the CTC

Destination marketing organizations (DMOs) promote their cities, regions, provinces, or country. Our national DMO is the CTC. Recent government cuts have left the CTC short of funds, which translates into less advertising. A projected loss of 30+% of the American market means convincing travellers from Europe and Asia to enjoy their holidays here. The big problem is that Harper has not signed the MOU with China giving us Approved Destination Status. This means the loss of Chinese conferences, conventions, and groups to Canada. With the Olympics less than two years away, signing this agreement is vital.

Marketing services use a variety of tools to sell a destination: commercials, posters, perhaps even a safari hat.
(Photo: Paula Kerr.)

In 2005, the CTC began to revitalize Canada's branding, giving it a new focus and name: Canada—Keep Exploring. The CTC has also developed a new five-year plan which identifies what it believes are the key areas of concentration:

- The continuing animation of the branding
- The development of a new system called the Explorer Quotient (EQ) that will quickly tell the organization about visitor behaviours, values, and motivators while in Canada
- Focusing on Canada's global image of Canada as a green destination
- Support for Meeting and Conferences and International Travel (MC&IT)
- Using both the 400th anniversary of Quebec City (2008) and the 2010 Olympic Games to expand on Canada's global image.[3]

Working for a DMO is challenging and can be exciting. Workers must have good knowledge of their region and strong marketing and communication skills.

RESEARCH AND CONSULTING

Not all products appeal to all people. How do you figure out who will use your products? Will your product suit their needs? Those questions are answered through market research and analysis. Research can be done informally, simply by asking clients about their satisfaction, but many guests are reluctant to give negative responses. Tourism research firms usually focus either on tourism products in general or on specific products, providing important information to help guide decision making. Here are some of the questions that product research should answer:

- Is the product unique?
- How does the quality of the product measure up against similar products?
- Does the product have enough capacity to handle demand?
- What are the benefits of purchasing the product?
- What drawbacks have been identified with the product?
- Is the product sustainable? Easily accessible?
- What do clients expect when they purchase the product?
- What needs does the product fulfill for the client?
- What needs are left unfulfilled?

Research also provides the sector with a track record of its performance, and it measures the impact of tourism on the economy. Some companies, such as Air Canada, have their own research divisions. Others hire consulting firms. Many large multinational consulting firms, such as PricewaterhouseCoopers and KPMG International, work with the sector. The non-profit Conference Board of Canada is the lead agency responsible for research in Canada. The board's Canadian Tourism Research Institute (CTRI) concerns itself with tourism issues. Its members' mandate is to "assist their customers in the Canadian tourism sector to anticipate and respond to emerging trends in a manner that will enhance their competitiveness."[4]

Consultants may work for a large firm but they are often entrepreneurs with specific expertise. For example, if you have worked extensively in the food and beverage

www.conferenceboard.
ca/ctri

industry, you may be able to use your knowledge of foods to help a restaurateur create an exciting menu using colours, shapes, and good descriptive copy. Perhaps you are an accountant with a specialty in food and beverage labour cost control. Whatever your field of knowledge, being a consultant means you sell your expertise to those willing to pay for your services. When you work for yourself, you can have greater flexibility with your work hours, but you must also have a strong skill set and the willingness to take a risk—because unemployment may be just one contract away. Many consultants find that the satisfaction of being their own boss outweighs all of the risks.

MISCELLANEOUS SERVICES

Miscellaneous services is the final component of the tourism services industry. Below is a short list of some of these businesses and occupations:

www.cthrc.ca

- **Education and training services** for tourism are provided by a variety of institutions and businesses: high schools, colleges, and universities; private trainers; and organizations such as tourism education councils (TECs) and the Canadian Tourism Human Resource Council (CTHRC). TECs focus on **front-line training**—that is, training staff who deal directly with the tourist. Because tourism businesses are also interested in creating and maintaining a professional workforce, they will often provide in-house training for staff.

- **Media opportunities** exist for travel writers, photographers, television personalities, and documentary writers and producers. These artists combine their love of travel with their creative or artistic abilities. A travel writer or photographer may work for one magazine (such as *Canadian Geographic*) or may freelance. Food photographers working with culinary or tourism magazines preserve for all time outstanding dining experiences found in Canada. Cable television has channels dedicated solely to travel and culinary shows. Many networks include at least one travel documentary and culinary demonstration in their schedules because of the popularity of these shows. Having an education and background in the industry provides you with expertise other applicants will not have.

- **Webpage and website designers** are quickly becoming indispensable to the industry. With so much of our business based on marketing through the internet, people who design and maintain—and can sell through—this medium are indispensable. Good web designers must have not only strong computer skills, but also a thorough knowledge of the tourism industry, the variety of products it offers, and the different target markets the seller is focusing on. Web design wages for large contracts can be quite lucrative.

- **Duty-free shops and retail merchants** provide opportunities for travellers who love to shop. Many department stores are offering SuperHost training to their floor staff to provide good customer service.

- **Construction engineers and architects** design and build facilities for the tourism sector. Often a firm will specialize in the construction of restaurants, cruise ships, or hotels.

- **Specialty food producers** such as farms and cheese factories (Balderson), vineyards (Inniskillin), and food distributors (Summit Foods) all help to make Canadian foods a culinary adventure.

- **Auto clubs** around the world are important to any vacationer who uses a private vehicle. Auto club counsellors design travel routes to help CAA (Canadian Automobile Association) customers avoid construction areas and bypass large cities. Counsellors must have knowledge of the region, updated highway information, and the skill to explain a route.

- **Manufacturers** produce items used by different businesses in the industry, such as commercial ovens, machines, furniture, and amusement park rides.

The list goes on. So many people work in and with tourism services that it is easy to see why it is known as a labour-intensive industry. The work can be fun, and the rewards—even just a warm hello or hearty thanks—make a tourism job a special event every day.

CASE STUDY

Claudia's Late Shift

When Claudia got her first job at a local fast food chain, she was thrilled. She had great bosses, good training, and enthusiastic co-workers. Claudia soon became an important part of the team when she showed maturity well beyond her age. She handled responsibility easily, never had problems with her cash register, and had a special knack for working the drive-thru window. By the time she was 18, she was a junior shift supervisor, which meant that she made more money, but also often had to work the closing shift. Even though company policy dictated that either a manager or an assistant manager had to be on duty with her during these closing shifts, her mother worried about her, especially when another fast food restaurant two blocks away was robbed. Claudia, however, felt safe even late at night because either her parents picked her up or she walked the two blocks home with friends from

her shift. One night, the assistant manager was called away to an emergency at home and left the responsible late shift team to close up. Claudia's parents were out of town and her friends had other plans, so she found herself walking home alone. Though she walked quickly and was alert for danger, she did not arrive home safely. Her brother called the police when he discovered her missing and a search party was raised. Claudia was found hours later a few kilometres from her home. She had been attacked and abandoned on the side of the road.

While this is not a true story, it is based on events that have occurred in Canada recently. As a result of these events, many fast food restaurants have made efforts to change current company policies to include safety measures for employees who work the late shift.

1. What is the root problem in this case study? Is it a common problem in the fast food industry?
2. What options did the assistant manager have when she was called away to an emergency?
3. What would you have done if, like Claudia, you had been faced with walking home alone?
4. Should the fast food chain have had a policy regarding the safety of employees working the late shift? Why or why not?
5. How much responsibility should a company take for ensuring safety for its employees in situations like these?

Summary

The tourism services industry includes a wide range of occupations that are instrumental in creating a quality Canadian tourism product. The industry can be broken down into five components: government agencies, tourism associations and organizations, marketing and promotional firms, research and consulting firms, and miscellaneous services. All levels of government become involved in the tourism sector through research, development, promotion, education, funding, and legislative and regulatory initiatives.

Tourism associations are either promoters of or advocates for the sector. They provide information to members and help set the direction of tourism. TIAC has published a paper that shows the extreme difficulty the industry currently faces without immediate government intervention. Marketing and promotional firms know how to sell the sector's products. Understanding the unique characteristics of the tourism product is essential. Canada's DMO is the Canadian Tourism Commission. They hope to use the Olympics to promote the animation of Canada's new brand. Research and consulting firms provide the industry with a wealth of information, including an analysis of current market trends and projections for the future. The remaining occupations that keep the sector progressing and running smoothly fall into the miscellaneous category and include educators, architects, construction engineers, and companies that supply the tourism sector with products such as fresh produce, cleansers, and landscaping services. Although those parts of the tourism services industry remain behind the scenes, they play a vital role in the tourism sector.

Questions

1. The government of any country plays a crucial role in the planning, development, maintenance, and promotion of a country or region.
   a) Summarize briefly the roles played by: i) the CTC; ii) your provincial government; and iii) your municipal government.
   b) List two regulations or pieces of legislation created by provincial and municipal governments that help or hurt the tourism sector as a whole, or the tourist as an individual. Explain why you believe this legislation is helpful or harmful.

2. Research your city's convention and visitors bureau and describe four different services it performs for the tourism sector in your region.

3. Tourism services provide the sector with many different support services.
   a) Choose any five services that appeal to you from this industry and explain why you might be interested in this line of work.
   b) Would you require further education to work in each of these businesses? If so, what courses would you be looking for?

4. Define the following terms as they relate to the tourism sector: *familiarization tour*, *site inspection*, DMO.

Notes

1. Canadian Tourism Human Resource Council, *The Student Travel Map,* 1995, pp. 102–103.

2. *Report on Canada's Tourism Competitiveness–A Call for Action,* www.tiac-aitc.ca.

3. *Strategy 2008–2012,* www.corporate. canada.travel.

4. www.conferenceboard.ca/ctri.

Challenges and the Future

Key terms

code of ethics   time poverty

Learning objectives

Having read this chapter you will be able to

1. Identify and explain the impact of current trends in lifestyles, travel, and technology on the tourism sector.

2. Explain the importance of ethical behaviour in the tourism sector.

3. Explain how the eight concerns/challenges identified by the CTC for the tourism sector may slow or expand the sector's growth rate.

4. Outline the trends and challenges in each component of the tourism industry.

Tourism is like a snowfall. During blizzard periods, the sheer number of tourists makes life for a community difficult. Tourism produces overcrowded streets, hour-long waits for restaurant tables, and overbooked flights and hotels. The Olympic Games is a good example of an event where all the planning in the world cannot lessen the strain on the entire community. As with a massive snowfall, the aftermath of such an event requires a tremendous amount of cleanup. At other times, Canadian snowfalls are beautiful, soft and steady; this is the equivalent to tourism's high season, when the number of tourists is constant but workable. Attractions are busy, hotels and restaurants are full, and the crowds are friendly. At times, the snow falls sporadically, enough to tell us that it is snowing, but not enough to bother us—the equivalent of tourism's shoulder or off-peak period. The tourists are still coming, but there is no inconvenience to residents. Hotels and restaurants experience a slow cycle, and often the airlines cut back on their flights. Finally, there comes a time when no snow falls at all. Not all destinations experience a total lack of tourists, but some inaccessible resorts must close for the winter. This is equivalent to tourism's low season when prices are lower, top attractions are easier to get into, and tourists are not constantly bumping into other tourists on the street.

Snowfalls are similar to tourism in other ways: just as no two snowflakes are alike, no two tourists are alike; the impact of a snowfall is affected by external factors (winds, time of day, day of the week, amount of snow already on the ground), just as tourism is affected by factors beyond its control. The past eight years have illustrated that, despite our efforts, tourism is often deeply affected by the unpredictable factors of politics, weather, and other environmental issues and disease. The terrorist attacks on the World Trade Center, and in London, Egypt, and Thailand; the SARS epidemic; and the tsunami in Southeast Asia followed by Hurricane Katrina are just some of the unexpected and destructive events that have focused attention on and brought about concern for the tourism industry. Despite these negative impacts, it is human nature to focus on the positive and hope for the best. Professionals were certain the industry would bounce back, and it did between 2004 and 2007.

Canadians have no choice about how much snow they get—but they do have a choice about the quality and size of their tourism industry. Political moves, some made by other countries, some made by our own government, have deepened concerns for the financial stability of our tourism industry. No expert could have predicted the fast rise in value of the Canadian dollar in 2007, or the leap in the price of gas, or the impact WHTI (Western Hemisphere Travel Initiative) legislation would have on tourism in Canada. Those three moves, along with a number of other political choices (including refusal to sign the Chinese MOU and our prime minister's not attending the opening and closing ceremonies in Beijing in 2008) may have set for us a very difficult future.

This chapter examines the future of tourism. Why does Canada believe tourism will continue to grow? Where is the sector going and how will it get there?

SOCIETAL CHANGES THAT IMPACT TOURISM

Each generation develops its own style of living based on a great many different factors. Family life structures have changed, impacting the social fabric of our North American society. People are choosing to marry later in life or not to marry at all. The financial need for two incomes adds stress to all members of the family. Due to widely distributed family members, people are seeking "familial people ties" by looking outside the family circle, linked via computer and cellphone. The exchange of information made possible by sites like Facebook and YouTube has helped show how many world cultures there are, and has, perhaps, made the desire for travel stronger. Generation Y members are willing to leave their jobs for an extended period of time to include distant destinations. Money in the bank, while important, is considered positive only if it is being spent on pleasures, one of which is travel. In the 1950s–1970s, destinations relied on celebrity endorsements to sell vacations. This advantage has disappeared as younger generations choose a destination with little consideration of its celebrity status.

Even the boomers have not aged as experts had forecast. While some remain true to predictions—retiring to quiet lives with travel that suits their aging needs—others have grabbed their new freedom with a gusto not foreseen by the experts. They are retiring earlier and using the internet to research and book trips. The new breed—some experts are now calling them "zoomers" because of their need to stay busy—want to take part in whatever activities are found at the destination. Not only are these zoomers interested in seeing the sights, they are looking to be challenged by travel. They have a need to give back to society as volunteers, helping build homes, schools, water systems, and home businesses in developing countries instead of sitting on the beach. Some choose to become more involved with tourism by investing in homes abroad that they rent out when they are not there. Most travellers are concerned about the ecosystem and want to better understand biodiversity and what actions they can take to help slow global warming. They may choose to buy carbon credits, give thought to using a "greener" mode of transportation, or pick tourism companies that have strong eco-conservative backgrounds. Of course, many boomers still look at vacations as times when they are looked after and pampered.

FOOTPRINT

Are You a True Eco-tourist?

The International Ecotourism Society (IETS) recently published the results of a survey taken in Berlin by the University of Eberswalde based on guest responses at an eco-travel show. The results were not surprising:

- 75% of those surveyed said they believe tourism is a contributor to climate change.

- Only 6% of travellers said they offset their carbon footprints related to their travel experiences.

- Exhibitors agreed that they also have concerns for the environment and try to create packages that meet green standards. The cost of implementing eco-changes would determine if those changes were set in place.

- Less than 3% said they had carbon offsetting plans in place.

- 66% noted that their business has changed because of the impact of climate changes, but seldom is anything done about it.

The IETS suggested that eco-trotters incorporate the following into their travel plans: choosing destinations that can be reached without flying, preferring travel by bus or train; using public transportation at their destination rather than renting a car or using a taxi; selecting eco-friendly hotels whose operations focus on recycling/reducing waste policies; buying locally produced souvenirs; and eating local, not packaged, food products. Travellers note that fresh, local foods not only taste better and support the local economy, but are also generally healthier.

What this survey suggests is that both travellers and tourist businesses are concerned about climate change, but are not often committed enough to making major lifestyle changes.

Technology is an ever-growing part of the tourism puzzle. Ecommerce drives the industry as the younger generation researches, books, and then posts comments on their trip choice—good or bad. A bad experience can now be quickly broadcast to the world, not just the next-door neighbour. Travel has been made easier with the online booking system, "ticketless travel," and machines that check people through immigration faster. Because trips are easier to book and promotions are plentiful, there has been a rise in "impulse buying," or trip deals that are just too good to turn down.

ETHICS AND TOURISM

This book has already addressed ethical standards and why they are so important to the tourism sector. In North America, we have legislation that protects tourists from some forms of unethical behaviour. Laws against false commercial claims, and laws that protect travellers when tour operators or airlines go bankrupt are just two examples. Yet how easy it is, with computer technology, to create a brochure that shows mountains in the backyard of a cute little chalet, when in truth they are 30 km away! Another marketing deception is the so-called "bait and switch," in which a company advertises a deeply discounted price for, say, a cruise, but sets aside only a few cabins at this price. Once potential customers are on the line, a good salesperson can easily sell a space at a higher price.

Tourism workers, by necessity, have a very close relationship with tourists. Few businesses are given this type of trust, and it is important to tourism services and products everywhere that this trust is not misplaced. The tourism product is intangible and cannot operate well without that trust. The tourism worker is the only link between the product and the tourist. Tourists entrust their lives, their security, and their possessions to tourism professionals. Individuals who enter the tourism sector must accept this responsibility and serve with honesty and concern for their customers' welfare. The reward is happy clients, a profitable business, a sense of pride, and the satisfaction of a job well done. In addition, having risk management policies in place ensures your establishment has the highest regard for safety. The importance of these concepts, the **code of ethics**, needs to be instilled in employees from the very beginning of their employment, ensuring that safety, as well as enjoyment, tops the list of successful requirements.

ISSUES CAUSING CONCERN IN THE SECTOR

A decade ago, the CTC addressed eight key tourism issues that the sector felt needed the federal government's attention.[1] All these issues still exist; in fact, some have been exacerbated by government action and inaction. If not resolved, they will likely weaken the Canadian tourism product in the next decade. This section will explore those key issues.

Transportation Easy, reasonably priced access to and around a country is critical if tourism is to flourish. Canada's transportation system is slowly deteriorating. The quality of highways, roads, and roadside facilities has diminished, and upgrading is slow. Deregulation appears to have helped create a near-monopolistic air system, with

Air Canada our only remaining national carrier. Air travel has become increasingly expensive as governments and the airlines tack on additional taxes and surcharges. One of the latest examples is the surcharge placed on checked baggage by many of the world's larger airlines. Charges vary, but checking a bag at Air Canada costs $15 for the first and $25 for each additional bag. In addition to these charges, the maximum weight of your checked item has dropped from 50 kg to 40 kg. WestJet has dropped the weight allowances, but has yet to institute a checked bag surcharge. So, while a less expensive ticket price would encourage travel within Canada, reasonably priced air transportation is becoming a rarity.

In truth, the impact of rising oil prices has forced all modes of transportation to increase their pricing structures, and while they adjust to new pricing structures, people are thinking twice before taking even short trips by car. As mentioned, concern for the ecosystem is another factor. Aircrafts are big polluters, and while newer models are more eco-conscious, they are not pollution-free. Faster, eco-friendly train systems are available, but their expense will likely ensure that Canada will not invest in this technology. In fact, Canada has been very slow to make any advancements in this area. High-speed trains between Calgary and Edmonton or Toronto and Montreal would cut down on the number of flights between these major cities, reduce pollution, and provide a comfortable journey for clients. It would take just 45 minutes on the *Maglev* to get from Edmonton to Calgary, normally a three-hour drive. Here is a perfect example of how a tourism product moves from the mature stage into decline. Even though there has been some investment into our older rail system, a new option like the *Maglev* is not being considered. New investment in all areas of transportation is necessary, however, if we are to maintain our position as a world leader in tourism.

The Role of Parks, Historic Sites, and Crown Lands National parks and historic sites are important to the tourism sector because many product offerings have some natural or historic significance. However, conflicts arise when Parks Canada, for example, attempts to balance the need for better tourist accessibility with the need to preserve land, flora, and fauna for future generations. The tourism sector has raised concerns because demand for our national parks experience is growing (Banff and Jasper are perhaps the most pressured), while deteriorating facilities threaten the overall quality of the tourist experience. Wilderness areas such as Nahanni and Tatshenshini-Alsek national parks are already showing the strain of more adventure-seeking tourists. To add to these problems, the dilemma caused by world oil supplies is encouraging some politicians and businesspeople to reconsider using land currently under government protection for development.

The use of land tenure systems on Crown land is creating great concern among some people in Canada's Western provinces. The oil sands in Alberta, while producing over a million barrels a day, are expected to quadruple output by 2020. With oil in such demand, and the billions of dollars already spent to extract it, there is little thought of slowing development of this land even though the ecological impacts will be felt for hundreds of years.

While a small fund has been set aside to return the land to its natural state, there are no criteria defining what that natural state is. Granted, this is not an area high on the eco-adventure list for tourists, but what if the desecration of the land continues? Another province, British Columbia, is also facing a major power struggle between tourism and the coal reserves found in its Flathead Valley. Coal, still a major source of energy, could be strip-mined from the area, destroying one of the world's last great ecological treasures. How far should Canada go to protect its vast and globally important ecosystems?

The Evolving Role of Canada Customs and Immigration More than two million border crossings take place daily between the United States and Canada. While Europe reduces the formalities at border crossings, making travel on the continent easier, borders in North America are moving to stricter controls that make it more difficult and time-consuming to cross our border. The United States has expressed concern about Canada's immigration system because, in the past, several known terrorists have entered the United States through Canada. Officials are being given broad powers to ensure that anyone crossing the border has proper papers and legitimate business. By 2009, WHTI legislation will require all Canadian citizens travelling to the United States to have valid passports in their possession. It is ironic that in the past 10 years, European countries have eased border restrictions, making travel more convenient across the continent, while the so-called open border between the United States and Canada becomes increasingly difficult to cross. Is the Canadian government willing to invest the hard dollars required to upgrade technology at our borders? Will these changes ensure a smoother, safer border crossing for tourists, while eliminating potential terrorist threats? While the NEXUS card is already being accepted, it will be years before border improvements ease the situation.

The Tax Issue Taxes have always been a thorn in the side of tourism, and with the introduction of the goods and services tax (GST) in 1991, they became a major concern for tourism. Since the GST is not levied on Canadian exports, and tourism is one of Canada's biggest exports, why is the GST charged on tourism products? Even if a foreign tourist purchases a Canadian tour package outside Canada, the GST must still be paid. Tourism advocates feel strongly that this discriminates against tourism products that are already costly. In 1998, after lobbying by TIAC, the government agreed to remove the GST paid by international conferences choosing a Canadian destination. Delegates must still pay GST on any purchases while in Canada, but TIAC also lobbied for remuneration rights for tourists on any GST they pay while in Canada. The program set up in 1998, allowing visitors who kept their receipts to fill out the correct paperwork and receive an instant rebate at the border (which was usually spent on duty-free goods on the Canadian side) or a cheque in the mail. Almost a decade ago, Ken Hine, who was CEO of the International Hotel and Restaurant Association, described the tax situation as it once existed in New York City and warned Canada it was moving quickly in this direction. When taxes in New York City reached a high of 21.25%, the industry was able to prove to both municipal and state governments that they were driving more business away than they were generating in tax revenues.

Consider the case of tourists visiting Ontario who must add 13% (PST and GST) to all their purchases, plus a liquor tax, and a hotel tax. In 2004, some larger destinations allowed hotels to add an additional 3% promotion tax to help pay for future advertising campaigns. Add to that an entertainment tax levied on some forms of entertainment, airport improvement fees, CATSA and NAVCAN charges, and numerous municipal taxes. It is like killing the golden goose—when taxes become too high, tourists choose other destinations, and tourism revenues drop. With the dollar resting at 65 cents, perhaps taxes were not a concern for U.S. tourists. At even par, as it was in 2007, all of our markets look at other destinations for a less expensive vacation. Bringing in more tourists is the answer to this problem, not raising another tax.

Training of Tourism Workers Quality of service has been identified as one of the most important features consumers look for when purchasing any product, and it remains one of the biggest problems faced by the tourism sector today. Because many workers have direct contact with the tourist, proper training is essential. If Canada is to compete in a global market, our tourism professionals must have the skills, knowledge, and attitudes (SKAs) to deliver the product effectively. In 2010, the world comes to our door with the Winter Olympics. Are our workers ready to be the outstanding hosts they need to be?

Training programs developed by the tourism education councils and the sector are an important advancement. With the CTHRC's *emerit* certification process now online, getting certified is even easier. Once a business's workers are certified, an owner can display his workers' individual certificates and allow them to wear their certification pins—showing the individual's personal investment in training.

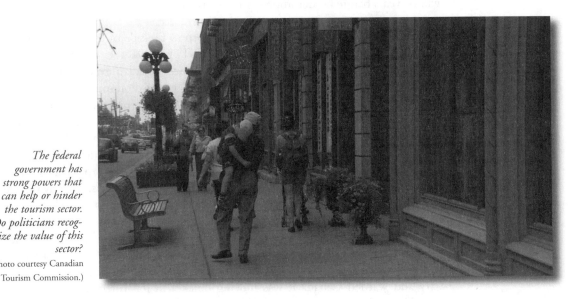

The federal government has strong powers that can help or hinder the tourism sector. Do politicians recognize the value of this sector?

(Photo courtesy Canadian Tourism Commission.)

Financing the Future of Tourism The financial community has never perceived tourism to be a sound financial investment. There are several reasons for this perception. First, tourism is made up of mostly small businesses, many of which have a track record of financial difficulties or bankruptcy. Second, it is difficult to define the tourism business and its potential revenues in a financial statement, although the new NAICS system will help. And third, financial institutions have never possessed a clear vision of the tourism sector (a problem that also exists within the sector itself). As tourism moves front and centre in the world of financial investment, Canadian lending institutions and the government of Canada must reconsider their position and invest the dollars needed to maintain the quality of Canadian tourism products.

Aboriginal Tourism Both the federal and provincial governments, along with the tourism sector, recognize the growing demand for experiences centred on the cultural heritage of Aboriginal Canadians. All too aware of the harm tourism can bring, the sector strongly supports the development of Aboriginal tourism as long as it meets the government's requirement for sustainability. This development must enhance Aboriginal culture, respect Aboriginal lands and lifestyle, and produce viable employment for our First Nations. In the end, Aboriginal tourism, already in high demand, should help improve the quality of life, both financially and culturally, for Aboriginal Canadians.

www.projectplanetcorp.
com

TERRORIST THREATS

In the past decade, the threat of terrorism has increased against many nations. Terrorist acts have plagued U.S. facilities on foreign soil, and the destruction of the World Trade Center in 2001 brought the fear of terrorism home to Americans. In the 1970s, hijackings were more common than they are today, but passengers were used as hostages, allowing terrorists to bargain for certain demands. The events of September 11, 2001, turned the airplanes themselves into bombs and wrought massive destruction.

Israel's tourism sector has suffered more than most from terrorist actions, and in Malaysia, tourists were captured and held for more than three months while their captors' demands were being considered. In Bali, two Canadian tourists died when a nightclub was bombed. Terrorism is taking a toll on tourism around the world.

Travel in less-developed countries is more dangerous than it was, and ironically, Canada has actually benefited indirectly from these events. We still view our country as a safe place for travel, but there is no doubt that if terrorists continue to make headlines around the world, tourism everywhere will suffer.

OTHER GLOBAL CONCERNS

Climate Change

Our climate is changing and that is having an impact in many areas. Ski resorts in Europe, open just 40 years ago from November through April, are now finding their season lasts from late December through to February. The snow line is decreasing and the quality of skiing is deteriorating. Many resort areas have already started to expand summer season activities in order to stay profitable.

Rising waters may not have had a big impact on Canadian shores, but they are threatening islands with low water lines such as the Maldives. Historic cities like Venice are slowly "sinking" into the sea. Concerns are high in the Netherlands and Mexico City regarding the possibility of major flooding. Rising temperatures are also causing problems. Climates once considered "warm" are now hot with temperatures reaching and exceeding 43 C (100 F). Warmer, dry weather is causing drought that is harming crops and spawning major forest fires across the west coast of North America. Southern European countries like Spain are seeing their first major forest fires. Hurricanes of greater magnitude and frequency batter the Caribbean islands and Central/North America. More tornadoes are being reported and, in Asia, hurricanes are becoming more intense. Africa is suffering from unusual drought that threatens most of the continent and its delicate ecosystems. Weather is one of those factors beyond our control, so why discuss it here? We cannot change it, but we must be prepared for it and try to prevent any destruction that we can. Dikes, dams, and levees need strengthening; campfires are forbidden in many parks; modern forest fire fighting equipment needs to be developed and purchased by provinces like B.C. and Ontario; hotels and attractions must be built to withstand strong winds; and risk management plans must be in place for evacuation of guests if their safety is threatened.

Cultural and Economic Concerns

The internet has opened up whole new areas of tourism, with one of the most disturbing being the sex trade. Tourism has benefited in some developing countries where exploitation of women and children in the sex trade is tolerated. Some countries such as Great Britain have passed legislation allowing it to prosecute British tourists who travel to these countries for the purpose of accessing any aspect of the sex trade.[2]

TRENDS IN THE TOURISM SECTOR

Peter Yesawich, a leading expert in the field of marketing research, has identified some of the trends in lifestyle, travel, and technology we have looked at and his comments sum up these changes well.[3] He reminds us that contemporary customers are better educated, have more knowledge about the products they are purchasing, and demand and expect more value for their dollar than customers of past years. The internet has made them smarter shoppers, and they know how to search out the best price for the products they want.

As business becomes more competitive and as companies try to produce more for less, our society becomes more burdened by **time poverty**. Many people find they have less time for everything, including vacations; indeed, the average North American lunch "hour" is just 28 minutes long! How well will restaurants handle the need for quicker service or the working lunch? The number of hours that most people work is increasing, while the time we allot for vacation and business trips is getting shorter. As a result, the need for efficient service is greater. Today's consumers are willing to pay more for convenience. With the workweek getting longer, time at home is focused on family and family activities. Research has shown that our priorities have changed. We want more control of our lives and what we do with our time. We are concerned about our health. We want to be able to take time off work when needed, to have successful relationships, and to experience a better quality of life. These desires are becoming more important to younger generations than is personal wealth.

Happy tourists take pleasant memories of their vacation home, share these memories with friends and, hopefully, return to visit again.
(Photo courtesy Canadian Tourism Commission.)

Over the years, North Americans have become increasingly jaded in their view of government, authority, and the media. Advertising enjoys even less credibility. Consumers are more willing to complain if a product or service does not meet expectations. This erosion of trust in the marketplace can easily affect tourism because tourism is a product that is both expensive and intangible. Tourism businesses that want to succeed and thrive in the future must deliver a product that surpasses customer expectations.

Businesses that survived the World Trade Center attack or the SARS epidemic may still be struggling with the current economic downturn caused by the collapse of technology stocks, or recent stock scandals among large, respected businesses. Although business travel has largely rebounded after September 11, 2001, studies conflict about the overall trend in business travel, with some studies projecting a continued decline. Trips may be shorter or less frequent, or they may be extended to cover more than one objective. The internet and teleconferencing have the potential to replace face-to-face business practices. (This effect applies mostly to individual trips and small meetings rather than conferences and conventions.)

Having successfully hosted the G-8 Conference at Kananaskis in August 2002, with no major disruptions, Canada is being recognized as a safe alternative to U.S. destinations. Growth is forecast for the business meeting market.

As branding becomes important to sales, small businesses are having more difficulty staying profitable. The growing demand for high-profile brand names is expressed by the forming of alliances and associations, and the buyout of smaller businesses by larger ones. Using a brand name provides customers with a familiar product, one that they have confidence in. Fifty-one to seventy-one percent of consumers choose a brand name over an unknown name, especially when dollar values are similar.

Consumers are looking for products that are easy to purchase and use, and tourism businesses can fill this need by creating partnerships. Package deals—for example, putting accommodations together with a rental car and some entertainment and dining options—are growing in popularity. This kind of package is seen not only in the tourism sector, but also in many aspects of the North American lifestyle. Consider the new mega-stores that sell groceries, clothes, furniture, appliances, and drugs under one roof. This trend reflects the longer workweek and the erosion of personal, discretionary time.

Travel packages that provide short, relaxing holidays are expected to gain a greater share of the market. For example, hotels should be looking at strategic pricing: a Sunday-through-Thursday stay coupled with a Thursday-through-Sunday package. This fills the need for business travellers looking to reduce the cost of their travel, and the vacation traveller who wants to take a four-day weekend.

Transportation trends include ticketless air travel; do-it-yourself, computerized check-in; and discount airlines that offer little or no service. Aircraft manufacturers are designing larger, much faster planes. Expect to see continued alliances and code sharing between the major airline companies. Trains are becoming an attractive alternative to air travel because they seem less likely to attract terrorism. And with the added surcharges on an airline ticket in Canada, at least on short-haul runs like Montreal to Toronto, the train can be more affordable. VIA Rail has recognized the tourist demand for luxury train travel and has added newly refurbished cars and more service, making the trans-Canada trip more like a cruise—a total vacation package.

Cruise lines seem convinced that bigger is better and are making cruises even more luxurious and elaborate, including facilities such as wedding chapels, bowling lanes, ice rinks, jogging paths, and surfing pools. High-end cruise lines like Crystal are focusing on "smaller is better" for upscale clients looking for fewer people aboard, luxury, and different ports.[4]

Trends in the accommodation industry include creating a more home-like atmosphere in rooms with more comfortable beds, pillows, and furniture, while providing customers with a high level of personal service (delivered through enhanced training programs for workers). The high-end customer is looking for facilities that include a gym or spa and high-speed internet connection. Larger hotel chains are expected to continue their partnerships with and buyouts of smaller properties. Hotels are beginning to look at the airlines' surcharge strategy to keep rates low. A study by PricewaterhouseCoopers published in May 2005 reports that U.S. hotels expect to rake in more than $1.4 billion by adding surcharges such as "resort fees" (use of the parking lot, use of the pool and towels, and airport shuttle services); restocking of mini-bars (whether or not they have been used); additional fees for room service (in addition to the automatic gratuity); and even a charge for housekeeping. Hotels have lost money as more customers use the internet rather than the phone to contact customers and friends from their rooms; "free" internet may soon come with a hefty hook-up charge.

Since these surcharges are as frustrating as airline surcharges, many CVBs suggest that if customers wish to avoid or at least reduce them, they should negotiate the add-ons the moment they arrive at the front desk. Waiting until the end of the stay means likely not having much luck at reducing or eliminating charges for services that were not used.[5]

Food and beverage will remain a growing entrepreneurial industry. As baby boomers age, they become increasingly concerned about nutritious food. Fresh, local products will score high with this knowledgeable market, as will a good wine list. Smaller establishments will continue to struggle against the larger, well-known chains and must be able to reach a target market that believes that smaller is better.

Alliances and buyouts will continue to be commercially successful. Technology will play an ever-increasing role in this industry, and businesses will have to keep tight control of their food costs, using modern computers and cash systems. Menus are beginning to reflect consumers' interest in healthy eating by offering dishes that meet the standards of many diets.

Finally, the demand for contract food services and for food service aligned with upscale retirement homes will provide hospitality and culinary students with interesting career options.

Recreation and entertainment, the experiential components of tourism, will flourish as more baby boomers enjoy their retirement years. Attractions and special events that focus on culture and historical themes will be popular. More attractions are getting the visitor involved with hands-on workshops or seminars. Communities looking to expand their economic base are hosting a variety of special events to help extend their tourist season and increase revenue generation. Special events are not just important for the tourism sector; they are also a main source of revenue for charities, and bring needed recognition to local enterprises. While the rising dollar no longer gives this country a bargain advantage, Canada is still perceived as a safe and welcoming country—a perception that is sure to mean new growth in the conference and convention business.

www.workopolis.ca

Our challenges for the future must include respecting the environment and creating a world in which tourism and our natural wonders coexist comfortably from one generation to the next.
(Photo courtesy Canadian Tourism Commission.)

Adventure tourism and outdoor recreation have strong growth potential. Good risk management policies that provide a high level of safety will be important for much of this market. Ecotourism, in the true sense of the word, will continue to interest the adult market. Resorts that boast a unique natural setting will be held to a higher standard of sustainable development, and designs will have

SNAPSHOT

John Gow

With a love of skiing and the mountains, it is no wonder that John Gow set his sights high early in life. He began his career in 1964 at Sunshine Village in Banff, Alberta, as a ski instructor and mountain guide. He was soon recognized for his skill and knowledge, which were too great to leave him on the mountain. With his first promotion, he became director of ski school operations. From there he moved to director of marketing for Sunshine Village. Then he became its general manager and, finally, chief executive officer. John Gow was an integral part of the development strategies that led to Sunshine Village's great expansion (including one of the world's largest gondola systems) and its ability to operate at virtual capacity.

By 1981, John reached the pinnacle of success at Sunshine Village. His next move, along with several associates, was to purchase Silver Star Mountain Resort in British Columbia. As president of his own company, John discovered that his responsibilities included not only the day-to-day operations of the resort, but also the challenges of working alongside government agencies, planning for future expansion, and determining how to finance his ideas. How Silver Star Mountain Resort has changed under his guidance! What had once been a local ski hill has now become a major resort area for the Okanagan region and all of British Columbia. Gow added a themed village centre, hotels, restaurants and bars, shops, and special recreation facilities that satisfy the needs of both day visitors and tourists. Recently, he expanded the resort, tripling its ski-able acreage, installing

two express quad chairlifts, and increasing the vertical drop by 40%. Plans for the future include an 18-hole golf course, making Silver Star Mountain Resort a year-round property.

John Gow is not a man to sit around. In Banff, he became an active member of the chamber of commerce, serving on the hospitality board and the municipal council. During his 17 years in Banff, he was a major catalyst in the construction of two housing developments, improving the quality of life for residents who lived and worked in the mountain resort area. Working with local transportation companies, he formed a partnership with the ski schools, creating a joint marketing program with ticketing and transportation facilities, which allowed them to penetrate markets in Eastern Canada, Japan, and the United States.

When Gow moved to British Columbia, he became even more active. Among his current positions are chair of the Pacific Rim Institute of Technology and of Rendez-Vous Canada; board member with Tourism British Columbia; and past chair of TIAC.

Who is John Gow? He is an energetic man, with a passionate commitment to the ski industry, to the development of the western ski product, and to tourism as a whole. His ability to work with all levels of government and industry and his vision for a sustainable and profitable future have made him one of the most respected voices in Canadian tourism. There are few who can balance life and its challenges as well as John Gow.

---

www.tourism.govt.nz

to ensure minimum harm to the environment. Boomers looking for a healthy retirement will lead increasingly active lives that will include daily exercise. Golf courses and walking trails within suburban sites will become an integral part of the tourism experience.

Travel services will remain an important piece of the tourism sector, but methods of doing business will change. Customers' use of travel agencies will depend more on the agencies' expertise and accountability. Tour companies will need to align many of their products with an older audience, providing well-paced, intellectually stimulating tours.

Tourism services will expand with the other industries. As better service is demanded by consumers, employees will need better customer service skills. Good trainers and quality training programs will be increasingly popular with all service industries. Good consumer research and statistics will also be required. Niche marketing will become important for smaller businesses as they work against the tidal waves of branding and big business. If brands are to remain competitive, they will have to produce more cost-effective advertising campaigns that clearly address their target markets' needs.

www.hcareers.com

TOURISM CHALLENGES

Challenges provide opportunities for people to grow and expand their vision—and they frequently lead to greater achievement and new inventions. Some challenges are life-changing. Where would the world be if scientists did not challenge disease by searching for cures? Some challenges simply make life interesting—like walking the Great Wall of China. As mentioned, the biggest (and most silent) challenge for tourism is the continued threat of terrorism. Keeping tourists safe has always been important; now it has become a priority. The events of September 11, 2001, forced Canada to deal with the ongoing problem of fake Canadian passports, and forced the government and the airlines to take additional security precautions. However, investigative reporters have identified many different lapses in security still open to people intent on doing harm and promoting their cause.

The rising cost of fuel is likely the number one challenge for all modes of travel. Using Airport Improvement Fees (AIFs), airports are adding better facilities to reflect the demand for faster and more efficient services, and longer runways for larger jets. Taking steps such as reducing baggage allowances, charging for checked baggage, removing food service on flights under four hours, and removing pillows (the most frequently stolen item) from airplanes illustrates how hard airlines are working to control costs. Some airlines are considering removing entertainment systems as well. Note: Pillows, blankets, and meals may often be purchased from the airline.

Car rental companies will likely be stocking smaller, more fuel-efficient cars, with SUVs becoming less popular. Cruise lines face myriad challenges: too few ports, overcrowding at popular ports, and ports unable to handle the needs of the larger ships currently being built. Passenger safety becomes an issue—whether threats come from food poisoning, terrorism, or crime. A report by CNN, aired in 2007, reviewed treatment of crimes on-board a cruise ship and showed that crimes committed in international waters with no one country clearly in charge are a cause for concern. Cruise lines, unwilling to become involved, often ship the suspected perpetrator back to their own country once the ship enters a port. The party atmosphere, the temporary lifestyle on-board, and the wide variety of cultural norms on-board a ship are often used as excuses. With no investigative personnel on-board, the crime scene is not properly examined, the evidence is lost, and the crimes go unanswered. The cruise industry's final challenge is to reach that 85% of the population that has never cruised and persuade them that cruising is the best vacation buy.

Lodging facilities are facing many different challenges, including luring guests back and providing consistent, high-quality service. Businesses in this industry must begin to provide better facilities for the disabled and the elderly traveller, including wheelchair accessibility, ergonomically designed bathrooms, and brighter lighting. Analysts predict that over the next 20 years, baby boomers will begin to sell their homes and move into retirement communities. Already some small hotels have been converted to retirement condominiums, making good use of existing facilities such as commercial kitchens, dining rooms, a pool or exercise area, and meeting spaces. Resorts will need to think in terms of all four seasons. By adding spas, winter activities, and special events, resorts can extend revenue seasons and appeal to a broader clientele.

The food and beverage industry faces many challenges. Service and training will continue to be priorities. More competition means restaurants will need to make service a factor for the discriminating customer. Legal issues such as alcohol consumption and no-smoking bylaws will need creative solutions from restaurateurs. Perhaps the most important challenge is food safety. Incidents of *E. coli* outbreaks and other food poisoning incidents continue to plague the industry. One of the best ways to ensure safe food handling is to put into place the Hazard Analysis Critical Control Point (HACCP) system.

Strong growth in the recreation and entertainment industry means cities and regions must provide visitors with a greater array of attractions, events and conference facilities, and outdoor experiences. Tourists are beginning to look for unique educational experiences with hands-on activities such as weaving or wine making, or working on a ranch. A new area of growth—volunteer tourism—opens up a wide range of opportunities. Weather and other natural disasters of 2004 and 2005, such as the tsunami in Asia, earthquakes, flooding, and hurricanes, have inspired many people to travel to places where they can help other communities rebuild.

A shortage exists of trained, experienced event coordinators and meeting planners. The event business gets bigger every year as companies from all industries recognize the financial returns of a well-planned event. Can this country meet the challenge with newer conference facilities and well-trained staff? Canada has the opportunity to become an even more desirable destination as we head to the Olympics of 2010 and the positive promotion the Games will bring.

www.monster.ca

Adventure tourism and outdoor recreation have also seen tremendous growth. As boomers retire, exercise and fresh air become important health issues. Baby boomers will be looking for destinations that provide a wide variety of physical activities. Young, single travellers are searching for excitement while on vacation, and finding it backpacking around the country, hiking in the mountains, and boating on our beautiful lakes and challenging rivers. Canada is well positioned to take full advantage of this trend, but will we have the trained personnel to ensure the experience is not only exciting but also safe? Canadian colleges and universities now offer a wide variety of adventure tourism courses.

Use of the internet by potential travel service customers is quickly eroding business. With commissions lowered or dropped altogether, travel agencies and other businesses must find new streams of revenue. That great hotelier Cesar Ritz was finding new streams of hotel revenues at the turn of the 20th century; now travel agencies must use his techniques and find new ways to generate revenue for themselves. They must be aware of niche markets (e.g., travellers with disabilities) and provide services that meet customer needs in a professional and friendly manner. Keeping customer profiles will be more important than ever. Travel workers who have developed a relationship with customers, who know customers' likes and dislikes, also know that those customers will feel comfortable and well looked after, and will return again.

Tourism services, the support services for the sector, must meet the needs of the struggling tourism sector. Architects and designers must be more ecologically driven, ensuring that new products cause minimal harm to the environment. Research, consulting, and marketing firms; retail outlets; government services; educators; and trainers all must provide the tourism sector with the means to create a strong, sustainable product. The information they supply must be reliable and easily understood. The years ahead will provide many challenges for people entering the tourism business, but in the baby boomers there lies a ready, willing, and able group of travellers. Opportunities no longer lie just in Canada, but around the globe. Tourism needs new ideas, new energy, and new dreams.

CASE STUDY

The China Gem

Shannon had just graduated with her travel diploma and had the job of her dreams—acting as an escort for a large tour company. She had always loved working with people, and this job gave her the chance to see the world and get paid for it. This particular tour, "China Gems," was for retirees, and she found she had her hands full with 30 very active and talkative ladies. This high-end tour package used only five-star properties and attractions and moved at a leisurely pace for 18 days. Check-in at the first hotel in Honolulu had gone smoothly; now they were in China. Shannon took a moment to remind the ladies of the different cultural practices they should observe. In this bustling city of 10 million residents, so full of history, keeping 30 ladies on time and together would be enough of a challenge. The dinner arranged for them in the hotel restaurant had

been delicious, but exotic. Some of the ladies were uncomfortable with the style, preparation, and service of the meal.

Breakfast was included in the package, and Shannon got to the restaurant early. She wanted to know if the ladies had slept comfortably and whether they were tired. If they were, she would take them to their first site, the Palace Museum, also known as the Forbidden City, then bring them back to the hotel to rest. The ladies started arriving, and everyone seemed to be in good spirits. Then came the surprise: two of the ladies came down for breakfast in their bathrobes and with their hair in curlers. Before Shannon could reach them, they began complaining loudly about their room, the food, and the horrible coffee they had been forced to drink at dinner the night before. All eyes in the restaurant turned to them.

1. What do you believe is the core problem in this scenario?
2. As tour leader, what would you do first? Why?
3. Describe one positive and one negative outcome your action would achieve.
4. From the tour company's perspective, what impact do you think this situation would have on future arrangements? How might a similar embarrassing scene be avoided on future tours?
5. How might customers and staff in the dining room react to this display?
6. Brainstorm: think of something a foreign tourist might do to upset the Canadian cultural norm.

Summary

The tourism sector has experienced phenomenal growth over the past 50 years. Much of this expansion is due to changes in lifestyle brought about by technological advancements. With the retirement of the baby boomers, dramatic growth will continue for the next 20 years. Although the sector is looking at growth potential, it has also identified challenges. If it is to succeed, it must be aware of global trends and must clearly identify the motivations of its markets and be ready to meet their needs and expectations. The tourism sector is gearing up for a new era, and the snapshot of Canada's tourism future looks bright and exciting!

Questions

1. a) Look at the challenges identified by the Canadian Tourism Commission. Rearrange them in order of importance, as you see it.

    b) Provide a brief description of what you feel are the five most important issues.

    c) How do you feel each of these chosen issues might best be overcome?

2. For each of the following groupings, find one positive challenge that will help the CTC redesign/update their product to reach new clientele: generational changes; ethical changes; political changes; changes in business practices.

3. List all eight sectors of the tourism industry as studied in this text. Beside each one, explain the challenge you feel will be the hardest for that sector to overcome.

Notes

1. Aditus, *The Aditus White Paper: Facts, Issues and Trends in Travel and Tourism* (Toronto: Southam, 1996).

2. J. Christopher Holloway, *The Business of Travel* (Essex, London: Pearson Education Limited, 2006), p. 124.

3. Peter Yesawich, "Trends in the tourism industry," Address to the TIAC Conference, Jasper, Alberta, November 1996.

4. www.cruising.org/challenges.

5. Melinda Ligos, "Hotel add-on charges can cost you more than a good night's sleep," *Edmonton Journal*, September 5, 2005, p. A13.

Tourism Education Councils Contact Information

Canadian Tourism Human Resource Council (CTHRC)
Email   cthrc@cthrc.ca
Website   http://www.cthrc.ca/
Telephone   (613) 231-6949

Alberta Tourism Education Council (ATEC)
Email   info@atec.ahla.ca
Website   www.atec.ca
Telephone   1-800-265-1283 (toll-free in Canada)

Conseil québécois des ressources humaines en tourisme (CQRHT)
Email   info@cqrht.qc.ca
Website   www.cqrht.qc.ca
Telephone   (450) 651-1099

Go2—The resource for people in Tourism (B.C. representative)
Email   info@go2hr.ca
Website   www.go2hr.ca
Telephone   (604) 930-9770

Hospitality Newfoundland and Labrador
Email   hnl@hnl.ca
Website   www.hnl.ca
Telephone   1-800-563-0700

Manitoba Tourism Education Council (MTEC)
Email   general@mtec.mb.ca
Website   www.mtec.mb.ca
Telephone   1-800-486-9158

Ontario Tourism Education Corporation (OTEC)
Email   info@otec.org
Website   www.otec.org
Telephone   1-800-557-6832

Nova Scotia Tourism Human Resource Council (THRC)
Email   NSTHRC@tourism.ca
Website   www.tourismhrc.com
Telephone   1-800-948-4267

Tourism Industry Association of New Brunswick (TIANB)
Email   info@tianb.com
Website   www.tianb.com
Telephone   1-800-668-5313

Tourism Industry Association of Prince Edward Island (TIAPEI)
Email   tiapei@tiapei.pe.ca
Website   www.tiapei.pe.ca
Telephone   1-866-566-5008 (toll-free)

Saskatchewan Tourism Education Council (STEC)
Email   stec@sasktourism.com
Website   www.stec.com
Telephone   1-306-933-5900

Yukon Tourism Education Council (for Yukon, Northwest Territories, and Nunavut)
Email   yukontec@internorth.com
Website   www.yukontec.com
Telephone   1-800-667-4733

200 km menu—Indicates that all the major ingredients have been grown within 200 km of the restaurant.

activation—Guest's level of excitement, alertness, or energy, which is either high or low.

adventure tourism—Outdoor activities that present the participant with risk and challenge. Adventure tourism is divided into two types: hard adventure and soft adventure.

agricultural tourism—A tourism experience that teaches travellers about the agricultural industry in Canada through hands-on farm life experiences.

airfares—Set according to two very broad markets: the business traveller and the discretionary traveller.

all-inclusive tour—A tour package that provides the guest with transportation, food and beverage service, entertainment, and lodging for one price. Service charges may also be included.

allergy awareness—Consumer demand to know the ingredients used to create food products, in order to avoid allergic reactions.

allocentric—A traveller willing to take risks, and willing to go without the normal conveniences of life in order to gain a fuller travel experience. These travellers prefer to go where few people have been and are often referred to by marketers as *innovators*. They are first to try a new travel destination in its development stage.

American plan (AP)—A hotel room rate that includes the room, plus three full meals.

amusement park—A centre of entertainment that offers rides, shows, food, candy, and arcades.

aquarium—An aquatic zoo that features a wide variety of fish and sea creatures in tanks for viewing. It may also include marine mammals, such as porpoises.

art museum—An institution that exhibits a variety of artwork including sculptures, oils, watercolours, and carvings.

back of the house—Employees who do not come into direct contact with guests.

balanced development—A component of the integrated development theory in which one portion of the development can operate at a loss that is compensated for by a lucrative operation elsewhere in the resort.

bed and breakfast (B & B)—Accommodation that is generally family owned and managed, accommodates three to ten groups per night, and includes a family-style breakfast.

Bermuda plan (BP)—Room rate that includes a full American breakfast: juice, coffee, eggs, sausage or bacon, and toast.

bilateral agreement—In transportation, an agreement between two countries that often deals with the number of flights permitted from each country into a specific airport, the size and capacity of the airplanes, and special fares.

bistro—A small, casual restaurant that serves fresh, eclectic food.

breakout room—Smaller room made available for seminars or workshops at a conference.

BritRail pass—A train pass allowing unlimited travel in the British Isles.

buffet house—An all-you-can-eat restaurant that offers a wide assortment of hot and cold food, which customers can help themselves to.

bullet train—A high-speed Japanese train.

business guest—An individual travelling for work purposes, who usually has few choices in deciding where, when, how, and how long to travel.

cafeteria—A type of restaurant at which customers can choose their food from a serving line of different dishes, with the portions preset and served by kitchen staff.

campground—A place where campers can set up their tents or park their recreational vehicles.

cannibalization—A situation in which a franchiser allows two independent units to locate too near each other, causing loss of revenue.

Canadian Tourism Commission—Federal agency responsible for promoting tourism in Canada, reporting to Industry Canada.

Canrailpass—A discounted train pass that allows unlimited travel on Via Rail trains over specific travel periods; may be purchased by both domestic and foreign tourists.

carrying capacity—The maximum number of people who can use a site with only acceptable alteration to the physical environment and with only acceptable decline in the quality of experience gained by subsequent visitors.

cash bar—Alcohol service at a banquet at which guests pay for their own drinks.

casino gambling—Gambling including slot machines, roulette, craps, blackjack, poker, and other games of chance.

catalytic development—Development of a destination in which a single developer encourages complementary businesses in and around the property.

centralized development—A component of catalytic development; refers to the major developer who provides the basic facilities, major accommodation units, and promotion for the destination.

certification—Industry recognition of individuals who have demonstrated competencies relating to occupational standards for a particular occupation.

chain ownership—A single corporate identity that operates more than one property, with all properties reporting to corporate headquarters.

chamber of commerce—A city organization that promotes industry and retail development and markets tourism to the city.

charter—A bus, plane, or ship rented for the purpose of transporting people from one location to another, usually at rates lower than regularly scheduled rates.

children's museum—A museum that involves young children in activities to educate and entertain them. May be one component of a larger museum.

circle trip—A type of round trip in which the routes taken to and from the destination differ.

civic event—Event sponsored by a government organization (e.g., swearing in a new prime minister, Remembrance Day).

clustering—Locating a variety of tourism sites and products in one area to create easy access for visitors.

coattail development—Development of a destination that occurs naturally, without community planning. A lack of common theme often means duplication of services and a general lack of direction in the development of the destination.

code of ethics—A system of beliefs based on the values of right and wrong in a specific culture.

coffee house—A type of restaurant that serves a variety of specialty coffees from around the world, but little food.

commercial food service—A division of the food service industry that serves the public and is available to anyone wishing to eat out.

commission—The percentage of a selling price paid to a retailer by a supplier (e.g., from an airline to a travel agency).

common currency—Credit cards, traveller's cheques, and other currency dispensed by automated banking and currency exchange machines, which allow travellers easy access to money and credit while on vacation.

condominium—An individually owned, apartment-style residence located in an area filled with recreational amenities; may be rented out to other travellers when not occupied by the owner.

conference—A large meeting where delegates from the same industry or occupation come together to learn, network, and exchange ideas.

conference appointment—Permission to conduct business in a travel agency.

conference centre—A location specifically designed to provide a quiet, working environment for a conference and its delegates. Conference centres have accommodations within the complex.

conference hotel—A hotel with conference facilities that caters to large groups, usually in the downtown area of major cities.

confirmed reservation—An oral or written confirmation by a hotel that a room has been reserved, usually with an agreed-upon time of arrival (e.g., 6 P.M.); also called *tentative reservation.*

consolidator—An operator that purchases a large number of airline seats every year from individual airlines at a low price, which it then sells to tour operators and travel agents at discounted prices.

consortium—A group of independent businesses who work together for a common purpose (e.g., independently owned travel agencies who promote their products through the brand name of GIANTS).

continental plan (CP)—A hotel room rate that includes the room and a continental breakfast.

contract food service—A division of the food service industry that serves a specific clientele, not the general public; found in establishments whose main purpose is something other than serving food, such as museums, stadiums, airlines.

convention—A large meeting where delegates from different occupations come together to share ideas and achieve some form of consensus.

convention and visitors bureau (CVB)—A municipal or private organization that promotes tourism and provides convention facilities and information services for visitors to the city.

convention centre—A location specifically built to handle groups of more than 1000 people but that does not provide accommodations.

corkage fee—A fee charged by restaurants for opening a bottle of wine brought to the restaurant by customers.

corporate rates—Reduced rates designed to encourage sales to companies.

corporate travel agency—An agency that deals almost exclusively with business travel arrangements, as opposed to leisure travel.

Crown land—Land that is not privately owned. Crown land may be owned by the province or by the federal government, but unlike protected parklands, it often does not fall under specific protective legislation. Much of Canada's wilderness is designated Crown land.

culinary tourism—Tourism—such as a tour of wineries, a short course at a cooking school, or a series of lectures on foods of a region combined with a local food festival—that focuses on culinary products.

cultural motivators—A desire to know and learn more about the music, architecture, food, art, folklore, or religion of other people.

cultural tourism—See *heritage tourism*.

customer profile—Information about customers used by service providers to identify client needs and expectations.

day rate—A hotel room rate charged between 9 A.M. and 8 P.M. (no overnight stay).

day tour—A bus tour that lasts less than 24 hours and has no accommodation arrangements, usually in one specific region.

demand—The need or desire for goods and services; the number of people who wish to purchase a product.

demographics—Statistics that include age, marital status, gender, occupation, income, and place of residence, used for understanding who the travellers are to a particular site.

destination life cycle—The stages through which a destination moves: conception, growth, maturity, and decline.

destination marketing organization (DMO)—A tourism organization that is responsible for creating a marketing plan for a destination and promoting it. The CTC is Canada's federal DMO, with CVBs usually representing a city or region.

direct flight—A flight that carries a traveller from one destination to another, making at least one stop along the route.

discretionary income—The money that one may spend as one pleases.

discretionary time—Time away from work and other obligations.

domestic tourist—A person travelling in the country in which he or she resides, who stays for a period of 24 hours and travels at least 80 km from home.

double—Two people staying in one room.

double double—A hotel room with two double beds.

dude or guest ranch—Accommodation that is either a working ranch where guests help in the everyday work, or a luxury ranch resort for horseback riding, swimming, hiking, or tennis.

ecotourism—Responsible travel aimed at learning about the interrelationships and physiology of organisms and their environment; focuses on nature-related experiences that help people appreciate and understand our natural resources and their conservation.

ecotourist—A person who believes in responsible travel to natural areas and who aids in conserving the environment and improving the welfare of local people.

elastic demand—Demand that changes significantly when price changes (e.g., demand drops when price rises).

emerit—Online training program overseen by the CTHRC and provincial TECs that provides easy access to these organizations' certification training modules.

empty nest—The life stage of married couples whose children have grown and left home.

escorted tour—An organized tour led by a professional tour guide.

ethics—A system or code of morals of a particular person, religion, culture, group, or profession.

ethnic restaurant—A restaurant that serves food from a specific culture, country, or region.

Eurailpass—A discounted rail pass allowing travel by train. Certain restrictions apply. Must be purchased outside Europe. May also include other forms of transportation, such as ferry service, buses, etc. in 16 European countries.

European plan (EP)—A hotel rate that includes the room, with no meals.

excursionist—Any person who travels at least 80 km from the place of residence, stays less than 24 hours, and is not commuting to work or school or operating as part of a crew on a train, airplane, truck, bus, or ship.

exhibition—At a convention or congress, a display of goods and services used by the delegates in their workplace.

external locus of control—A personality dimension of believing that events are determined by other powerful individuals, fate, or chance.

extrovert—An individual who is outgoing and uninhibited in interpersonal situations.

fair—A special event with a theme, such as an agricultural fair, historical fair, trade fair, or World's Fair.

familiarization tour (fam tour)—A free or discounted trip for travel professionals, designed to acquaint them with an area in order to help them choose a convention site.

family life stage—A person's position in his or her lifetime.

family plan—An accommodation plan in which there is no extra charge for children under a given age to stay with their parents at a hotel.

family-style restaurant—Restaurant, often located in the suburbs, that offers full, fast, and friendly service, "comfort" food, and a welcoming environment for children.

fast food restaurant—A restaurant where customers place their own order, pick up their own food, and clear their own tables when finished. Prices are low and menu is limited.

festival—A public celebration centred on a theme of local, regional, or national interest or importance.

fine dining—Restaurants that provide elegant decor, high-quality food prepared from scratch, and professional, attentive service.

fly/coach tour—a tour that combines airfare with an escorted bus tour.

forecasting—The process of attempting to determine future demand in an area.

foreign tourist—A person visiting a country other than the one in which he or she usually resides, and staying for a period of at least 24 hours.

franchise—A business purchased as a turnkey operation, with everything in place.

franchise advisory councils (FACs)—Bodies that represent franchisees, providing them with a forum through which to address concerns with the franchise contract or the franchiser.

franchisee—The purchaser of a franchise operation.

franchiser—The company that owns the franchise rights to a product and sells it to other operator/investors.

Freedoms of the Air—Global rules regulating aircraft and airline activity and addressing rights of passage for an airplane, traffic rights, and the granting of special rights to certain airlines under specific circumstances; also known as *rights of the air*.

front of the house—Employees who deal actively with customers, usually in a hotel or a restaurant setting.

front-line training—Training provided for staff members who deal directly with the public.

full-service travel agency—A travel agency staffed and equipped to answer and serve all categories of traveller needs.

functional form—Within integrated development, adherence to a common theme.

fundraising event—Public event that encourages people to participate in order to raise money for a specific cause or organization.

gateway—The welcoming sign to a destination that informs tourists they have arrived; e.g., an information centre providing tourists with friendly assistance brochures and help in arrange their stay.

gateway airport—Airport from which major international flights arrive and depart.

gateway city—The city where a tour begins.

Green Plan—Created 20 years ago, a commitment to solve Canada's complex environmental challenges and implement sustainable economic development, identifying tourism as an important partner in the plan. It recommended that 12% of

Canada's lands be protected space for parks, historic sites, and wildlife, still a priority for the government.

greenwashing—Using the so-called "eco" label to lure unsuspecting tourists into believing that a company uses sound environmental practices.

ground/land package—A tour that includes the land arrangements of a tour but no air transportation.

guaranteed reservation—A reservation that has been made with one night pre-paid to ensure the room is available for any arrival time.

guests—Another term for tourists.

hallmark event—Major happening that brings tourists from around the world to a destination and has a huge economic impact on the community (e.g., the Olympics).

hard adventure—Tourism activities that often take place in an unusual, exotic or remote setting, requiring pre-training, a high level of physical activity, risk and may require specialized equipment.

haute cuisine—An elegant and expensive style of restaurant noted for its outstanding food, opulent atmosphere, and highly trained staff.

heritage tourism—Immersion in the natural history, human heritage, arts, philosophy, and institutions of another region or country. A trip that educates the visitor on the architecture, food, folklore, or religion of another culture. Also called *cultural tourism*.

higher value traveller—A tourist looking for upscale destinations and experiences and willing to pay more for them.

historic site—A place of special historical interest.

historical museum—A museum depicting some historical event or place.

hospitality of host—An intangible concept referring to the genuine warmth extended to visitors by the host destination.

hospitality suite—A hotel room with a parlour that has a bar and sitting area for guests.

hosted tour—A tour on which participants travel between destinations without a guide but are met at each destination by a host guide from that community.

hostel—A lodge with communal wash-rooms and bedrooms designed for four to twenty people.

hosts—People, communities, or regions that entertain visiting guests.

hotel—Accommodation that provides access to guest rooms from a central lobby.

hub and spoke—A pattern of transportation in which an airline uses one airport as the collecting point for incoming and outgoing flights. This system is also used in the motor coach industry.

inbound tour—A tour that brings guests from a foreign country to Canada, generating jobs and revenue for Canadians.

inbound tourist—See *foreign tourist*.

incentive travel—The practice of using a trip as an award for performing to a certain set of standards.

industrial tourism—Tourism that includes visits to industrial sites, such as the oil fields of Alberta or the salmon fisheries of British Columbia.

infrastructure—A basic system that includes facilities such as roads, sewage systems, electricity, and water supply.

inn—Smaller hotel/accommodation, often using a historic building that has been renovated to meet the expectations of travellers looking for upscale but homelike accommodations. Most inns are located in the countryside rather than in large cities.

integrated development—The development of a large parcel of land by a single individual or company to the exclusion of all other developers.

interdependency—A component of catalytic development; entrepreneurial activities of other businesses within the development succeed because the initial developer succeeds, and the initial developer succeeds because of the entrepreneurs. Each is dependent on the other.

interline connection—Air travel between two destinations during which the traveller is forced to change airline companies in order to complete the journey.

internal locus of control—The belief that people are in charge of what happens in their lives.

International Air Transport Association (IATA)—A privately run international organization whose principal function is to facilitate the movement of persons and goods from and to any point on the world air network by any combination of routes.

International Civil Aviation Organization (ICAO)—An agency of the United Nations that ensures safe, orderly the development of the global air travel.

interpersonal motivator—A reason for travel based on family and friends and the seeking of comradeship.

introvert—A person who is more concerned with personal thoughts and feelings than those of others.

isolation—A component of integrated development; a development is located away from existing settlements.

Jetway—A hallway that joins a plane to the airport terminal.

joint venture—An arrangement between two partners in which one partner supplies the expertise in a business and the other partner provides the financial investment.

landing fee—Fee charged by an airport to an airline for the right to land and use airport services.

land package—See *ground/land package*.

"le grand tour" —An educational tour of Europe undertaken by young English noblemen in the seventeenth and eighteenth centuries.

leakage—A community's need to import workers or goods in order to sustain its tourism industry.

living history museum—A museum in which people act the parts of historical characters.

load factor—The percentage of seats filled on an airplane by paying or revenue-producing passengers.

low-impact camping—A type of camping in which every item carried in is carried out; every item created on the trip is carried out; enclosed fires and biodegradable products are used; no souvenirs are taken from the area; and the area is left virtually untouched and ready for the next group of adventurers.

management contract—A method of hotel management and operation in which one company owns the property and another company operates it.

marketing—A continual, sequential process through which management plans, researches, implements, controls, and evaluates activities designed to satisfy both customers' needs and wants and the organization's objectives.

marketing mix—Controllable factors that may be selected to help satisfy customer needs or wants (product, price, place, promotion).

marketing plan—A written plan used to guide an organization's marketing activities for a period of one year or less.

market match—The satisfactory situation in which the product on offer meets the needs of the target market.

market segmentation—The division of the overall market into groups of people who share common characteristics or have similar needs.

medical tourism—A branch of spa tourism, involves travellers choosing a destination to gain access to a specific medical practice unavailable at home.

Meeting Planners International (MPI)—A professional association of meeting planners.

mega-mall—A large shopping and entertainment centre offering a wide assortment of services including retail stores, restaurants, and accommodations as well as a variety of entertainment facilities such as indoor theme parks, game rooms, wave pools, minigolf courses, cinemas, etc.

menu—A list of all the products a restaurant sells.

midcentric—In the tourist personality classification system, the halfway point between allocentrics and psychocentrics. Most people fit into this category.

modified American plan (MAP)—A hotel room rate that includes the room plus breakfast and lunch or dinner.

motel—Tourist accommodation that provides free parking and access to a guest's room directly from the parking lot.

motivator—A "promoter of action" whose purpose is to fulfill a need or want.

motor coach package—A bus tour that lasts from 3 to 30 days and includes one or more of these four components: accommodations, meals, attractions, sightseeing.

multiplier effect—the mechanism whereby the benefits of tourism dollars spread through a community, profiting businesses and residents not directly involved in tourism.

multi-unit corporate restaurant—A chain of restaurants in which one person or company controls all the units; typically, all restaurants have similar decor, menu, and management style.

museum—A building that displays a wide assortment of memorabilia ranging from artwork and historical or scientific items, to agricultural tools or cartoons.

national parks system—a countrywide system of representative natural areas of Canadian significance, protected for public appreciation, enjoyment, and education. Operated under the jurisdiction of by the federal government, national parks have strict rules and regulations, which are enforced by park officials, to ensure they are maintained in an unimpaired state for future generations. The system has 41 established parks with an additional 10 under consideration.

natural resources—The physical means of supporting and attracting tourists, such as land and agriculture, a habitable climate, a water supply, and natural beauty.

niche (target) marketing—Creating products to fulfill the needs of a specific segment of the total market; also known as *target marketing*.

non-commercial food service—Often referred to as **social** and **contract caterers**, includes food and beverage services found on airlines and railways, in stadiums, museums, and department stores, and at recreational events and recreational camps.

non-consumptive tourism—A type of tourism in which the tourist takes nothing away from the destination and leaves nothing behind.

non-stop flight—A flight that does not stop between point of departure and destination.

occupational standards—Documents that outline the skills, knowledge, and attitudes that an individual must demonstrate and practise to be deemed competent in a given job.

oceanarium—An aquatic zoo located on the shores of an ocean, which features saltwater fish and animals such as dolphins, seals, whales, and shore birds.

online connection—Air travel between two destinations during which the traveller is forced to change aircraft but not airline in order to complete the journey.

open bar—Alcohol service at a banquet at which the host pays for the alcohol consumed.

open-jaw trip—A type of air travel in which travellers can fly to one city but return from a different city.

Open Skies Agreement—Bilateral agreement between the United States and Canada for North American airlines, which provides tourists with greater choice of carrier and types of flights.

organically grown foods—Foods raised without the use of chemicals or foreign substances.

Orient Express—A historic train, noted for carrying royalty, political leaders, and the wealthy, which operated between Paris and Istanbul between 1833 and

1977. Its cars have been refurbished to their original luxury and the train is now considered a destination in itself, rather than a simple mode of transportation.

outbound tour—A tour in which Canadians travel to a foreign country.

outbound tourist—A Canadian who travels to a foreign country as a tourist.

outdoor recreation—Activities that take place outdoors, such as hiking, backpacking, canoeing, sailing, kayaking, bicycling, horseback riding, wildlife viewing, and heli-hiking.

overbooking—The practice of selling more hotel rooms, airplane seats, etc., than exist, on the assumption that not all reservations will be picked up. This practice can leave guests without a room at the hotel or a seat on the airline.

overnight/short tour—A bus tour that is two days long.

override—A bonus or extra commission earned for doing volume business.

parimutuel gambling—A betting pool in which those who bet on the winners of the first three places share the total amount, minus a percentage for management.

Parks Canada—Agency that oversees national parks, historic sites, marine conservation areas, heritage rivers, and national battlefields, and that reports to Environment Canada.

partnerships—Alliances formed among various sectors of the tourism industry. By working together, the partners ensure a better quality product for the consumer and shared business opportunities for the industry.

physical motivator—A health-related reason for travelling to an area, including relaxation, sports participation, recreation, medical exams, or health treatments.

place—One of the marketing Ps, referring to the location in which a product is sold; also known as *channel of distribution.*

planning—organizing the future to achieve certain goals.

pleasure guest—Someone travelling for pleasure on discretionary time and money.

price—One of the marketing Ps: the amount charged for a product, which includes all costs and profit.

product—One of the marketing Ps; the good or service being sold.

product capacity—The number of facilities, the accommodations or rooms available, and the transportation system capacity.

product/market match—See *market match.*

promotion—One of the marketing Ps, referring to advertising and other means of generating customer interest in the product.

psychocentric—An often-anxious traveller who enjoys travel only when it is just like home; the so-called armchair traveller.

psychographics—Marketing information based on people's activities, opinions, motives, behaviours, and interests.

pub—Small casual restaurant that emulates an English, Irish, or Scottish bar, including the ambience, the menu, and the types of beer and whiskey available.

pull factors—Tangible reasons for travel choices, such as friends, mountains, and beaches.

push factors—Intangible reasons for travel choices, such as the need to escape, the need for culture, or a need for physical fitness.

qualitative forecasting—The use of experts and their accumulated experience and knowledge to predict the likely outcome of events.

quantitative forecasting—The analysis of numerical data (current and historical) to help predict the future.

rack rate—A standard day rate for a hotel room.

rapid development—A component of integrated development; refers to the speed at which development can occur because a single developer can make decisions quickly.

recreational sports—Major sports that affect the tourism industry, including skiing, golf, tennis, and water sports.

referral system—independently owned and operated hotels working together under a brand name in order to receive brand-name recognition, access to a global reservation system, and global marketing strategies, e.g., Best Western.

REITs (real estate investment trusts)—A company that buys hotel or resort properties, and then sells shares of the property on the stock market.

Rendez-Vous Canada—A trade show that brings together Canadian tourism suppliers and international tour operators.

resort—A destination hotel that is usually located in the countryside, near water or the mountains. Resorts provide their guests with a wide variety of outdoor recreational activities, indoor services such as spas, pools, and workout rooms, and a variety of in-house dining experiences.

round trip—An airline routing that originates in a city, goes to a destination, and returns to the original city.

run-of-the-house rate—A discount rate for block bookings.

same-day visitor—See *excursionist*.

scheduled air carriers—Airlines that operate on defined routes at specific times, whether domestic or international, for which licences have been granted by the government or governments concerned.

scientific museum—A museum centred on some study of science, ranging from dinosaur bones to space ships.

secondary developers—Developers who build complementary facilities near a primary development, such as a major resort.

sector—A composite group of industries.

seminar—An informal meeting in which participants share ideas, knowledge, and expertise under the supervision of a leader or presenter.

sense of place—The special feeling of a destination, created by its unique feature(s), and used in marketing it.

sightseeing tour—See *day tour*.

single—A hotel room occupied by one person.

site inspection—First-hand view of a potential conference site by the organizers to determine whether it meets the group's needs.

site specific—A museum located where an historic event took place.

soft adventure—Outdoor activities, such as hiking and snorkelling, designed to give participants the thrill of hard adventure, without the risk. These activities require no pre-training, are usually less strenuous, and equipment if needed is supplied by the operator.

spa—A hotel or resort that encourages healthy, rejuvenating activities such as massage therapy, body wraps, steam baths, aerobic exercise classes, etc. As part of the vacation package, guests often are provided with low-calorie gourmet meals.

spa tourism—Focuses on the overall health and well-being of the traveller.

special event—A one-time or infrequently occurring event outside the normal program or activities of the sponsoring or organizing body.

special interest cruise—A cruise that focuses on a specific topic of interest, usually from an educational standpoint, such as ecotourism, history, or opera.

specialty restaurant—A type of restaurant that serves one kind of food, such as chicken or ribs.

specialty travel agency—An agency that specializes in a particular type of travel, such as adventure travel or cruises.

spectator sporting event—A sporting event that has audience appeal, such as professional hockey, baseball, or basketball.

status and prestige motivators—Reasons to travel related to a need for recognition, attention, appreciation, and good reputation; same as social and ego factors.

step-on guide—A sightseeing guide who has particular knowledge about the history, people, and events that have shaped a region and who is specifically trained to show the sights of the region.

suite—A hotel room with one or more bedrooms and a sitting room or parlour.

summit—An international meeting of high-level government leaders.

supply—The amount of product available.

suprastructure—All of the buildings located at the destination; that is, structures that are "built up" from the ground, such as lodging facilities, restaurants, terminals, and stores.

sustainable tourism—When tourism development and operations meet the needs of current tourists and host regions, while protecting and enhancing opportunities for the future.

target marketing—See *niche marketing*.

tentative reservation—See *confirmed reservation*.

theme cruise—A cruise that focuses on a particular event or topic (e.g., Super Bowl Cruise, Rock and Roll Cruise); also called *special-interest cruise*.

theme park—A family entertainment centre oriented to a particular subject or historical area, which combines the continuity of costuming and architecture with entertainment and merchandise to create a fantasy-evoking atmosphere.

theme restaurant—Restaurant that transports customers to a different time or place through ambience, server costumes, menu, and entertainment reflecting the theme (e.g., Medieval Times).

time poverty—Having too much to do and too little time in which to do it.

time-sharing—Buying a vacation segment, usually of two weeks, in a condominium unit.

tour operator—A company that contracts with and pays in advance for services provided by hotels, transportation companies, and other suppliers in order to create a tour package.

tour wholesaler—A company that contracts for space with hotels, transportation companies, and other suppliers to create a tour package. Historically it differs from a tour operator because no money changes hands until the space is purchased by a client. Today, there is no noticeable difference between the two types of operation.

tourism—The activities of persons travelling to and staying in places outside their usual environment for not more than one consecutive year for leisure, business, and other purposes.

tourism education councils (TECs)—Organizations that work with provincial mandates to stimulate and coordinate the development of tourism training in their provinces.

tourism illiteracy—The condition of not knowing or understanding the benefits of the tourism industry.

tourist court—Tourist accommodation that provides customers with a small cabin and a parking space.

tourist dollars—Revenue produced by the tourism industry.

trade show—A marketing and sales tool used by many industries to display and sell their products.

transfer—Any change in transportation, between modes or within the same mode, during a journey.

transportation systems—The vehicles that use the travel infrastructure of a destination.

travel counsellor—A person who has satisfactorily completed the certification process of the Canadian Institute of Travel Counsellors.

travel deficit—The difference that occurs when the dollar amount spent by tourists choosing to vacation outside their country (outbound tourists) exceeds the revenue generated by foreign tourists (inbound tourists) who visit the country.

trend—Current style or preference; in tourism, a popular destination or activity.

trend analysis—The use of historical data to predict future trends.

trinketization—The process of producing and selling cheap, mass-produced, imported goods as if they were genuine artifacts of local culture.

trip—Any travel that takes a person 80 km away from his or her place of residence for any reason, other than a commute to work or school, travel in an ambulance to a hospital or clinic, or a trip that is longer than one year.

turn-down service—Service provided by luxury hotels, in which the bedspread is folded down and a chocolate placed on the pillow.

twin—A hotel room with two single beds.

unescorted tour—A tour in which the group travels without a company representative.

UNESCO World Heritage Site—A place designated by the United Nations Educational, Scientific, and Cultural Organization in recognition of its outstanding universal value.

unlimited kilometres—A car rental package that charges travellers a flat fee regardless of distance driven.

upselling—A sales technique used by servers to increase the amount of a bill, by encouraging customers to purchase items not included in the cost of the meal (e.g., appetizer, baked potato, coffee).

variety—Change or novelty, which the guest either seeks or avoids.

Via Rail Canada—A Crown corporation, created by the merger of Canadian National Railways and Canadian Pacific Railway, responsible for most of the passenger rail travel in Canada.

Visit Canada—A trade show that introduces travel writers from around the world to the Canadian tourism product.

visitor—A generic term used for both domestic and foreign tourists in Canada.

visitor use—The total number of tourists or excursionists to visit a destination or attraction or to attend an event over a specified period of time.

volunteer tourism—tourism that arranges volunteer opportunities with a specific purpose or cause (e.g., building homes for Habitat for Humanity).

walking—The practice of sending guests who have reservations that cannot be honoured to other available hotels.

weekend rate—Special discounted rates used by hotels that rely upon corporate business during the week. These discounted rates encourage business people to bring their families in for a weekend vacation, or encourage locals to use the hotel and its services for a quick weekend getaway.

workshop—A small group session in which participants learn new skills or techniques.

World Heritage Site—see *UNESCO World Heritage Site*.

INDEX